French sacred drama from Bèze to Corneille:

Dramatic forms and their purposes in the early modern theatre

J. S. Street

Cambridge University Press

Cambridge

London   New York   New Rochelle

Melbourne   Sydney

Published by the Press Syndicate of the University of Cambridge
The Pitt Building, Trumpington Street, Cambridge CB2 1RP
32 East 57th Street, New York, NY 10022, USA
296 Beaconsfield Parade, Middle Park, Melbourne 3206, Australia

First published 1983

Printed in Great Britain by New Western Printing Ltd, Bristol

Library of Congress catalogue card number: 82–14691

British Library Cataloguing in Publication Data
Street, J. S.
French sacred drama from Bèze to Corneille:
Dramatic forms and their purposes on the early modern theatre.
1. Religious drama, French – History and criticism
2. Drama, French – 16th century – History and
criticism   3. Drama, French – 17th century
– History and criticism
I. Title
842'.0516'09   PQ573
ISBN 0 521 24537 0

NWP

Contents

iii

Acknowledgements

This book has developed from a doctoral thesis undertaken at Birkbeck College, London. My supervisor was Professor William Barber: I wish to thank him in particular for his patient and constructive guidance and criticism. My external examiner, Professor Richard Griffiths, also offered many pertinent comments, for which I am especially grateful. I wish also to thank particularly Peter Bayley, who performed no small work of supererogation in reading and criticising an earlier version. The other debts of gratitude that I contracted are too numerous to catalogue; Christopher Smith and Tony Gable in particular gave generously of their time. If I have not profited from all the advice that was so willingly given, the fault is mine alone. I wish also to thank my pupils at Cambridge for obliging me to clarify my ideas; and the staffs of the various libraries I used for their unfailing cooperation.

I embarked on the thesis on a part-time basis, and am glad to thank my various employers over the years for their tolerance of such an engrossing hobby. I was fortunate also to receive grants from several bodies to facilitate intervals of full-time study, and wish here to record my gratitude to Birkbeck College, the University of London Central Research Fund, the Jebb Fund of Cambridge University, the French Ministère des Affaires Etrangères, and the Department of Education and Science.

Finally, it is a pleasure to thank my father for his constant support; and my wife, Maureen, for encouragement, consolation, tolerance and practical help beyond anything I deserved. To her I dedicate this book.

J.S.S.

Tonbridge, May 1981

Abbreviations

In addition to the standard initials for the titles of periodicals, the following abbreviations will be used:

Antiquities	Flavius Josephus, *The Jewish Antiquities*, trans. by H. St J. Thackeray, R. Marcus, A. Wikgren and L. H. Feldman, 6 vols, London and Cambridge, Mass., 1967–9 (Loeb Classical Library)
Dabney	Lancaster E. Dabney, *French Dramatic Literature in the Reign of Henri IV: a Study of the Extant Plays Composed in French between 1589 and 1610*, Austin, Texas, 1952
DBF	*Dictionnaire de biographie française*, Paris 1933 – (in progress)
Du Verdier	*Les Bibliothèques françoises de La Croix du Maine et de Du Verdier*, ed. Rigoley de Juvigny, 6 vols, Paris 1772–3
Forsyth	Elliott Forsyth, *La Tragédie française de Jodelle à Corneille (1553–1640): le thème de la vengeance*, Paris 1962
Haag	E. and E. Haag, *La France protestante*, 10 vols, Paris 1846–58; or, where appropriate, 2nd ed., 6 vols, Paris 1877–88 (incomplete: A–G only published)
History I	Henry Carrington Lancaster, *A History of French Dramatic Literature in the Seventeenth Century: Part I, The Pre-classical Period, 1610–1634*, 2 vols, Baltimore and Paris 1929
History II	ibid, *Part II, The Period of Corneille, 1635–1651*, 2 vols, Baltimore, London and Paris 1932
La Croix du Maine	see Du Verdier

La Vallière
Louis César de la Baume le Blanc, duc de la Vallière, *Bibliothèque du théâtre françois depuis son
origine*, 3 vols, Dresden 1768

Loukovitch
Kosta Loukovitch, *L'Evolution de la tragédie
religieuse classique en France*, Paris 1933

Michaud
*Biographie universelle ancienne et moderne pub-
liée sous la direction de M. Michaud*, 2nd ed., 45
vols, Paris 1843–65

Mystères
Louis Petit de Julleville, *Histoire du théâtre en
France: les mystères*, 2 vols, Paris 1880

Pascoe
Margaret E. Pascoe, *Les Drames religieux au
milieu du XVIIe siècle, 1636–1650*, Paris 1932

Soleinne
P. L. Jacob [i.e. Paul Lacroix], *Bibliothèque
dramatique de M. de Soleinne* and *Suppléments*,
5 vols, Paris 1843–4

Stone
Donald Stone, Jr, *French Humanist Tragedy: a
Reassessment*, Manchester 1974

TR
Raymond Lebègue, *La Tragédie religieuse en
France: les débuts, 1514–1573*, Paris 1929

VT
Le Mistére du Viel Testament, ed. James de
Rothschild and Emile Picot, 6 vols, Paris 1878–91

Introduction

The French Classical theatre has always been the object of study, almost of reverence, and interest has recently revived in humanist and baroque drama, but the many sacred plays in this tradition have been largely neglected. This says more of modern taste than of the preference of contemporaries, who relished the sacred drama, as records of performances attest, even while Corneille's Roman tragedies were triumphing on the Parisian stage. Apart from the importance they derive from their popularity, the sacred plays are of value to us in offering a key to much that seems strange in the theatrical practice of the time. Of paramount importance in the conception of literature in the Renaissance was the idea that it was instructive, that it afforded access to moral and even metaphysical truths. The masterpieces of the time contain many practices – conscious artificialities, nonchalant manipulation of plot and character – which strike the modern mind as disconcertingly unnatural and undramatic. In fact these devices had their purpose, which contemporary taste appreciated. Many of the most artificial were directed towards ensuring that the edifying implications of the dramatic action should emerge clearly. It is perhaps easier to grasp how these devices worked in the sacred theatre, in which their instructive function is obvious; having seen how they were used in a deliberately didactic genre, we shall be closer to understanding what effects were intended in the more familiar masterpieces of the day. If the theatre contains any significance beyond the immediate thrill of vicarious experience, the sacred theatre offers a key to understanding how the dramatists arranged for the play's sense to emerge, how they expected it to work on the audience.

I shall be studying the nature of the various dramatic forms current in the late Renaissance and the effects that they were designed to produce on the spectator, as these were illustrated in the sacred plays. These effects, as I have suggested, were somewhat remote from the modern expectations of the theatre, and for this reason the plays of the time have been much misunderstood. In this century, and particularly following the experiments with deliberate alienation of the audience with which Brecht is principally credited, it should not need saying that emotional identification of the spectator with profoundly-characterised protagonists is not the only way a play can work on an audience, and yet much critical opinion, at least in the fields of sixteenth-century and seventeenth-century French studies, and, in my experience, much teaching, have remained based on this assumption. It is not difficult to understand how this should have happened: this expectation has dominated the European stage, generally speaking, from 1600 at least until the beginning of this century. It was developed first in the late Renaissance from the plays of ancient Greece and Rome, which had concentrated on a human crisis. But where the ancient dramatists had appealed to the spectator's religious emotion, aroused by the pattern of the disaster as a whole, the neo-classical authors attended increasingly to the emotional states and psychology of the human figures involved in the action, and sought to allow the spectator to experience for himself what it feels like to be in the position of the hero.[1] Despite many superficial differences the same basic assumption has underlain the main stream of European drama since the Renaissance: neo-classical, romantic and bourgeois drama all invite the spectator to share in the character's emotional life, and all use the proscenium arch to serve as a 'fourth wall', behind which the actors are required to behave naturally and unselfconsciously, as if no audience were present, so that there should be no obstacle to the spectator's believing in the characters and surrendering his identity to theirs. The dominance of naturalness as a critical value has been reinforced by the success of the nineteenth-century novel, which has imposed character-delineation as a *desideratum* even on other genres. As a consequence we are still more inclined to discuss the personality of Hamlet than the pattern of the play as a whole; and where the characters seem unnatural or fail to communicate their emotions we categorise the play as 'avant-garde' or even condemn it outright, while any deliberate breach of naturalism can still transfix us with embarrassment.

However, these conventions only apply in modern Europe. The ancient Greeks had no expectation of profound and humane characterisation and accessible emotions, and we quite accept that in judging their drama we cannot rely exclusively on such criteria, any more than we would dream of applying them to a Japanese Noh play. In studying the works of the beginning of the modern theatre we have not always remembered to discard our modern assumptions: we have looked for such features as lifelike characterisation or a compelling plot and, not finding them, have recorded only disappointment, instead of registering what else was present. The result has been the unjustified neglect or condemnation of genres which operated by standards different from our own. In this study I shall be attempting to give full value to the unfamiliar conventions which the men of the time appreciated, rather than attending to what we feel they ought to have preferred.

I am hardly the first to suggest that the conventions of one stage of the development of a tradition do not necessarily provide helpful criteria for judging the art of a previous period. Among art-historians it is now a commonplace – see for example the writings of Sir Ernst Gombrich – that the failure of medieval painters to achieve the same degree of realism as their successors in the Renaissance does not automatically make medieval painting inferior; they simply had other objectives. In the study of the English theatre of the sixteenth and seventeenth centuries it has long been recognised by scholars such as Professor Bradbrook that naturalness is not the only, or even the most useful, touchstone for understanding the poets' creation. It is curious that in the world of French studies the first attempts to overthrow judgements based on standards imported from a later period were made only relatively recently.[2]

The obvious difficulty in seeking to allow due importance to what contemporaries actually liked, rather than judging by some supposedly absolute but potentially inappropriate notion of how a play should be, is that we shall be left without any basis for critical assessment, any practice being good by its own standard. One way out of this difficulty is simply to take a sufficiently large sample. Confronted with a play of, say, 1580, in which the characters address each other in tirades so long and ornate that they more closely resemble arias than dialogue, we are hardly in a position to consider what effect was intended by this strange technique and whether the play achieves it; all we can do is record testily that such speechifying does not appeal to us. If, in analysing such a play, I inform the reader that contemporaries actually liked the bombast, I may not be believed, so strong is the modern expectation of a natural dialogue. However, when from a larger sample we see that almost all the plays of the same time used the same technique, we are bound to admit that contemporaries thought such rhetoric essential to their plays, no less and perhaps no less rightly than we consider natural characterisation essential, and bound to set out to discover what effects they intended by it. Having seen a sufficient number of examples of the style to understand what a generation expected of its theatre, we shall also be better able to judge to what extent individual playwrights were successful. These considerations have led me to undertake an exhaustive survey of the sacred theatre in the century in which it underwent the transformation from medieval to modern. I shall discuss each work separately, where necessary demonstrating what features a play in a given style did and did not contain by summarising the plot, so as to allow the evidence of the texts themselves to show how the various dramatic styles worked. The analysis *seriatim* of over 100 plays may occasionally seem a tedious method, but only thus have I felt able to demonstrate with authority what the men of the time expected, and found in the theatre.

This is the first attempt at such a comprehensive survey of the French sacred theatre: previous studies have excluded certain types of play or have offered a more limited temporal or geographical coverage.[3] Kosta Loukovitch alone studied the genre over a longer period, but defined his subject as *L'Evolution de la tragédie religieuse classique* and excluded or dismissed all plays not participating in the evolution towards Classicism, so depriving himself of the opportunity to realise that many dramatists preferred other styles to the one which he took as his yardstick.[4] This, as I have suggested, has been the weakness of many studies of the sacred theatre: brought up on the Classical style which instituted the drama of personality that has dominated the European stage until this century, previous critics have allowed its familiarity and the fact that it produced masterpieces to blind them to the possibility that it is not the only way to write for the theatre, and have condemned dramatists by Classical standards which they had no intention of fulfilling. Recent attempts to re-evaluate the pre-Classical theatre without applying post-Classical standards, mentioned above, have concerned only the humanist theatre: my study is the first to attempt to apply this approach to other forms, such as the *mystère*, and the first to apply it to the sacred theatre, the genre which has been most consistently condemned by post-Classical standards and in which a re-evaluation seemed consequently most necessary and potentially most fruitful.

I shall be arguing, then, that if many pious dramatists adopted forms that were at variance with our Classical norm, it was not necessarily the case that they did so out of backwardness, ignorance or incompetence, as has too readily been supposed, and I shall be working from a more charitable view of their artistic integrity by assuming, unless there is evidence to the contrary, that they chose these forms because they seemed best suited to their dramatic purposes. In arguing thus I do not wish to exalt the second-rate; the effect is a reassessment, not so much of the individual plays and playwrights, as of the various dramatic styles available at that time. I have fixed the period covered by this study so as to permit consideration of the crucial transition from the medieval to the modern conception of the theatre. The opening date, 1550, marks the appearance of the first French play showing the systematic influence of ancient tragedy, Bèze's *Abraham sacrifiant*; but

in 1550 the *mystères* were also still popular. The study embraces the
humanist theatre and the chronicle dramas of the first years of the
seventeenth century. It ends at the point when the Classical style
was established, soon after the appearance of *Polyeucte*. To put it
another way, I shall start from what was essentially a theatre of
ideas in the *mystères* and end with the style that appealed first to the
emotions.

Since my purpose is to explore what features of the various dramatic
forms available induced a playwright to choose one rather than another,
I shall not be concerning myself in detail with the literary origins or
evolution of the dramatic forms themselves. Studies of these matters
are in any case already available.[5] Similarly, the question of social and
church attitudes to the theatre, though important, is strictly tangential
to my theme and will have to be left aside; here, too, adequate accounts
are already in existence.[6] My concern will be with the author's selection
of a dramatic form in the light of the way he wished to work on the
audience.

Many of the plays to be studied were described as tragedies by their
authors. The question whether a play can be both religious and tragic
has long aroused controversy; the predominant opinion is that it cannot,
despite the religious basis of Greek tragedy. I prefer to leave the
examination of this question until after some examples have been
considered. For the moment it need only be remembered that the
playwrights themselves saw no incompatibility between a religious
subject and a tragic treatment.

In studying the sacred theatre of this time a problem of definition arises,
for it was considered that every play had or at least ought to have an
instructive purpose and the instruction offered was customarily
Christian: the difficulty is to exclude any play from the category of
religious drama. For the present purpose I have limited the field to
plays on subjects drawn from the Bible or the lives of saints; for this
reason I prefer the more exclusive designation 'sacred drama' to
'religious drama'. I have extended this definition in certain cases: it
would have been perverse, for example, to exclude a play about Joan
of Arc on the ground that she was not canonised until 1920. Also
included are plays on abstract matters of belief, such as the Incarnation.
Plays treating Christian morality, on the other hand, are excluded,
even where they had a biblical origin (the Prodigal Son, for example):
the *moralités*, which had fictional and symbolic subjects treated
allegorically, formed a dramatic tradition quite separate from that of
plays about historical or at least legendary human figures. The exclusion
of the moralities does not encompass all allegories; allegorical treat-

ments of matters of belief are discussed. Only plays in French are considered. There was a considerable body of neo-Latin sacred drama, but since the genre was cultivated by scholars throughout Europe it is impossible to identify a French tradition within it. The neo-Latin theatre followed conventions of its own, and had little direct impact on the French tradition: its importance lay in awakening dramatists in the sixteenth century to a possibility by showing that modern poets could successfully imitate the masterpieces of ancient Greece and Rome. Since my concern is the dramatic forms themselves rather than their literary origins, the neo-Latin theatre is in any case peripheral to my subject.[7] A few neo-Latin plays, however, were also published in French versions: these are taken into consideration. Only plays that were printed are discussed: the texts surviving in manuscript are frequently incomplete and usually are not contemporary copies but contain emendations from later centuries: only texts that were sufficiently popular to be fixed by printing give a reliable indication of what contemporaries appreciated. All the extant French sacred plays printed between 1550 and 1650 are considered, including those written by Francophones outside the French Kingdom.

Appended to this study are a descriptive bibliography of these editions, and a chronological table showing the dates of composition, performance and printing of the plays, with locations. Bibliographical and chronological information is not duplicated in the body of the study: for my authority for stating that a play was printed or performed at a particular place on a given date, reference should be made to the Catalogue or the Chronology.

In the Catalogue the original orthography and punctuation are retained, save that the long s is not reproduced. Elsewhere the original orthography is likewise followed, but the long s is not shown, abbreviations are resolved, and the modern distinctions between i and j, u and v are introduced. I have not presumed to interpolate corrections, except in the titles of plays: the punctuation of title-pages was particularly erratic, and in referring to them in the text (though not in the Catalogue) I have allowed myself to remove such features as full-stops in the middle of phrases. Given the habit among printers of the day of making new editions without reference to the author, quotations and references are regularly taken, unless it is stated otherwise, from the first edition described in the Catalogue, that being the only one certainly approved by the author.

The authors' own spelling is retained for the names of characters, while the English version is used to refer to the historical personage: thus Nabuchodonozor for Garnier's villain, Nebuchadnezzar for the Old-Testament figure.

1. The inheritance of 1550: the *mystères*

Although 1550 saw the appearance of the first French neo-classical tragedy, the medieval style was far from having been superseded. By an *arrêt* of 17 November 1548 the Parlement of Paris had prohibited all performances of the 'mystère de la Passion Nostre Sauveur, ne autres mystères sacrez',[1] but outside Paris the *mystères* continued to flourish, dying out only at the Revolution. It is difficult to estimate their popularity because of the lack of systematic records, but even the incomplete documentation we possess shows the impressive total of some 190 performances between 1550 and 1650.

However, the prohibition of 1548 is not to be disregarded entirely: though it was far from killing off the *mystères* overnight, it was important as a symptom, and consequence, of a decline that had already begun. The *mystères* had attained gigantic proportions: they could require casts of over 100; rehearsals and construction of the stage took some weeks and could occupy a whole community, while the performance itself lasted a number of days.[2] Time, energy and money were never easily available on such a scale and would certainly not be forthcoming during the religious wars.[3] The *mystères* had in any case fallen into disrepute both for the impropriety of many scenes and for the irreverent behaviour of the crowds.[4] The performances after the middle of the sixteenth century were more subdued than previously: few lasted more than a single day, and probably none exceeded four.[5] Only short *mystères* or excerpts from the great compilations reached the stage. The *mystères* survived, certainly, but in diminished form.

Moreover, of the many *mystères* composed earlier and still performed, few were printed. When a community wished to present a *mystère*, its usual course was to procure a copy of the text and have it revised in accordance with local circumstances and modern conditions by the best-educated resident (known as the *fatiste*); after the performance the new version would be printed. After 1550 the process of revision and performance continued, as local records attest, but the resulting texts were rarely printed.[6] The great compilations of the fifteenth century were neglected by the printers, and in fact only five *mystères* were judged sufficiently important and interesting for revised texts to emerge from a press; only those five will be considered here.

These were modest *mystères*, using relatively small casts and occupying no more than two *journées*. They were also distinguished from the productions of an earlier period by their subject-matter and theme. Grace Frank defined the purpose of the churchmen under whose guidance plays first emerged from the liturgy as a 'desire to make visible and potent to the people the story of the Resurrection and the hope of the Redemption...to strengthen the understanding of the services by the unlearned and to make manifest by ceremonials of various kinds the allegorical content of the liturgy'.[7] The aim was nothing less than to elucidate the whole of the Christian understanding of the conditions and purpose of human life. This was accomplished in the developed *mystères* by showing the events on which this under-standing is founded – principally the Fall and the Passion – and introducing God Himself to explain how human history is directed by His will: this was the approach in the *mystères* of the *Viel Testament*, the *Passion et résurrection* and *Apocalypse*, and the *Actes des apôtres*, which together set forth the whole of the Christian version of history from the Creation to the Last Judgement. Though still performed after 1550, these were no longer printed: the plays which attracted the greatest public favour were those which took as their subject-matter the careers of individual men.[8]

This choice of material excluded any attempt to set out God's grand plan for mankind; the playwrights who maintained this tradition, studied in Chapter 3 below, used material of a different type. In the new *mystères* God appeared only fleetingly, if at all, to explain how He was directing events. The playwrights were not concerned with elucidating the providential significance of history. Instead, they concentrated on the incidents of the career of the individual who was their subject. This was not simply an attempt to present every revered act of the saint, for the technique was applied equally to Old-Testament figures to whose deeds no reverence attached, while the saint-plays contained many incidents not concerning the saint himself. Whatever the pious intentions of the man who first wrote a play about an exemplary human, in the second half of the sixteenth century the *mystères* were appreciated principally for the sensational incidents the subject's career contained.

Of the five *mystères* reprinted after 1550, three concerned the acts of popular saints and martyrs. One seems incomplete; the others trace the whole of the subject's career, in exhaustive detail. Saint Barbara was the object of a special cult, being numbered among the Fourteen Holy Helpers and credited with the power to protect her devotees from lightning. The *Vie de Madame saincte Barbe* was printed twice after 1550 and performed twice in 1597.[9] It is a compact *mystère* of some 4000 lines, with a cast of forty. A detailed analysis will give a graphic illustration of the nature of the *mystères* in the latter half of the six-teenth century.[10]

A Prologue explains what each *mansion* on the stage represents, and introduces the characters. A farcical prelude follows. First a Folle Femme sings of her life of luxury, then the Emperor Marcien leads his court to sacrifice at the Temple of Mahom, to the delight of the priests who appropriate his offerings. They present a burlesque spectacle for his benefit, in the course of which Satan, hidden within an idol, orders Marcien to kill all the Christians.

The *mystère* proper commences: King Dioscorus announces to his wife that he intends to make a pilgrimage to the Temple of Mahom, leaving their daughter Barbe at home. Their conversation turns to Barbe's nubile beauty and virtue; in consultation with the court they decide to find her a husband. They despatch a Messenger to fetch her. He crosses the stage to her *mansion*, not omitting to pause for a drink on the way, delivers the summons and returns with her to the palace. Dioscorus tells her of his wish that she should marry. She replies unambiguously:

> Je ne vueil copulation
> D'homme ne habitation,   (f. 10ʳ)[11]

and rejects all her parents' blandishments. Dioscorus has his Messenger fetch some masons, whom he orders to build a tower with two windows. He announces that it is time to set out on the pilgrimage. Barbe is summoned by the Messenger and left in the charge of three Pucelles, who settle down to drink and gamble as soon as the King is out of sight. Barbe slips away to see the masons, and begs them to incorporate a third window into the tower; they agree when she promises to take responsibility for altering Dioscorus's design.

Barbe returns to her own *mansion* where she prays for enlightenment. She makes the sign of the cross on a stone: her finger sinks in and leaves a cruciform impression. The miracle decides her to seek baptism at once. She goes to a hermit in the mountains, who instructs her briefly in the doctrines of the Trinity, the Fall and the Redemption and baptises her with no more ado. In Hell, Lucifer curses his devils for permitting her conversion. They promise to make her father torment her. Dioscorus decides to return home, and is angry to find that his tower (which has been built on the stage) has been completed with three windows. Learning that Barbe was responsible, he promises himself to punish her, and sends his Messenger to fetch her.

At this point there is a second Prologue: this perhaps marked the beginning of a second *journée*, though the first would in that case have been disproportionately short, or perhaps indicated that all the preceding material could be omitted in an abbreviated performance. After this Prologue, the Messenger summons Barbe to her father, who asks why she had a third window added to the tower. She explains that she wished thus to honour the Trinity. He is outraged to discover that she is a Christian: 'Il descend de dessus son cheval, et tire son espée pour la vouloir battre' (stage direction, f. 22ʳ). She prays for protection: the tower splits in two, creating a passage through which she can escape, then closes before she can be pursued. Undeterred by this miraculous proof that Barbe enjoys divine protection, Dioscorus gives chase. He meets two shepherds who set him on her track. When they turn round, they find that their sheep have disappeared. Barbe returns and explains that they have been punished thus for betraying her to her father, but when they kneel in contrition she prays God to forgive them; the sheep reappear.

Dioscorus catches up with Barbe. 'Il la lie à la queuë de son cheval' (stage direction, f. 25ᵛ) and leads her back to his palace, where the Queen urges her to desist from her rejection of marriage and paganism. Barbe remains inflexible, so Dioscorus, losing patience, has her taken by the Messenger to prison, where she is admitted by the Chartrier.

The Emperor Marcien, in consultation with his court, decides to order the execution of all Christians. His Messenger proclaims the edict. Dioscorus orders his Messenger to fetch Barbe from gaol; he does so, and leads her before the King. She informs him defiantly that incarceration has not shaken her faith. Baffled, Dioscorus consults his courtiers, who suggest sending her to the Emperor for punishment. Dioscorus agrees and has two Chevaliers lead her before Marcien. Marcien is surprised that so beautiful a girl should reject marriage and favour Christ. She retorts that his words will never daunt her; Marcien orders a beating. Four Tyrans gleefully strip, bind and beat her, accompanying their blows with taunts and insults, but Barbe is unmoved:

> Mauvais tyrans plains de tristesse,
> Vostre tourment m'est grand liesse ...
> Mon ame en sera bien plus saine.   (f. 35ʳ⁻ᵛ)

She prays for protection. In Heaven, God hears and orders Michel and Gabriel to descend and console her. At their arrival the Tyrans fall insensible. The angels exhort Barbe to endure her torments patiently, for she will be rewarded in Heaven. They leave; the Tyrans recover, and report that they are unable to harm Barbe because the devil is protecting her. Marcien has her brought before him and, when she continues to defy him, has his Messager lead her to prison. There she again prays for assistance, and God sends down the angels to heal her wounds.

When Barbe is led before Marcien again, having been fetched from gaol by his Messager, he is amazed to see no marks of the beating. He offers to arrange a rich marriage for her but she refuses, explaining that she loves only Christ, who healed her wounds. Marcien consults his courtiers to know how to convert her; at their suggestion she is suspended by her feet and whipped. When this produces no effect, the courtiers suggest scorching her with flaming brands; and when this too fails, Marcien personally beats the Tyrans for their incompetence then has them return her to gaol. In response to Barbe's prayers, God sends the angels to assure her that she will be martyred and received into Heaven. Marcien invents a new torment: Barbe's head shall be beaten with hammers against an anvil. The Tyrans fetch her from gaol and inflict this with their habitual gusto. In response to Barbe's prayers, God sends Michel and Gabriel to confirm that after martyrdom she will enter Paradise. Encouraged, she defies Marcien afresh, at which he orders a new torture which the Tyrans inflict with a will: they tie her to a post, tear off her breasts with pincers and throw them to the dogs. Nevertheless, Barbe continues to defy Marcien, who finally has her led back to gaol.

In Hell, Lucifer reproaches his devils for failing to overcome Barbe. They promise to inspire Marcien with a new scheme to corrupt her: to give her a whore as companion. Lucifer approves, so Satan goes and suggests this to Marcien in his sleep. Marcien wakes and repeats the idea to his courtiers; they approve, so the Messager is sent to fetch the Folle Femme. In her *mansion* she sings of the pleasures of her way of life, in the intervals of eating and drinking. The Messager finds her and leads her to Marcien, who orders her to initiate Barbe into these pleasures. The Folle Femme advises Barbe to take advantage of her beauty to live a life of luxury, and offers to set up in business with her.[12] Outraged by the proposition, Barbe warns the Folle Femme that her sinful life will lead her to Hell. She offers to prove her point by showing the whore the devil inhabiting her. At Barbe's command the devil vacates the Folle Femme's body; Barbe beats him, ordering:

> me promettras qu'en tous lieux
> Qui de moy fera remembrance
> N'auront nul mal celles ne ceux
> Qui me requerront en aidance,

> Esclair, ne foudre ne tonerre,
> Ne cherra en lieu ne en place
> Sur ceux qui me voudront requerre
> Que mal ne ennuy leur face.   (f. 59ʳ)

The devil promises and wins his release; the Folle Femme, converted, swears loyalty to Barbe and her faith.

Wishing to know if his device has succeeded, Marcien has Barbe fetched by his Messenger from prison, but she informs him defiantly that she has converted her intended corruptor. Marcien orders both to be executed. The Messenger leads them to the Prevost, who, after consulting his retinue, decides first to have Barbe whipped naked through town. The Tyrans set about this with even more enthusiasm than usual. Barbe prays God to hide her shame: He orders His angels to cover her with a robe. The Tyrans fall insensible at the angels' arrival; these cover Barbe with a cloak embroidered with the message, which a hermit reads out, that she will soon enter Heaven. The Tyrans recover and report that they cannot harm Barbe; despairing of executing his orders, the Prevost has her led back to Marcien. Marcien too is baffled; he has his Messenger take Barbe back to Dioscorus. Unmoved by her pleas for mercy, her father decides to behead her at once. Barbe commends her soul to God and requests that her devotees should be spared from lightning and headaches, using the same formula as previously. Dioscorus kills her. God orders the angels to descend and lead her soul to Heaven, which they do, to the accompaniment of carols.

Dioscorus suddenly feels himself a prey to a consuming rage. He calls on Lucifer:

> A toy me rend comme mon sire
> Pour t'obeïr j'ay faict mainct mal
> Mon ame en aura bien du pire
> Du feu d'enfer...
> Lucifer m'as-tu point ouy?
> Faire me devez telle feste
> Je suis vostre sans nulle ressort
> Mettez mon corps à grand diffame
> Venez à moy tout d'un accord:
> Et m'emportez et corps et ame.   (f. 72ʳ)

In turn Marcien, the Prevost, the Chartrier and the four Tyrans consign themselves to Hell; with much rejoicing, Lucifer and his minions carry off their souls.

L'Aveugle and Le Boyteux pray to Sainte Barbe and are miraculously cured. They praise her, and with the Hermit's help carry her body into a chapel where they bury her, singing the Te Deum which, as custom required, closes the performance.

In the cycles setting out God's design for mankind, the *fatistes* had narrated the events on which our understanding of His purpose is based. Although the material was now the life of an individual, the same technique was retained: *Sainte Barbe* tells the story of the whole of the subject's career from conversion to martyrdom. The narrative is simply conceived: events are related only by paratactic succession, with no sense of subordination. The *fatiste* did not feel the need to make events convincing. There is no explanation, for instance, of why Dioscorus is transformed from a loving father into his daughter's executioner, or of why Marcien uses torture instead of persuasion. Legend assured that events were so, and the *fatiste* did not find it necessary to endow his account with any inherent plausibility: the authority of the legend was sufficient. The *fatiste* was indeed prepared to go quite beyond the bounds of realism where religion required: he showed Barbe arranging with God for her devotees to be protected from lightning and he showed Dioscorus and the others consigning themselves to Hell. A saint would never presume to strike such a bargain with God, and men do not naturally describe themselves as monsters; but the *fatiste* knew that his audience was interested in the religious significance of the subject and would not be disturbed by the breach of realism needed to make this significance clear. This was the essence of his technique: the *naïveté* of the narrative, the improbabilities and the symbolic actions, all responded to and indeed were required by the spectators' reverent approach. The spectators had no need of plausibility because they accepted the legend, and they expected the action to symbolise their appreciation of its religious meaning whether or not the result was realistic on a human level. The whole construction of the *mystère* implies the spectators' faith.

However, reverence is not the atmosphere that the play conveys. God's role is limited to sending His angels down to comfort Barbe; He does not explain His purpose in permitting her to suffer. The play does of course show the miracles associated with Barbara, but in their presentation attention is focussed principally on the spectacular aspect. The tortures which the saint endured are likewise shown with a degree of anatomical detail that is closer to prurience than reverence. There is, moreover, a great deal of material that is not related to the subject's saintly career; the *fatiste* took particular delight in exhibiting cameos of disreputable figures, such as the pagan priests, the Messagers and the Folle Femme.[13] Although the dramatic technique in the *mystère* was dependent on the audience's reverence, the choice of material to fill the scenes was dictated more by the spectators' delight in the sensational, the comic and the spectacular.

In the mechanism of the action another principle is apparent:

despite the spectators' acceptance of implausibilities sanctioned by religion, where a physical action was concerned nothing could be left to the imagination, because they expected to witness every stage. If Dioscorus desires to speak to Barbe when she is in prison, it is not enough for her to be led on in response to his wish: Dioscorus orders his Messenger to fetch her, and the audience watches the Messenger cross the stage to the gaol, pausing to drink, eat and joke on the way, then deliver his orders to the Chartrier, who goes in and repeats the summons to Barbe herself, then leads her out and gives her into the charge of the Messenger, who leads her back across the stage and announces her to Dioscorus in his palace. This procedure is repeated on each of the many occasions when Barbe is fetched from prison or returned there. In his zeal to ensure that no link in the chain of events should be hidden from the audience, the *fatiste* was not afraid of repetition; thus in the episode of the Folle Femme, the audience first hears Satan propose to Lucifer the use of a whore to corrupt Barbe, then hears Satan repeat the idea to Marcien, then hears it a third time when Marcien repeats it to his court, before witnessing the scheme being put into effect.[14] A major determinant in the handling of the material was the audience's unimaginative curiosity about events.

The convention on the post-Classical stage has been that the characters behave like real people engaged in their own lives, quite unconscious of the audience. The *fatiste* allowed his characters no such autonomy: when Barbe strikes her bargain with God or Dioscorus consigns himself to the devil, the words do not well up from within the character but express the audience's opinion of him. The characters describe themselves, not from within, but as the audience sees them: they are mouthpieces of the audience's faith. The implausibilities of the narrative of the saintly career are also reflections of the audience's reverent acceptance of the legend. The play does not stand on its own but is comprehensible only as a projection of the audience's faith. However, the *fatiste* combined this deeply symbolic technique with a minutely realistic treatment of incident: far from implying reverence, the details of the tortures and the comings and goings of the Messagers answer to the audience's curiosity and taste for spectacle. Whatever the capacity of the *mystère* for expressing the spectators' religious feelings, it had come to be quite overwhelmed by the sensational detail of the plot.

Like Barbara, Margaret is numbered among the Holy Helpers, and the *Vie de Madame saincte Marguerite* retained some popularity into the seventeenth century. It is another compact *mystère*, presenting forty-four characters and occupying some 5000 lines. The action is more extensive than in *Saincte Barbe*, for it commences at Marguerite's birth. It recounts her brief life, the miraculous conversions she effected, the deaths of her disciples and her own martyrdom. The play ends with her persecutors condemning themselves to Hell.[15]

Marguerite is the daughter of a pagan lord but is brought up by a Christian wet-nurse. On the death of Marguerite's parents, the Nourisse says to the young girl:

> Ma fille, et moy demeurerons,
> Elle et moy donques garderons
> Les brebiettes par les champs,
> Avecques les autres enfans,
> Et tous les jours irons de suitte.
> Et aussi, pucelle petite,
> Il vous faut croire en Jesus Christ,
> Qui les portes d'enfer rompit
> Apres sa resurrection:
> Tresdouce fille de renom,
> Son sainct Baptesme recevoir,
> Et ses sacremens pour tout voir,
> Que ses apostres ont presché:
> Et par tous les pays noncé:
> Ma fille, ceux qui le croiront
> En paradis sauvez seront,
> Douce pucelle seure et bonne,
> Ne croyez pas la loy felonne,
> Voicy un homme d'austere vie,
> Par qui vous serez baptisee,
> Vous plaist-il bien, pucelle tendre?   (pp. 13–14)

This is all the instruction in the content and meaning of the Christian faith that Marguerite needs to reach her commitment. She replies without hesitation:

> Il me plaist bien, sans plus attendre,
> Son sainct baptesme recevoir
> Mieux me vaudra que nul avoir,
> Depuis que c'est si noble chose
> Je m'y oblige, et mon coeur pose,
> Et renonce la loy payenne
> Pour estre plus vraye chrestienne,
> Du tout me donne à Jesus Christ.   (p. 14)

The priest (the 'homme d'austere vie' mentioned by the Nourisse) is satisfied on the strength of this declaration that Marguerite is a true Christian, for he baptises her without further ado. An equally sudden conversion is effected by Marguerite herself when eight pagans, having observed that God sustained her as she was tortured, ask her for baptism: she instructs them as follows:

Vous faites bien vostre devoir
De delaisser la loy payenne
Pour recevoir la loy chrestienne,
Agenouillez vous, baissez la teste,
Car voicy de l'eau toute preste
Je vous signes, et vous benis,
En disant in nomine Patris, et Filii,
Et Spiritus sancti. Amen.   *Elle les baptise*
Or mes amis ayez bon coeur,
Et gardez bien que a malheur
Vous ne renonciez point Jesum,
Qui mourut en croix sans raison
Pour le forfaict du premier homme
Adam, qui mordit en la pomme
Pour sa grand inobedience.   (p. 102)

It is inconceivable that Marguerite's or the Nourisse's elliptical references to the Fall and the Redemption could be understood by their
pagan disciples, let alone give them sufficient grasp of doctrine to turn
them into full-fledged Christians. These speeches are clearly not
designed for the benefit of the pagans to whom they are addressed, but
for the spectators, who are predisposed to accept that the simple naming
of elements of doctrine is enough to produce conversion as if by magic.
The depiction of action and character is governed by and reflects the
spectators' reverent acquiescence, but, as in the case of *Saincte Barbe*,
the *mystère* is not a schematic representation of their faith: it consists
of a copious narrative of sensational events. The *fatiste* presented as
many spectacular scenes as possible, notably one in which Marguerite
is swallowed by a dragon but escapes unscathed when it splits in two
on her making the sign of the cross in its belly.

Although not a Holy Helper, Mary Magdalen was the object of
special veneration in France, for legend held that with her sister
Martha, their resurrected brother Lazarus and Saint Maximinus she
landed near Marseilles and converted the Duke and his serfs to
Christianity.[16] A *mystère* on this subject was printed under the somewhat inaccurate title, *La Vie de Marie Magdaleine* (Lyons 1605); as
Petit de Julleville suggested, this is probably all that survives of a
larger work narrating the whole of Mary's life.[17] In the complete
Life Marie herself would no doubt have been the principal character,
but as it stands the *mystère* is chiefly concerned with the activities of
the Duke, while Marie and the other Christians figure only at the
beginning and end. The Duke longs for an heir: Marie promises that
her God will give him one. When his wife becomes pregnant, the Duke
embarks with her on a pilgrimage to Rome; but the Duchess dies in
childbirth during the voyage, and the baby with her. The bodies are

left on an island which is so rocky that they cannot be buried. The Duke completes his pilgrimage and on his way home puts in at the island, where he finds his wife and son alive and well, having been miraculously sustained by Marie whom he had left in Marseilles. The Duke and Duchess are converted and return home to seek baptism.

These miracles are recounted without any sensational emphasis: there are no supernatural interventions and we see only the result of a miracle, not its occurrence. The play does of course have its spectacular element, in the scenes of sea-crossings, storms and devilry, but there is little of the lurid or the bawdy found in other *mystères*. The *fatiste* was perhaps a relatively sensitive soul; certainly his depiction of the dashing of the Duke's hopes for an heir is touching. However, these qualities of the play show the *fatiste* failing to attend to his ostensible reason for staging the legend, its religious significance: in his zeal to exhibit the miracles by which the saint showed favour to France, he almost forgot the saint herself to provide a detailed narrative of the career of the individual who was the object of her intervention. Whatever the emphasis this subject might have received in the hypothetical *Life* of Mary Magdalen, when this episode was extracted from it to stand on its own the *fatiste* was perhaps more concerned to do honour to France than to God. The chronicle of miracles as a dramatic form could be used for a purpose that was at most marginally religious.[18]

The Old Testament establishes the need for the Redemption by its account of the Fall and contains innumerable instances of the intervention of providence in the lives of individuals. However, in treating Old-Testament material, the *fatistes* of this period were not concerned to draw attention to the operation of the divine plan in human history: as in the saint-plays, they provided instead circumstantial accounts of the lives of the subjects.

The *Patience de Job* remained one of the most popular *mystères*: it was printed no fewer than ten times after 1550 and performed on at least six occasions.[19] It staged the whole of the Book of Job. Job's trials, narrated briefly in the Bible, are presented in great detail, occupying about half the play. The devils first propose to assault Job at line 1431. The scene shifts between Heaven, Hell and various locations on earth as the devils first obtain God's permission then proceed to try Job. They incite the Roy de Sabbée to raid Job's stock. The King is shown deliberating and mustering his army. The raid is staged. An interlude is provided by a misunderstanding between the forces of Sabbée and the Caldyens, who imagine that it is their stock that is being stolen; a skirmish is fought before the truth is explained. Job finally learns of the loss of his stock and the deaths of his children at

line 3104, some 1700 lines after it is first decided to put him to the test;
the interval is devoted to the comic and spectacular activities of devils,
soldiers and herdsmen, in which every stage of the mechanism by
which Job is afflicted is presented in copious detail. After the first
disaster, we turn again to the court of the Roy de Sabbée, and only
after the devils have brought his captains to an evil end fighting over
booty do we return to the story of Job.

Job accepts these first trials with exemplary constancy: he thanks
and praises God and urges his wife to do the same. However, after
God authorises Sathan to afflict Job in his own body, resignation comes
less easily. He avoids suggesting that God is unjust, but asks repeatedly
what he has done to deserve such suffering and even wishes that God
had never given him life. He admits nevertheless that he deserves
punishment for his sins, while remaining confident that God in His
mercy will spare him the eternal torment he merits. At length he is
abandoned by his friends and cursed by his wife. He complains:

> Hellas! Qu'ay je peu mesfere
> Envers Dieu, qui me veuille desfere?
> J'ay tousjours heu patience
> Et bonne foy et esperance,
> Et ce que Dieu m'avoyt donné
> Aux pauvres gens habandonné.   (ll. 5738–43)

When God is thus reproached for permitting Job to suffer despite his
blameless life, He replies in person, warning Job not to resist His will.
Job sues for forgiveness and God, mollified, explains that He has
permitted Job's sufferings so that he may serve as an example of
patience. Job praises Him.

This detailed account of how Job's faith withstands the trial and
enables him to accept his sufferings is in fact no more than a dutiful
transcription of the biblical narrative. This part of the play seems to
have been imposed on the *fatiste*. It provides only half the action.
Apparently he judged the biblical account insufficiently interesting to
stand on its own as a play, and, though obliged in conscience to reproduce it, added for pleasure all the activities of the Sabbéens, the stock-
men and the devils. These episodes are highly spectacular and no
doubt appealed strongly to an audience which saw its own life mirrored
in them. For the audience and the *fatiste* this material was indispensable
for the success of the play, and at least as important as Job himself.

The other Old-Testament *mystère* that was sufficiently esteemed to
be reprinted after 1550 was an episode extracted from the *Mistére du
Viel Testament*. Little was changed when the *Hystoire de Saincte
Susanne* was separated from its source. In the *Viel Testament* the

stories of Daniel and Susanne were intertwined, and by extracting only scenes concerning the latter the *fatiste* left Daniel's intervention to save her from being stoned somewhat unprepared; otherwise the plot suffered little by being removed from its primitive context.[20] No incident in the biblical narrative is omitted. Some are slightly embroidered; the servants are given large comic roles, and Susanne is shown instructing them and her children. The intervention of God, on the other hand, though present in both the Bible and the *Viel Testament*, is omitted here. Virtue triumphs over evil by human means: there is no suggestion that Susanne's vindication is an instance of God's protection of the innocent. Like the saint-plays, the later biblical *mystères* concentrated on the incidents of the plot rather than their significance.

Instead of providing a drama of human emotions, as we expect of a modern play, the *mystères* were designed to do honour to God through a narrative of His miraculous interventions in human affairs. In the presentation of the narrative the *fatistes* combined an implausible treatment of action with unnatural characterisation: for its acceptability the play relied, not on any inherent *vraisemblance*, but on the spectators' reverent acquiescence. In this stage world deeds and words are symbolic. The speeches do not epitomise what a real person might have said and felt in a given situation, but express the significance of the action from the point of view of the spectators: thus Dioscorus can describe himself as a servant of the devil, and conversions can be effected simply by naming points of doctrine. The technique of the *mystère* was quite opposed to the convention by which the characters are supposed not to know an audience is watching: everything is designed explicitly from the spectators' point of view, and what occurs on the stage is a projection of their faith. Thanks to its implausibilities and its symbolic actions, the *mystère* makes sense only when viewed with believing eyes: the dramatic form did not only express, it positively required the spectators' faith.

In the *mystères* as they survived into the late Renaissance, this potent dramatic form was applied to presenting a lurid and exhaustive chronicle of events, in which reverence is the last emotion implied. The *fatistes* seem to have retained the traditional form without realising how unsuitable it was where its religious purpose had been so far forgotten that scenes of torture were developed far beyond the length necessary to make the religious point, and where the account of the miracles of Mary Magdalen could be diverted into patriotism. The result was an unresolved conflict: a style devised for the symbolic presentation of faith was used for a realistic presentation of events. Such a combination of realism and symbolism, of course, is not necessarily disruptive: it has been used recently with striking success in Peter Nichols's *A Day in the Death of Joe Egg*, for example, where the characters at some moments address the audience directly and at others behave in the correct post-Classical realist manner, as if no audience were present. However, when a martyr converts the by-standers by naming Christian doctrines while undergoing gruesome tortures, it is hard to see her as a symbol since her sufferings are all too real, and equally hard to sympathise with her as a suffering human since her actions are too patently symbolic. The *mystères* of this time lack the artistic coherence that would guide the spectator's response; without this, it is impossible to appreciate the martyr's sacrifice either on the human or the religious level.

It was not just in the number of *journées* or the size of the cast that the *mystères* as they survived into the second half of the sixteenth century were diminished. Though the old plays retained some popularity in performance, almost no one attempted to write a new *mystère*; contemporaries felt that the genre was ripe for replacement rather than renewal. A few dramatists were attempting perhaps to return to the original spirit of the *mystères* when they wrote plays setting out Christian doctrine. These will be the subject of Chapter 3. First, however, it will be appropriate to say something of the alternative dramatic form that was first used in French in 1550, though it had been available in Latin for some time: this was the Renaissance interpretation of the classical style.

2. Bèze and the classical tradition

Théodore de Bèze in his *Abraham sacrifiant* was the first playwright working in French to attempt a new approach. Rather than retailing the events of sacred history he concentrated instead on the crisis that Abraham experienced when ordered to sacrifice Isaac. Unlike the *fatiste* of the *Mistère du Viel Testament*,[1] he did not cause Abraham to express the audience's opinion of himself, but presented him as an autonomous and living character with whose anguish the spectator is enabled to sympathise. Identification with the protagonist was not central to the ancient Greek and Roman drama, but it was from the ancient playwrights' concentration on the crisis that the imitators of the classical tradition in the Renaissance and later developed what became the drama of the hero's emotional life; Bèze thus wrote the first neo-classical French play. However, *Abraham sacrifiant* is not simply an offshoot of an alien tradition, unconnected with anything in the existing French theatre. Like the primitive *fatistes*, Bèze was concerned to explain God's will, and adopted a device from the technique of the *mystères* to do so, the intervention of supernatural figures. In order to make his religious meaning clear, Bèze combined classical and medieval techniques in a new form.

The attempt to stir the spectators to sympathy with the protagonist, on the other hand, was not a feature of the *mystères*; in this respect *Abraham sacrifiant* constituted a major departure from the existing French tradition. In concentrating on the emotions generated by the crisis Abraham endures, rather than on the incidents of his life, Bèze could draw for inspiration not only on the Greek and Roman theatre but also on a modern tradition of neo-classical drama in Latin. In the first half of the sixteenth century, writers throughout Europe had established that it was possible for a modern poet to write a play in imitation of the ancient masterpieces, and even that it was possible to imitate their style while using non-classical subjects, including biblical and hagiographic material. Individually the neo-Latin sacred plays were of no great importance in the development of the French genre, as I have said; once the possibility of reproducing the classical style was established, writers using it in the vernacular naturally turned for models more to the ancients themselves than to their modern imitators.

Two of these early Latin sacred dramas appeared in French versions as well, and so fall into the province of this study. These are the *Jephthes sive votum* and *Baptistes sive calumnia* of the Scot, George Buchanan, who between 1539 and 1543 taught at the Collège de Guyenne, where he translated Euripides's *Alcestis* and *Medea* into Latin and wrote his biblical plays. Later he taught in Paris, where he met the men who composed the first French neo-classical tragedies, Jodelle, Grévin, La Péruse and Bèze himself. *Jephthes* was not printed until 1554, in Paris, and *Baptistes* appeared from London only in 1577, but the texts had long circulated in manuscript.[2] They were probably known to Bèze before he wrote *Abraham sacrifiant*, and are more conveniently analysed here before that play is discussed further.[3]

The Latin text of *Jephthes* was frequently reprinted, and it was quickly translated into French, by Vesel (Paris 1566, *privilège* 1560), by Florent Chrestian (Orléans 1567), by Mage de Fiefmelin (Poitiers 1601) and by Brinon (Rouen 1614);[4] the version by the Protestant Chrestian was reprinted three times.[5] The play's popularity is attributable in part to its connection with the civil wars: it reflects on a theme which preoccupied many dramatists at this time, God's punishment of the nation's sin by the scourges of war and other disasters. Buchanan anticipated the consequences of the doctrinal strife of his day.

The theme is established by the angel who delivers the Prologue. In prosperity, the Jews forget that they owe their happiness to God and worship false deities; He punishes this ingratitude with war, famine or plague, but before the Jews' afflictions can cause them to despair He sends a champion or a prophet to lead them back into His favour. They have recently been punished by subjection to the Ammonites, but now God has relented. Lest the Jews fall again into pride, He has sent as a champion an outcast bastard, Jephté, so that they should realise that they owe victory to God, not the unworthy human agent. Jephté vowed, if victorious, to sacrifice to God whatever element of his household he should first see on his return from battle: to protect him from deriving any pride from his victory, God will arrange for him to be met by his daughter, Iphis.

Jephté is not forgetful of God. Marching home, he praises His justice in punishing the Jews for their sins and His mercy in relenting. He takes no credit for the victory, ascribing it to God alone. In gratitude, he renews his vow to offer a sacrifice. On his daughter's approach, although he laments his misfortune, he does not rebel, but insists in arguments with his friend Symmache, the Chorus and a Priest that he must perform the sacrifice. But having triumphed over himself and his advisers, Jephté still has to face his wife, symbolically named Storge,[6] and Iphis herself. He resists their arguments and pleas, and concludes:

> Si ta mort se pouvoit racheter par la mienne,
> Je mettroy volontiers ma vie pour la tienne.
> Suis-je par dessus vous à vostre avis heureux?   (ll. 1523-5)

From his anguish Iphis appreciates that he has not undertaken frivolously to kill her, and accepts that she must be sacrificed. Her heroism redoubles Jephté's grief, but he does not waver: the play concludes with a *récit* of Iphis's death. Whatever his anguish, he remains steadfast in his determination to do his duty before God. He rejects the advice that his vow is not binding, and never expresses any resentment against God for requiring this sacrifice. In personal disaster as in victory, he is God's dutiful servant.

The play owes relatively little to the brief account in the Bible;[7] its power derives, so far as it derives from anything other than Buchanan's genius, from imitation of classical models.[8] Buchanan's principal invention, based on Euripides's *Hecuba*, was the pathetic figure of Storge, who struggles unavailingly to save her daughter and hears the *récit* of her death. Indeed all the pathetic confrontations between the two women and Jephté were added to the source. Although the Bible provided the basic irony of the vow, Buchanan invented, helped by the classical models, all the scenes in which the characters' innocent hopes emphasise the pathetic implications of the destiny set for them in the Prologue, and in which they exhibit the most extreme grief and the most noble devotion to duty. Unlike the *fatistes*, Buchanan did not expand on the biblical story with a wealth of incident, but so arranged his plot as to involve the spectators' sympathies with the anguish endured by the characters.

These emotions are allowed to subside, however, while Jephté discusses the sacrifice with Symmache and the Priest. These scenes were not contrived for their emotional power or their necessity to the plot. In the first Jephté wishes he had not won the battle, and even that God had never elevated him to lead the Jews from his previous lowly estate, the pleasures of which he extols; at this Symmache inveighs against the faint-hearted who ungratefully reject the good fortune God sends. The argument possesses a certain irony, because Symmache does not yet know the cause of Jephté's grief; but the characters concern themselves principally with debating the relative merits of the

exalted and humble estates, a conventional issue[9] developed more for
its own sake than for its application to Jephté's predicament. The
Priest, in his discussion with Jephté, argues that the latter could not
please God by fulfilling a vow when this would involve a crime, but
Jephté answers robustly that one cannot break a vow in any circumstances and dismisses the Priest, saying

> J'aime mieux une simple et sotte verité,
> Qu'une sagesse belle en toute impieté.   (ll. 1295-6)

At a time when the monasteries were under attack, the legitimacy of
vows was a subject of controversy: Jephté evinces a distinctly Protestant
preference for individual conscience over the casuistic teaching of the
Church as a guide to right and wrong.[10] The scene demonstrates Jephté's
steadfastness, but this quality is amply exhibited elsewhere: the debate
seems to have been included more for its relevance to contemporary
Europe. The inclusion of debates which were to be appreciated for
themselves more than for their relevance to the speakers' circumstances
was not an idiosyncrasy of Buchanan's: it was a regular feature of the
dramaturgy of the bookish poets of the humanist school.[11]

Excepting these irrelevancies, the play is carefully arranged to arouse
the spectators' emotions by exhibiting those of the characters. Having
witnessed Jephté's anguish at the ironic result of his vow, the spectator
observes his heroic steadfastness in overcoming the appeals of a series
of characters with successively stronger moral claims on him; simultaneously we are moved by the grief of Storge and Iphis. Indeed, so
intense is the grief of father and daughter that they approach tragic
status: in making the sacrifice in the confidence that whatever God
requires is just, they transmit the tragic insight into the rightness of an
order that seems cruel to men. Concentration on the characters'
emotions also provided an effective technique for presenting religion
on the stage: instead of being contributed, as in the *mystères*, by the
audience's reverence, religion is active in the play as Jephté struggles
to place his love of God before love of his daughter.

Baptistes does not contain such a drama of the hero's faith.[12] More
than *Jephthes*, *Baptistes* contains speeches with only an indirect bearing
on the ostensible subject, the execution of John the Baptist. It consists
largely of monologues and debates concerning the injustice of persecution by the established church of those who point out its defects.[13]
This theme had an obvious relevance to contemporary Europe, but not
to the historical John: to insert it, Buchanan modified history, arranging
that the Levites rather than Herod's wife should instigate John's
persecution.[14] John himself appears in relatively few scenes: a large
part of the action concerns the priests' plot to turn Herod against him.

However, the play is not a court drama of the kind familiar to the student of Corneille: Buchanan did not seek to draw his effects from the characters' reactions to the pressures to which they are subjected. On the other hand, *Baptistes* does not contain the detailed physical action found in the *mystères*. In order to express his opinion, Buchanan devised his own dramatic form which, though lacking in action and emotion, would allow him to make clear the iniquity of the church.[15]

Bèze followed in the same tradition as Buchanan's *Jephthes* in handling the story of Abraham's sacrifice of his son. Because of the happy ending he was uncertain whether to call the play a tragedy or a comedy, but he was clear that in the conduct of the plot and depiction of character it conformed to the classical practice of concentrating on the hero and his crisis, and so endowed it with elements of the classical form:

> Or pour venir à l'argument que je traicte, il tient de la Tragedie et de la Comedie: et pour cela ay je separé le prologue, et divisé le tout en pauses, à la façon des actes des Comedies, sans toutefois m'y assubjectir. Et pource qu'il tient plus de l'un que de l'autre, j'ay mieux aimé l'appeller Tragedie.
> (Aux lecteurs, ll. 67–72)

However, he abandoned one conventional component of Renaissance neo-Latin tragedy, its richly ornamented language. By adhering to a simple style Bèze forfeited the literary esteem of his peers, but he preferred to write for the common people:

> je n'ay voulu user de termes ny de manieres de parler trop eslongnées du commun, encores que je scache telle avoir esté la facon des Grecs et des Latins.   (ll. 79–82)

In this he had a special purpose. He had recently fled France to join the Protestants in Switzerland, and *Abraham sacrifiant* was written during the first year of his new life to fortify his embattled fellows.[16] He explains that he found in the Bible 'une multitude d'exemples, desquels le moindre est suffisant, non seulement pour enhardir, mais aussi pour rendre invincibles les plus foibles et descouragez du monde' (ll.10–13): among these Abraham was outstanding as an example of the kind of faith the Protestants needed. Bèze's decision to concentrate on the emotional life and particularly the religious emotions of his hero was inspired by the desire to encourage his fellow Calvinists no less than by the neo-classical tradition.

The Prologue's description of the play's contents makes it clear that Abraham's willingness to sacrifice his son is intended to symbolise the victory of faith over the temptations of the world:

> vous verrez estranges passions,
> La chair, le monde, et ses affections

> Non seulement au vif representées,
> Mais qui plus est, par la foy surmontées.   (ll. 35-8)

Abraham shows how faith, triumphing over the flesh, justifies sinful mankind: 'Vous le verrez par foy justifié' (l. 33). The Epilogue too emphasises the role of faith:

> Or voyez vous de foy la grand'puissance,
> Et le loyer de vraye obeissance   (ll. 973-4)

and goes on to invite the audience to imitate Abraham's example. The emphasis on faith was a sufficient hint for a Protestant audience; Bèze felt no need to state the implicit contrast with the powerlessness of works to save the sinner.

However, Abraham is not simply a remote example to be observed dispassionately: he endures intense anguish as he struggles to accept God's order to kill Isaac, and the play is arranged to allow us to enter into his feelings. The action unfolds principally in Abraham's heart. It begins when he reproaches himself for his insufficient diligence in demonstrating his gratitude to God. Immediately he is invited to do so: an angel orders him to sacrifice his son to God. Abraham promises to obey, but not without repugnance:

> Brusler! brusler! je le feray.
> Mais, mon Dieu, si ceste nouvelle
> Me semble fascheuse et nouvelle,
> Seigneur, me pardonneras tu?
> Helas, donne moy la vertu
> D'accomplir ce commandement.
> Ha bien cognoy-je ouvertement
> Qu'envers moy tu es courroucé.   (ll. 290-7)

His submission is not perfect: he does not accept that God's order is necessarily for the best, and can only understand it as a punishment. Nevertheless, he wishes to obey, and knowing his weakness prays for the necessary strength. In his next scene he has received it, and is about to set out with Isaac. Sara, though ignorant of the real purpose of the journey, is unhappy at the prospect of temporary separation from her young son, and objects that the journey will be dangerous for him,

> Auquel gist toute l'asseurance
> De nostre si grande esperance,   (ll. 437-8)

to which Abraham replies simply:

> Mais en Dieu.   (l. 439)

His words are more momentous for himself than for Sara: he has accepted that God's will must be obeyed with complete trust, even if He demands the life of his son.

When the moment comes, Abraham again hesitates, and sends Isaac to build the altar while he deliberates alone. This is not the conventional monologue of Senecan tragedy: rather than giving grandiloquent expression to emotions conceived on an epic scale, the speech sympathetically traces the father's struggle to bring himself to accept God's will. Three times he doubts if it can be right to kill his son, but each time he reminds himself that God's will must be obeyed, however repugnant to human judgement, in the confidence that He knows best:

> ô Dieu! puis que l'as ordonné,
> Je le feray: las, est-il raisonnable
> Que moy qui suis pecheur tant miserable,
> Viene à juger les secrets jugemens
> De tes parfaicts et tressaincts mandemens?   (ll. 720–4)

With God's help, he concludes, he will do as he was ordered:

> ô Seigneur, tu scais qu'homme je suis,
> Executer rien de bon je ne puis,
> Non pas penser, mais ta force invincible
> Fait qu'au croyant il n'est rien impossible.
> Arriere chair, arriere affections:
> Retirez vous humaines passions,
> Rien ne m'est bon, rien ne m'est raisonnable,
> Que ce qui est au Seigneur aggreable.   (ll. 811–18)

From Abraham's agonised heart-searching arises this triumphant declaration of faith. He desires only what God wills, and will demonstrate this with the greatest sacrifice he can make.

It remains to take the most difficult step of all: he must tell Isaac of the nature of the sacrifice. Having built the altar, Isaac approaches, addressing Abraham naturally as 'Père'. Abraham's grief is redoubled by this innocent trust but he masters himself and tells the boy he is to be the victim and – the final twist – that the knife will be wielded by his own father. Isaac protests only briefly before submitting to God's will; he grieves more for his parents than himself. At this Abraham is almost overcome, but he perseveres. The triumph of spirit over flesh is symbolised in physical action, as Abraham embraces his son, explaining:

> Isac mon filz, le bras qui t'occira,
> Encor' un coup au moins t'accollera.   (ll. 911–12)

But the flesh is not perfectly obedient: the knife falls from his hand. Isaac encourages him:

> Ostez toutes ces peurs
> Je vous supply, m'empescherez vous doncques
> D'aller à Dieu?   (ll. 934–6)

Abraham prepares again to strike, but the angel intervenes.

In tracing the course of the struggle of Abraham's faith, I find that
I have summarised almost the entire plot: action and theme are
coextensive, since both consist of the hero's battle with himself. This
is quite different from the practice in the *mystères*: in the *Patience
de Job*, which also treats submission to God's will, most of the action
does not relate to the theme at all. Moreover, instead of setting forth
a catalogue of miracles for the audience to revere, Bèze traced the
operation of faith within his hero. Abraham does not present the
spectators' opinion of himself in his speeches, unlike his equivalent in
the *Viel Testament*, who repeatedly describes his own exemplary
significance.[17] Bèze was at pains to maintain the illusion that Abraham
lives an independent life; the severe and protracted struggle he endures
to bring himself to obey God's will is portrayed with a sympathy that
compels involvement. Where the *mystères* offered a mirror of the
spectator's faith, the neo-classical technique showed the protagonist's
faith in action and invited the spectators to identify with him.

However, Bèze was not concerned only with stirring the spectators'
emotions: he also wished to ensure that the significance of the triumph
of Abraham's faith should not escape the Protestant audience. He made
the theme explicit, not only by having a Prologue and Epilogue state
it, but also by incorporating into the action two roles – Sathan and
the Chorus – with the function of commenting on events. Sathan is
always on hand, until he leaves at line 907, to describe Abraham's state
of mind. He hopes to force Abraham to commit a sin, because although
'Il a au vray Dieu sa fiance' (l. 255),

> s'il n'a ferme perseverance,
> Que luy pourra servir son esperance?
> Je feray tant de tours et cà, et là,
> Que je rompray l'asseurance qu'il a.   (ll. 259–62)

The implication is clear: Abraham is in a state of grace. During the
scene in which Abraham is thrice tempted,[18] Sathan again provides a
commentary. The Chorus too describes the quality of Abraham's faith
and holds him up as an example. The use of supernatural figures like
Sathan to elucidate the significance of events was common in the
mystères; although the play was conceived in the classical tradition,
Bèze freely combined its techniques with the medieval where these
suited his purpose of propagating Protestantism. Although the play
was the first attempt at classical tragedy in French, it would be an
error to suppose that the admixture of medieval techniques resulted
from an imperfect assimilation of the new style. As Bèze established in
the Aux Lecteurs, he had good reasons for not bowing to all the neo-
classical conventions. By fusing the presentation of Abraham as a

sympathetic living figure with the medieval practice of commenting explicitly on the action, Bèze was able simultaneously to present the triumph of faith vividly embodied in the emotions of the hero and a gloss ensuring that no spectator insensible to this unarticulated account of the theme should miss the point.

Bèze and Buchanan chose not to exhibit the incidents of the lives of the patriarchs and their families, nor did they have their heroes explain the religious significance of their own deeds, as was the habit in the *mystères*. They created instead a dilemma between obedience to God and a legitimate human affection, paternal love. Their subject was not the events of sacred history nor their exegesis, but the struggle of faith made accessible to the spectators' sympathy. Where the *mystères* presented in their heroes symbols of the audience's belief, Bèze and Buchanan traced the emotions of representatives of mankind thrown into contact with the divine; rather than symbolising a system of belief, their plays expressed what it feels like to be a believer. The *mystères* depended on the spectator's intellectual complicity; the neo-classical system required his emotional participation. The *mystères*, at least as originally conceived, instructed the audience, while the neo-classical play offered an image of the protagonist's inner state and permitted the spectator to incorporate this vicarious experience into his own being. Bèze, however, found the latter technique insufficiently instructive, and combined it with devices for addressing the audience directly. The didactic urge of the Middle Ages was not diminished in the Renaissance, even among playwrights with no propagandist intentions: in the work of those who followed in the tradition exploited by Buchanan and Bèze, it gave the neo-classical style a particular didactic inflection which it retained until the end of the sixteenth century, and which was so distinctive as to require scholars to give this genre a name of its own, the humanist theatre.

3. The explicit representation of Christian doctrine

It is easy with hindsight to see *Abraham sacrifiant* as the first step on the road to the masterpieces of the Classical theatre in the following century, but for contemporaries the dramatic style that Bèze adopted was simply one possibility among many. The playwrights of the second half of the sixteenth century were not limited to the two major inherited traditions described in the two previous chapters, and indeed Bèze himself exemplified their willingness to innovate when he combined medieval and neo-classical elements to create a form suited to his particular purpose. It was above all those fired by special purposes who chose not to use the neo-classical conventions, which otherwise were quickly adopted by the scholarly class that composed the world of letters at this time. Two groups can be distinguished among those who found the neo-classical form unsuited to their needs: those who used the theatre to set out the essentials of Christian doctrine, and those who used it for sectarian propaganda during the religious wars. The two groups developed distinctive dramatic forms for their various purposes, which from our point of view as inheritors of the neo-classical tradition can all too easily be seen as dead-ends leading off the path to the Classical triumphs, though each had its own validity. Since these plays stand apart from the main tradition, and are in many ways closely related to the works discussed in the two previous chapters, it will be convenient to consider them separately in this chapter and the next, abandoning chronological order temporarily to do so, before returning in Chapter 5 to the study of the neo-classical theatre as it developed after 1550.

The venerable *mystères* representing such key events as the Passion and the Resurrection were still performed outside the area governed by the Parisian Parlement, but the simple texts which had emerged from the liturgy had grown to contain copious narratives of events while obscuring their significance by the very detail in which they were presented. A number of pious dramatists felt that, rather than revise these texts again, it would be better to replace them. The new plays, unlike the *mystères* by this time, were brief and to the point.

For their purpose of elucidating the basic tenets of Christianity, the dramatists chose to present summary enactments of key events, such as the Fall; a few preferred to use allegory. In this they diverged completely from the classical concentration on a crisis in the lives of men, and consequently had no need of such devices as the unities, designed to promote that concentration. The dramatic form they adopted was the chronicle, habitually wide-ranging and often symbolic in its treatment of events.

Little is known of the conditions in which these plays were staged. Buschey's *Incarnation* was written for performance in church (see below); this was perhaps the destination in some other cases as well. Six performances in Collèges are recorded, though the texts do not survive (see below, n. 1 on p. 302, and p. 35). No doubt other performances in such establishments have left even less trace. Ville-Toustain's *Creation*, on the other hand, was printed in a set apparently consisting of productions from the professional stage (see p. 34 below). In all cases, the staging was probably somewhat rudimentary, consisting of little more than boards, a backcloth or two, and a few elementary props and costumes.

The authors were in many cases friars or priests. None was a Parisian, moreover. These circumstances have given rise in a number of studies accepted as authorities on the theatre to the erroneous opinion that they neglected the neo-classical style through rustic ignorance or clerical obscurantism; in fact, however, they appear to have in mind purposes which the classical conventions would not have met.

The first surviving doctrinal play published after 1550[1] is the *Mystere de la saincte incarnation de nostre redempteur et sauveur Jesus-Christ, par personnages* (Antwerp 1587) of Henri Buschey, an Observantine Franciscan, which before being printed had been performed in church at Bastogne 'le mercredi des quatre-temps avant Noel'.[2] In the Dedication Buschey explains that his purpose was to celebrate the Incarnation by explaining why it was necessary, and so to magnify God's mercy in sacrificing His Son to save man from the punishment he brought on himself in Eden. The emphasis is on man's offences rather than the Incarnation, which occupies only a few lines: like many dramatists who witnessed the denominational strife (in the Dedication Buschey mentions the sacking of his monastery), the author was preoccupied with men's sinfulness, by which they had caused God to unleash the scourge of war.

Buschey starts with the original sin, enacted in summary form. Eve eats the fruit of the tree of knowledge as soon as Lucifer prompts her, and Adam hesitates equally little: it was not Buschey's intention to study the mental states of his human characters. Adam immediately realises the consequences of this first sin:

> Voicy un povre changement,
> Je voy de mes yeux clerement
> Ma nudité: mais qui plus est,
> Ma chair faict tout ce quil luy plaist,
> Rebellant fort contre raison.   (p. 26)

In the fallen state, reason no longer rules the flesh: Adam never fails to explain the significance of his own actions for the audience's benefit. God punishes the couple but promises to send a Saviour; while they await His coming in Limbo, Michiel protects them from the despair Lucifer tries to induce. Buschey next summarises the Messianic prophecies contained in the Old Testament, introducing Abraham, Moyse, Aaron and David in rapid succession and showing the miracles associated with them that betokened the Saviour's coming. Misericorde begs God to send the Saviour He promised, but Justice insists that man should make satisfaction for his crimes. Misericorde proposes the solution:

> Pour faire satisfaction,
> Il faut cercher autre moien,
> Ou du tout ce ne sera rien:
> Car une pure creature,
> Ne peult aider à la nature
> Humaine, estante ainsi damnée
> Et de misere environnée:
> Celuy qui doit racheter l'homme,
> Il faudra quil soit Dieu et homme:
> Car Dieu seul mourir ne pourroit,
> L'Homme seul la mort ne vaincroit:
> Le fils de Dieu, donc, soit faict homme.   (p. 59)

God accordingly sends Isaie, Michée and Daniel to prophesy the Saviour's advent. A canticle 'represente les grans desirs des anciens Patriarches, Prophetes, et Saincts Peres, souspirans et crians pour la venuë du Mesias' (stage direction, pp. 65–6). Marie too prays for His coming. Her faith is rewarded: God sends Gabriel to announce that she will bear His Son. Gabriel explains how she will conceive and give birth while preserving her virginity. The Aucteur delivers an Epilogue praising God.

Buschey studded his simple narrative of the key incidents leading to the Incarnation with explanations at every point of the significance of events. God Himself contributes largely to this exposition, as do the allegorical figures, angels and demons. The human characters are no less informative: thus Moyse glosses the miracle of the burning bush as an earnest of the virgin birth. Adam, Moyse and the rest display a superhuman understanding of God's purpose and their own role in it; viewing their own actions objectively, they explain their symbolic significance to the spectator at every stage. The play provides a remarkably clear and vigorous account of how God's design was worked out through the actions of men.[3]

The Fall and the Redemption were again dramatised by Jean Gaulché of Troyes, who in 1601 obtained permission to print *L'Amour divin, tragecomedie, contenant un bref discours des Saincts et sacrés mysteres de la Redemption de l'humaine nature.* Where Buschey had staged a summary of biblical history, Gaulché preferred an allegorical approach. The five acts correspond to different stages in man's redemption. They show the Creation and man's Fall; his punishment; the decision of the Saviour to intervene; the satisfaction He made for man; and man's rehabilitation.[4]

The brief play (some 450 lines) offers a simple exposition of the events by which the Christian believes his redemption was first made necessary and then effected, and the allegorical figures explain clearly why these events occur thus. Gaulché even omitted such personages as the Virgin in his concentration on the essentials of doctrine. However, this spare account of dogma is combined with a large patriotic element which obtrudes throughout and dominates the last act, where a hyperbolic encomium of France as the home of peace, justice and truth quite overshadows man's reconciliation with God: veneration for God's self-sacrificial mercy is diverted into patriotic self-congratulation.

Jean Moucque of Boulogne adopted the pastoral allegory to celebrate the triumph of divine love in *L'Amour desplumé, ou la victoire de l'amour divin, pastorelle Chrestienne* (Paris 1612). This concerns a competition for mastery over the shepherds and shepherdesses between Cupidon, representing worldly love, and Amour divin. Cupidon seduces the mortals by charms, at which Supresme puissance intervenes: He summons Cupidon and Amour divin to settle their differences before Him in single combat. Amour divin triumphs; Cupidon is 'desplumé' and consigned to a dungeon. The shepherds and shepherdesses forget their love-affairs and unite in praising the Supresme puissance.[5]

The greater part of the action – almost the whole of acts II, III and IV – traces the disruption caused by Cupidon, aided by a lecherous Satyre who turns a shepherdess who resists him into a rock. The spectacular element is large; Cupidon flies until his defeat, and spells are cast. The lovers utter long plaints about their unrequited passions. The brief scenes at the beginning and end where Amour divin explains his purpose seem to be only the excuse for the pastoral and spectacular material which is the most important element in the play, and was highly fashionable at this time.

The theme of the consequences of man's sinfulness returned in a play by one Ville-Toustain, *Tragédie de la naissance, ou Creation du Monde, où se void de belles descriptions des Animaux, Oiseaux, Poissons, Fleurs et autres choses rares qui virent le jour à la naissance de l'Univers* (Rouen 1612–14).[6] He represented this theme through a simple narrative of the first sin and its first consequence. The first act shows the Creation and the prohibition of the tree of life.[7] The second act presents the Temptation and Fall. In act III Adam and Eve are expelled from Eden. The last act, the fourth, concerns the results of their sin: first Adam and Eve are seen labouring to eke a living from the soil, then Cain, encouraged by Sathan, kills Abel. The play ends with God cursing Cain and reflecting on man's ingratitude.[8]

Ville-Toustain condensed the biblical narrative slightly, particularly in neglecting the deeds of Adam's children, their marriage and Abel's sacrifice. These omissions make the connection between the original sin and its first consequence clearer than in the *Mistére du Viel Testament*, where the intervening episodes are narrated in copious detail. On the other hand Ville-Toustain expanded the role of God and added interventions of devils and an angel: these figures perform the important function of demonstrating the significance of events and explaining how God's justice acts. The play is carefully contrived simultaneously to remind the audience of the events of the Fall and to explain its importance for later generations.

This simple work of devotion has attracted severe criticism from two authorities, who started from the premise that it ought to have been a tragedy of the Classical kind, concerning the emotional life of the characters. Loukovitch consequently lamented the lack of psychology:

On ne remarque nul effort pour étudier les caractères ou les sentiments. L'auteur n'a même pas songé à expliqué [*sic*] psychologiquement le péché d'Adam et d'Eve, ni même la jalousie de Caïn.   (p. 77)

Similarly, he regretted the lack of concentration on any one crisis:

Ville-Toustain a voulu écrire une tragédie, mais elle est fort irrégulière. Nous assistons à quatre actions successives...   (p. 76)

Lancaster too found fault with the play's form, which 'rambles like a medieval mystery'; he also complained at the inclusion of the essential figures, God and the devil, on the ground that it is medieval.[9] While factually correct, such criticisms are unjustified because they do not take into account that Ville-Toustain had no intention of dramatising the emotions of an individual hero. The plot consequently has no need of the Classical concentration: it deliberately 'rambles' to admit all the incidents Ville-Toustain thought necessary to demonstrate his theme. The characters are made to explain the theological significance of their own actions, and so lack natural psychology; any psychological explanation of Adam's or Cain's sin would only have obscured the divine interpretation Ville-Toustain wished to offer. His play may lack the intensity of Racinian tragedy, by which standard Loukovitch and Lancaster judged it; but it possesses a clarity of purpose which confers a dignity of its own. It is of course true, as Lancaster concluded, that 'the play is of no importance in the evolution of the theater',[10] but Ville-Toustain no doubt did not worry unduly to know whether he was a precursor of Racine: his concern was to find a form suited to expressing his religious purpose. Through his symbolic summary of biblical history with supernatural glosses he was able to demonstrate clearly the nature, enormity and effects of the first sin.

Even after the end of the civil wars, Ville-Toustain was still preoccupied with the theme to which they had given rise, man's sinfulness and the punishment it deserves. As the memory of the fighting faded the dramatists continued to write about Christ's sacrifice, but now approached the subject in a mood of celebration in place of the penitence which had predominated earlier; celebration was perhaps the mood in Moucque's *Amour desplumé,* so far as that play had a religious sense at all. At the same time dramatists inclined to treat the theme of man's redemption by showing the life of the Redeemer, rather than the sin which made His intervention necessary. The apostle of the more confident approach to Christ was François de Sales, in whose presence a play by D. Candide was performed at the Barnabite College at Annecy in 1618. The text seems not to have survived, but the title suggests jubilation at Christ's triumph: *Daphnis, célébrant l'Ascension du Christ.* Celebration was probably again the mood at another performance at the College, in 1633: *Le Retour des trois Mages après l'adoration du Christ,* by Cyrille Borella.

The more traditional approach was retained by Denis Coppée, of Huy near Liège, in *La Sanglante et pitoyable tragedie de nostre sauveur et redempteur Jesus-Christ* (Liège 1624). This is not divided into acts, as Coppée explains in a Preface, 'a raison qu'elle êt de longue haleine, et que le Sauveur de nos ames fut tourmenté sans relache' (p. 11); he adds, nevertheless, that the 4500 lines may be presented in one, two or even three *journées.* Coppée considered using the classical form but rejected it, finding the *mystère* more suitable for this subject.[11] The play narrates in detail the final stages of the Passion, from Christ's betrayal by Judas to the entombment. Transitions form a large part of the action: Christ is seen several times being led across Jerusalem by His captors, and many scenes detail the errands of messengers. Considerable attention is given to incidental figures, who assume great importance for a few scenes before being forgotten altogether.

Amidst so much business, Christ is a little overshadowed. However, His anguish at Gethsemane is presented with great sympathy: three times (as in the Bible) He prays His Father to release Him, but eventually submits to death. Coppée also took care to emphasise the pathetic aspect of the tortures and humiliations to which Christ was subjected; these, like the Crucifixion, are presented on the stage.

Coppée's sympathy for Christ's sufferings is thwarted by an equal determination to present His actions as symbolic. At every stage the figures surrounding Him compare events to Old-Testament precedents and explain their significance for later generations. The Virgin, the chief vehicle of these glosses, even promises Pierre that she will intercede with God on behalf of all who turn to her (p. 80). Under the weight of these glosses the deeds shown appear to be performed principally so that they should serve as symbols for generations unborn; this had been the usual approach in the primitive *mystères*, but it assorts ill with the naturalistic presentation of Christ's agony. Like the later *mystères* studied in Chapter 1 above, the play founders in indecision as to whether the hero is to be seen as a symbol or an object of sympathy.[12]

A major instance of man's sinfulness, the Flood, was dramatised by Hugues de Picou, a Parisian lawyer,[13] in *Le Deluge universel, tragedie, ou est compris un abregé de la Theologie Naturelle* (Paris 1643). Picou was not attracted to the subject as an opportunity to extol the combination in God of justice and mercy, nor, despite the title, did he treat other theological matters. He declared in an *Advis* that he wished to summarise the arguments that Noah and his family might have used to dissuade men from sin as they attempted to avert the Flood. To provide extra opportunities for moralising, Picou invented a number of involved amatory intrigues concerning Noah's family.[14] Picou limited himself to sermonising and neglected the religious and human issues the Flood raises.

Grateful celebration of the Nativity occasioned two plays which appeared in close succession from the mountains on either side of the Rhône; in the absence of documentary evidence, one can only speculate that they may be the only survivors of a regional tradition of nativity plays. One Sainct André, an Embrunois, published an *Histoire Pastoriale sur la Naissance de Nostre Seigneur Jesus-Christ* (Béziers 1644) representing the adoration of the shepherds. Strangely, when they visit the stable, the text indicates no lines for the holy family, which must have been represented by models in a crib before which the play was performed.[15] The Prologue and Epilogue address a popular audience: the play was doubtless performed in Embrun at Christmas.

Three shepherdesses discuss the day's labours. They are joined by some shepherds, and all experience a strange feeling – a 'sainct feu', a 'divine flame' – whose origin they cannot understand. The beauty of the stars leads them to lament man's exclusion for his sin from enjoying the universe God created for him. They look forward with confidence to the day when God will send a Saviour to free man of the burden of his error. Their faith is rewarded: an angel announces the Saviour's birth and tells them to go and adore Him. They discuss what gifts to take. One declares

> Je ne luy puis donner plus belle oblation,
> Qu'un coeur remply d'amour, et de devotion.   (I iii, p. 10)

All agree; but they also prepare more concrete offerings of cheese and flowers.

In the second act each shepherd in turn adores the infant, offering himself to Him heart and soul, and thanking Him for His love in coming to lead men to Heaven. Two Ambassadeurs du Ciel explain that Christ will save them, but the worldly, who have ignored His birth, will be damned. The Ambassadeurs order them to spread the glad tidings. After the shepherdesses leave to go home, two of the shepherds quarrel and come to blows, but are reconciled by a third. One announces suddenly 'Je veux estre Martyr' (II iv, p. 25). They depart amicably to get drunk: 'Je voudrois en beuvant devenir tout divin' (II iv, p. 25).

The last act presents new characters. It shows the reaction of other shepherds to the news of Christ's birth. One persuades his fellow, with some difficulty, that He has indeed been born in a stable. They go to adore Him, and on the way meet a third shepherd, who disbelieves this news. Four Ambassadeurs du Ciel confirm it, foretell Christ's passion and explain that He has come to save mankind from the effects of sin. The three shepherds go to adore Him and pray Him to protect them from Hell.

This disjointed plot was assembled with complete disregard for the Classical conventions, by now established on the Parisian stage. These would, indeed, have been quite inappropriate to Sainct André's purpose, which was not to extract a conflict of personalities from Christ's birth, but to lead the spectators in celebration of the fact and remind them of its significance for themselves.[16] The play is scattered with Noëls sung by the shepherds and angels, and with speeches explaining man's need of the Saviour. Sainct André laid special emphasis on Christ's favour for the humble, such as his audience: the play conjures up the rejoicing with which they greet His birth.

The second nativity play, *Le Triomphe des bergers* (Lyons 1646), was written by the curé of Saint-Genest-de-Malifaux (Loire), Louis Jaquemin.[17] Here too the plot is somewhat disjointed, and the adoration of the shepherds, despite the title, occupies only the last two acts. The three previous acts show the Emperor deciding to take a census, the arrangements for raising a tax, and the removal of Joseph and his wife to Bethlehem.[18]

Unifying this material are two preoccupations of the author's, expressed equally in the prefatory material: vilification of the rich, especially office-holders, and praise of humble reliance on God. The scenes concerning César Auguste, although they contain some gratuitous spectacle, are mostly devoted to showing him to be intent on serving his people, even to the extent of offering to resign his throne if this would benefit them.[19] Having established that his quarrel was not with the King, Jaquemin bitterly criticises the tax farmers, who are shown plotting to strip the the poor for their own profit while sparing those rich enough to bribe them. The uncharitableness of the rich is further evidenced by their refusal to lodge Joseph and Marie. The latter exhibit perfect patience, trusting that God will provide. The bystanders point out the exemplary significance of their meekness: relying patiently on God, the humble are proof against any worldly disaster. Jaquemin's strictures against the rich were inspired more by Christian disdain of worldliness than by political consciousness.

The theme is also evoked by a Raby and Saint Simeon, who are introduced for one scene only (II i) for this purpose. The Raby is convinced that God has forgotten His people in allowing them to be enslaved by the Romans, but Simeon warns him sternly not to despair or blame God when the fault is man's. The stories which the shepherds tell each other to while away the night are *exempla*, again showing that God does not fail those who rely on Him. Throughout the last two acts the shepherds and angels reiterate the praise of humility, which Christ exemplified by His choice of the manner of His birth: He does not reveal Himself to the worldly, who will be damned, but He will save the humble and poor.

As Loukovitch does not fail to point out, the play is deficient in characterisation and unity of plot:[20] yet these ideals of Classical dramaturgy would not have served Jaquemin's purpose. The loose plot allowed him to introduce both rich and poor in support of his praise of the latter, and the rejection of naturalistic characterisation assisted him to make the significance of their actions clear. Jaquemin's play was skilfully designed to set forth his country parishioners' faith in the Saviour and trust in God to compensate them in the next life for the hardships of this.

While Sainct André and Jaquemin celebrated the birth of Christ, the abbé Chevillard mourned His death in *La Mort de Théandre, ou la sanglante tragedie de la Mort et Passion de Nostre-Seigneur Jesus-Christ* (Orléans 1649).[21] Starting from Judas's betrayal of Christ, Chevillard chronicles His prayers in Gethsemane, His arrest, the use of false witnesses to accuse Him, Pilate's refusal to condemn Him, and the ascent of the Mount of Olives; the Crucifixion is recounted at the end.[22] A large part of the action is devoted to demonstrating the iniquity of Caiphe and his fellow priests in attempting to secure Christ's conviction. Considerable space is also devoted to Pilate, who attempts to behave justly but dare not cross the priests. Amidst these intrigues Christ is somewhat neglected; only in the last act does Chevillard's intense devotion emerge. Christ is led on having been whipped; He is taunted and goaded by the soldiers at the priests' order, then driven across the stage with kicks and shouts under the burden of the cross. The details of His agony are recounted by Véronique, Salome, Joseph d'Arimathie and Nicodème with anguished horror; their words are filled with revulsion and grief at the torture of the innocent Christ and His gentle submission.

Chevillard's passionate devotion is expressed only by the transposition of the events of the Passion onto the stage. These acts are not glossed: no figure explains the importance of Christ's sacrifice, and there is no elucidation of the figurative significance of events. Chevillard perhaps considered such explanations unnecessary, though earlier Greban and Michel in their versions of the *Mystère de la Passion* had found it helpful to introduce God to explain His intentions at every stage of the action. Chevillard felt no need to express the spectators' beliefs directly; he took these as given and, in the closing moments at least, concentrated on the feelings of the believer.

In the century from 1550 to 1650 few doctrinal plays are known to have been written, despite the importance of such material and its popularity earlier. As with the development of the *mystères* outlined in Chapter 1, taste had shifted away from a drama of ideas towards a drama of the deeds of men. Indeed, the continuation of this evolution of taste after 1550 can be seen even among the few doctrinal plays that were written: Buschey's account of the original sin, printed in 1587, includes allegorical figures, while Ville-Toustain's treatment of the same material, printed twenty-five years later, does not employ allegory, and where both these plays introduced God to explain His purpose,

Coppée (1624) and Chevillard (1649) excluded Him in their versions of the Passion, the latter concentrating particularly on evoking the emotions of the characters.

Despite a certain convergence with this taste, however, the doctrinal plays stand quite apart from the neo-classical tradition: their authors wished to express their ideas directly, rather than through the medium of accounts of the deeds of heroes of Jewish or saintly history, and for this they required an entirely different dramatic form. Where the doctrinal playwrights did use Jewish history, moreover, they handled it quite differently from the neo-classical dramatists: while Bèze requires us to share Abraham's feelings, Buschey or Ville-Toustain present Adam as strictly symbolic and use him to give an objective account of the significance of his own deeds for future generations. Only Gaulché and Moucque went so far as to use allegory, and the latter was perhaps motivated more by the vogue of the pastoral than the desire to expound doctrine clearly; the majority of the doctrinal playwrights preferred to provide a more concrete account of the main tenets of their faith by representing the historical events – the Fall, the Passion – on which it is founded. As a matter of course they accompanied the summary narrative of these incidents with glosses intended to make their significance clear, delivered by God Himself, by allegorical and supernatural figures, and by the human characters equally. Where Chevillard neglected these devices in favour of a more naturalistic presentation of plot and character, the result was a confused emotional outburst, pious, no doubt, but ill-directed.

In the successful doctrinal plays the symbolic enactment of cardinal episodes combines with the devices for explaining their significance to yield a vivid reminder for the Christian of the fundamentals of his faith. The result may seem undramatic to the spectator accustomed to participating in the emotional life of the hero, but to the believer to whom they are addressed these plays encapsulate the whole meaning of life and death. They involve the spectator directly rather than vicariously: he witnesses the drama of his own salvation. In this century we ought to experience no difficulty in recognising this effect on the spectator as dramatic, the breach of naturalism notwithstanding; it would perhaps have been instantly familiar to the ancient Greeks. The practitioners of this genre may not have followed the more familiar conventions of the Classical stage, and undoubtedly were not so gifted as Corneille or Racine; but the dramatic form they adopted was not inherently a less valid way of writing for the theatre.

4. The theatre of sectarian propaganda

The didactic urge also determined the form devised by those who used the theatre as a vehicle for sectarian propaganda during the long period of religious strife. There were indeed almost as many forms as dramatists, but in their attempt to present their position clearly one element is constant: they rejected the neo-classical conventions in favour of a consciously symbolic handling of their historical subjects.

Some of the propagandists were happy nevertheless to adopt certain features of the classical tradition: Henri de Barran, for example, divided his *Tragique comedie francoise de l'homme justifié par Foy* (1554) into acts, for reasons that he gave in the Au lecteur:

> Touchant la disposition et ordre que j'ay tenu en la Tragique Comedie, je l'ay disposée par Actes et Scenes, non tant pour l'imitation des Poetes comiques, que pour la division des propos et des dialogues: afin aussi qu'on puisse faire pose en certains lieux, si d'adventure on la faisoit lire ou proposer par dialogues publiques... (f. A3ʳ)

Barran was not overawed by the prestige of the classical system of divisions, but used it because he thought it would help his audience follow the articulation of his argument. Conrad Badius, on the other hand, presented a single continuous action, as he explained in the Au lecteur of his *Comedie du pape malade et tirant à la fin, où ses regrets et complaintes sont au vif exprimees, et les entreprises et machinations qu'il fait avec Satan et ses supposts pour maintenir son siege Apostatique et empescher le cours de l'Evangile sont cathegoriquement descouvertes* (Geneva 1561):

> quant à ce que j'intitule ce present jeu Comedie, et toutesfois je ne retien point la mode des anciens Comiques, qui ont distingué leurs Comedies en Actes et Scenes, je laisse au jugement de ceux qui s'entendent en telles choses, à cognoistre s'il ne m'estoit pas aisé de le faire, veu l'argument que je traitte, et les divers personnages que j'introduy. Toutes fois, ayant esgard que j'escrivoye

pour les simples, j'ay pensé qu'un fil continuel leur plairoit plus que ces interruptions qui se font ès Scenes, et l'artifice qu'on tient ès Comedies.[1]

Badius's defensive tone reflects his awareness that his rejection of the classical formalities would earn him the scorn of his peers in the world of letters, but he felt, like Bèze, that it was more important to avoid confusing his audience. Other propagandists chose forms falling between these two extremes. None was swayed by respect for the classical models; their first consideration was effectiveness, not literary fashion. From the Renaissance interpretation of the classical tradition they took only those elements that they thought would help them to put their point over, and all rejected the neo-classical concentration on the emotional life of a hero, preferring to attend to the sectarian argument, expressed directly by the characters themselves and by the exemplary pattern of the play as a whole.

(i) PROTESTANT PROPAGANDA

The use of the theatre for criticising the church was a venerable tradition; on the French stage it stretched back at least to the *Mystère du Concile de Basle*, composed in 1434. As dissatisfaction intensified into schism and finally war, the French Protestants were happy to continue the tradition. The first theatrical assaults on Catholicism were launched in the form of the allegory and the morality, in which the church was satirised directly.[2] In the second half of the sixteenth century allegory continued to be used enthusiastically for propaganda: old allegories were still performed and printed, and new ones were written. Their usual burden was to show that the Pope was a servant of the devil.[3]

Two plays went beyond satire to provide in allegorical form full expositions of the Calvinist understanding of the route to salvation. One was the *Tragique comedie* of the pastor Barran, already mentioned. Here l'Homme pescheur, unable to obey Loy, despairs of being saved. The Raby (i.e. the Catholic priest) therefore helpfully veils Loy's face: l'Homme now finds it easy to believe that he is obeying her, and known as l'Homme pharisien (i.e. hypocrite) exults in his virtue, describing himself as one of the elect and demanding his place in Heaven. Paul informs him, however, that although he obeys the Law in his external acts, he neglects her in his heart, which is inhabited by Peché and Mort, and he tears the veil from Loy's face: l'Homme again despairs of ever satisfying her. Paul prays with Foy for Grace to intervene: Grace informs l'Homme that Christ has made satisfaction for mankind, and Loy relents. L'Homme places his trust in God and, known now as l'Homme chrestien, succeeds in driving away Peché and Mort and mastering the temptations of Concupiscence. A less abstract treatment of the same theme was offered by the Protestant martyrologist Jean Crespin, who in 1558 issued from his own printing house in Geneva the first of several editions of his translation of the *Mercator* (Antwerp 1540) of Naogeorgus (i.e. Thomas Kirchmayer) under the title *Le Marchant converti, tragedie excellente, en laquelle la vraye et fausse religion, au parangon l'une de l'autre, sont au vif representees, pour entendre quelle est leur vertu et effort au combat de la conscience, et quelle doit estre leur issue au dernier jugement de Dieu.* Summoned by the angel of death, the Marchant is warned by Satan that he will be damned for his sins, of which Satan has a list. The Marchant confesses to a Curé, listing all his good works, but these are unavailing, even when the Curé administers them in a potion of all the Marchant's masses, fasts, indulgences and other merits: the Curé is unable to break Satan's hold on his victim, and Satan mocks him with a series of farcical pranks. Having shown Catholicism to be ineffective, the author presents the Protestant system for comparison. Christ sends Paul to instruct the Marchant to trust to the Saviour rather than his own merits. When he dies, the Marchant is judged beside a Prince, a Bishop and a Franciscan, who all find that their cargoes of merits weigh less heavily in the balance than their sins; the Marchant, trusting exclusively to Christ for salvation, is welcomed into Heaven. Both plays, while turning Catholicism to scorn, offered remarkably comprehensive expositions of the Protestant alternative, and Crespin's at least enjoyed a deserved popularity.[4]

The great majority of Protestant propagandists in this period, however, preferred to use Old-Testament subjects. Bèze was the first playwright working in French to use such a subject for propaganda, and other Protestants quickly appreciated the advantages of this type of material in lending concrete reality and scriptural authority to their message. On the other hand they did not imitate Bèze's harrowing depiction of the near-failure of Abraham's faith: they preferred to offer more unequivocal encouragement. They eschewed drama of the hero's emotions, conceiving him instead as an example; and to present him as such they retained the medieval devices for explaining his exemplary significance, principally the interventions of supernatural figures and the convention by which a character can comment objectively on himself. On the other hand, the propaganda plays differ greatly from the *mystères*, above all in not recounting the whole of the subject's life: here one may detect classical influence. Ultimately, however, to seek to describe precise filiations and proportions of classical or medieval influence in the propaganda plays does not give an accurate representation of how the dramatists worked: although the plays contain elements of both traditions, it is more helpful to attempt to understand them as the product of the authors' concern to convey their meaning with all possible clarity and vigour.[5]

In the year following the appearance of *Abraham sacrifiant*, Joachim de Coignac, a pastor, used the defeat of Goliath to encourage his flock.[6] *La Desconfiture de Goliath, tragedie* (Geneva 1551) closely follows the account of the incident in I Samuel xvii. The scene moves from one camp to the other, as in the source. The direction 'Pause' divides the play into eight episodes.[7]

The dedicatory epistle, likening Edward VI's destruction of Catholicism in England to David's defeat of Goliath, makes it clear that Coignac wished his David to show that God never fails those who rely on Him for protection from oppression. David confesses that the Jews' sins render them unworthy of God's support, but never loses confidence that with His help they are capable of defeating the superior Philistine forces; and if God wills death, David will accept that with equal joy:

> je suis certain et seur,
> Qu'il n'est à DIEU difficile,
> Contre le fort aggresseur
> De renforcer le debile.
> Et quand par la rude espée
> De ce Geänt tant hautain,
> Ma teste seroit couppée,
> De salut je suis certain. (p. 59)

David is certain of victory because he trusts to God's strength, whereas Goliath relies only on his own muscles, as David explains before attacking him:[8]

> tout le peuple verra,
> Que l'homme pervers et injuste
> Avec ses armeures cherra,
> Combien qu'il soit fort et robuste:
> Et que DIEU donne la victoire,
> Quand il veut, sans charnel moyen. (pp. 63–4)

David speaks always of what 'le peuple verra' by his deeds: he explains the significance of his own actions for the benefit of the audience. Thanks to this device the message of support for the oppressed Calvinists is very clear; nevertheless, the other Jews repeat it. The heart of the play is a long prayer, led by Samuel, in which the Filles d'Israel beseech God for deliverance. This is the only substantial passage Coignac added to his source: it makes explicit the play's reference to the plight of the Huguenots. The Jewesses beg God to protect them because they are defending His cause against the worshippers of images:

O Createur, ton Eglise à toy crie
A ce besoing, et tres-ardamment prie,
Pour l'entretien de la pure doctrine
De ta Parole, et de ta Loy divine,
Que ton plaisir soit de la regarder:
Et à present te plaise la garder,
Que le cruel tyran ne l'engloutisse.

(p. 57)

Their prayer for the safety of the 'Eglise' refers more to the position of the Protestants in Europe than to their own plight confronted by Goliath. Coignac was not concerned with the emotional life of the personage involved. David is serenely undaunted by the danger he faces, and his confidence is of course rewarded: in him Coignac presented a sublimely encouraging example.

God's protection of the oppressed believer was again exemplified by Antoine de la Croix, a member of the household of the King of Navarre,[9] who in 1561 published a *Tragi-comedie* concerning the three Jewish youths cast into a furnace by Nebuchadnezzar for refusing to worship his image as a god (Daniel iii).[10] The three brothers triumph over their oppressor because they place their trust exclusively in God, while He humbles the mighty Nabuchodonozor, who relies only on human strength to defy him. The brothers state this doctrine explicitly in a canticle they sing in the furnace, and Nabuchodonozor is finally forced to admit that God's power is greater than his own. In case the characters' own statement of the moral should be insufficiently clear, a Chorus repeats that whatever the might of the persecutor, God's strength is always greater; and at the end an Epilogue drives the same point home.

La Croix added to his source a long scene in which Sidrach advances reasons for obeying the King's order to worship his image, thus obliging his brothers to rehearse the justifications for rebelling against the King when his orders are not consonant with the service of God.[11] Sidrach then reveals that he was playing devil's advocate so as to test his brothers' faith, but there is no reason for him to wish to do so: the episode was contrived so as to catechise the audience rather than the brothers. Like the *fatistes*, La Croix did not conceive of his characters as autonomous beings, but as examples. The play as a result does not generate the sort of tension Bèze created in *Abraham sacrifiant*, but La Croix was concerned only with religious truth, as the Prologue's stern description of the contents of the piece makes clear:

On n'y orra aussi mensongeres merveilles,
Qui oignent de plaisir des asnes les oreilles:
Voire, il n'y fault encor ou peu ou rien chercher,
Qu'un follastre ris espande sur la chair:

> Bref, on n'y entendra rien qui les corps contente...
> D'un zele ardant à Dieu voz corps abandonnez,
> Et souffrez qu'à plaisir vos ames or s'esgayent
> En la felicité qu'iceux meschans corps hayent.   (f. B^r)

The play was strictly an example for the mind and spirit.

A rather different use of biblical material was made by Jacques Bienvenu, who besides the two satires mentioned earlier published *Le Triomphe de Jesus Christ, comedie apocalyptique* (Geneva 1562), a translation of John Foxe's *Christus Triumphans* (1556). Using figures from both Testaments and allegorical personages, the play recounts the whole of human history from the Fall to the time of writing.[12] The play is principally a satire, devoted to showing the Pope to be the devil's agent, rather than an investigation into the operation of providence in sacred history.

Louis Desmasures took the more conventional course of treating the biblical subject as an example. In the dedicatory epistle to his trilogy of *Tragedies sainctes* (Geneva 1566),[13] he explains that he considers David an example to all Christians and an inspiration especially for Protestants such as the dedicatee, Le Brun, and the author himself, who have suffered oppression for their faith: like David, if they rely on God they will triumph.

To place the example on the stage Desmasures rejected the classical concentration on the crisis in order to present large episodes of David's life, and neglected the division into acts in favour of indicating 'pauses'. Being associated with many members of the Pléiade he was quite aware that he courted the disapproval of his colleagues in the world of letters,[14] and took pains to justify his choice of form:

> l'action presente
> J'ay cependant rendue entierement exempte
> Des mensonges forgez, et des termes nouveaux
> Qui plaisent volontiers aux humides cerveaux
> Des delicates gens, voulans qu'on s'estudie
> De rendre au naturel l'antique Tragedie.
>   Moy, qui de leur complaire en cela n'ay souci,
> Pour l'histoire sacree amplifier ainsi
> De mots, d'inventions, de fables mensongeres,
> J'ay volontiers quitté ces façons estrangeres
> Aux profanes autheurs, ausquels honneur exquis
> Est par bien inventer, feindre et mentir acquis:
> Et à la verité simple, innocente et pure
> (Pour envers le Seigneur ne faire offense dure)
> Me suis assujetti. Car qui invente et ment,
> N'acquiert en cest endroit deshonneur seulement,
> Ains au scandale ouvert de maint fidele, attente
> Encontre Dieu commettre impieté patente.[15]

He shared Bèze's objection to the embellishments of the neo-classical style, its flights of rhetoric which he approximates to lying, and its mythological allusions which could lead to obscurity. On the other hand he was glad to retain the classical chorus for its capacity to deliver comment.

David himself is the principal exponent of the idea that even the weakest of men can with God's support withstand oppression by overwhelming human forces. As usual in the propaganda plays, he describes his own sentiments with great objectivity. In his first speech in *David combattant*, a monologue, he informs the audience that 'C'est Dieu, c'est Dieu, que j'ay tousjours au coeur' (l. 60). He explains the workings of grace within himself, and rapidly justifies the Protestant doctrine of the inability of human merit to attract God's favour:

> Car quel en moy, quel eust esté le bien
> Dont j'eusse peu meriter d'estre sien?
> Par quel bien-fait en nul jour de ma vie
> Ay-je de Dieu la faveur desservie?
> Donc de sa grace et bonté le Seigneur
> Est de sa crainte à mon coeur enseigneur:
> Et ce qu'encor je l'ay en souvenir,
> D'ailleurs ne peut que de luy me venir.
> C'est luy qui met son honneur en ma bouche...   (ll. 85–93)

In gratitude for this bounty, David never ceases praising God. Yet despite his meekness, he has no qualms in taking on the giant: with God's support he is certain of victory:

> Mais, ô Dieu tout-puissant, non en ma force, non,
> Je ne vien, ne m'y fie: ains, Seigneur, en ton nom,
> En toy seul suis-je fort, soustenant ta querele.
> Invincible est quiconque entre au combat pour elle.   (ll. 1643–6)

His humble dependence on God contrasts with Goliath's proud self-reliance, expressed in the defiant speeches in which he challenges the Jews:

> Quel Dieu me peut aider ou nuire en aucun poinct?
> Non, il n'est point de Dieu qui s'oppose à ma rage,
> Ne qui ose l'attendre.

> Pour Dieu vay-je adorant les forces de mes mains:
> Par lesquelles, maugré les dieux et les humains,
> Me feray voye au ciel.   (ll. 998–1003)

As he cuts off Goliath's head David utters a pæan in God's praise, repeatedly driving home the moral:

> C'est à toy seul, non à moy, qui rien suis,
> Toy, en qui tout, et sans qui rien ne puis,

> C'est à toy seul, mon Dieu, ma force, à toy,
> C'est toy à qui la victoire je doy.   (ll. 1709–12)

By humble reliance on God David triumphs over the proud self-reliance of the stronger heathen.

The victory exposes David to the temptation of pride in *David triomphant*. He is honoured by the whole kingdom as the destroyer of Goliath, and Saul proposes to marry him to his daughter. Rightly, David does not expect his favour to last.[16] He continues to insist that the victory was God's doing and to take no credit for himself, but despite his wish the Jewish women at the victory parade praise not God but David:

> Chantez, filles de la ville,
> Saul en a tué mille,
> Et David, homme plus fort,
> En a mis dix mille à mort.   (ll. 1573–6)

The comparison offends Saul: David is disgraced and forced into exile. He laments at this sudden disaster, but without recrimination; indeed, he indicates in a prayer that he welcomes disgrace as a punishment for his sins, while remaining confident that God will forgive him. Secure in God's mercy and love, he fears nothing:

> Tu es mon fort, tu es mon asseurance.
> Asseuré suis qu'en la vive esperance
> Qui seule en toy au combat me valut,
> En toy encore auray joye et salut.
>   Or je m'en vay, sans rien craindre au contraire,
> Sous ton support, en ce bois me retraire.   (ll. 1961–6)

David finds security even in the wilderness: depending exclusively on God, he is undaunted by any worldly disaster or danger.

In *David fugitif* he is still the victim of Saul's unjust persecution. David and his band have been trapped in a gorge by Saul's army, and must die either by starvation or the sword. To human judgement their plight seems hopeless, but David does not despair because he trusts in God's support:

> En toy sans fin, Seigneur, nous esperons.
> Seure est en toy nostre vive esperance,
> Et nulle en nous des hommes l'asseurance.   (ll. 406–8)

His confidence is of course rewarded: Saul's army is miraculously enveloped in a deep sleep, so giving David the opportunity to prove, by not taking advantage of their defencelessness, that he is not seeking to kill Saul and supplant him on the throne.[17] Saul's jealousy of David evaporates and he allows him and his band to leave peacefully. David praises God for supporting His servants:

Rien ne peut des hommes l'effort
Encontre ceux que ton confort
    Fortifie et conforte.
Les hommes vains ont conjuré:
Mais le fidele est asseuré
    Sous ta main seure et forte.   (ll. 2299–304)

Thanks to the objectivity with which Desmasures endows him,
David is able to analyse his own actions and the course of events as a
whole in terms of God's purpose; indeed almost all his speeches consist
of elucidation of God's role. Other figures are introduced to provide
additional comment. Each play is endowed with a Chorus, a Prologue
and an Epilogue glossing the action. Satan too plays a considerable
role in instructing the audience. It is he who prompts Goliath to defy
the Jews and their God. After Goliath's death Satan's agent is Doeg,
a courtier, who turns Saul against David. Doeg himself explains in a
monologue:

J'ay tant fait par finesse et dol,
Par ma langue, duite à tout vol,
Vaine et legere comme vent,
Par flatter et mentir souvent,
Dont j'ay une science exquise,
Que j'ay du Roy la grace acquise.
De lui faire pour vray tenir
Ce qui n'est, ni peut convenir,
J'ay une astuce nompareille...   (David fugitif, ll. 515–23)

Just as Doeg is made to condemn himself out of his own mouth, so
Desmasures had all his characters explain the moral value of their
actions to the audience.

Desmasures was more concerned with the capacity of his figures to
offer explicit instruction than with their emotional life, which is slight.
The only point at which a character's emotions are allowed some
importance is when Satan tempts David. In *David combattant* Satan
insinuates while David is praying that his God is false:

SATAN: Povre insensé, ce que tu ne peux voir,
    Trop follement l'imagine ta teste.
    C'est un Dieu vain.
DAVID: O Dieu, quelle tempeste
Me bat le coeur! ô mon Dieu, ne permets
Que ton sentier j'abandonne jamais.
Trop je sen fort et rude l'adversaire.
Làs, ton secours, mon Dieu, m'est necessaire,
Avec lequel invincible seray.
En ta vertu le fort je forceray,
Comme à present en ay eu la puissance.

> Dont je me veuil, par grand'resjouissance,
> Victorieux en ta force vanter,
> Et de victoire un hymne te chanter.   (ll. 536–48)

David proceeds to sing a canticle in God's praise: the only result of
Satan's efforts is a stronger expression of faith. In *David triomphant*
Satan similarly attempts to induce pride in David (ll. 1060–3), and in
David fugitif tempts him afresh with despair (ll. 1837–54): on each
occasion the result is a renewed affirmation of faith after only the
briefest hesitation and anguish. Where Bèze explored Abraham's doubts
at length, Desmasures preferred to present an exemplary reaction to
tribulation. He used David to show how the Christian should meet any
and every situation: thus, walking towards the camp burdened with
provisions for his brothers, David announces:

> Ce temps pendant que mon chemin je passe
> (Et ja passé en ay la mi-espace)
> Je ne sen point sur mon espaule forte
> Estre pesant le fardeau que je porte.
> Rien ne me greve ou poise en aucun lieu,
> Quand je travaille au service de Dieu.
>
> *(David combattant, ll. 1009–14)*

At every turn David utters similar unprovoked homilies and declarations of faith. Bèze had exhibited the triumph of faith over doubt and
trial, whereas Desmasures did not seek to show how David's faith arises
from his experience. The latter approach was less dangerous: David's
affirmations of belief may be less powerful and moving than Abraham's,
but thanks to the absence of doubt and weakness the trilogy offers a
serenely encouraging example, in word and deed, of God's protection of
His servants.

Desmasures also wrote a brief allegorical *Bergerie spirituelle* (Geneva
1566), in which Verité and Religion argue with Erreur (though it is
never established what the latter's beliefs are or how they are erroneous)
until Providence Divine steps in to announce that He will support the
faithful in the face of adversity. But for the inclusion of music, which
suggests that a performance was intended, it would be difficult to think
of this piece as a play; it more closely resembles a catechism spoken
by four voices, though it has not even the virtue of clarity. It can
hardly have succeeded in giving enlightenment or encouragement to
the Protestants; for this purpose the author's indirect expression of his
convictions through the medium of the biblical story was more eloquent
by far.

Political as well as personal encouragement was offered by one
Philone in *Josias, tragedie, vray miroir des choses advenues de nostre*

temps (Geneva 1566).[18] As the title indicates, the subject lent itself to identification with the plight of the Protestants. The play represents the accession of King Josiah at the age of eight, the rediscovery of the Book of the Law and destruction of the cult of Baal, and the death of the King.[19] In France, Charles IX had come to the throne in 1560 at the age of ten; during his reign the policies of Catherine de Médicis (Idida in the play), influenced by Michel l'Hôpital (Chancellor Saphan), raised the hopes of the Protestants, and early in the year in which the play was published the Ordinance of Moulins had satisfied many of their grievances.[20]

Philone departed from the biblical account only to add passages of edification. In act I Idida asks why her husband was killed. In a speech of some 130 lines Saphan explains that the misfortune must be accepted as God's will; the late King was idolatrous and his death a punishment. In act II Josias has been crowned in succession, and Joa (a 'secretaire') invites Ahican (Saphan's son) to watch the rehearsal of a spectacle he has prepared for the young King's instruction. For the space of some 300 lines three Princes, speaking in turn, proceed to describe the virtues required of a King; they emphasise that he must obey God's law, and declare that he becomes a tyrant if he departs from it.[21] In act III (which occurs thirteen years later) the prophet Jeremie describes God's anger against the Jews, who have been misled by unworthy priests and have abandoned Him to worship false gods.[22] Jeremie's words do have a historical basis,[23] unlike the other additions, but Philone made no atempt to motivate his sudden intervention: this and the other authorial interpolations needed no justification other than their edifying content.

Philone returns to the historical narrative in act IV: the Book of the Law is recovered and the cult of Baal destroyed. The priests of Baal, who figure briefly, are grotesquely caricatured: they are made to condemn themselves out of their own mouths as wholly unworthy and ignorant. Act V is devoted to the death of Josias, which is treated with all the trappings of classical tragedy: the King's death in battle is described in detail by a messenger and lamented copiously by Jeremie and a Chorus of Jewish girls. Lebègue criticised this act as having 'aucun rapport avec la destruction du culte de Baal' and surmised that it was written to permit the author to style his play a tragedy.[24] If Philone's theme was the destruction of the cult of Baal the last act would indeed be irrelevant, and the first no less so; however, all five acts illustrate the larger theme of the controlling influence of God's will in human affairs, for which Philone was happy to sacrifice the classical circumscription of the action. Saphan, Jeremie and the Chorus emphasise throughout that all the events of the somewhat tenuously unified plot illustrate the principle that apparent disasters must be welcomed as triumphs since God ordains them. The extensive account of history enabled Philone to elaborate the parallel with French political circumstances, to provide an opportunity to express his opinion of how a King should rule, and to offer confirmation of the encouraging belief that the disasters of human history are ordained by God for the best.

An Old-Testament subject was again used in 1572 to encourage the Protestants during the siege of La Rochelle, where Catherine de Parthenay's *Holoferne* was performed. The text has not survived. This play almost marks the end of the Protestant propaganda theatre. The Protestants had always looked somewhat askance on the theatre because the performance could be an occasion for immorality among the spectators,[25] and where the subject-matter was sacred there was the danger that it might be profaned by their irreverence.[26] These reservations were encapsulated by Barran, in the Preface to *L'Homme justifié par Foy*:

Je n'ignore pas Chrestien lecteur, les grans abuz qui sont commis journellement, tant en ceux qui jouent Comedies, Tragedies, et autres semblables histoires prinses de l'Ecriture sainte, que en ceux qui y assistent. Car les uns ne regardent qu'au profit temporel, ou bien imprimer és entendemens des auditeurs quelque opinion de leur bonne grace, mettant souvent choses prophanes et dissolues avec les saintz propos. Les autres se contentent d'occuper le temps en quelque chose plaisante, se delectant plus en la grace des personnages, ou bien en propoz joyeux et facecieux, qu'en l'utilité et edification qui leur en peut venir. C'est pourquoy, communement apres telz Dialogues on joue quelque farce dissolue, n'estimant rien le tout si la farce joyeuse n'y est adjoustée. Je me tay de plusieurs autres grans abuz qui y peuvent estre faitz, pour lesquelz ces actes (quelque espece d'edification qu'ilz portent) sont illicites à tous Chrestiens. Pour ceste cause plusieurs bons espritz laissent a composer telles comedies ou semblables histoires, car combien qu'elles soyent saintes et tres-utiles, toutesfois la corruption des hommes est telle, qu'ilz en abusent en une sorte ou autre. Pource aussi doutoye-je publier ceste Tragique comedie, tellement que je l'ay gardée presque deux ans, ne deliberant jamais la manifester. Mais apres considerant que tous fidelles savent user des bonnes choses à l'honneur de Dieu et edification du prochain: je n'ay craint les presenter: estant certain qu'ilz ont l'honneur de Dieu en telle recommendation, que pour rien du monde ne voudroyent que telles histoires prinses à l'edification servissent à destruction. Je prie donc les lecteurs, et au nom de Dieu les admoneste, n'abuser point de ses saintes Escritures en fols passe-temps, mais qu'ilz considerent diligemment, voire et espreuvent en leurs consciences d'où vient nostre justification et salut eternel. Car combien que par le ministere de la parole nous ayons cognoissance des articles de nostre foy, si est ce que ce moyen d'enseigner par Dialogues y peut aucunement servir. Et pourtant que l'article de justification est le fondement de toute la Doctrine Chrestienne, j'ay pensé que ceste maniere de parler par personnages ne seroit inutile pour nous mener à quelque cognoissance de celuy.   (f. A2^{r-v})

Barran concluded that the instruction an audience might derive from a play outweighed the risks, and avoided the danger of profaning Scripture by inventing his own allegorical action. By 1572, however, mistrust of the theatre had grown to such a point that the delegates to the Synod of Nîmes added to the Discipline of the church a new clause prohibiting the theatre in general and the biblical theatre in particular; it was permitted only in the schools for its pedagogical value, and even there biblical subjects were proscribed.[27] In 1579 the Synod of Figeac renewed the prohibition of biblical subjects, though without repeating the general proscription of the theatre, which was already sufficiently clear.

Les livres de la Bible, soit Canoniques ou Apocryphes, ne seront point emploiés en Comedies ou Tragédies par aucune representation des Histoires Tragiques, ou des autres choses qu'ils contiennent.[28]

Since only one Protestant biblical play had appeared since the first ruling (La Taille's *Famine*, 1573, probably written earlier),[29] the new prohibition was perhaps not prompted by infringements but by the desire to make explicit a regulation which had previously figured only incidentally among more general considerations.

Only three new French biblical plays are known to have been written by Protestants after the Synod of Nîmes: all were published, and presumably written, outside the jurisdiction of the French Synods. The name Philone appeared again on a play published at Lausanne in 1586: *Adonias, tragedie, vray Miroir ou Tableau et Patron de l'Estat des choses presentes et que nous pourrons voir bien tost cy-apres, qui servira comme de Memoire pour nostre temps, ou plutost de leçon et exhortation à bien esperer.*[30] The strong parallel, emphasised in the title, between the subject and the situation in France after the death of François d'Anjou, perhaps helped the author to overcome the Protestant scruples about biblical drama. With support from abroad, Adonias, the general Joab and the high priest Abiathar rebel against the weak King David to prevent the succession of Solomon, the legitimate heir (I Kings i 5–ii 29); the similarity with the machinations of Guise, Mayenne and the Cardinal de Guise is patent.[31] David bitterly criticises the rebellious trio, spillers of innocent blood, and on his deathbed advises Solomon to kill Joab. On succeeding to the throne, Solomon kills Adonias as well as Joab, and exiles the scheming 'Papelard' Abiathar, so as to pursue the sacred 'OEUVRE' begun by his father. The ruin of Adonias and his faction expresses the author's hope that the Protestant heir-apparent, Henri de Navarre, will ascend the throne despite the Ligue.

Although the author used the neo-classical form with all its trappings,

the result is quite remote from the classical effects: rather than presenting a crisis in the life of Adonijah, the play consists of a continuous
narrative of the biblical story (arbitrarily divided into five acts) in
which Nathan and the Chorus, rather than the Princes, have the largest
roles, since they could comment on the exemplary significance of the
action. When they first learn of Adonias's plot against the legitimate
heir, the Jewish girls of the Chorus are horrified, but console themselves
with the thought that

> RIEN ne se meut que par vouloir
> De celui, qui a tout pouvoir,
> DEPENDONS de sa Providence.
> Quand propre le temps il verra
> Justice à son point amerra.
> Nous pechons par impatience.   (I, f. B3ᵛ)

The evils of Kings must be endured patiently, for by patience God's
servants will triumph: God will eventually punish the evil-doer, whose
worldly might will not save him:

> C'est dessous la conduite
> Du grand Dieu D'EXERCITE
> Qu'un CHEF se treuve heureux.
>   MAIS si Dieu en son Ire
> Ceste Faveur retire,
> Tous ces forts et grand CHEF
> D'un peu de vent foudroye,
> Et fait tomber en proye
> Des subites meschefs.   (III, f. C5ʳ)

Such commentaries were the only substantial passages the author added
to his source. All distractions are avoided: the play consists simply of
a transcription of the biblical narrative with glosses explaining its
application to the plight of the Protestants.

The two other Protestant biblical plays written after the Synod of
Nîmes were the work of Pierre Heyns, a schoolmaster of Antwerp, who
when the town fell to Farnese in 1585 transferred his establishment
to Harlem, whence he published three plays he had written for performance by his pupils in Antwerp, including two on biblical subjects.[32]
The third was a *moralité*,[33] and in the other two he paid special
attention to moral instruction, as befitted his profession.

*Jokebed, Miroir des vrayes meres, Tragi-Comedie de l'enfance de
Moyse, representant les afflictions que les enfans de Dieu ont à souffrir
avant que parvenir à salut* (Amsterdam 1597)[34] illustrates the usual
themes of Protestant propaganda, defined in the Prologue:

Combien sagement, puissamment et fidelement le Dieu tout-puissant, fidele et
sage, conduit et dresse toutes choses par sa providence eternelle à tresbonne

fin, et au salut de ceux qui croyent en luy, et se confient en sa promesse, mesmes celles là qui souvent semblent et paroissent aux yeux des hommes mauvaises et pernicieuses. Item que ce bon Dieu n'inspire personne à mal, ou ne le fait mauvais, mais sait user merveilleusement de la malice des hommes au salut et conservation des bons, la perdition desquels les mauvais cerchent de tout leur pouvoir. Et avec ce, que le secours fidele de Dieu tout-puissant n'est jamais plus prochain de l'homme, que lors qu'il semble qu'il en soit du tout esloigné, et que c'est fait de luy. De sorte que l'amour de Dieu assiste, defend et sauve, quand il semble vouloir destruire, extirper et aneantir.   (p. 4)

The principal example of God's protection of the faithful is His thwarting of mighty Pharaoh's attempt to kill the helpless baby Moses, but the same theme is repeated in innumerable incidents Heyns added to his subject. In the first act Disposition Divine speaks a long mono-logue extolling God's providence, by which all events serve His purpose. Gent-Israelite enters, wishing to complain in solitude to God about the sufferings of the Jews, but the presence of Disposition Divine inhibits her. The latter identifies herself, and by a series of questions and answers forces Gent-Israelite to concede that she has no right to complain against God's providence. She teaches her to accept patiently the suffering He sends, since it is for her good, and promises that the Jews will soon be freed from Egypt. When Gent-Israelite leaves, Cruauté (daughter of Anxiété, and *chambrière* to Pharaon's con-cubine Sagesse Humaine) enters with complaints about the failure of her attempts to afflict the Jews. Disposition Divine informs her that God will turn her cruelty to the benefit of the Jews; Cruauté naturally does not understand. At this point, in fulfilment of Disposition Divine's promise, Sagesse Humaine enters with orders from Pharaon for Cruauté to persecute the Jews. Sagesse Humaine boasts that this is her doing, since Pharaon obeys only herself.

The rest of the play is in similar vein. The main plot follows Exodus i 8–ii 10: Pharaon orders all male Jewish babies to be killed, but Jokebed's child Moïse, thanks to Disposition Divine, is rescued by Pharaon's daughter, who gives him to Jokebed to nurse, not knowing her to be the mother.[35] Around the simple story, as in the first act, Heyns embroidered a rich tissue of incidents and cameos, which per-mitted him to catechise the audience thoroughly on the matter of reliance on God to protect the faithful from apparently overwhelming oppression, and a host of connected virtues.

In 1582 Heyns's pupils performed another play, *Le Miroir des vefves, tragedie sacrée d'Holoferne et Judith, representant, parmi les troubles de ce monde, la pieté d'une vraye Vefve et la curiosité d'une follastre* (Amsterdam 1596). As in *Jokebed*, the historical subject, the lifting of the siege of Bethulia by Judith's assassination of Holofernes, was the principal illustration of the theme, which was reiterated, together with innumerable other points of instruction, by the allegorical figures the author contributed. Heyns was more concerned with the homely virtues than the military, and neglected soldiers and generals to concentrate on the exemplary reactions to the siege of the allegorical figures representing more or less courageous elements of the *bourgeoisie* of the city: his lack of male actors was thus no inconvenience.[36] As in *Jokebed*, the figures provide a thorough education in virtue, by word and deed. Heyns showed considerable pedagogical genius in inventing personages and situations to illustrate so many points.

By introducing explicitly allegorical figures Heyns went further than most other writers of Protestant biblical propaganda in the direction of didacticism; but the difference was one of degree only. Other playwrights caused their human figures to state their own significance with no less objectivity; the Davids of Coignac and Desmasures are hardly less symbolic than the Cruauté or the Vefve Mondaine of Heyns's plays. The Protestant propagandists had no use for the convention that the characters are living beings whose troubles the audience shares: as Coignac's Prologue made clear, their prime concern was not to speak to the sensibilities of their spectators but to address their intellect with an irrefutable example supported by a clear exposition of the success of relying on God for protection when oppressed for their faith.

(ii) CATHOLIC PROPAGANDA

During the period of religious wars, the Catholics made strangely little attempt to answer the Protestants on the stage. From the appearance of Bèze's *Abraham sacrifiant*, the Protestant propaganda went unchallenged until the publication in 1575 of Chantelouve's *Tragedie de feu Gaspard de Colligny* (Paris). Of course, any play about a saint or the Virgin could be construed as Catholic propaganda, even if it contained no polemical passages. Many plays on such subjects were performed, but it is doubtful whether any was a new composition: most if not all were reworkings of the old *mystères*.[37] If any new saint-play was written, it was not printed: from 1550 to 1596 the only saint-plays to emerge from the presses were the few *mystères* considered in Chapter 1. Only after the fighting had stopped did the first new saint-plays appear,[38] but they cannot be seen as a response to any Protestant challenge, because by this time Protestants had effectively abandoned the propaganda theatre. During the period of most severe denominational conflict, the Catholics did not assert their beliefs by dramatising the lives of saints.

Only one Catholic attempted to answer the presentations of the Protestant position contained in such plays as Barran's *L'Homme justifié par Foy*. Simon Poncet, secretary to the *Ligueur* Aumale,[39] published a *Colloque chrestien* in dramatic form (Paris 1589). A man whose faith has been destroyed by all the contradictory arguments advanced in the doctrinal controversy is catechised by a student of theology, who answers the Protestant objections to the real presence, images, communion under one kind, purgatory and prayers for souls there, the value of hearing mass, prayers to saints, the value of works, the validity of priestly absolution, celibacy, fasting, and the unique authority of the Church of Rome to interpret the Scriptures.[40] Although the dialogue is spirited, the author did not endow his personages with even the presence of allegorical figures: the piece has no more life than a catechism.

The Catholics refrained equally from using biblical subjects for propaganda. They did of course write biblical plays, which will be considered in the next chapter, but only one Catholic imitated the Protestants in using the Bible to encourage his fellows, and even this play was directed less against the Protestants than the Valois. With this one exception, the Catholic biblical drama of the time of the religious wars was not primarily polemical in intention.[41]

The sole example of Catholic biblical propaganda is Adrien d'Amboise's *Holoferne, tragedie sacrée*, which was printed in Paris in 1580 with a Dedication stating that it was written four years earlier (f. A2^r). The biblical account of the assassination of Holofernes (Judith vii–xiv) is followed very closely; indeed several speeches are almost verbatim transcriptions. The first act consists mostly of a monologue, in which Holoferne vaunts his might as a general. For act II the scene shifts to Bethulia, where the priests discuss the restiveness of the citizens, who have forced them to agree to surrender if assistance does not come in five days. Judith intervenes to insist that to set such a limit to God's action is sinful. She promises to take a hand, and in the third act prays for strength, then goes to the Assyrian camp, where she is presented to Holoferne. In act IV he describes his passion for her and invites her to a banquet; Judith prays for the strength to kill him. The last act is occupied by her triumphant return to Bethulia, brandishing Holoferne's severed head.

D'Amboise followed the action in both camps rather than concentrating on any one figure;[42] his subject was not the emotions of any individual but the exemplary significance of the story as a whole. Holoferne is presented as a proud tyrant. He describes himself as

> regissant le sort
> Des filandrieres seurs, le destin, et la mort   (I, f. 4^{r-v})

and defies God to thwart him. The Jews refer constantly to God as the destroyer of tyrants; Judith in particular prays to Him as the avenger of oppressed innocence, and cites the example of His protection of the Jews from the tyranny of Pharaoh in the Exodus. Where previously the Protestants had written in these terms against the Catholic Kings, by 1576 the Valois court had so outraged Catholic opinion that the Ligue was formed and d'Amboise felt justified in putting on the stage his hope that the Catholics would be delivered from the tyranny of Henri III.[43]

Catholic propaganda was dominated by the Ligue, and directed more against the Valois than the Protestants. The only Catholic propaganda play to appear in France before the Ligue was formed, Chantelouve's *Colligny*, consisted of a salvo against the Admiral's family and Protestantism in general, with a vindication of the Saint Barthélemy. Also probably anti-Protestant was a play entitled *Calvin*, which does not survive: it was performed at the Jesuit College of Pont-à-Mousson, then outside the French kingdom, in 1577. After the formation of the Ligue the French Catholics wrote against the Valois Kings and Henri IV. Only Pierre Matthieu used a sacred subject for this purpose, when he rewrote his *Esther* to yield two firmly anti-Valois tragedies, *Vasthi* and *Aman* (Lyons 1589);[44] in the same year he also published *La Guisiade*, depicting Henri III as a bloody murderer. The latter approach was the more common: the supporters of the Ligue in the majority used modern subjects and a blunt satirical method.[45]

The Catholic propaganda theatre of the long period of denominational strife did not address itself to the religious issues involved. Only Poncet attempted to present any account of Catholic doctrines and to refute the Protestant positions. While the Protestant propagandists illustrated what they held to be the correct reaction to persecution, their Catholic counterparts offered vituperative caricatures of contemporary events and personalities. Other Catholic dramatists were of course moved by France's suffering to reflect on the mysteries of God's injustice, and many examples of this concern will be studied in the next chapter, but the Catholics never combined an assault on the doctrines of the opposing sect with the exemplification of correct beliefs and action, as did the Protestant propagandists.

The dramatists who used historical material for propaganda tended to take large episodes and trace their development *in extenso*, following the action, for example, in both Jewish and Philistine camps. They were able thus to present both righteousness and vice, the humility of David and the boastfulness of Goliath, the better to illustrate their message by both positive and negative examples. They had no use for the classical concentration.

The propagandists combined the extensive action with devices for making its significance clear: the commentaries of angels and demons, of Prologue, Epilogue and Chorus (borrowed of course from the classical tradition), even in some cases of allegorical figures. More important, they caused the historical figures themselves to comment on the significance of their own actions from the point of view of the audience. A realistic illusion was not what the propagandists required to make their message clear, any more than Brecht found realism suitable for a similar purpose; they needed a dramatic technique that allowed them to address the audience more directly.

It might seem that in not attempting to present a living example of faith in action, such as Bèze offered in Abraham, the propagandists were to some extent defeating their own purpose in choosing historical subjects, which might be expected to endow the lesson of reliance on God with the force of real experience: thanks to the devices for addressing the audience directly, this message is stated with illustrations instead of being lived. However, the propagandists perhaps found Bèze's presentation of the inner workings of faith and the near-triumph of doubt too rarefied and dangerous an approach: they preferred a more robust form of encouragement, and writing for a restless crowd in the market place thought a clear statement more likely than an attempt to build emotional empathy to be successful in transmitting it. The historical subject provided the authority of the Old Testament and was combined with a dramatic style designed to make the meaning of the example clear: thanks to this combination the propagandists were able to convey their message of encouragement with great force. By the very serenity of the heroes who are unmoved by tribulation and comment dispassionately on their position, the propagandists perhaps spoke with special vigour to the souls of the spectators who knew no such calm in their own lives.

5. Humanist drama: the themes and forms of the wars of religion

The last two chapters were concerned with two rather specialised types of play in which the authors purposely adopted a non-naturalistic dramatic style in order to express their themes. Here we return to the deliberately classicising theatre, and to chronological order, with the other plays that were written during the religious wars.[1] These were hardly less didactic and artificial than the doctrinal and the propaganda plays.

During the religious wars the playwrights were naturally preoccupied above all with the nation's agony; indeed reflection on the nation's suffering and its origins in the people's sinfulness remained the inspiration for some even after the restoration of peace, until the memory of strife began to fade. This brooding concern with men's cruelty and violence was shared by poets such as Sponde and d'Aubignac. Among the dramatists it was reinforced by the bloodthirsty plots of Seneca and the Italians to whom the French turned for literary models in the Renaissance; indeed the prestige these authors enjoyed was founded in part on the violent content of their plays[2] and their concern with the moral implications of the horrors they depicted.[3] Even the authors of the sacred dramas, who of course did not draw their plots from Italian or classical sources, turned to them as literary models and imitated their violence of language and spectacle.

The pious dramatists naturally sought the explanation of the horrors they depicted in God's justice, and adopted dramatic styles that would allow them to expound the connection between suffering and providence. Two playwrights, Grezin and Du Monin, chose to state the connection plainly by means of allegory. Other dramatists preferred a less uncompromisingly didactic approach, at least to the extent of using human heroes and historical material. Their handling of this material, however, was intended first and foremost to make the significance of the action clear. For this purpose, like the propagandists, they

used the comments of a chorus and other onlookers, and frequently
caused the principal characters to reflect objectively on their own
actions for the benefit of the audience. They also exercised considerable
ingenuity in blocking out the action in such a way that examples
of vice would stand contrasted with instances of virtue, and retribution
would be seen to be connected to sin. Action and character were firmly
conceived as exemplary: this was the essence of the humanist dramatic
style. The theme to which it was applied was the reflections to which
the civil wars gave rise. Where a modern audience responds to the
evocation of emotional states, the humanists thrilled to the explicit
delineation of major religious and philosophical issues illustrated in
history.

The authors in question were in many cases teachers or lawyers.
Of the schoolmasters, only two from the Low Countries, Macropedius
and Vivre, seem to have had a juvenile audience in mind (pp. 74–6
below); the language of the other schoolmasters, like that of the authors
from the university and legal worlds, was clearly designed for ears that
were not only adult but also highly literate. La Taille and Garnier, in
publishing their works, made it clear that they aspired to see them
performed at court;[4] Rivaudeau may have had the same idea in
dedicating *Aman* to the Queen of Navarre. The others no doubt
wrote for the main in the expectation of performance by students in
the halls of schools, colleges and law-courts, using improvised scenery
which, though on occasion sumptuous, was not realistic. The humanist
plays were also presented by the professional troupes, which were in
existence by 1550 and included such material in their repertoires.[5]
Contemporary illustrations most commonly show the professional
troupes playing in the open air on small stages of boards raised on
trestles to the height of the heads of the spectators, who were standing;
the scenery consisted of simple backcloths and one or two props.[6] It
was perhaps not part of the humanist dramatists' intention that their
plays should be taken round the market places of France, but it is
important to bear in mind that, although they were written for a
highly cultivated public, they were enjoyed as entertainment by the
ordinary unlettered people.

The earliest play exploring the pious reaction to the outbreak of war
was the work of a provincial priest,[7] Jacques Grezin: *Advertissements
faicts a l'homme par les fleaux de nostre Seigneur, de la punition à lui
deuë par son peché, comme est advenu depuis trois ans en ça*
(Angoulème 1565). Grezin explains in the Au lecteur that the nation's
suffering is an instance of God's benevolence: He has sent famine,
plague and war to punish the French for their sins, but mercifully
refrains from chastising them as severely as they deserve, in the hope

that the warning will suffice to encourage them to return to righteousness.

The play demonstrates this interpretation of events by means of a simple allegory. In turn Famine, Peste and Guerre reproach L'Homme, who represents the French, with abandoning himself to sin and ungratefully neglecting his Creator, and warn him of the punishment God will administer by their agency if he does not amend. L'Homme ignores them separately, so they assail him in unison. L'Homme bewails the piteous plight to which they reduce him, and prays God for mercy. An angel informs him that it is too late to escape chastisement by repenting; he should be glad to evade eternal punishment by suffering in this life. L'Homme regrets that all the French, innocent and wicked alike, must suffer because of the sinners. He reflects on his offences and rejoices that God has given him this warning so that by repentance he may escape the eternal suffering he deserves; he hopes piously that his body may suffer so that his soul may be saved. He is confident that Christ can redeem his sins. The angel tells him to do penance. L'Homme confesses the sins of the Church, the Nobility and the Third Estate, by which he has offended God, and throws himself on His mercy.

The allegorical figures are able to offer a clear account of the divine purpose; indeed, the play is scarcely less explicit than the Au lecteur, where the author speaks with his own voice. Despite the possibility of clarity that such an approach offered, the great majority of dramatists preferred not to speak to the audience quite so directly: they abided by the literary convention of hiding the authorial presence and worked obliquely through biblical and hagiographic material, apparently judging suggestion more effective than direct statement. Nevertheless, their manipulation of plot and character was hardly less transparent than Grezin's.

This was the case in the Aman, tragedie saincte (Poitiers 1566) of André de Rivaudeau, despite the author's adoption of all the neo-classical conventions, except the most fundamental, established in Bèze's Abraham sacrifiant, which was the treatment of the hero as an autonomous figure. This was not to Rivaudeau's purpose: he wished to treat his characters as examples. In this he was perhaps motivated partly by a desire to make propaganda on behalf of the Protestants,[8] but he was also acting in accordance with the predominant literary fashion: all the humanist dramatists opted for this exemplary approach. The formalities of the neo-classical style, on the other hand, were to Rivaudeau's taste, and he adopted wholeheartedly the adherence to Greek and Roman forms that was commonplace in the humanist theatre. He was in fact the first dramatist writing in French to

enunciate and practise the unity of time, which he derived from Aristotle,[9] and *Aman* was the first regular French sacred tragedy. Rivaudeau's classicising intention is made clear in the Avant-Parler:

je me suis rengé le plus reservement et estroictement que j'ay peu en escrivant ceste Tragedie à l'art et au modelle des Anciens Graecz... (ll. 183–5)

As the Dedication to the Queen of Navarre establishes, his aim was to write, not a replica, but a French equivalent of the work of Seneca and the Greeks. In form, *Aman* follows the pattern elaborated by the humanists from those models: it has a long historical Prologue, monologues open the four succeeding acts while choruses close all five, the action commences *in medias res*, and there are many elaborate tirades.[10]

Starting *in medias res*, indeed almost *in fine*,[11] Rivaudeau chose to show only one episode of the story, the banquet, which contains the only peripeteia and is reserved for the last act. Physical action is reduced to a minimum: the plot consists rather of a series of object-lessons, in which each character shows whether he relies on God or, ignoring Him, trusts to his own muscles, and is suitably rewarded in the last act.[12] Aman is an example of pride. His first appearance establishes that he has received a divine warning that he will be humbled: he tells one of his faction that Mardochée has refused to honour him according to his rank, and that he has been forced instead to honour Mardochée by the King. Rather than heeding the warning to place no reliance on his position as favourite, Aman swears to punish Mardochée and all his race. The Escuyer reminds him that

"Les Dieux qui peuvent tout entrerompent le cours[13]
Souvent de nos desseins, les tournans au rebours (ll. 439–40)

but Aman replies

Je n'ay que faire aux Dieux, car ma grande puissance
Me promet à part moy la fin de ma vengeance. (ll. 441–2)

With irreligious pride, Aman is confident that he is master of his own destiny and no divinity can thwart his intentions: 'On est Dieu à soymesme' (l. 1583) is his creed. His self-confidence is punished when, far from seeing Mardochée hanged, he is himself executed on the gibbet he had prepared for his enemy.

As a mighty King, Assuère might have more justification for self-confidence than Aman. His first speech, however, shows him to be aware of the impermanence of good fortune: he reflects on the disasters endured by his predecessors, and concludes:

bien qu'un peuple grand soubz ma puissance tremble,
Et le Soleil m'ait veu naistre homme et roy ensemble,

> Je suis douteux pourtant en atendant des Cieux
> Sur mon sceptre et sur moy, l'ordonnance des Dieux.   (ll. 609–12)

Unlike Aman, Assuère has a proper mistrust of the permanence of his present power: he is a model of the humble, God-fearing King.

The Jewish figures, of course, are conscious of the need to fear God. In the long monologue which he delivers as a Prologue, Mardochée recalls the whole of Jewish history and describes the afflictions the nation has brought on itself by its sins and its neglect of God, culminating in oppression by Aman; he concludes with resigned humility:

> Mais Dieu dispose tout, une humble patience
> Peut surmonter d'Aman la roide violence:
> Au fort, s'il faut ployer soubz nos persecuteurs,
> Je ne suis pas meilleur que mes predecesseurs.   (ll. 225–8)

For all Aman's might, Mardochée retains perfect confidence in God's ability to overthrow him:

> tu peux tirer des tiens et leur foiblesse
> De quoy vaincre les Rois, et baisser leur hautesse.   (ll. 1683–4)

Esther shares her uncle's faith that God can confound Aman:

> la main trespuissante
> De Dieu destournera ton emprise meschante,
> D'un Dieu plus fort que toy, et que les plus grans Rois,
> Qui se moque là haut de vos trop foibles loix,
> Qui des hommes n'a cure, et leurs desseins renverse,
> Et en la creuse fosse ireusement les verse,
> Qu'eux mesmes ils ont fait.   (ll. 791–7)

Since she is a woman, her faith is less steadfast than Mardochée's, and she permits herself to speculate that Aman might triumph, even suggesting that God would be unjust to allow this result; but her confidence returns and she rebukes herself for her sinful lack of faith (ll. 917–28).

Even the minor figures refer to the theme of God's might and men's weakness. Zarasse, Aman's wife, features in one brief scene to warn Aman that God is more powerful than he (ll. 1329–38); but since she says this without entire conviction, she is justly punished by Aman's death. Rivaudeau reinforced the theme by introducing two roles, Simeon (an old Jew) and a Chorus, to offer explicit comment. Simeon reflects sententiously on the benefits of humility (ll. 493–8). The Chorus explains why God permits Assuère and his favourite to persecute His people:

> Les Rois Ministres souvent
> Et bourreaus du Dieu vivant

Executent sa justice
En chastiant nostre vice.   (ll. 1001–4)

The reward for submitting patiently to His correction is eternal life:

Celuy qui prent sobrement
Du grand Dieu le jugement
Pour un peu de temps endure,
A fin que tousjours il dure.   (ll. 1025–8)

The Jews must even accept death, if God wills it:

Le Seigneur Dieu ne peut rien que pour le mieux faire,
Quant tous les Juifs mourront, si s'en faudra-il taire.   (ll. 915–16)

The comments of the onlookers reiterate the moral of the main plot: the whole play is arranged to recommend humble submission to God.

The characters are presented firmly as examples. The speeches in which they express pride or humility are often unprovoked: Assuère's humble monologue in act II, for instance, is not necessary to the plot, and its only function is to show the King being humble. The intervention of Zarasse is similarly unconnected with anything before or after, and has no bearing on Aman's subsequent course of action: she is introduced to exhibit Aman's pride. The characters speak at the author's behest to exemplify pride or humility, rather than obeying any inner imperatives: Rivaudeau had no interest in endowing them with any such independent emotional life. The figures are mouthpieces of exemplary sentiments. Unlike Bèze's Abraham, the Jews experience no difficulty in reconciling themselves to God's will, even though until the last act it seems that He intends to allow them to be massacred. Only Esther expresses any anxiety, fleetingly; for the most part, the Jewish protagonists speak of themselves as dispassionately as the Chorus. Aman likewise gives no impression of real feeling: he speaks with an unchanging vindictive rage, and his one hesitation as to his right to kill the Jews (ll. 425–7) is so abrupt that it is clear Rivaudeau introduced it simply so as to prolong the debate with the Eunuque. The spectator is not intended to identify imaginatively and emotionally with the characters: their dispassionate and self-analytical turn of phrase encourages him instead to judge them as object-lessons of pride and humility and the rewards these qualities receive. Having been denounced by Esther, Aman states the truism that his fate illustrates:

ô Fortune, ô ingrate,
Aveugle, passagere, eventée, ô Honneur!
D'un bien pauvre valet tu tailles un Seigneur,
Et d'un bien grand Seigneur, retailles un esclave.   (ll. 1978–81)

Despite using the neo-classical form, Rivaudeau subscribed to the convention familiar from the *mystères* by which the characters do not speak for themselves, but in their words express the lesson the spectator may draw from their careers.

So intent was Rivaudeau, however, on incorporating the formal features of neo-classical tragedy that he was capable of disregarding their congruity with the play's religious import to include them for decorative effect. When Simeon, newly arrived, asks why Aman hates the Jews, the Chorus first explains how Esther came to the throne, prefacing this with an ornate description in forty-eight lines of the sumptuous scene at the banquet at which Assuère repudiated Vashti (ll. 1391–438). The scene at the banquet Esther gives for Assuère is also described at length by a servant, who includes a long apostrophe to Beauty, inspired by the Queen (ll. 1775–811). With the crisis approaching it seems hardly the moment for this interruption, but Rivaudeau's audience was happy to wait for the banquet scene while thrilling to the poet's skill:

> A a BEAUTE, quel pouvoir tu as sur tous les hommes,
> Beauté par ton moyen à nousmesmes ne sommes,
> Ains nos vaincus esprits demeurent chez autruy,
> Foibles en leurs maisons, sur toy cerchent apuy.
> Tu nous fais desirer les choses non loisibles,
> Tu nous rends soucieux, patilleux, mal paisibles,
> Meschans, injurieux, sans force et sans honneur,
> Larrone du repos, de la paix, et de l'heur...   (ll. 1775–82)

In fact Rivaudeau's poetry is less than outstanding, but the apostrophe has a second *raison d'être*: it is the opportunity for a disquisition about the dangers of beauty and the passions it provokes. The sentiment is scarcely apt, since the beauty by which Esther captivates Assuère saves the Jews from extermination, but Rivaudeau and his audience were clearly content with morsels of conventional wisdom and grandiloquent poetry, almost irrespective of their appropriateness to plot and situation. The expectation of the humanist theatre was that it should air philosophical questions in passages of fine poetry, and it was not uncommon for a dramatist to attend so closely to this requirement at every stage that the sense of one scene was unconnected with or even ran contrary to that of another or of the play as a whole.

Rivaudeau's self-conscious adoption of the full panoply of the devices by which the extent of the classical play was restricted so as to encourage concentration on the hero and his crisis was somewhat at odds with the effects he sought to create. The fundamental requirement of the humanist technique was that the spectator should not sympathise with individual characters but should stand back and judge the various elements presented as exemplifying different aspects of a theme; from his detached position he could also appreciate the author's rhetorical skill. Devices such as the unities of action and time have the effect of promoting involvement with the hero in his agony. The humanists perhaps adopted the classical style more for its prestige than its suitability to their purposes, and many indeed abandoned such features as the unities and even the individual hero so as to present extensive examples for analysis; Rivaudeau himself, for all his classicising intentions, built his *Aman* round a collection of object-lessons rather than any one protagonist.

In the light of the humanists' preference for presenting the action as exemplary, Jean de la Taille's *Saül le furieux, tragedie* (Paris 1572)[14] must have struck contemporaries as somewhat unorthodox, because it did admit a degree of sympathy with the hero; and La Taille was perhaps also less inclined than his peers to indulge in philosophising and grandiloquence for their own sakes. There is no doubt, though, that La Taille was following in the general direction of the Pléiade when he wrote *Saül*,[15] to such an extent that scholars have tended to see it as an exclusively neo-classical work with no Christian content. Hall and Smith have summarised critical opinion of *Saül* and its companion-piece, *La Famine*: they 'are not religious tragedies, but classical ones with scriptural plots'.[16] *Prima facie*, however, it is not plausible that La Taille should have chosen biblical subjects if he had no religious intentions whatsoever.

The principal action in *Saül* concerns the King's struggle to come to terms with God's anger. In place of the conventional Senecan monologue, the play opens with the startling apparition of Saül, who rushes onto the stage mad, lunging with his sword at his followers and even his sons. His first words refer to the heavens: he sees his enemies there, and will climb up to attack them. He runs off, but at his next appearance he again looks heavenwards:

> Je veux monter au ciel, que mon char on attelle,
> Et comme les Geants entassants monts sur monts,
> Je feray trebuscher les Anges et Daemons,
> Et seray Roy des Cieux...   (ll. 254–7)

The discreet allusion to classical mythology makes it clear that Saül is guilty of the sin of pride. Rather than expanding repetitiously on Saül's frenzy, La Taille now allows him to recover his senses and reflect. He laments at the recollection of God's withdrawal of His favour, which drove him mad; but rather than submitting meekly to His wrath, Saül asks angrily what he has done to deserve it:

> Helas tousjours le vent la grande mer n'esmeut,
> Tousjours l'hyver ne dure, et l'air tousjours ne pleut.[17]

> Tout prend fin, faut-il donc que ta longue cholere,
> O grand DIEU, dessus moy sans cesse persevere?
> Je suis hay de toy, et des hommes aussi:
> J'ay cent mille soucis, nul n'a de moy soucy:
> Mais dy l'occasion d'une si grande haine,
> Dy la raison pourquoy j'endure telle peine?
> Mais helas qu'ay-je fait, qu'ay-je lás merité,
> Que tu doives ainsi tousjours estre irrité?   (ll. 292–300)

Saül's Escuyer answers: his offence was sparing the life of Agag, in defiance of God's order. Saül protests:

> "O que sa Providence est cachee aux humains!
> Pour estre donc humain j'esprouve sa cholere,
> Et pour estre cruel il m'est donc debonnaire!
> Hé Sire, Sire, lás! fault il donc qu'un vainqueur
> Plustost que de pitié use fier de rigueur...?   (ll. 312–16)

Saül knows that God's designs are hidden from men, but still suggests that He is unjust. The Escuyer warns that in judging God's actions men are guilty of pride, and reminds Saül of all he owes to his Creator.[18] Saül admits that he has no right to judge God's purposes:

> Je sçay bien qu'aux mortels appeller il ne faut
> De son Arrest fatal decidé de là haut,
> Mais il a maintenant esmeu la Palestine,
> A fin d'executer l'Arrest de ma ruine,
> Donc je veux assouvir sa rigueur, et suis prest
> De mourir maintenant, puis que ma mort luy plaist.   (ll. 399–404)

The Escuyer detects the note of rancour rather than submission in the conclusion of this speech, and warns Saül to abandon his mistaken conviction of his innocence and accept that God is just in punishing him:

> Mais sans tant desguiser les maux qu'avez commis,
> Priez Dieu qu'ils vous soient par sa bonté remis,
> "L'invoquant de bon coeur: à l'heur qu'on l'invoque
> "On gaigne sa faveur: mais lors on le provoque
> "Au juste accroissement de sa punition,
> "Quand on se justifie avec presumption.   (ll. 415–20)

Saül refuses to admit guilt in order to beg forgiveness; in any case he believes his sins too great to be removed by God's mercy.

Deprived of God's support, on which he has always relied, Saül has lost his confidence. Rather than joining his sons in the battle against the Philistines, Saül is paralysed by uncertainty until he can discover what God intends for him. In seeking to know God's will Saül contravenes the principle he admitted earlier, as his Escuyer is quick to point out:

"Mais on peche en voulant sçavoir son adventure. (l. 454)

Knowing his fate would not enable him to avoid it; but Saül replies:

"Le prudent peut fuir sa fortune maligne. (l. 457)

Saül pits human prudence against God's will; he has refused God's help
by rejecting the Escuyer's advice to seek His pardon, and now trusts
to his own wits to enable him to evade what God has ordained. Com-
pounding this temerity, he proposes to discover the future by the
forbidden art of necromancy. The Chorus makes it clear that the
attempt to know God's purpose betrays a pride equivalent to that
which caused man's first sin (ll. 517–20).

Through the witch of Endor, Saül consults Samuel, who confirms
that in seeking to know the future Saül has only compounded his sin.
Saül, his children and his line will all die shamefully:

Et le tout pourautant qu'à la divine voix
Obeï tu n'as point ainsi que tu devois,
Qu'execute tu n'as sa vengeance dépite,
(Comme je t'avois dit) contre l'Amalechite [i.e. Agag]. (ll. 773–6)

Saül faints, but on recovering he continues to question God's justice
with undiminished vehemence. He accuses God of having elevated
him to the throne specially for the pleasure of dashing him down:[19]
he rejects as cruel and unjust the destiny God has ordained for him.

Returning to the camp, Saül gives tongue to his awareness that God
intends to place David on his throne, and concludes:

Tu eslis donc des Roys de mes ennemis mesmes:
Et bien ayme les donc et favorise les:
Mais je vas, puis qu'ainsi en mes maulx tu te plais,
Finir au camp mes jours, mon malheur et ta haine. (ll. 912–15)

His sulky defiance is immediately answered by the news that his three
sons are dead. Saül recognises that he is responsible:

O lamentables Fils, ô defortuné Pere!
Fault-il que dessus vous tombe le triste fais
Des peches et des maux que vostre pere a faicts! (ll. 960–2)

For once, he does not accuse God of injustice. However, when he is
advised to flee since the battle is lost, his defiance returns: he decides
to commit suicide, affirming that he, not God, is master of his destiny.
He asks the Escuyer to kill him, again rejecting the latter's advice that
he should submit to God and seek forgiveness; but the Escuyer refuses
to harm the King whom God appointed. Since the Escuyer will not
oblige him, Saül goes off with the intention of dying in battle; there,
as we learn in act v, he is so weakened by his wounds that to avoid

capture he is obliged to fall on his sword. The last words he speaks on the stage suggest no submission to God's will, but rather a Stoic defiance: he will go to meet his death because it would be unworthy of a King to avoid it:

> Je ne veux abbaissant ma haute majesté,
> Eviter le trespas qui prefix m'a esté...   (ll. 1085–6)

From first to last, Saül remains insubmissive: he thinks only in terms of human justice, prudence and courage and nowhere shows any capacity for gladly embracing God's mysterious will. Unlike Rivaudeau's Aman, Saül is not simply an unchanging example of a moral quality: La Taille traces the human evolution by which a man, having forfeited God's favour, by his own misguided actions cuts himself off from any possibility of retrieval and forgiveness.

When Saül pits himself against God's will, he is 'furieux' not just in the clinical but also in the theological sense: he embodies the merely human wisdom that is contrary to the true wisdom of God and in His sight is folly, as Paul puts it in 1 Corinthians. However, Saül is also 'furieux' in imitation of Hercules. The scenes of his frenzy are modelled on Seneca's *Hercules furens*, and the play abounds in classical allusions.[20] There is a certain ambiguity in La Taille's conception of the subject, expressed by the two sonnets accompanying the text.[21] In one, placed at the beginning, La Taille states that his intention is to glorify God; in the other, at the end, he holds Saül up as an example of the mutability of fortune. Saül may well be seen as an undeserving victim of an arbitrarily harsh fate which he comes to face with exemplary fortitude.[22] La Taille wished his play to be a tragedy, not just an object-lesson in the doctrine of reprobation, as the *Art de la tragédie* he prefaced to the play makes plain. He knew of Aristotle's recommendation that the tragic hero should not be undeserving of sympathy, and applied this principle to Saül by to some extent justifying his sins. When the Escuyer reproaches Saül with sparing Agag, La Taille gives the King a powerful speech advocating clemency in the name of humanity, quoted above. Nothing could be more humanly excusable than the wish not to survive his sons, which drives him to the sin of suicide. Above all, Saül is presented as a hero, even by his closest critic, the first Escuyer, who follows him into battle, there to die with him. The second Escuyer, left behind, describes Saül as a model of patriotism and Stoic fortitude in going out to meet certain death (ll. 1099–112). He is immediately corrected by the Chorus, which points out that the suicide is a sinner, not a hero, but when in the last act the second Escuyer describes Saül's destiny in purely pagan terms as an example of the mutability of fortune, the Chorus does not demur. David, on learning of the two suicides, reflects conventionally on the vanity of worldly power and praises Saül as a hero, even extolling his valour in killing himself (ll. 1491–500). The defiance which marks him as a sinner in the first acts is hailed at the end by David and the Escuyers as the quality which distinguishes him as a heroic representative of humanity resisting an unwarranted fate. Is his death the action of divine justice or blind fatality? La Taille seems to have been undecided. In the Argument explaining the events which caused Saül's death he is non-committal, and David in his elegy likewise refrains from naming the agency he considers responsible for the disaster. As Lebègue has concluded,

> il nous est impossible de savoir s'il tombe sous les coups de l'aveugle et cruelle Fatalité ou d'un Dieu juste, et si, en épargnant Agag, il a commis un crime ou un acte généreux: ce point essentiel reste obscur, parce qu'il y a conflit dans l'âme de l'auteur entre l'influence de la Bible et la morale chrétienne et celle d'Aristote et du théâtre grec.[23]

There was perhaps also a religious reason for this confusion: having made Saül sympathetic, La Taille felt that to make God responsible for his death would make Him seem unjust, and so brought in fate to take the blame. By attempting to exonerate God, La Taille only compromised the religious sense of his play.

In making Saül sympathetic rather than an object-lesson, La Taille diverged from his humanist colleagues. There are few of the conventional passages of abstract generalisation on philosophical commonplaces; when commonplaces do occur, they are usually treated briefly and directed *ad hominem*, as in the instances noted above. The play is arranged rather to encourage the audience to understand Saül as in the name of humanity he defies God; this is quite different from the approach Rivaudeau expected his audience to take to Aman. The scenes not involving Saül are also designed to have an emotional impact. After Saül's first brief appearance, the bulk of act I is given over to a discussion between his three sons, who decide to fight the Philistines despite the King's incapacity to lead the Jews. The scene perhaps has some religious import, reminding us that the three Princes, for all their virtue and vigour, cannot rescue the Jews once God has decided to punish their King, but the main effect of the scene is to induce tension by reminding the audience that while Saül is hesitating the crucial battle is already being fought. The long scene devoted to the witch and her incantations seems to have been intended to provoke a *frisson*, though it also no doubt answered to La Taille's special interest in necromancy.[24] The other major scene not focussing on Saül, the disconcerting episode in act v in which David orders the

execution of an Amalekite soldier who first claims to have killed Saül
and then confesses that he did not but hoped by claiming so to in-
gratiate himself with his successor, seems to have been intended to
serve another purpose again. The scene may have a religious function,
either by illustrating the folly of human calculation or by reminding
us that David too is capable of injustice and will lose God's favour, but
this is improbable because the first point is illustrated adequately
elsewhere and the second is at odds with the use made of David in the
rest of the play. One is driven to conclude that La Taille included the
episode principally because it figured in the Bible. Here we approach
the weakness of the play: although the greater part of it is devoted to
the human exploration of Saül's reprobation, at other points La Taille's
attention was dominated by other considerations, the desire for
sensational effects, concern with fidelity to his source. Although it is
less fragmented than Rivaudeau's *Aman*, *Saül le furieux* lacks complete
imaginative integration.

Thanks principally to the power with which La Taille depicted
Saül's emotional state, which the modern age finds more sympathetic
than the usual humanist drama, the play is enjoying a resurgence of
critical acclaim. With its contemporaries the play was not a success, to
such an extent that the successor of the first printer was still trying to
sell off sheets of the first edition thirty years after it had been made.[25]
La Famine, ou les Gabéonites (Paris 1573)[26] was not more popular,
despite being closer to the humanist conventions. The play opens with
a monologue, the last act contains a long messenger speech, and much
space is given to grandiloquent tirades. More important, *La Famine*
is not centred on an individual whose emotions drive the plot: it
presents a number of figures whose role is passively to endure their
fates while expanding poetically on their griefs. Many lines are
imitated from classical sources,[27] and the action, which La Taille
invented on the basis of a few lines in the Bible,[28] is arranged to follow
the model of Seneca's *Troades*.

Nevertheless, La Taille imposed a Christian rather than a pagan
interpretation on events, in the first acts at least. In the opening monologue, David laments the Jews' afflictions. He wishes God had not
selected him to be their King, and asks why He has so frequently
saved the Jews if He intends now to let them die of famine: will He
abandon His people? Unlike Saül, David recollects at this point that
men may not criticise God's hidden purposes:

> Mais lás, que di-je? où suis-je? Há je te prie, ô Sire
> Pardonner à ton oinct, si la faim luy fait dire
> Chose qui t'ait dépleu. Je sçay bien qu'il convient
> Souffrir (soit bien ou mal) tout ce qui de toy vient.   (ll. 143–6)

He reaffirms his faith that God's will is just, and surmises that the
Jews have brought the famine on themselves by their sins. Joabe, the
Connétable, enters and suggests that the Jews should escape starvation
by moving to other pastures, but David rejects this prudent stratagem
in favour of strict attendance on God's will:

> Nous ne partirons point,
> Si le Dieu d'Israël ne l'a premier enjoint.
> C'est luy qui nous a faict en ce lieu cy venir,
> Pareillement aussi nous en doit il bannir.   (ll. 209–12)

The Chorus reflects that Israel's sufferings are a divine punishment.

The second act presents Rezèfe, Saül's mother. She accuses God of
nursing 'hayne' and 'bouillante ire' against Saül (l. 282), but unlike
David she does not correct herself after thus taxing God with injustice.
She reveals that Saül's ghost has warned her that his offspring will be
sacrificed. Although Saül stated that God willed it (l. 347), Rezèfe has
no intention of permitting the children to be killed. Rather than
submitting, she asks resentfully if God's anger will never end and
laments that the children will not live to avenge their father, thus
again impugning God's justice in killing him.[29] With Mérobe, Saül's
widow, she hides the children in Saül's tomb, hoping to save them.
The Chorus declares that it is impossible to thwart God's will, citing
among other instances Saül himself.

Joabe brings David the prophets' pronouncement that God will end
the drought only when the Gibeonites are appeased, and the Prince
de Gabon demands as satisfaction the death of all Saül's male descent,
to which David agrees. Despite Rezèfe's precautions, Joabe discovers
the children in the tomb. The Chorus reflects that God is just: He is
slow to anger in order to give the sinner time to repent, but if he persists
His punishment is sure.

To this point La Famine has evoked the same theme as Saül: no
man may with impunity doubt the justice of God's will or attempt to
evade its effect. As the play advances this theme becomes less important:
hardly mentioned in act III, it is entirely absent from acts IV and V.
The characters lament, but do not deliver any understanding of how
God's justice operates in the disaster. Rezèfe blames David, Fate, the
Gibeonites, God and Joabe indifferently, and never tries to come to
terms with the central problem the play raises, the acceptance as just
of God's apparent cruelty. The only figure to confront this problem is
David, who has to decide whether to obey God's order to sacrifice the
children, but he resolves the difficulty after the briefest hesitation and
does not appear again. The question of obedience to God's will when
His purpose is mysterious is thus shelved, and never becomes the
dramatic kernel of the play.

In the last acts La Taille turns from showing the characters' acceptance or rejection of God's will to depicting the pathos of their fate; throughout, indeed, his major concern is lamentation of the disaster more than reflection on its cause, and the play accommodates a large number of pathetic tirades. Act II has no historical basis: it was invented (following classical models) to allow Rezèfe and Mérobe to lament their lot. Act III deals rapidly with the action, then passes on to the pathetic scene in which Joabe discovers the children; this occupies half the act. In act IV the pathos is redoubled: to Rezèfe's dismay the children are heroically determined to submit to their fate. Finally their death is recounted to Mérobe; the Messenger emphasises the pathetic steadfastness of the victims, who were unmoved save by the sight of Rezèfe's desolation. The formal dignity of the Messenger's account, and indeed of the language throughout, enhances the pathetic effect of the actions described.

The action of *La Famine* is very simple: it is decided to sacrifice Saül's offspring, and they duly die. Various impediments are invented to create opportunities for the characters to expand on their feelings; variety is ensured by each expressing a slightly different reaction. David submits easily. Rezèfe resists, while Mérobe endures passively. Joabe carries out his duty efficiently, though not without compassion. The children themselves submit with heroic fortitude. This display of a gamut of emotions was in accordance with the principle La Taille enunciated in the *Art de la tragédie*: 'La vraye et seule intention d'une Tragedie est d'esmouvoir et de poindre merveilleusement les affections d'un chascun' (ll. 31–2). What is notable here is La Taille's omission of the usual humanist preoccupation with instruction, although he subscribed to this convention in the first acts of *La Famine*. In *Saül* and the last two acts of *La Famine* La Taille played on the 'affections' of the audience through the emotions of the powerful individual protagonist and of the wretched group, but in both plays the emotions are exhibited to no very good purpose because of the lack of an integrating and consistent thread of serious reflection, religious or otherwise, which would give them point.

La Taille was unusual in concentrating on emotional impact. A more representative example of humanist dramaturgy in one way at least was the *Joseph* (Antwerp 1544) of Georgius Macropedius, which inclined in fact to the opposite extreme of didacticism, as befitted the profession of the author, a friar and schoolmaster.[30] Apart from its didacticism, however, this play is unusual in the humanist theatre in not being a tragedy: Macropedius thought the *comoedia* a more suitable medium for instructing his young audience. He wrote a number of Latin *comoediae sacrae* for his pupils to perform; only *Joseph* falls into the ambit of this study, because it was translated into French by Antoine Tiron[31] and published in 1564.

Tiron's title, *L'Histoire de Joseph, extraicte de la saincte bible et reduitte en forme de Comedie*, indicates that the subject includes a large part of Joseph's life: his service with Potiphar, his entanglement with his master's wife, his imprisonment and his liberation (Genesis xxxix–xli). The action is simply arranged to recount these episodes. In his treatment of his hero Macropedius avoids suggesting any religious difficulties or dilemmas such as Bèze's Abraham endured; Joseph is seen principally in his role as a servant and is a model of the homely virtues in which Macropedius wished to coach his pupils. Scenes concerning servants and the other secondary characters bulk larger than those involving the hero himself: on the basis of a relatively slight action Macropedius wrote an expansive *comédie de moeurs*, well adapted to inducing his juvenile public to adhere to the path of rectitude and simplicity in domestic life, and especially to the virtue of chastity.

Gérard de Vivre of Ghent, a schoolmaster at Cologne,[32] likewise wrote plays for his pupils. He explained the pedagogical value of 'Comedies' in a Preface: performing them helps a child to learn French, to overcome youthful timidity, and to acquire assurance in speaking, while the subject-matter provides moral instruction. Vivre published three comedies he had written with these aims in mind: *Les Amours pudiques et loyales de Theseus et Dianira*, *La Fidelité nuptiale*, and *Le Patriarche Abraham et sa servante Agar*.[33] They are written in simple French prose and deal with the homely virtues. The first two have as their major themes fidelity in marriage and steadfastness in adversity, but many other points of morality are mentioned in passing; such skilful introduction of incidental instruction recalls the work of Heyns, to whom some editions of the plays were dedicated.

The same manner is used in the biblical play. The subject is the rejection of Abraham's illegitimate son Ishmael and the mother Hagar after the birth of Isaac (Genesis xxi 6–19). In the first scene Abraham and Sara rejoice at the birth of a son in their old age. However, Ismael has mocked the baby Isaac: Sara urges Abraham to dismiss Ismael and Agar. He is unwilling to banish his son, but is ordered to obey Sara by the voice of God, which explains that the displacement of Ismael by the younger brother symbolises the supplanting of the old law by the new. Although Abraham does not understand this reference to the coming of Christ, he promises to obey. In the second act, after ascertaining Sara's will, he obediently orders Agar to leave with her son. Preparations are made in the third act, and they depart in the fourth. In act v, Agar despairs as she wanders in the desert with

Ismael, despite knowing that God promised Abraham that He would
support her. An angel assures her that God has not forgotten her and
shows her where to find water. Refreshed, mother and son journey
on with renewed strength and faith.

At the beginning attention is concentrated on Abraham, but by
the end the focus has shifted to Agar, who dominates the last act. By
dramatising the whole of the biblical episode without concentrating on
the emotions of any individual, Vivre was able to present two instances
of confidence that God knows best and will provide, in Abraham's
rejection of Ismael and in the provision of water for Agar. This action,
being slight in itself, gave Vivre the opportunity to have his characters
moralise about a wide range of topics, notably servants' duty of
obedience and the achievement of domestic harmony. Vivre emphasised the homely virtues that his pupils would need.

These two comedies, like Heyns's more polemical *Judith* and *Jokebed*,
were written by natives of the Spanish Netherlands for performance
in schools, and reflect a local tradition as well as the special concerns
of schoolmasters.[34] Moral or religious dilemmas suggested by the source
are glossed over and the subject is treated as an uncomplicated example
of virtue. The major action is surrounded by a tissue of minor incidents, each a cameo of *moeurs* with its own instructive significance.
The action consists mostly of homely activities and the heroism of
Judith, Moses's mother, Joseph and Abraham is allied with more
domestic virtues. To impart this instruction the authors adopted a free
form which admitted allegorical figures and extensive actions, and
provided a clear account, unclouded by emotion, of the virtues they
wished to instil.

The humanist dramatists who had no need to adapt their work to
juvenile audiences generally preferred the tragic to the comic mode
and addressed themselves to larger philosophical themes, but their
plays resembled those of the pedagogues in their didactic tone. That
the theatre should be instructive was essential to the humanists' conception of the literary genre. In constructing their plays according to
this principle they were capable of neglecting other considerations, as
was the case in Rivaudeau's *Aman*; this tendency was perhaps more
marked in plays written later in the century. It was exhibited by
François de Chantelouve in his *Tragédie de Pharaon* (Paris 1577),[35]
which is more typical of the humanist style than any of the plays
examined so far; I shall analyse it at some length.

An Angel, as Prologue, opens the play thus:

> Le haut tonnant qui de sa dextre bride
> Tout ce qui est, de la race abramide
> Se souvenant, et du pacte promis

A l'Isacide, et leurs ayeux amis:
Du Trosne sainct de l'argentine voute
Le Roy prophane en ses desseins escoute,
Et d'Israël les complaintes, et cris,
Ont justement ses bras rouges aigris.   (f. A^r)

This sets the tone of emphatic declamation; it also establishes the theme
of God's protection of the Jews. The action proper is begun by Terinisse,
Pharaon's daughter, who delivers a monologue of lamentation:

Ah! ah! infortunee, et chetive pourquoy
Cest astre blandissant raionne dessus moy?
Pourquoy d'un doy rozin l'Aurore matiniere
Espanit a mes yeux sa purprine lumiere?
O dolente Princesse, ô miserable moy
Si vivante, souffrir un tel forfait je doy.   (i i, f. A3^v)

True to Senecan convention, she reveals that the cause of her anxiety is
a dream, which fills her with fear for her adoptive son Moïse. Pharaon
enters, and she disguises her feelings. He plays with the boy, placing his
crown on his head in sport; but Moïse rejects the honour by throwing
the crown to the ground and trampling it. Héliopole, an Egyptian
priest, warns Pharaon that Moïse will be his ruin, as this action
portends. Pharaon is sufficiently alarmed to consider killing the boy:

Des misteres secrets, et sacrifices saincts
De noz dieux ô grand prestre! ô des pays Nilains
Le souverain appuy je cuide que serappe
T'inspire sa fureur afin que point n'eschappe
Ce Genne dangereux: et mon coeur qui ba-bat:
Pour toy contre l'amour en moi-mesme debat.   (i iii, f. A5^v)

The hesitation is a formality, for Pharaon quickly demonstrates himself
to be a tyrant by deciding to kill Moïse. Terinisse engages in a stichomythic debate with her father, maintaining that Moïse has committed
no crime to deserve death, while Pharaon insists that he must die since
the gods will so. Exasperated, Pharaon draws his sword to execute
Moïse on the spot, but Terinisse interposes her own body. Euloge, a
courtier, intervenes:

les dieux ne veulent pas
Que leurs Autels divins, se rougissent ça bas
Du sang aimé de l'homme...   (i iv, f. A7^v)

He makes a strong plea against persecution, arguing that if the gods
intend Moïse to destroy Pharaon, simple murder will not prevent it.
He proposes that they should test Moïse's obedience by requiring him
to eat a flaming brand; when the boy executes this order, Pharaon

declares himself satisfied with his loyalty. A Chorus of captive Jews praises God for saving Moïse.

Having shown Pharaon to be a godless tyrant, and in passing reflected on the ineffectiveness of persecution as a policy, Chantelouve turns to the virtuous Jews for the next two acts. Act II consists entirely of a monologue spoken by Moïse. First he announces:

> Ja desja plusieurs ans ont leur course fuyarde
> Parachevee, ja cest Astre qui nous garde
> Sa lumiere journelle, és chariots donez
> Attelant maintes-fois les roussins Eritrez
> Et ja l'ombreuse nuict, à la Lune cornue
> Veu maintes-fois trainer par la trace cogneu
> Les brillotans flambeaux par les douze maisons
> Le Soleil repassant, des anneuses saisons
> Bon nombre a desja faict depuis que Terinisse
> (Royne que le grand Dieu m'a fait estre propice)
> M'enleva du rivage...   (II, f. B^v)

In this vein he recounts the whole of his life up to his present exile, concluding with a prayer that he may see his people again. The Chorus prays God to free the Jews, not because they deserve His favour, but for His own greater glory.

In act III Aaron recounts that he was meditating on the inevitability of suffering in the human lot, thinking of the example of the Jews, when God ordered him to go to find Moïse. Moïse enters, recounts the miracle of the burning bush, and tells Aaron that God ordered him too to help the Jews. They go to carry out His will. Despite its 170 lines, this scene consists of only two speeches. Chantelouve omits the brothers' interview with Pharaon: in the next scene a messenger reports Pharaon's refusal to free the Jews to the Chorus, which closes the act with a plea to God to relent in His anger against His people, since they repent for their sins.

The last two acts return to Pharaon and his daughter. Act IV is opened by Terinisse lamenting for Pharaon's harshness towards her son. She fears that he may kill Moïse, and fears also for Pharaon's own life; this leads her to reflect on the impermanence of Kings and kingdoms:

> Comme du large Protee
> L'onde vitrine ne peut
> Estre coisible, ains se meust
> Sans cesse, au Nort agitee,
> De la race ainsi humaine
> L'Estat glissant se promaine
> Ores parmy le bon-heur
> Ores parmy le mal heur.   (IV i, f. C2^r)

In the following scene Euloge reproaches Pharaon for appearing to agree to release the Jews then changing his mind, calling down a fresh plague by each vacillation.[36] For the good of Egypt he implores Pharaon to end the persecution, which is ineffectual, and release the Jews. A messenger enters; after the conventional hesitations and regrets, he declares sententiously that lost riches can be recovered but death is without remedy, and finally reports the death of all the first-born sons of Egypt, including Pharaon's heir. Pharaon laments vociferously. Euloge tells him a Prince should never be daunted by fortune's blows, but

> "   cognissant que c'est vengeance des Dieus haute
> "Pourvoit à l'avenir, repentant de sa faute.   (ɪv iii, f. c6ᵛ)

Pharaon agrees to release the Jews, then as soon as Euloge leaves to give the necessary orders decides to destroy them instead with his army, which he goes to prepare. The Chorus reflects on the mutability of fortune and rejoices at the Jews' release.

Terinisse opens the last act with fresh lamentations following a premonition of disaster. A messenger delivers a long account of the death of Pharaon and his army in the Red Sea, emphasising the King's foolish presumption in pitting human forces against God. Terinisse laments until grief overcomes her. In a brief final scene, Moïse leads the Chorus in praising God for delivering them from the tyrant.

Pharaon is an example of how God punishes those who ignore Him. Chantelouve makes it plain that Pharaon entirely deserves his fate, for his assaults on Moïse, his rejection of the pleas for mercy, his persecution of the Jews and his refusal to heed divine warnings. The Chorus presents every stage of his career as an instance of the operation of providence. The other side of the coin is illustrated by the Jewish figures, shining examples of virtue for which they are rewarded. This contrast, however, is never made concrete in any confrontation between Pharaon and the Jews, except the brief scene at the beginning in which Moïse spurns Pharaon's crown; otherwise Pharaon and the Jews do not meet. Where Bèze showed a representative of humanity struggling to choose between good and evil, Chantelouve presented each side separately, to be weighed as an example by the spectator, who is left to make the connection between them, aided by the Chorus which points the moral. The contrast between Pharaon and the Jews is exclusively material for reflection: Chantelouve's was an austere conception of the theatre.

In addition to this major example, the play contains lengthy discussions on a wide range of other philosophical and moral issues: whether one may kill an innocent man in obedience to a divine injunction, the merits of policies of rigour and clemency, the effectiveness of persecution, and the mutability of fortune. The debates have little relevance to the action and their resolution does not influence the subsequent course of events: like the apostrophe to beauty in Rivaudeau's *Aman*, these items seem to have been introduced for their own sakes. Audiences clearly relished passages of philosophising no less than flights of elaborate poetry,[37] and worried little over their appropriateness to the action. The practice contributed to the deliberate alienation of the audience, which was invited to exercise judgement rather than sympathy.

Although the play is named after Pharaon, Moïse, Aaron and Terinisse are equally important. Chantelouve's concern was the exemplary significance of the story as a whole, not the personalities and emotions of individuals. The Jewish figures exhibit a heroic indifference to their suffering, which they describe with little emotion. The extensive panorama, unclouded by questions of psychology, allowed Chantelouve to present an unequivocal example of unwavering reliance on God, which is duly rewarded, and of evil, which is suitably punished.

Chantelouve preferred to avoid the disturbing possibility that the Jews might deserve their afflictions for their sins. This was however a common theme. It was present to Thomas le Coq, a curé of Normandy, when he explored the connection between Adam's guilt and the murder of Abel. When he published his *Tragedie representant l'odieus et sanglant meurtre commis par le maudit Cain à l'encontre de son frere Abel* (Paris 1580), he must have been an old man, for he had first been appointed to a cure at Falaise sixty years earlier.[38] In style and language his tragedy is somewhat old-fashioned: it is not divided into acts, it has no chorus, and the lines are octosyllabic and decasyllabic couplets, as in the *mystères*. Indeed Le Coq drew on the *Viel Testament* as well as the fourth chapter of Genesis for his material, but the structure of the play is his own, as is the sense he gave to the story.[39] In the *Viel Testament* the murder of Abel is part of the large illustration of God's direction of human affairs; in Le Coq's hands the episode is a crime whose origins lie in men's actions.

Accordingly, he omitted God (unlike the *Viel Testament*) and concentrated on the human figures. Cain is carefully drawn. From the first he insists on his pre-eminence as elder brother, and lives in constant anxiety lest Abel should usurp his status; Abel of course has no such intention. Cain's farming does not prosper and he refuses to waste a tithe of his harvest to sacrifice to God, but offers only worthless straw instead. When God rejects this but accepts Abel's sacrifice, Cain is doubly angry:

> Quoy, Dieu: me veux-tu faire honte:
> Veux-tu ma disme despriser
> Pour mon frere favoriser...?   (f. B6ʳ)

God, he concludes, is unjust:

> Car s'il estoit juste, il voudroit
> M'eslever en plus grand honneur,
> Et biens, que mon frere mineur...
> Or le face, je l'en despite
> Sa faveur et grace je quite.   (f. B6ᵛ)

His envy turns into a murderous rage, and though he is not deaf to the remonstrances of Remors de Conscience he is soon persuaded by Satan to kill his rival. Although an angel reproaches him, Cain remains unrepentant; Peché and Mort inform him of the foulness of the deed and his sufferings to come, but Cain ends the play, proud to the last, cursing himself, his parents, and the whole of creation.

This psychological explanation of Cain's sin did not satisfy Le Coq. A major figure in the play is Adam, whose principal function is to regret his own sinfulness. He opens the play with a long lamentation recognising the magnitude of his offences, for which he has been justly condemned, and praising God's mercy in promising to send a Saviour. So conscious is he of his unworthiness that he almost despairs of returning to God's grace; but he quickly corrects himself:

> Pardonne moy mon Dieu et me retire
> De desespoir, ou mon peché me maine,
> Delivre moy Seigneur de ceste peine,
> N'est-ce pas toy qui m'as faict et forgé?
> Ne m'as tu pas sur la terre logé?
> Mon but, mon tout, mon Dieu, mon esperance
> Si je ne t'ay porté obeissance,
> Ny tel honneur, que je devois porter,
> Ay-je pas tort? doy-je à toy disputer?
> Nenny, pour vray, dont pardon te demande.⁴⁰   (f. A7ᵛ)

His consciousness of guilt increases his sense of his debt to God and his gratitude for His mercy.

By juxtaposing Adam's remorse with Cain's crime Le Coq indicated the connection between the first sin and all subsequent sins. In thus combining separate episodes to illustrate his theme, Le Coq's approach was characteristically humanist, despite his use of the language of the *mystères*. He also supplied a vivid psychological portrait of how this inherent evil manifests itself in Cain's envy.⁴¹ However, Le Coq lacked the confidence to depart from the *mystère* tradition to make the form of his play reflect his theme: like the *fatistes*, he included the intermediate episodes in his characters' lives, despite their irrelevance. The brevity with which he treated the marriages of Cain and Abel and their choice of ways of life compared with the length of these episodes in the *Viel Testament* suggests that he was aware of the irrelevance, but he felt constrained to follow tradition in staging all the events associated with his heroes. The copiousness of Le Coq's account detracts from the austere analysis of the moral origins of Cain's crime.

Father Fronton-du-Duc, S.J., addressed himself more purposefully to expressing his perception of the cause of the nation's afflictions. In *L'Histoire tragique de la Pucelle de Dom-Remy, aultrement d'Orleans, nouvellement departie par Actes et representée par Personnages* (Nancy 1581)[42] he used a subject drawn from an earlier war on French soil to show the connection between this scourge and France's sins. The choice of subject was unusual: the pious dramatists (apart from the propagandists) habitually took their material from the Bible or the lives of the early saints. Fronton-du-Duc was influenced by local pride: as he did not fail to remind the audience, Joan was a native of Lorraine.[43]

Fronton-du-Duc traced the whole of Joan's career from her acceptance of her mission to her death. This chronicle is presented in the humanist form. Each of the five acts is opened by a lengthy monologue and closed by a chorus. In act I the French King and his courtiers express their dependence on God. Jeanne, helped by the archangel Michel, decides to obey the divine order to rescue France, and introduces herself at court. In act II the Council discusses whether to accept her help, in her absence; in order to permit a proper debate, they designate one of their number to argue against her mission. She is given command of an army, and raises the siege of Orléans. Charles thanks God for the victory in act III and prays that the French may continue to deserve His favour, but news comes of Jeanne's capture: Charles attributes this to the sins of his people. The last two acts are set in Rouen and show the ruthlessness of the English in securing Jeanne's conviction and execution.[44]

Although the action is an extensive historical narrative, the military and political events are not shown on the stage: in the humanist theatre, in distinction to the *mystères*, historical episodes were material for analysis, not spectacle.[45] The play differs equally from the Classical form, in that the characters do not express their emotions, but discourse on conventional themes such as the mutability of fortune. Reflection is dramatic in the way that the later age expected only during Jeanne's first appearance, when she hesitates modestly to put herself forward as France's saviour in obedience to God's command; but the intervention of grace, through the agency of Michel, resolves this dilemma and she never again wavers.

Fronton-du-Duc did not seek to make a tragedy out of Jeanne's dilemma between obedience to God and her natural human fears; the tragedy is rather that the innocent should suffer along with the guilty in expiation of the nation's sins. The theme of the nation's guilt is present throughout. In the initial monologue, Louis de Bourbon laments for France, 'un Royaulme battu par le courroux du ciel' (i i, p. 1). The King sees the hand of God in all the events of history. After Jeanne's first victories, he praises God's providence:

> de ce qui se fait comme par adventure,
> Tu te sers pour dresser nostre foible nature:
> Affin que, chastié en ses calamitez,
> Elle sente les maulx, quelle avoit meritez:
> Et revenue à soy a toy elle revienne,
> Et seslongner de toy jamais ne se souvienne.
> Ainsi, las, nous t'ayant tant de fois irrité
> Par diverses façons de toute iniquité,
> Tu nous as faict sentir tes verges punissantes,
> Recueillant contre nous les haynes croupissantes,
> Et cause de desbatz de nos vieulx ennemys,
> Qui jà presque accablez soubs leur joug nous ont mis:
> Mais or si nous avons, congnoissans nostre faulte,
> La clemence franchy de ta Majesté haulte,
> Et si ayans asses porté sur nostre dos
> Le fleau de ton courrouz, nous meritons repos:
> Et qu'acordant le veu de nostre humble priere,
> Tu veuilles mettre à fin nostre longue misere,
> C'est toy, qui de ces maux seul Sauveur je congnois
> Comme ilz venoient de toy, et de toy recognois
> Avoir de mes combats obtenu la victoire...   (iii i, p. 23)

Charles submits himself entirely to God: he ascribes both victory and defeat to His justice, and thanks Him for both equally.

As King and principal exponent of the religious understanding of France's agony, Charles plays a most important role; but it ends abruptly with act iii. Jeanne's role, too, is quite small: she appears in only seven scenes, all relatively brief, and not at all in acts iii and v. Like Chantelouve, Fronton-du-Duc concentrated on no individual but presented a panorama, displaying both the iniquities of the English and the virtues of the French. The spectator was required to make the connection between the two, to observe the operation of providence in the punishment of the sins of the French and reflect on the chastisement awaiting the English in their turn for their iniquities.

Garnier's treatment of the same theme was somewhat less cerebral. In *Les Juifves, tragédie* (Paris 1583) he reflected on the connection between sin and the scourge of war, which he made clear in the Dedication:

Or vous ay-je icy representé les souspirables calamitez d'un peuple, qui a comme nous abandonné son Dieu. C'est un sujet delectable, et de bonne et saincte edification. Vous y voyez le chastiment d'un Prince issu de l'ancienne race de David, pour son infidelité et rebellion contre son superieur: Et voyez aussi l'horrible cruauté d'un Roy barbare vers celuy qui battu de la fortune, est tombé en ses mains par un severe jugement de Dieu.   (p. 10)

God permits Nebuchadnezzar to punish the Jews and particularly the King under whose leadership they neglected Him. However, unlike his contemporaries, Garnier combined the illustration of the theme with an exploration of the hero's feelings, from which the play derives much of its impact: the result is an unusually coherent exemplification of God's justice and an exceptionally powerful play.

The nature of the Jews' offence is at once established by the first act, which consists of a historical monologue (true to Senecan example) in which an anonymous Prophete recalls the Covenant by which God engaged to protect His people, and laments that by failing to honour their side of that bargain and forgetting God the Jews have forfeited His favour.[46] The Chorus reflects on human sinfulness, and particularly the Fall and the Flood, prime examples of the punishment that follows man's failure to heed God's commands. Lest there should be any mistake, the Chorus reminds the audience throughout the play of the religious basis of the action: the Jews have offended by neglect of God and are being punished.

Sedecie is perfectly aware of the origin of the disasters:

> C'est pour avoir peché devant ta sainte face,
> O pere, et n'avoir craint le son de ta menace:
> Te reputant semblable à ces Dieux que lon fond,
> Ou qu'en pierre et en bois les statuaires font,
> Qui n'ont ame ny force, abominable ouvrage,
> Aux hommes abestis qui leur vont faire hommage.
> J'ay failli, j'ay peché...   (ll. 1287–93)

The High Priest Saree, whom he is addressing, can only agree. On several occasions Sedecie repeats his conviction that his people's sufferings were caused by their sins and his own offences above all, and he even defiantly tells Nabuchodonozor that his defeat is attributable to God's just anger, not Nabuchodonozor's prowess (ll. 1391–412). After Nabuchodonozor has punished Sedecie for his rebellion by killing his children before him and then putting out his eyes, Sedecie returns to the stage and asks rhetorically:

> Voyez-vous un malheur qui mon malheur surpasse?   (l. 2100)

The Prophete replies gravely:

> Non, il est infini, de semblable il n'a rien.
> "Il en faut louer Dieu tout ainsi que d'un bien.   (ll. 2101–2)

The blinded King responds without hesitation:

> Tousjours soit-il benist, et que par trop d'angoisse
> Jamais desesperé je ne le deconnoisse.
> Je sçay bien que je l'ay mille fois irrité,
> Que j'ay trop justement mes peines merité,
> Que j'ay son ire esmeuë, et que par mon seul crime
> J'ay incité à mal toute Ierosolyme. (ll. 2103–8)

Sedecie remains heroically confident that God is just in thus atrociously punishing him.

One question still disturbs Sedecie, despite his submission to God's will: why does God punish him through the triumph of Nabuchodonozor, a man infinitely more sinful than himself? The Prophete explains that God will punish Nabuchodonozor in his turn. Sedecie acquiesces, accepting that God's action is perfectly wise and just. That God uses even the evil of tyrants for good is not just a principle stated abstractly by the Chorus, as in Rivaudeau's *Aman*: it is a belief that Sedecie acquires through painful experience.

Nabuchodonozor never considers that God or any other agency could put an end to his power. Sedecie attempts to warn him at their interview not to place much reliance on his present good fortune: when Nabuchodonozor answers his plea for mercy by asking

> Quelle grace veux-tu qu'à mes haineurs je face? (l. 1455)

Sedecie replies:

> Que voudriez qu'on vous fist estant en nostre place. (l. 1456)

The Chorus at the end of the act repeats the warning:

> "Ne t'orgueillis de l'heur de ta victoire,
> "   Car c'est un don de Dieu,
> "Qu'il peut reprendre, et t'en ostant la gloire
> "   Mettre un malheur au lieu. (ll. 1801–4)

Nabuchodonozor does not see the possibility that he might one day find himself, like Sedecie, at the mercy of another King, and so refuses to show him clemency; far from being humbly aware of the precariousness of his position, he is inclined to think himself no less powerful than a god. In his famous first tirade he compares himself to the gods explicitly:

> Pareil aux Dieux je marche, et depuis le réveil
> Du Soleil blondissant jusques à son sommeil,
> Nul ne se parangonne à ma grandeur Royale.
> En puissance et en biens Jupiter seul m'egale:
> Et encores n'estoit qu'il commande immortel,

> Qu'il tient un foudre en main dont le coup est mortel,
> Que son thrône est plus haut, et qu'on ne le peut joindre,
> Quelque grand Dieu qu'il soit, je ne serois pas moindre.
> Il commande aux éclairs, aux tonnerres, aux vents,
> Aux gresles, aux frimats, et aux astres mouvans,
> Insensibles sujets: moy je commande aux hommes,
> Je suis l'unique Dieu de la terre où nous sommes.[47]   (ll. 181–92)

This immediately follows the sombre warnings in act I against pride and idolatry; Nabuchodonozor compounds the two sins in self-idolatry.

Where other humanist dramatists were capable of including debates on such commonplaces as the mutability of fortune as adornments appreciated for their own sakes without regard to their relevance to the whole, Garnier integrated the commonplace into the thematic movement of his play and christianised it: by refusing to recognise that fortune, or rather God, could one day strike him down like Sedecie, Nabuchodonozor demonstrates his sinful pride. The other characters devote their energies to urging Nabuchodonozor to pardon Sedecie. This would require him to recognise the frailty of his own present success: the many scenes of argument about the humanist commonplace, whether a King rules more securely by a policy of rigour or clemency, which form the bulk of the action, are thus directed at the theme of pride.

The debate between Sedecie and Nabuchodonozor, mentioned above, is the climax of a series of debates in which the characters reveal their positions on the scale of pride and humility by their attitudes to the punishment of Sedecie. The series starts in Nabuchodonozor's first scene, a debate with his Lieutenant General, Nabuzardan. Nabuchodonozor insists that Sedecie shall be punished for his rebellious 'outrecuidance', and Nabuzardan replies:

> "Celuy qui entreprend d'estre plus qu'il ne peut,
> "Souvent, trompé d'espoir, dechet plus qu'il ne veut.   (ll. 205–6)

Nabuchodonozor has just been equating himself to Jupiter, but fails to reflect that Nabuzardan's warning could apply to him, or that he is himself guilty of 'outrecuidance' in relation to God.

After a Chorus, Amital, Sedecie's wife, enters to lament her misfortunes with a Chorus of Jewish women. Wife and mother of Kings who have all been killed or deposed, and herself now a slave, Amital is a living example of the frailty of the gifts of fortune. Her lament is interrupted by the entrance of the Queen, Nabuchodonozor's wife, who rejoices at the victory. However, when she sees the wretched Jewesses, she does not exult: she remarks to her Gouvernante:

> Que voyla, ma compagne, un beau miroüer pour tous.   (l. 586)

Unlike Nabuchodonozor, she recognises in the Jews' plight a warning
that the same misfortune could befall her. She explains her sentiments
to Amital:

> "Il ne faut que Fortune eleve nostre coeur,
> "Pour vous voir maintenant esprouver sa rigueur,
> "Que tous hommes mortels doivent sans cesse craindre,
> "Soit Roy, soit laboureur, le grand plus que le moindre.
> Helas! que sçavons-nous si ce jour seulement
> Ternira point nostre heur de quelque changement?   (ll. 613–18)

She promises to intercede with her husband, but first explains to Amital
the grounds on which she expects him to justify his rigour. This produces a piquant variation on the rigour/clemency topos, as the merciful
Queen makes the case for harshness; but her nature provides her with
few arguments and she soon turns to discussing Amital's misfortunes.
They debate another conventional topic, whether any situation is so
desperate as to warrant suicide; this is followed by another set-piece,
Amital's *récit* of the fall of Jerusalem to Nebuchodonozor. By emphasising how far Amital has fallen from her throne, these two conventional developments reinforce the theme of the impermanence of
worldly fortune. The Queen is sympathetic, but her Gouvernante asks

> Pourquoy vous gesnez-vous d'inutiles douleurs?
> Madame, et que vous sert d'affliger vostre vie
> Pour les calamitez d'une tourbe asservie?   (ll. 802–4)

Her uncharitable attitude recalls the harshness of Nabuchodonozor.
    The confrontation in the following act between Nabuchodonozor and
his Queen develops the theme of pride. Nabuchodonozor brutally
rejects his Queen's entreaties to treat the Jews mercifully. Playing on
his inclination to see himself as a god, she implores him to imitate
divine mercy: he replies proudly:

> Dieu fait ce qu'il luy plaist, et moy je fais de mesme.   (l. 928)

Greatly alarmed, the Queen warns him of divine wrath:

> "Dieu rabaisse le coeur des Monarques hautains
> "Qui s'egalent à luy, et qui n'ont cognoissance
> "Que tout humain pouvoir provient de sa puissance.
> Vous voyez par ce Roy (dont les ancestres ont
> Porté si longuement le diadême au front,
> Et ores vostre esclave, accablé de miseres)
> Combien les Royautez sont choses passageres.   (ll. 930–6)

Nabuchodonozor is unmoved by the warning or the example, but having
no wish to quarrel with his wife he callously allows her to form the
impression that he will spare Sedecie. He is equally heartless towards

Amital, who enters at this point to beg for mercy for her son: Nabuchodonozor plays with her, forcing her to contradict and abase herself,
until he tires and allows her too to think Sedecie will be spared.

Amital appeals to Nabuchodonozor's vanity: since he is god on
earth, let him show the divine quality of mercy (ll. 989–1002, 1026,
1028–32). Even Sedecie uses this approach: he informs Nabuchodonozor
that

> vous estes en ce lieu
> Le temple, la vertu, la semblance de Dieu...   (ll. 1465–6)

and begs him to be merciful accordingly. This *leitmotif* draws attention
to the difference between the true God and the Emperor who sets
himself up as a god. The Jews have constantly on their lips examples
of God's mercy, but Nabuchodonozor is deaf to all appeals. The minor
figures who entreat him to show mercy – Amital and the Queen – and
their debates all play their part in Garnier's meditation on pride, no
less than the principal characters.

Sedecie himself appears in only three scenes, two in act iv and one
in act v. Although Sedecie embodies the personal application of the
abstract theme of pride and provides the climactic movement of the
play, for Garnier the sympathetic hero was clearly not the all-
important figure that he was to be for later generations. The theme for
Garnier was larger and more important than any one character, and
it is approached from a variety of angles throughout the length of the
play, principally through the numerous debates about rigour, clemency
and the mutability of fortune of which the action consists. These
debates do little to advance or delay the dénouement, and could almost
be presented in a different order with equal effect: Garnier was not
concerned with plot in the sense of the inexorable working-out of a
chain of cause and effect. He was equally little concerned with developing character and showing its inevitable manifestation in events. Logic
of plot and character was not a preoccupation of the humanist dramatists, whatever its importance in later theatre. *Les Juifves* is tightly
bound together, however, by a logic of theme, and it is only by reference
to the theme that the structure of the play makes sense. The humanist
playwright required the spectator to reflect on the material presented
and to apply the lessons learned from, say, the interview between
Amital and the Queen to the situation of the protagonist, and *vice
versa*; it is only by such a process of reflection, rather than by reference
to development of plot and character, that the relevance of the scenes
to each other becomes clear.

Les Juifves is exceptional among humanist dramas in the extent to
which Garnier unified his material. As a rule the humanist playwrights

inclined, like Rivaudeau and Chantelouve, to include philosophical commonplaces and passages of elaborate poetry at every opportunity, with little or no regard to their relevance to the march of the whole. *Les Juifves* contains a great deal of conventional material in the debates about rigour, clemency and fortune, but this is always thoroughly integrated with the thematic movement and never included for decoration alone. Garnier's meditation on the nation's sufferings and its sins is a work of unusual imaginative and intellectual power and coherence. He illustrated his theme through the sweep of the plot as a whole and in Sedecie provided a living example of its meaning for the suffering individual.

Les Juifves does not address the audience directly: the characters do not pass judgement on themselves, as was customary in the humanist drama, nor is there the usual transparent manipulation of plot and character, such as Rivaudeau used in introducing Zarasse and Simeon. Unlike other humanist dramas, *Les Juifves* does not constantly remind the audience that its material has been carefully arranged by the author to make a point; Garnier exercised more skill than most in so constructing his play, but always hid its operation. Accustomed as we are now to a realistic theatre as our norm, in which no authorial voice disrupts the illusion, we are apt to praise Garnier for his self-effacement; but it is not certain that it was for this quality that his tragedies enjoyed unique popularity among contemporaries.[48] The evidence of the other humanist plays, and indeed of the surviving *mystères*, the doctrinal and the propaganda plays, suggests that audiences preferred to be addressed directly in the theatre; this remained the almost universal approach until the emergence of the Classical style in the next century. Garnier's extraordinary popularity is perhaps to be ascribed more to the copious provision of well-placed sententiae and the numerous and decorous debates of major philosophical questions that his work offered than to the relative realism for which we are inclined now to praise his plays. The alternative hypothesis – that for the fifty years during which Garnier's vogue lasted other dramatists were trying but failing to imitate his indirect approach – is untenable unless one takes an exaggerated view both of Garnier's genius and of the incapacity of all the other writers of the day: untenable particularly if one takes into consideration their consistent success in achieving other objectives. No other dramatist at this time possessed an imagination as vigorous and as well-directed as Garnier's, but it is a far step from this to supposing that the others all disdained realism and addressed the audience directly because they were unable to do otherwise, with Garnier alone exempted from this general incompetence. The basis of Garnier's popularity among contemporaries was not the same as the origin of our modern appreciation of his work. *Les Juifves* speaks to us with exceptional power, but it was perhaps not this power that contemporaries appreciated in the play: as a rule they preferred a more explicit approach. The next four plays that chronology presents confirm this taste.

Jean-Edouard du Monin went to the opposite extreme, by using allegory to express his view of the role of divine justice in the civil wars in *La Peste de la peste, ou jugement divin, tragedie* (Paris 1584). Igine (Santé, according to the key provided with the list of characters), daughter of the Emperor Théodice (Jugement divin), has been kidnapped by Celte (the vassal King of France). Théodice is dissuaded by his wife Phronoée (Providence) from destroying Celte, and sends a warning by Limomart (Famine guerre) which Celte ignores. Peste is then sent to punish Celte; she succeeds in freeing Igine, but her uncontrolled forces ravage not only the Celtes but also the Aristes and the Contrits, virtuous servants of Théodice who live among the Celtes. Théodice puts an end to the destruction by banishing Limomart and executing Peste.[49] Du Monin saw in France's afflictions a divine punishment, and hoped that God would soon lay aside His scourges, which afflict guilty and innocent alike.

Du Monin's meaning is quite unclear, despite his use of allegory. The youthful author cultivated a reputation for erudition.[50] His characters speak an inflated language containing many abstruse neologisms and classical allusions: their tirades are often nearly incomprehensible, if impressively erudite. The action is frequently confused. Théodice's outrage at the kidnapping of Igine provides a thunderous speech, but at the cost of showing that God lacks foresight. Similarly, Théodice's hesitation over how to punish Peste – he determines to kill her, is persuaded to pardon her, then again to kill her, wavers once more and finally has her executed – gives splendid scope for arguments *pro* and *contra*, but at the cost of showing God to be unable to make up His mind. Like many humanist dramatists, Du Monin was so intent on displaying his rhetorical skill and erudition that he did not notice that many of the passages he introduced for this purpose ran contrary to the general intention of the play.

Pierre Matthieu took a more conventional approach in using historical material for his plays, which, like his fellow humanists, he arranged visibly to present examples. The didactic tone was in keeping with his profession: although he is remembered now as a historian, he had started his career as a teacher.[51] In 1583 his pupils at the Collège at Vercel, where he was principal, performed his play *Esther* (Lyons 1585). This traced the whole of the story, starting with a portrait of the wedded bliss of Vashti and Ahasuerus and ending with the Jews' slaughter of the whole of Haman's faction. Perhaps because of the play's excessive length (some 6000 lines), Matthieu was dissatisfied with it: in 1589 he republished it as two separate plays, *Vasthi* and *Aman*.[52] These reproduced almost all the scenes of *Esther* and added a little new material: they must be treated as the definitive version.[53]

Matthieu was particularly inclined to value each speech in isolation for its poetic and didactic content, perhaps by virtue of his profession.[54] This is clear from the first act of *Vasthi*. It opens with a monologue in which Assuere compares Kings to the gods. There follows a debate with Vasthi, who disputes her husband's proud claim. This has no bearing on the action and is even misleading, since Vasthi evinces a humility which is at variance with her later behaviour, but the scene permitted Matthieu to introduce a formal debate, complete with such ornaments as stichomythia and an extended simile. The following scene is described thus by the author:

Toute ceste Scene est comme un Assueropedie, ou institution du Roy, pour bien regner, selon la forme presentee par la sagesse et prudence de son conseil, composé de Princes sages, qui ne visent qu'à la prosperite du Roy, et à la chose publique, mesprisant leur advancement, pour l'advantage de son estat, avec une modeste liberté dont ils façonnent leurs remonstrances à fin de tenir leur maistre au branle de la vertu, par de belles et gentilles comparaisons.[55]

The Princes advise Assuere that God appointed him King to serve his subjects, not for his own gratification; he must not tax them too heavily, and must be guided by Justice rather than personal whim. A King is compared at length to a mirror, silvered with virtue and reflecting honour on his subjects. The Princes also fulminate against flattering courtiers concerned only with self-advancement. Assuere assures them that he desires to rule virtuously and peacefully. This long scene (some 300 lines) bears scant relation to the plot, and indeed Assuere's pacific sentiments are at odds with his later willingness to countenance the slaughter of the Jews. The scene has no equivalent in the Bible or Josephus: Matthieu invented it so as to express his opinion of Henry III, and to stage another formal debate. Even in act II, where events have some function in the action since they show stages leading up to Vasthi's repudiation, the episodes Matthieu presented were chosen for their opportunities for didactic and grandiloquent writing. The 'argument' of the first scene is

Les delices des Roys, et les passetemps ne doivent servir à la volupté, ains à la recreation de leurs esprits, apres les serieuses affaires des Provinces. Il faut donner quelque relasche au travail de l'entendement, et ne le bander si roidement que sa force, par ceste severe continuation, s'en diminue. Excellence de l'apprest du festin d'Assuere. Belle loy contre la dissolution des beuveurs. Vitupere de l'yvrognerie, du luxe et de l'intemperance.   (II, p. 21)

After lengthy discussion of pastimes suitable for a King and severe
condemnation of drunkenness, the conclusion is that Assuere shall give
a banquet: the plot advances in a few lines, but the bulk of the scene
consists of ethical debate. In the following scene the banquet takes
place and another debate occurs: Assuere declares that the meal should
be accompanied by food for the mind and proceeds to discuss Woman
with his guests. At every stage Matthieu's first concern was to provide
opportunities for flights of rhetoric and ethical discussion.

So intent was Matthieu on the content of the individual speech that
he admitted many inconsistencies, of which minor instances have been
noted. Another arises from the criticism of drunkenness, for when
Assuere proceeds to get drunk at the banquet no one thinks to blame
him. More grave is an inconsistency in *Aman*, when the villain tries to
persuade Assuere to order the slaughter of the Jews (II, pp. 42–51).
Assuere refuses, declaring it impossible to defeat the God who protects
them and citing from Jewish history many examples of His invincibility.
Aman objects that there is nothing a King cannot do, and Assuere in
reply authorises him to kill the Jews. Each of Assuere's speeches airs
the ethical issues involved, but no attempt is made to connect the two
statements through the life and behaviour of the speaker, while the
larger moral issue, Assuere's responsibility for the crime for which he
executes Aman, is ignored. As in the criticism of drunkenness, the
characters speak of right and wrong but their comments are not
related to what goes on in the play: the consideration of moral issues
remains quite abstract.

The expression of emotion is similarly abstract: the phrases give scant
impression of referring to a concrete situation. Characteristic is the
tirade in which Assuere, having repudiated Vasthi and combed the
kingdom for a replacement, expresses his feelings for Esther, whom
he has just selected:

> Dieux, que je suis content! ô fortune prospere!
> Le ciel, que je pensois courroucé, se tempere:
> Qui eust jamais jugé, qu'apres si peu de nuits
> La liesse viendroit repousser mes ennuits,
> M'embrassant en son sein, et me faisant entendre
> Que tout vient à propos à cil qui veut attendre?[56]
> Ainsi que le soleil sortant du pavillon
> De l'aube, qui rougit son front de vermillon,
> Se plaist à flamboyer par l'escharpe azuree,
> Et monstrer aux humains sa lumiere etheree,
> Sans laquelle tousjours l'homme seroit en dueil,
> Et ne pourroit sommer pour le sommeil son oeil,
> Quand on la voit chasser de la nuit tout le sombre
> Et nous faire admirer la grandeur de nostre ombre

Comme l'on voit Titan apres les froids glaçons,
Apres qu'il a laissé les estoillez poissons
Plus beau, plus pur, plus clair, esparpillant au monde
Les tortillons dorez de sa perruque blonde:
Ainsi je cognois jà que mon ombre s'estend,
Combien l'ennuy me fuit, que le bon-heur m'attend,
Souz le soleil d'Esther, qui dechasse la pluye
Des nues de Vasthi, dont la presence essuie
Les larmes de mes gens, et semble que ses yeux
Esgalent en clarté les deux flambeaux des cieux.
Autant que par l'ardeur de la chienne brillante,
Le ruisseau est soulas à la bouche beante,
Qui reduit nos esprits en premiere vigueur,
L'hastif bat-bat du coeur corrigeant sa langueur,
Autant j'ay de liesse, en regardant la grace
D'Esther, qui mes regrets d'un doux pinceau efface:
Esther soeur d'Apollon, perle de l'univers,
De laquelle les pris paroissent descouvers
Hors du vermeil bouton, comme l'on voit la rose,
Des Charites l'honneur, sur le printemps desclose
De bien loin exceller les primaveres fleurs,
Et le blanc decorer les voisines couleurs,
Des joyaux precieux que le ciel me presente:
Sa face seulement sur toutes me contente,
Et pour effectuer mon mandement Royal,
Ma femme elle sera, je luy seray loyal.   (*Vasthi*, iv, pp. 87–8)

In such a monologue Matthieu clearly did not hope to excite sympathy
with Assuere's passion, but sought rather to display his own poetic
gifts by such devices as introducing no fewer than four extended
similes; that his control of syntax was not equal to the task of making
this material comprehensible seems not to have dismayed him unduly.

The Jewish characters too state emotions and reflect on ethical
questions in elaborate terms without giving any impression of personal
involvement in what is said. Mardochee, for example, delivers a tirade
vilifying the court and praising the simple life (*Aman*, i, pp. 10–11).
This has no obvious application to him, since he has no position in the
court: the commonplace is reproduced for its own sake. When Mardochee urges Esther to become a candidate to replace Vasthi, she
promises to accept the throne if God wills, at which Mardochee
launches into a tirade of some ninety lines in which he urges her to
accept the marriage by describing the Creation and the exemplary
love of Adam and Eve, who were married by God, which proves that
marriage is a divine institution and state (*Vasthi*, iv, 73–8). The
encomium of wedlock is unnecessary, since Esther has already agreed;
but it makes a pretty speech. Jews and pagans all mouth decorative
commonplaces.

Matthieu expected his audience to appreciate the reflections on conventional issues for themselves. When Vasthi rejects her ladies' advice that she should obey Assuere's order to appear at the banquet, Matthieu explains in the 'Argument' of the scene that she 'rejette toutes les belles et saines remonstrances des Princesses' (*Vasthi*, II, p. 39). The 'sain' is part of the concept of what makes a play 'belle': even the didactic passages are ornamental. From the airing of moral issues the spectator did not expect to receive a new enlightenment: his pleasure consisted in recognising old friends. The issues were commonplace and were presented in small isolated parcels; they did not always refer to the speaker's situation or the moral problems generated by the plot. There was little sense that the moral reflections derived from or bore on the action and circumstances of the characters: the plays offered truisms stated abstractly, rather than enriching the spectator's understanding of life by suggesting how the experience contained in the play may illustrate the moral and philosophical basis of human life. The failure to integrate the characters' statements of moral truths with their lives may be attributable to a myopic quality in Matthieu's imagination, but in less extreme form this was a recurring feature of the taste of the age. The authors and spectators of humanist tragedy did not expect the sweep of the play as a whole to contain a distillation of human experience hinting at the universal laws governing men's lives; they preferred abstract reflection on truisms. They similarly preferred brilliant individual lines to a poetic structure running through the whole. Matthieu's plays, lacking any grand moral or poetic movement, and offering innumerable discrete passages of ethical reflections and elaborate verse, answered well to this taste.

The work of Jean George, the schoolmaster at Saint-Julien,[57] confirms the taste for abstract didacticism. His *Tragique comedie augmentee, en laquelle l'histoire de deux tresgriefves tentations desquelles le S Patriarche Abraham a esté exercé est representee* (Montbéliard 1609; performed at Montbéliard in 1588) consists largely of a transcription of Bèze's *Abraham sacrifiant*, which provides the account of the second temptation, the order to sacrifice Isaac. George prefaced this with a narrative of another trial, the order to dismiss Hagar and Ishmael, and added a new ending. In the Dedication George explains that he found Abraham an example of the triumph of faith, but (like the schoolmasters of the Low Countries) he was also concerned to inculcate the homely virtues:

Ceci [la Foy] est principallement traitté en ce livret, et quant et quant il y a des exemples comment on se doit bien gouverner es mariages et mesnages, en ce qu'Abraham faict son devoir alendroit de tous les siens: Sara semblablement se gouverne selon qu'il affiert envers son mari, voire en telle sorte que S. Pierre (en sa 1 ep. ch. 3. v. 6.) la propose comme un patron aux femmes chrestiennes: Isaac est un exemple d'un enfant obeyssant et patient:[58] Et les serviteurs de cette maison sont un miroir, auquel il seroit bien à desirer que les servans, et servantes de nostre temps prinssent esgard. (f. A3ᵛ)

George set out to illustrate these qualities, giving particular attention to the behaviour of servants. The effect of his additions is to transform Bèze's exploration of the struggle of the patriarch's faith into a moralising chronicle of the exemplary deeds of the hero and his family.

The action is opened by Abraham, who delivers the first speech from Bèze's play (ll. 49–78); then he turns to discuss the state of his herds and household with his steward. They leave, and a Philistine vents her resentment that Abraham prospers without worshipping Dagon. Agar complains that Sara treats her harshly and wants to drive her away; she will resist, because she is as much Abraham's wife as Sara, and Ismael no less his son than Isaac. Ismael offers to give Isaac a beating. The Philistine encourages them. Sara enters with her son and announces that she will not tolerate her servant's insubordination; meanwhile Ismael insults Isaac and strikes him. Abraham returns from the fields and Sara begs him to send Agar and Ismael away, but he is unwilling to reject his son. An angel intervenes to tell Abraham God wills that Agar and Ismael be cast out. He replies:

Seigneur puis que telle chose te plaist
Je suis tout prest de la mettre en effect. (f. B5ʳ)

Abraham calls Ismael and Agar and tells them to leave, since God wills; he is unmoved by their pleas. As they walk across the desert, Ismael reassures his mother that God will protect them. He falls in a faint from thirst, and Agar moves away so as not to see him die. An angel announces that Ismael's faith has not gone unheeded and shows her where to find water. Refreshed, mother and son walk on.

At this point George transferred to Bèze's text, starting at Satan's first intervention (l. 195). He tidied Bèze's order of events. The prayer of thanksgiving with which Sara and Abraham begin Bèze's play (ll. 79–194) is moved to the end, where they have more about which to be thankful, and the scene in which Sara worries while her husband and son are absent (ll. 678–704), which Bèze could place in the middle of Abraham's reflections as he prepares for the sacrifice thanks to his use of the system of simultaneous setting, is moved so as not to cause an interruption. At this point George has a servant comfort Sara; he exhibits exemplary loyalty and sympathy. After the sacrifice of the ram, with which Bèze ends, George continues. Sara expresses renewed anxiety, so the servant sets out to find Isaac and Abraham; he quickly meets them returning. Husband, mother and son greet each other affectionately, and Isaac gives Sara a lengthy account of the sacrifice, forgetting that the audience has already witnessed it. Together they thank God, in Bèze's words (ll. 79-194), and the play is concluded by Bèze's Epilogue.

George felt bound to spell out the details of the happy ending. He also added the edifying chronicle of the repudiation of Hagar, introducing many idealised characters as examples of how members of a family should behave. Bèze's spare but pregnant drama of Abraham's struggle to obey God's will is transformed into a chronicle of the exemplary paterfamilias, to which George added much incidental instruction. To the exploration of the patriarch's faith the humanists preferred an exemplary tale.

An extensive panorama containing both good and evil was also presented by François Perrin, a canon of Autun,[59] in *Sichem ravisseur, tragedie* (Paris 1589). This took the rape of Dinah and the vengeance of the Jews (Genesis xxxiv) as the vehicle of a serious inquiry into the moral origins of crime and counter-crime.

Emor, King of the Shechemites, describes dreams and other presages which lead him to fear for the safety of his house and kingdom. The scene shifts to Jacob's camp, where Jacob is a prey to a similar anxiety, then returns to Salem, the Shechemite town, where Prince Sichem tells his confidant of the suffering his love for Dine causes him. By the start of the second act Sichem has decided that he must enjoy her, come what may. Curiosity prompts Dine to visit Salem, though she knows she should not stray unchaperoned. She meets Sichem and rejects his advances, provoking him to threaten violence. In act iii[60] she has been raped, but Sichem's love is redoubled and he promises to marry her. Her parents curse her as a whore. Emor likewise laments at the dishonour the episode has brought on his house: his forebodings were justified. He meets the Jews and the marriage of Sichem to Dine is arranged; as a condition the Shechemites agree to undergo circumcision. However, in the following act Dine's brothers decide that the match would be shameful and determine to avenge their sister's honour by taking advantage of the Shechemites' weakness after the operation to kill them. In the last act they rejoice at the slaughter. Jacob is dismayed at their impetuousness in killing innocent and guilty alike, but his sons insist that their action was just.

The language is emphatic and rhetorical throughout. Perrin indulges on occasion in developments with little bearing on the matter in hand. When informed of her daughter's dishonour, Lea wishes that Dine had never been born, or had died when they started their wanderings:

> Que ne fus tu d'un somme eternel endormye
> En mettant le pied hors de Mesopotamye

Où tu voyais Euphrate et le Tigre ondoyants
Resjouïr la campagne et les prez verdoyants?
Où tu avois en front la riche Babilone,
Et à dos un caucase ou la Bize frissonne,
Qui infinis torrents vomit pour les mesler
Dans les fleuves qui font cent mille flots couler
Au travers du Medois esloigné de l'Affrique
Pour s'aller encofrer dans le gouffre Persique?   (III, f. 23ᵛ)

The wish that Dine were dead is succinctly expressed, but having
mentioned Mesopotamia Perrin was unable to resist the temptation to
describe the region, exhibiting his command of epithets and geography;
the ostensible subject of the speech, Lea's outrage, is forgotten.

Such excursions apart, the structure of the play was determined by
Perrin's moral concern. By tracing the action in both camps and presenting the attitudes of several figures Perrin explored the guilt of both
parties. In the first edition the play was prefaced by a meditation on
human sinfulness and the suffering by which God punishes it. In the
second edition this was replaced by an Argument explaining Dine's
behaviour as a consequence of God's withdrawal of His guidance from
the Jews because of their sinfulness, and blaming Dine for straying
from the camp 's'esmancipant de l'obeissance et du respect deu à Dieu
et à son Pere'.[61] In the body of the play, however, Perrin exonerated
Dine: in act II she chastely rejects Sichem, and when her parents call
her a whore the Chorus declares that they are unjustly harsh (III, f.
28ʳ⁻ᵛ). Emor and the Shechemite Chorus, on the other hand, blame
Sichem, and discourse on the ruinous consequences for the nation of
vice in the Prince. After the massacre, Jacob and the Jewish Chorus
upbraid Dine's brothers for their indiscriminate anger. There are faults
on each side. No individual is singled out as tragic: rather than extracting the tragedy of Dinah or Hemor from Genesis, Perrin ranged
over the whole cycle of crime and retribution to show how the sins of
the Prince, of the private individual and of the nation at large combine
to unleash general shame and horror.

The humanists commonly took extensive subjects which they treated
panoramically: only Rivaudeau, La Taille and Garnier chose to use the
classical unities, and even in their plays it is difficult to identify any
single protagonist, with the exception of Saül. Despite their use of
elements of the classical form, the humanists were not much interested
in the concentration on the hero and his crisis which that form is
designed to produce, and the conventions which increased that concentration were consequently of little importance to them. They preferred to take subjects which offered some parallel with events in France

and to apply to them a dramatic technique which would make their exemplary significance clear. Most of the plays concerned epic conflicts and civil war and traced the tragedies of nations; none was limited to the individual tragedy that was to interest Racine.

The humanists approached the historical material and personages as examples, then, rather than as the basis of a vicarious emotional experience: in Stone's epigrammatic phrase, their tragedies 'were destined to be food for thought, not tears'.[62] The characters were consequently presented as examples of qualities and attitudes and the rewards these reap. Each example was considered separately: the humanists had no special interest in the fireworks of personal clashes, and so made no particular effort to confront opposed figures. It was for the spectator to contribute the synthesis of what the various figures and events collectively showed; the play demanded his intellectual rather than his emotional involvement.

The habit of viewing each incident in isolation as an example was perhaps most strongly developed in the work of the schoolmasters of the Netherlands, who at every stage introduced such a wealth of instruction hung around the main events as to obscure the progress of the action. This inclination was shared by the other humanists: although the example provided by the main plot was important, they took every opportunity to introduce discussion of other issues in passing, as in the case of Chantelouve.[63] The convention of using typographical devices in the printed text to draw attention to *sententiae*[64] is indicative of the same inclination to value the play for its constituent parts, as is the inclusion of numberless bravura tirades. Rather than attempting to carry conviction by the breathless sweep of the action as a whole, the humanists wrote as if each scene, even each line, was going to be subject to separate dissection. The tolerance of irrelevance and even inconsistency confirms that each speech was written to be enjoyed in isolation. As Griffiths has observed,

To express a single emotion, a single mood, in one speech; to place oneself inside a character for a single moment of time; to produce a speech rounded and complete in itself; all these aims...tended to produce drama that was a series of 'set pieces' often unrelated to each other by anything but the general plot of the play. This explains the popularity of monologue in Renaissance drama; and it also explains why, in dialogue, the characters seldom seem to be listening to one another.[65]

Matthieu was unique in the extent of his imaginative myopia, but all the humanists excepting Garnier shared to some degree the attitude that so long as the constituent parts of the play were excellent the whole could look after itself.

Audiences were clearly not greatly perturbed that the characters' words could on occasion be unrelated to their situations. To the modern spectator it is disconcerting to find moral and philosophical verities simply averred as truisms: we expect a play to show how they emerge from and explain the experience of the speaker. Humanist audiences would perhaps have found only confusion in such an interpenetration of abstract universal truths and individual personality. They did not expect to find the theme embodied in the person of the hero: they preferred a more direct approach to philosophical questions. Jean George's adaptation of Bèze's masterpiece suggests how strong was the preference for a literal and even pedantic presentation of ideas.

Garnier was more unusual in giving his theme corporeal existence in Sedecie; and even Sedecie, though we are enabled to sympathise with him, is also presented as part of a larger exemplary pattern. The barrier between the spectator and the hero in the other humanist plays is more firmly established: the hero's behaviour and his fate are strictly material for analysis, not empathy, and in many cases the hero comments objectively on his own exemplary significance, like Rivaudeau's Aman. The Chorus too delivers comment. The structure of the play is equally calculated to make the theme clear. The incidents presented do not necessarily make sense if we seek developing plot or character, but do speak clearly when analysed as examples: thus Le Coq's *Cain et Abel* devotes considerable attention to Adam, who would be quite irrelevant if the effect of the play depended on our understanding of the chain of events or of the personalities of Cain and Abel, but contributes vitally to the curé's theme of human sinfulness and its consequences. Where each separate component of the play performed a poetic or exemplary function in its own right, there was little incentive for the dramatists to integrate their material into coherent wholes; but the humanist style in the hands of a poet like Garnier with sufficient power of imagination was capable of exploring the philosophical issues surrounding human life with great directness, clarity and power.

6. Peace: new themes and forms

The preoccupations aroused during the long years of war did not evaporate instantly when Henri IV succeeded in pacifying the country. The dramatists inclined still to serious reflection on moral and philosophical questions and retained the humanist style which permitted them to articulate their ideas through historical examples, while for material they continued to turn to the Old Testament, the prime source of examples of national sin and divine retribution. However, on the restoration of peace some playwrights began remarkably quickly to experiment with new subjects and forms. During the fighting the pious dramatists had concentrated almost exclusively on Old-Testament or allegorical subjects:[1] now new types of material appeared on the stage, and with them new dramatic techniques replacing the panoramic illustration of a theme.

During the first few years of the new reign, perhaps the bleakest period of the civil wars, no new sacred play was printed. In 1596, however, two years after peace returned, three new plays appeared, two treating hagiographic material and the other retaining the old preoccupations. Each used a different dramatic style.[2]

Bernard Bardon de Brun dramatised the career of St James. He was a priest at Limoges and had founded a company of Confrères Pélerins de Saint Jacques,[3] who performed his play on the saint's feast in 1596; it was then printed at Limoges as *Sainct Jacques, tragoedie*. Bardon was aggressive in championing his saint. He wrote a long Dedication in his praise, and an address warning the reader that the play is not intended for those who do not hold with the veneration of saints; the Prologue repeats the caution, and in the course of the action S. Jacques himself defends the use of images (III, pp. 117–18).

Although the play exhibits the outward form of classicism, being

divided into five acts each beginning with a monologue and the first
four ending with a chorus,[4] in content and treatment it is closer to the
mystères. Like them, it celebrates the cult of the saint by chronicling
the prodigies of his career, starting from his dedication of his life to
God and showing his ministry in Spain, the miraculous conversions he
effected and the miracles which occurred during his ministry and at
his martyrdom in Jerusalem.[5]

At the outset S. Jacques expounds his faith. He insists on the Fall
and the sacrifice God made for our redemption, and decides to devote
his life to service of God in gratitude:

> Prenez revenche telle
> De vos biens-faicts sur moy, Qu'en moy nulle parcelle
> Hault, bas, en ame, en corps, du Principe, à son bout,
> Ne me puisse rester, qu'à vous ne soit le tout.
> Ainsin prenes mon estre, ô seul estre supreme,
> Puis que mon tout ne vient d'ailleurs que de vous mesme...
> Seigneur, rien ne me plaist, sinon vostre plaisir.
> Brusles, Sacrifies, Divises moy en pouldre...
> Je veux ce qui vous plaist. Envoyez moy par tout
> Autour cest Univers, de l'ung, à l'autre bout,
> Faire ouyr vos grandeurs.   (I, p. 13)

Such self-abnegation is the kind of faith that produces miracles: S.
Jacques launches himself into the air and flies from Jerusalem over
Rome and France (not failing to praise Limoges in passing) to Spain,
where the pagan images miraculously topple on his arrival. He presents
himself at the court and sets about proselytising the Queen and her
entourage by asserting Christian doctrine, starting with the Creation:

> Avant que ce soleil, qui nostre air environne,
> Et que lastre argentin qui aux ombres rayonne
> Des taciturnes nuictz, et avant que les cieux,
> Et que les Elementz, et que voz mesmes Dieux,
> Et bestes, et humains, fussent en la nature:
> N'ayantz ny estre en eux, ny d'estre la figure:
> Ung Dieu tousjours estoit: seul tout dedans soy mesme:
> Seul heureux dedans soy: Seul tout grand: Seul supreme,
> Seul, qui seul n'estoit pas: Car tout en luy estoit,
> Avant que tout fust faict soubz le coeleste toict.   (II, p. 35)

He recounts the Fall, and tells how God made Himself man and died
in order to make men immortal:

> Sa mort na envahi l'immortelle existence.
> Mais Dieu ayant en soy nostre nature uni,
> En nature mortelle à sa mort defini:
> Affin que dans sa mort noz mortz fussent ravies:
> Et dans la mesme mort il ensema noz vies.   (II, p. 39)

His eloquence has instant effect: half the Spanish courtiers declare themselves converted.

In the historical part of the play S. Jacques uses the same technique. He tells Philete of the sacrifice God made for him, and urges him to love God in return:

> Je t'adjure, et conjure, adviser dans ton ame,
> Dou es tu: qui es tu: ou il te fault aller.
> Ne fay point tes pensers sinon sur toy rouler.
> Voy le grand praecipice ou ton peché te jecte.
> Voy ton Dieu, qui sans fin d'icelluy te rejecte,
> Createur, Redempteur, Toute cause en nous tous.
> Mon Dieu, inspires le. (III, p. 64)

Philete is instantly converted, and goes to catechise his master, the sorcerer Hermogene, by whom he is tortured for his pains. Later S. Jacques shows Hermogene the true nature of his infernal familiars and warns him of damnation: Hermogene becomes a good Christian on the instant. As in the *mystères*, it is enough for the saint to name items of doctrine to turn his hearers into complete Christians: rather than being appropriate to the interlocutor, what is said is really a reflection of the audience's faith.

Bardon was not writing for the humanists' intellectual audience and so did not present material for analysis. He preferred to remind his parishioners of God's miracles and to call forth their faith by representing events in a way that was comprehensible only when viewed with reverence; at the same time he carefully introduced expositions of the basics of doctrine, of which they no doubt needed reminding. In addition, a moving example of faith is provided by the intense lyricism with which S. Jacques speaks of self-annihilation in grateful service of God. Despite the recent wars, the play does not present an example of God's justice for intellectual analysis, but through the chronicle of miracles calls forth the audience's belief in God as Saviour.

Hagiographic material was arranged in the humanist fashion as an illustration of a theme by Pierre de Laudun, sieur d'Aigaliers, better known for his *Art poétique*. His *Diocletian* (Paris 1596) concerns the life of the Emperor, his persecution of the Christians (including St Sebastian) and his death. Although Laudun gave a large place to the martyrs, the preponderant role, as the title indicates, is that of Diocletian, whose destiny is traced.[6]

The theme, of which Diocletian is the prime example, is the impermanence of worldly goods. The Prologue puts the matter plainly:

> Vous verrez l'Empereur qui du peuple en honneur
> Sera craint, respecté, despitant tout malheur,
> Il sera caressé, puis en une mesme heure

Son dessein renversé changera de demeure,
Et ceux qui ont l'esprit oppressé de douleurs,
Ils verront espancher de Serena les pleurs,
Ils verront prodiguer de maint homme la vie,
Ils verront des Seigneurs la puissance asservie,
L'infortune ils verront d'un Tyran Empereur
Qui d'un glaive meurtrier s'offensera le coeur.   (f. 7ʳ⁻ᵛ)

At the start Diocletian is master of the world and decides that his
subjects shall adore him as a god; the Christian courtiers who protest
are executed. By the last act he has surrendered his throne and sought
peace as a gardener (an opportunity for lengthy praise of rustic bliss
against the cares of court life) but he receives news that his wife has
been executed as a Christian; he condemns himself as a 'meurtrier
inhumain' (f. 29ᵛ) and is finally reduced to suicide.[7] Throughout the
play, the Chorus emphasises that Diocletian's descent illustrates the
mutability of fortune; it says nothing of providence. The Christians
as they are sent off to martyrdom echo the same theme: typical is the
comment of Sebastien:

"En ce globe arrondi la mort est plus certaine
"Qu'autre chose qui soit, mais l'heure est incertaine
"Que sert de dilayer veu qu'il nous faut mourir?
"C'est esloigner la mort d'un sommeilleux martir.   (IV, f. 25ᵛ)

Facing martyrdom, the Christians say almost nothing of the service of
God, but declare that worldly fortune is so transitory that life is indifferent to them and not worth preserving: their deaths are less
Christian than Stoic, and are contrasted to Diocletian's failure to
achieve the state of apathy. Laudun compared various philosophic
reactions to misfortune and provided much incidental instruction; that
some of the individuals concerned happened to be martyrs did not
provoke him to any exploration of the subject's providential sense. The
humanist manner was not limited to expressing the preoccupations
aroused by the civil wars.

These concerns are amply reflected, on the other hand, in the third
play of 1596, Jean de Virey's *La Machabee, tragedie du martyre des
sept freres et de Solomone leur mere* (Rouen), which had been conceived during the period of war.[8] However, Virey did not offer the
usual humanist reflection on abstractions such as divine justice; as a
soldier,[9] he was unable to take so detached a view, and presented a
picture of intense horror. The subject is the execution of seven Jewish
children and their mother for refusing to abandon their faith (II
Maccabees vii). Virey contented himself with transcribing the biblical
narrative almost without change, in one continuous scene.[10] He had

some difficulty in handling so many protagonists: each proposition is answered by all seven brothers, speaking in turn, eldest first. When they refuse to abandon their faith the seven are tortured to death on the stage, in the same order; finally their mother, who has witnessed all this, is similarly killed. This scene of torture occupies nearly half the play's 1700 lines. Praise of steadfastness is the unvarying topic of the speeches, which are as repetitious as the action. Virey no doubt considered eight martyrdoms eight times more effective than one to illustrate unwavering faith. In this he may have been mistaken, but his play with the others of 1596 serves as a reminder that dramatists devised different techniques according to their purposes: Bardon celebrated miracles in a *mystère*, Laudun used the humanist style to reflect on a theme and Virey created his own form to exemplify steadfast faith.

The theme of divine wrath was also absent from Jean Behourt's treatment of an Old-Testament subject. He published three plays that he wrote as *régent* at the Collège des Bons-Enfants at Rouen for his pupils to perform. Two, *Hypsicratee* and *Polyxene*, were moral tales based on fictional plots, and the biblical *Esau ou le chasseur, en forme de tragoedie* (Rouen 1598) likewise provided instruction on the rewards reaped by different moral qualities.

The subject is the enmity between Esau and Jacob. The incidents recorded in the Bible occupy only act v and the last scenes of act iv;[11] the remainder consists of scenes Behourt invented to establish a moral distinction between the brothers. Esau is worldly and intemperate, fond of the violent pleasures of the hunt; Jacob is a peaceful and modest farmer. Esau believes in the influence of the stars; Jacob insists that God directs all. Despite establishing this opposition in the mores and beliefs of the brothers, Behourt did not arrange a confrontation: when they finally meet in act iv, they discuss only Esau's hunger and do not touch on religion. Behourt did not wish to make dramatic capital of the opposition: it is established in the spectator's mind, but not enacted on the stage.[12] In the usual humanist fashion, the play offers an abstract demonstration of the moral difference between the protagonists and its consequences.

Jean Heudon too followed the humanist convention of using his characters principally as examples of moral qualities in *S. Clouaud, Roy d'Orleans, tragedie avec des Choeurs* (Rouen 1599). Despite the title, the saint takes a small role. The subject is a struggle for power in sixth-century France. The King has died, leaving three young sons. During their minority the regency is exercised by his brothers, Childebert and Clotaire. Childebert persuades Clotaire that they will lose their power when their nephews come of age; he agrees to collaborate in killing them. The children are removed from the care of their grandmother, Clotilde, despite her suspicions, and brought to court. Clotaire, now grown more ruthless than his brother, kills the elder two, but a courtier saves the third, Clouaud. The play ends with Clouaud's decision to renounce his kingdom and become a hermit.[13]

The dominant theme is ambition, illustrated by Childebert and Clotaire, and also by the two Princes they kill, who unlike Clouaud are impatient to rule and are duly punished. Childebert and Clotaire are first alerted to the precariousness of their power by the attitude of their mother, who evinces a vicarious ambition to place her grandsons on the throne in place of her two sons: her ambition too is punished when it is left unfulfilled and she is left desolate. The Chorus and the secondary figures at the court comment throughout on the baneful effects of ambition. Heudon's vision is bleak: the court is left a blood-bath, and the only escape from the horror of this world is religious solitude. However, Clouaud's motives in abandoning his throne to serve God are not explored: like the other characters, the saint is introduced primarily as an example of moral qualities and their reward.

The theme of divine punishment for men's sins reappeared in two plays published in 1600. Virey's *Tragedie de la divine et heureuse victoire des Machabees sur le Roy Antiochus, Avecques la Repurgation du Temple de Hierusalem* (Rouen) was a dramatisation of a second extract from the author's verse translation of the Book of Maccabees.[14] Virey sets out his theme in the dedicatory epistle to the local bishop:

Aussi tost que le peuple de Dieu se retire de l'observance de ses Com-mandemens, il se peut asseurer de ne tarder pas long temps sans éprouver sa main justement vengeresse: mais pour monstrer que ce chastiment ne procede que de sa paternelle visitation tout incontinent qu'il vient à resipiscence, il est visité de la douceur de sa misericorde, et voit reluire sur luy un beau et lumineux rayon de sa faveur.   (p. 3)

The subject[15] illustrates God's mercy in helping the Maccabees to triumph over their persecutor. The Maccabees accept that their sufferings under Antiochus were merited by their sins: they thank God for punishing them, and for restoring their fortunes when they have been punished enough. Eleazar sums up their opinion (as youngest, he always speaks last: the Maccabees never speak separately, but always one after the other, in order of seniority):

> Dieu qui nous est vray pere de famille
> Honore ses enfans d'une vie tranquille:
> Il visite les siens de son oeil de bonté
> Quand il les a punis pour leur iniquité:
> Nos enormes pechez, nostre coupable offence
> Meritoyent chastiment et dure penitence.   (p. 10)

The characters simply aver the providential interpretation of events.

The limits of the play are set by the division of the biblical narrative into chapters: everything falling into the six chapters Virey selected is presented. We see not only the activities of the Maccabees, but also events at court in Antioch and the doings of the Philistine captains in Jerusalem and in the field. Even irrelevancies are included: thus the narrative extends beyond the Jews' victory to include the purification of the Temple. At one stage the Jews are nearly exterminated because they refuse to break the Sabbath to defend themselves from a cleverly-timed Philistine attack. In the Bible at this point there is some discussion of the conditions in which the Sabbath may be broken: Virey included even this, though it had no importance for his audience or his theme. All this material is presented as a continuous narrative, without division into acts or scenes. To illustrate God's mercy towards His erring servants Virey did little more than transcribe word-for-word six chapters from the Bible, adding some edifying glosses.

A much more thoughtful treatment of the same theme was undertaken by Pierre Thierry, sieur de Montjustin, in *David persecuté, tragedie* (Pontoise 1600). The subject is the rape of Tamar, the murder of Amnon in revenge by his brother Absalom, and Absalom's death (II Samuel xiii, xv–xvii), but Thierry used the humanist form to direct attention away from these brutal events and towards reflection on their moral origin in David's sins.

These are expiated in the agony of his offspring and of the country as a whole, as the prophet Nathan makes clear in a long protatic monologue. Nathan recounts the whole of history from the Creation, emphasising the frequency with which men offend against God and the regularity with which He punishes them. He reflects on David's sins, and laments in anticipation for the punishment to come. The Chorus regrets the distractions a King endures and praises the state of the humble man with no worldly cares to divert him from the service of God.

In act II, David recalls that before he was King he was never distracted from God's service. He confesses and repents for his sins; fearing that he is to be further punished, he prays God to show mercy, while submitting to His justice:

> Restrain ton juste fleau. En la mort du pecheur
> Tu ne vas point fondant ton eternelle gloire.
> Oste donc mon peché de ta saincte memoire.
> Mais toutesfois mon Dieu, non point noz vains desirs
> Soient faicts, mais les vouloirs de tes divins plaisirs.   (p. 18)

The scene immediately shifts to the agency by which David is to be punished. Amnon describes the torment of passion: he cannot satisfy his love for his sister, but not to enjoy her is torture; the only solution is suicide. His confidant, Jonadab, urges Amnon to preserve himself, if necessary by satisfying his lust, since incest is a lesser sin than suicide, and suggests that he should inveigle Thamar into his bedroom by simulating illness. The Chorus reflects that idleness turns youth to crime.

The rape occurs in the *entr'acte*. Act III opens with the lament of Thamar, who prays God to avenge her. Seeing Absalon, she makes the same plea to him; he agrees. The Captain of Absalon's guards reflects on the horrors afflicting David's household as a result of his sins, and laments that he has been ordered to add to them by killing Amnon. Amnon and David's other children are ushered in by Absalon and at his invitation sit to dine; Amnon is killed by the guards. Absalon exults at the completion of his vengeance. The Chorus laments for the suffering by which God is punishing the whole people for the King's sins and their own transgressions.[16]

In act IV David laments at this fresh crime. God punishes sinners: Absalon had no right to take vengeance himself. David surmises that Absalon was aiming to clear his path to the throne: he will ensure that his ambition is thwarted. The horror has engulfed the whole nation: his subjects are in revolt; this is a fresh instance of God's anger. Cusai advises him not to lose patience as God tries his faith, and offers to join Absalon's revolt so as to sow confusion in the enemy camp. There, Absalon justifies his action in punishing Amnon. He consults Cusai and one of his captains, Architophel, to know whether to atack David: Cusai advises him to bide his time, but Architophel recommends an immediate offensive. Absalon inclines to Cusai's opinion, at which Architophel hangs himself from pique. The Chorus laments the civil war, and prays God to relent.

Thierry refrains from staging the battle in the last act, to concentrate on David's reactions. David reflects that his sufferings are merited. His latest humiliation was to be driven from Jerusalem by his own son. Joab proposes to fight Absalon, confident that God will give him victory over the larger rebel army. David consents, but recommends him to show mercy if he wins and charges him specifically to spare Absalon. Joab goes to war, leaving David with a premonition of further suffering. Semei bursts in and curses David for having hounded Saul to death; wearily, David admits the justice of the charge. A Messenger describes the defeat and murder of Absalon by Joab. David laments bitterly. He admits that the origin of these disasters is his own sins, and blames himself for having resisted Absalon's aspiration to the throne. He promises to punish Joab and hopes for a prompt death.

From the Bible Thierry selected episodes in which David is punished by the disasters overtaking his children. The theme of retribution and the figure of David unite the various incidents of which the action is composed. In accordance with the conventions of humanist tragedy, the characters discuss such issues as the vanity of life at court and the power of love; but far from being merely ornamental, these speeches are used by the author as additional instances of the general corruption into which Israel has fallen by David's sins.

To the rigorous demonstration of his theme Thierry added an attempt to present his hero's anguish. David is aware throughout that his crimes are the cause of the agony of his family and his people, and this redoubles his remorse. In his final lamentation over Absalon's body, he blames himself bitterly:

> Pardonne moy mon fils, n'aye point souvenance
> Dans le seing d'Abraham, de ma cruelle offence:
> Pardonne moy mon filz, et voy quelle douleur
> Va talonnant de pres l'effet de ma fureur.
> Je ne veux malheureux trop long temps te survivre.
> Non, le plus grand desir que j'ay c'est de te suivre.
> Pardonne moy mon fils, je scay bien que jay tort
> De demeurer vivant, ayant causé ta mort.   (v, p. 69)

David's agonised impotence to save those he loves from suffering for his crimes is depicted with considerable sympathy. However, David is not entirely the sympathetic hero to whom the post-Classical drama has accustomed us: he is presented primarily as one element of the exemplary scheme, and the play does not rely for its impact on establishing empathy with the suffering individual. As usual in the humanist theatre, the thread which binds the various episodes into an intelligible pattern is not the development of plot or character, but the theme.

The theme of divine retribution also appeared in Rolland de Marcé's *Achab, tragedie* (Paris 1601), concerning the death of Ahab following the murder of Naboth (I Kings xxi–xxii). The historical events occupy only the second and third acts; the remainder was invented by Marcé to reinforce his theme and to provide a tragic ending according to the lights of humanist dramaturgy.

The first act establishes the theme clearly. It consists of a protatic monologue delivered by a ghost, the Ombre de Naboth, which is couched in hyperbolic language and includes various developments of commonplaces, notably an apostrophe against Woman inspired by Jézabel. Naboth's burden is anger against Achab. He asks why God allows the murderer to go unpunished and tolerates his worship of false deities; he cites examples from the Old Testament of God's punishment of those who offend Him and prays for vengeance. The Chorus inveighs against cupidity, which caused Achab to kill Naboth.

Elie reflects in act II that Israel deserves punishment for having abandoned God:

> Mais à qui plaindras tu peuple ingrat ton martire,
> Veu que ton seul delict sur toy mesmes attire
> Le courroux du Seigneur, par ce que tu le suis
> Des levres seulement, et du coeur tu le fuys?   (II, f. 9ᵛ)

However, the nation's sufferings under Achab's tyranny are punishment enough; he hopes God will now relent.[17] He warns Achab that God will punish him, and when Achab ignores him predicts that the dogs will lick his blood where they licked Naboth's. The Chorus extols God's patience in warning the sinner so as to give him the opportunity to repent. Despite the warning, in act III Achab decides to go to war, following a lengthy formal debate with Jozaphat.[18] Achab ignores the prophet Michée's warning that he will die in battle, since it seems to contradict Elie's prediction; nevertheless, with futile prudence, he arranges to disguise himself as Jozaphat in the field. The Chorus reviles the impenitent. In act IV Jézabel ignores the efforts of her Nourrice to convert her and scorns Elie's admonition that she should repent if she is to escape God's anger. A Messenger enters at once with news of Achab's death.

To this point the play adheres strictly to the themes of sin, punishment and repentance, but from the announcement of Achab's death these are forgotten. The Chorus delivers a pagan lament for Achab. The fifth act consists of lamentations over his body by his loyal soldiers and his widow; again, the sentiments are exclusively pagan. Marcé considered that the correct ending for a tragedy was hyperbolic deploration composed of classical allusions: he abandoned his theme to provide such a conclusion. The fulfilment of Elie's prophecy is not mentioned, nor does Marcé point out the mysterious operation of providence in the accomplishment of both the contradictory prophecies regarding Achab's death, although this matter is explained in the Bible.[19] The religious theme is simply abandoned.

The plays produced during the first years of peace seem to exhibit no radical departure from the established themes and forms of the time of the religious wars, and yet of the eight considered in this section only two, Virey's *Victoire des Machabees* and Thierry's *David*, used the humanist method to reflect on divine wrath. Other dramatists used this style for reflection on other themes, such as ambition or the mutability of fortune, while Bardon praised God's mercy, for which purpose he chose the traditional form, the chronicle of miracles. The first years of peace saw some diversification away from the predominant concerns of the wars and the means of expression then used, but no striking innovations.

(ii) THE MOVE AWAY FROM ABSTRACTION

The turn of the century marked the beginning of the decline of the humanist style, so far as it is possible to assign such an event to any point in time, and the start of the establishment of a new concept of the theatre. In the humanist drama, and equally in the *mystères*, the propaganda and the doctrinal plays, there had been no pretence that the stage showed an autonomous world in which the figures pursue their lives oblivious of the audience: speech and action were transparently arranged by the author in such a way that the characters' behaviour conformed to the spectators' opinion of them, rather than being supposed to well up from the characters' own inner imperatives. Bèze's Abraham, on the other hand, was not presented as an extension of the attitudes of the audience, and to appreciate him the spectator was required, not to listen to his objective statements about himself, nor to view him as an example, but to experience what it felt like to be Abraham in his particular predicament. La Taille's Saül, Garnier's Sedecie and Thierry's David were similarly presented as autonomous figures and their emotional life made accessible to the sympathetic spectator; but these authors, uncertain perhaps of the clarity of such an indirect approach, arranged also for the characters to be seen as elements in exemplary patterns. In the seventeenth century the convention of presenting the characters as autonomous gradually established itself. Ultimately the effect was a revolution in the expectation of how a play worked on the audience: instead of seeing its beliefs projected in the figures on the stage, the audience sought to share the inner life of the characters. Where the theatre in the sixteenth century had spoken to the mind, in the seventeenth century it spoke first to the heart.

The wholehearted adoption of this new principle could hardly occur overnight. The immediate symptom of the new taste in the sacred theatre at the beginning of the century was a change in the subject-matter of the plays. The humanists had depicted the consequences of sin while taking the sin itself as given; their subject was reflection on what punishment of the sin taught about divine justice. Neither Saül nor Sedecie is shown embarking on sin: in each play the action concerns the results of an earlier sin and the lessons to be drawn. With the new century a new interest emerged in the sin itself, and where previously playwrights had sought the moral cause of misfortune they now traced its course. Some movement in this direction had already occurred: the plays of Perrin, Thierry and Virey showed an increased interest in scenes of violence and passion rather than reflection. Antoine de Montchrestien moved perhaps a little further in this direction: his plays showed the perpetration of sin and treated the Kings who were his subjects as individual sinners rather than tracing the more epic connection, which had preoccupied earlier dramatists, between the King's sin and the nation's agony. Montchrestien explored divine justice, but as it affects the individual rather than the whole people.

Montchrestien retained the humanist forms. Of the two principal elements of the style, illustration of a theme and poetic expansion on the emotion of the moment, Montchrestien's personal bent inclined towards the latter, though the former was not neglected. *Aman* (Rouen 1601) is not centred on any one character. The scenes allow all the characters in turn to express a number of different emotions: the play consists mostly of lengthy tirades. Many of these are monologues, or are uninterrupted for so long as to be effectively monologues: Montchrestien's interest did not lie in the clash of personalities that was to be so important in later drama, and he aimed rather to give comprehensive expression to the character's state of mind at various successive moments of the plot.[20] Indeed, where a Matthieu had indulged in gratuitous elaboration of commonplace ideas, Montchrestien added similar scenes permitting him to vary the emotions expressed. Thus, as act IV of *Aman*, he showed Esther risking the pain of death by going to the King unbidden so as to invite him to her banquet. It was not necessary to stage this: the invitation could have been assumed, or mentioned in *récit*, while God's support of the weak, the point the Chorus derives from the scene, was already amply demonstrated elsewhere. The actual delivery of the invitation occupies few lines; as much space as possible is given over to the several tirades in which Esther expatiates on her anxiety. Throughout, Montchrestien maximised the opportunities for his characters to give copious and decorous expression to the emotions generated by the situation.

However, the tirades do not consist simply of whatever emotions could be fitted into the plot: they also refer to a theme. Montchrestien conceived tragedy as illustrating divine justice:

En tous les Actes Dieu descend sur le theatre, et joue son role si serieusement, qu'il ne quitte jamais l'eschaffaut, que le meschant Ixion ne soit attaché à une roüe, et que la voix lamentable du pauvre Philoctete ne soit exaucée, marques apparentes de sa justice et de sa bonté.[21]

Aman illustrates particularly God's punishment of pride; the original title was *Aman ou la vanité*.[22] All the characters reveal their positions on the scale of pride. Aman of course epitomises that quality. In his first speech he exhibits inordinate self-satisfaction and suggests that the gods must envy him. Later, when he promises himself to destroy the

Jews, he repeatedly defies God. He does not appear in acts III or IV but returns in act V with his pride undiminished. He is instantly humbled, first by being forced to honour Mardochee and then by being sentenced to hang. Assuerus too is proud, but he is a virtuous King: his pride is tempered by the consciousness of his duties. Mardochee is humbly aware of men's utter weakness and their total dependence on God, as is Esther, who adds to humility a perfect disdain for the pomp in which she lives as Queen. The Chorus draws attention to the degree of pride or humility the characters have expressed, and reflects on the fate that awaits those who do not submit to God.

The practice of conceiving each speech in isolation as an instance of pride or an expression of emotion led Montchrestien to admit inconsistencies. Aman evinces self-satisfaction, vengeful rage, and defiance of God: these are all in their various ways manifestations of 'vanité', but the author establishes no necessary connection between them in the life of the character, treating each tirade as self-sufficient. In act II Assuerus gives Aman authority to exterminate the Jews, but in act V he is so outraged to find that Aman has plotted against them that he sentences him to death. Although Montchrestien had a firm thematic purpose, he illustrated it in a series of discrete scenes.

David (Rouen 1601) concerns the murder by David of Uriah the Hittite, the husband of his mistress Bathsheba, and David's remorse when reproached by Nathan (II Samuel xi, xii 1–15). Here too the action is disposed to provide opportunities for speeches giving comprehensive expression to a range of emotions. However, Montchrestien did not take a random selection of passions for poetic expansion: as in *Aman*, the speeches also betray the speakers' positions in relation to the theme of the legitimacy of passion, suggested in the original title, *David ou l'adultere*. In the first act David describes how love has diverted him from his royal duties:

> C'est force, pour l'amour il faut que je m'oublie,
> Et que de mon Estat j'abandonne le soin.
> Adieu braves desseins, je vous rejette au loin;
> Je quitte le souci de sceptre et de couronne.
> A toy seule, mon coeur, desormais je me donne,
> Ton amour est ma vie...[23]

The Chorus reflects on the baneful effects of love, and describes David as an example of how it destroys a man's virtue.[24] The second act presents the warrior Urie, who laments at the rumour of his wife's adultery; but he resolves to do his duty as a soldier and permits himself no self-indulgence. Urie's speech is not only a poetic expression of sorrow: his attitude is chosen to contrast with David's lack of self-discipline. The Chorus praises chastity. In the third act David is so blinded by his love to his duty to protect his subjects as to propose to kill Urie, who speaks another tirade in which his virtue contrasts with the King's lack of principle. The Chorus reflects that God punishes those who abuse their power for their own gratification. David exults in act IV at the prospect of enjoying Bethsabee undisturbed, and hears the *récit* of the battle in which Urie died. The Chorus reflects on the danger for the subject in becoming embroiled with Princes. Bethsabee appears in the last act only, where she grieves for her husband. She is heartily ashamed of her infidelity; her self-reproach contrasts with David's exultation. The Chorus praises repentance and points out that the criminal's conscience prevents him enjoying the fruits of his crime. Nathan forces David to recognise that he did wrong, provoking him to repent. Nathan announces that God will forgive him, but will punish him by the death of the child Bethsabee will bear him. The various tirades giving poetic expression to a number of emotions are integrated into a powerful thematic movement concerning sin and forgiveness.[25]

Virtuous and vicious are not separated into opposed camps as in *Aman*. The result is a more complex moral movement than in the other biblical play, where the evil-doer is killed: in *David* crime and criminal are dissociated, and the crime is punished without the death of its perpetrator. However, Montchrestien's decision to present David as initially criminal and subsequently repentant seems not to have originated in any notion that a play ought to show the moral evolution of the protagonist. David's change of heart is abrupt: in one speech he exults in possessing Bethsabee (ll. 1031–40) and in the next he implores God's mercy (ll. 1153–220). There is no transition, no attempt to trace the process by which David learns how he has offended. Had Montchrestien wished to show his characters' moral development, he would have introduced Bethsabee earlier, so as to show her love for David turning into shame at her adultery. Although Montchrestien presented both crime and repentance in the single figure of David, he was not interested in how the two states were connected in the life of the man. He considered the two in isolation and wrote speeches exemplifying each, in accordance with the humanist preference for considering moral questions in the abstract. Although in both plays Montchrestien attended to individuals and forsook the humanist preoccupation with the sufferings of nations, he retained the humanist practice of illustrating a theme.

Nicolas de Montreux abandoned the presentation of any theme whatsoever in *Joseph le chaste, comedie* (Rouen 1601), which he published under his usual pseudonym, Ollénix du Mont-Sacré.[26] Montreux preferred to use the various threads of his plot – Joseph's entanglement with Potiphar's wife, his imprisonment and release[27] – as the basis of a copious *comédie de moeurs*. The action is very confused; indeed there is no visible reason why many of the scenes should not be presented in a different order. The location alternates between the court, Putifar's house and farm, and the gaol; the tone similarly veers between the heroic and the farcical. The play ends, not with Joseph's release from prison, but with a farcical trick played by a cunning farm-hand on his fellows. Montreux knew how to send his audience home happy. The play offers both pomp and slapstick: the lofty language and sentiments of the court are as much part of the entertainment as the comic antics of the labourers. Religion figures only in the sermons which are the habitual mode of speech of Joseph, a figure of impossible virtue who declines, for example, to speak of love because as a servant he has room in his bosom only for love of his master. The gaoler and Putifar receive no less attention than the nominal hero: the play is a panoramic entertainment based on the incidents of the biblical figure's life.

Where Montreux produced an entertainment, Antoine de la Pujade was content to narrate the incidents of the hero's career in *Jacob, histoire sacrée en forme de Tragicomedie retirée des sacrés feuillets de la Bible* (Bordeaux 1604). As La Pujade explains in the Dedication, he composed the play 'm'ayant esté commandé par ceste grande Princesse la Royne Marguerite,[28] l'unique perle et fleur de la France, de tirer l'histoire de Jacob en vers François, des sacrés cayers de la Bible, en forme de Tragicomedie' (p. 87). In accordance with this definition of the author's task, the play retails a large part of Jacob's life, from the theft of the blessing to his return to the paternal home; this matter is expanded with conventional material such as discussions about love and a *bergerie*.[29] La Pujade even transcribed the digressions in his source: thus Jacob's journey to the house of Laban is interrupted in III i, as in Genesis xxviii 6–9, by Esau's marriage to Meleth (i.e. Maha-lath). With the freedom of the historical narrative, the Bible traces the stories of two characters in parallel by devoting alternate phrases to each (Genesis xxx 1–21): La Pujade copied even this, bringing each figure onto the stage to speak only a few lines before making way for the other in a vertiginous alternation.

The Chorus provides a figurative interpretation of the copious narrative: thus the supplanting of Esau by his younger brother symbolises God's transfer of favour to the younger sect, the Christians. Religious sentiments are also presented by the characters, who frequently pray and praise God; but here more than in most humanist plays the words are unrelated to the speaker's circumstances and bear on no theme, while there is no sense that the disjointed action is arranged to illustrate any philosophical point. *Jacob* amounts to no more than a clumsily-told story with pious interjections; the author seems hardly to have undertaken any imaginative shaping of his material.[30]

Jacques Ouyn similarly presented a copious narrative of events. His *Thobie, tragicomedie* (Rouen 1606)[31] retails the whole of the Book of Tobit, in an account that is inevitably somewhat schematic.[32] Unlike La Pujade, Ouyn reorganised the historical material slightly to fit it to the stage.[33] He also gave some attention to characterisation: the figures are presented as autonomous, and the interest of the play derives not only from the account of sacred history but also to some extent from the access which is offered to the spectator to the state of mind of the believer confronted with tribulation.

Tobit's wife is a shrew. When he is blinded her first reaction is to blame him for having given his money to the needy instead of saving, with the result that the family will now starve; but when Tobit sends Tobias[34] to fetch money from Gabel she asks if it is not enough to have been blinded without exposing their son to danger as well. Tobit endures his wife's criticisms and his other afflictions with exemplary patience, born of faith. His initial reaction to blindness is to protest that he has always served God diligently and has done nothing to deserve it; but he quickly corrects himself:

> Toutesfois (mon Seigneur) je te pri' garde moy
> De murmurer jamais contre ta saincte loy.   (I, p. 16)

Difficult though it is for him to understand them, he accepts his afflictions as God's will and throws himself on His mercy:

> Seigneur je recognois que ta main liberale
> Soustient le juste poix et ta grandeur Royale
> En tous lieux se faict voir, je sçay que j'ay peché
> Devant toy mille fois, mais quoy estant taché,
> Tu me peux nettoyer de milles immondices,
> Que le maudit serpent causa par ces malices.
> Tu peux (ô Eternel) par ta seule vertu,
> Ranimer un esprit que la mort a vaincu,
> Et rien à ta grandeur ne se trouve impossible
> Pardonne aussi Seigneur à ma pauvre famille
> J'espere ainssi que Job à pres tant de tourments,
> Recevoir guarison par tes sacrez moyens:
> Nous fusmes expulsez de tous nos heritages
> Pour l'amour de ton nom, endurant mil' outrages,
> Puis tu nous renvoyas en ce pays icy
> Prendre posession de tout ce que voicy.
> Tu as cogneu mon coeur, ô Dieu des exercites,
> Tu le cognois encor.   (II, p. 18)

Tobit's reliance on God is reinforced by the blows he endures. Tobias sympathetically tries to shield his father from his mother's tongue and encourages him with the certainty that God will cure him. Both have an absolute faith which sustains them through their trials; their confidence is rewarded by Tobit's miraculous cure.

The act by Mlle des Roches contains a touching portrait of Sara, whose first seven husbands have died on their wedding nights. She wishes to marry Tobias, her rightful husband by Jewish convention, but dare not for fear that he will suffer the same fate. She supposes that she must have unwittingly sinned for God so to punish her, and prays:

> Las si j'ay offencé vostre majesté haute,
> O Dieu de mes parens, pardonnez à ma faute:
> Vous estes coustumier de recevoir tousjours,
> Les pauvres affligez qui vers vous ont recours,
> J'esleve jusqu'au Ciel mes yeux et ma pensee
> Esperant bien de voir ma priere exaucee
> Ayez doncques esgard en mon entiere foy,
> Desliez moy, Seigneur, Seigneur desliez moy
> Du reproche honteux qui bourelle ma vie.   (IV, pp. 43–4)

Her sad matrimonial history has so sapped her confidence that she accepts that men are right to mock and despise her, as her servant does; but she remains certain that God can make good her worthlessness, if He wills.

The play contains three portraits of the sustaining power of faith. These, however, are somewhat overwhelmed in the extensive plot, and are not the only source of interest.[35] To us, with the benefit of knowing *Polyeucte*, it may seem obvious that a religious drama should be founded in the hero's struggle to maintain his faith in the face of adversity, and we may be inclined to regret that Ouyn went only a little way in this direction. This seems not to have been Ouyn's purpose, however; the play offers rather a consoling picture of the support God gives to those who rely on Him and an encouraging narrative of the triumph of virtue. Ouyn did not wish to communicate to his audience what it is like to doubt; his aim was rather to prove with a historical example that God helps those who trust in Him.

In *La Ceciliade, ou martyre sanglant de saincte Cecile, patrone des Musiciens: où sont entre-mélés plusieurs beaux exemples Moraux, graves Sentences, naïves allegories, et comparaisons familieres, convenables tant aux personnages qu'au sujet* (Paris 1606) Nicolas Soret took the more usual course of chronicling the salient episodes of the saint's career with little account of her religious feelings. As in the *mystères*, the action consists of a series of miracles, first the conversions the saint effected, then the martyrdoms of her converts, and finally her own martyrdom accompanied by prodigies. Only the saint herself

figures throughout; other characters appear and disappear again as
the narrative dictates.[36]

The plot of a *mystère* is combined with philosophising in the
humanist manner. Soret was a priest and 'Maistre de Grammaire des
enfans de Choeur de l'Eglise de Paris' (Approbation, f. 1ᵛ), and wrote
the play for his pupils to perform. As a schoolmaster, he lost no
opportunity to adorn his work with copious moralising, erudite com-
parisons and examples of fine style, as he promised in his title. This
material is not always perfectly apposite. After Cecile has been contracted to marry Valere, he attempts to kiss her; she refuses thus:

> ne pincés cette corde,
> Elle est autant et plus d'avecques moy discorde
> Qu'une quarte en Musique, au simple contre-point,
> Qui contre un autre accord dissonne en tout point.   (II, p. 24)

Soret was no doubt glad to demonstrate his professional competence,
but the technicality Cecile mentions is hardly a suitable response to
Valere's passion, nor does it offer any insight into her feelings. Many
of the speeches consist of similes of this kind, which exhibit Soret's
extensive general knowledge and his particular acquaintance with
natural history. Soret's preoccupation with moralising similarly led
him into difficulties, notably in the first two acts, where Cecile's parents,
though Christians, force her to marry despite her dedication of her
virginity to God. Soret's purpose here was to provide an occasion for
sententious declarations about filial obedience, but so intent was he on
this that he failed to consider that he was giving obedience to one's
parents priority over obedience to God. Soret did not look beyond the
poetic or moral content of the individual line to the sense of the whole.[37]

Cecile is saved from breaking her vow by Valere's conversion, after
which he abandons his designs on her body, so sparing her the dilemma
between her duty to her husband and her duty to God. Valere and
his brother (also converted) are martyred, at which Cecile defies the
Governor Almachie and is martyred in turn. None of the martyrs
displays the slightest hesitation; indeed all vaunt their Christianity so
defiantly that Almachie seems quite justified in executing them as
rebels against the Emperor's authority. Soret refrained from endowing
his protagonists with any doubts or conflicts; such complications did
not attract him. He sought to edify the audience by the simple narration
of the saint's *acta*, which he combined with an exhibition of his
rhetorical skill and erudition.

The disjointedness produced by Soret's determination to adorn the
narrative with edifying and grandiloquent material at every opportunity is even more apparent in the anonymous[38] *Tragedie de Jeanne*

d'Arques (Rouen 1606), which provides an unconscious parody of the humanist style. Although the action traces the greater part of the saint's career, the acts open with monologues, the first three end with choruses,[39] the language is inflated and contains numerous classical allusions and compound neologisms,[40] while the whole laborious composition adds up to very little sense.

In act I Charles VII regrets the sufferings of France in the fighting against the English. He holds Neptune responsible for the war: peace ended, he says,

> Quand le pere des eaux escumant de courroux
> Arma ses flots grondans tout soudain contre nous:
> Et portant l'estranger sur son eschine enflee
> Regorgea sur le bord une moisson armee.   (I, p. 13)

He offers no hint as to what might have provoked Neptune's wrath. He takes a fearful oath by all the forces of Hades to rid France of the invader. At this Alençon intervenes to exhort the King to go to war against the English. Quite why the King needs encouragement after taking a mighty oath to do just that is never made clear; but, surprisingly, Charles now rounds on Alençon and argues in favour of peace. The author was happy to sacrifice consistency in favour of the stichomythic debate which ensues. The King is persuaded to fight. The Chorus reflects on the effects of ambition, and praises *aurea mediocritas*.

In act II Jeanne declares that it is time for her to forsake the rustic pleasures of life among the nymphs and turn to war. She exults in her military attire:

> Ce casque martial pressant ma chevelure
> Ne convient il pas mieux qu'une riche coiffure?   (II, p. 19)

An early supporter of the MLF, she scorns women who live decoratively at home; she looks forward to rivalling the men in 'gloire'. She thinks of nothing

>   sinon de manier
> En ma legere main, et le fer et l'acier,
> Briser la lance au poin, respirer sous les armes,
> Fendre le Ciel de dards, vaincre entre les gendarmes,
> Porter la parque aux uns, et d'un masle courage
> Semer les champs de corps, de testes et de targes.   (II, p. 20)

This ferocious mood was inspired, she reveals, by the 'messagers du tout-puissant Jupin' (p. 20), who appeared in a dream and ordered her to avenge France's misery. She convinces the Bastard d'Orleans that her mission is supported by God, and prays Him to inspire her as He inspired Judith in the defence of her country. The Chorus asserts that

> Celuy qui d'une ame loyalle
> Invoque les Dieux immortels   (II, p. 26)

need fear no danger,

> Car jamais les Dieux n'abandonnent
> Le juste en son adversité...   (II, p. 27)

The Chorus does not mention the Christian God.

For act III the scene shifts to the English camp, where the Conte de Suffort, in a monologue of eighty lines, vents his dismay at the cowardice of his troops before the French led by a woman. Despite his bluster, he takes to his heels when a soldier informs him that the French are victorious. Jeanne exults in violent terms over the vengeance inflicted on the English; although she refers to many classical deities, she does not mention the Christian God. The Chorus reflects on the mutability of fortune.

In act IV Talbot despairs at the plight of the English, in a tirade of ninety-six lines; he recounts the deaths of Suffort and the other English leaders, and resolves to kill himself. His confidant Allide tries to dissuade him; a stichomythic debate ensues. Talbot tricks Allide into leaving him alone and, after debating with himself as to the best method, kills himself with his dagger.

The final act returns to Jeanne. In prison, she complains at the injustice of the English, who have condemned her as a sorceress; but she is glad to die for her country, which she has preserved from the English monsters. She briefly commends her soul to God. The Filles de France utter a long lament for Jeanne the patriot, promising that her name will be immortalised in a play. The last word is given to a Gentilhomme Anglois, who rejoices that the English have exacted vengeance from the woman who had humiliated them, whatever the justice of the sentence; her condemnation as a witch will at least allow the English to claim that the French were victorious only by sorcery.

The play is conceived as a series of separate tirades in which the figures express the emotion of the moment in ornate and vigorous language. The result is not a little disconnected, the more so since no character except Jeanne herself appears in more than one act. This disparate material is not drawn together by any unifying theme, such as normally animated humanist drama. The author traced the sufferings of both French and English in the war, but any moral explanation of its cause is lacking; he hinted only that Neptune was angry. Religion is not presented in any other way; Jeanne is a virago rather than a saint, who mentions pagan deities more often than the Christian God. The author took the humanist formal devices – the elaborate tirades, the panoramic plot – and used them without the humanists' usual serious purpose; his aim was simply to introduce the maximum of pomp and spectacle into his play.[41]

Pierre de Nancel, a lawyer of Doué (Maine-et-Loire), had not forgotten France's agony. When the inhabitants of Doué commissioned him to write three plays for performance in the town's amphitheatre,[42] he chose Old-Testament subjects which he treated in the humanist manner so as to illustrate the connection between national suffering and the people's sins. The plays were *Dina, ou le ravissement; Josué, ou le sac de Jericho;* and *Debora, ou la delivrance,* each described as a 'tragedie' in the running titles when they were published as a volume of *Theatre sacré* (Paris 1607). In the Dedication, Nancel explained what he wished the plays to demonstrate to the French:

sous ces peuples icy opposés de creance, elle [la France] remarquera les jugements celestes, qui meinent à leur point les plus foibles essays de la Foy, et qui destruisent les plus puissants efforts de l'infidelité et de l'injustice. (f. ã3[r])

In the Recit pour l'entrée des jeux, a Prologue to all three plays, this point is amplified: the plays show

> la mort de maint peuple idolatre,
> Qui dessus le fidelle a long-temps dominé,
> Mais Dieu veut à la fin qu'il soit exterminé.
>   Par là nous apprendrons la divine puissance,
> Et la foiblesse humaine, et puis l'obeïssance,
> Quels effets elle rend, ce qu'elle opere en nous,
> Et son contraire aussi qui succombe dessous.
> Le vice et la vertu treuvent là leur salaire...   (f. A2[r])

The plays were designed to show God's support of the faithful and the punishment of sin; but so intent was Nancel on individual points of instruction that the declared theme is sometimes obscured or contradicted.

Dina is drawn from Genesis xxxiv, but does not follow the biblical narrative exactly;[43] in general Nancel omitted physical action so as to concentrate on his characters' reflections.[44] Jacob is constantly aware of God's influence in human affairs. In a long monologue, which forms act i, he meditates on historical examples of disaster and concludes that they are divine punishments for men's sins. After the rape he reflects again on human sinfulness; he summarises the whole of history since the Creation, dwelling particularly on the Fall and the Flood. He comes close to criticising God for creating woman, the source of all man's sufferings, but recollects that responsibility for the rape lies with men, not God:

> Las! que dy-je mon Dieu, pardonne moy ma faute,
> Dequoy je m'en veux prendre à ta Magesté haute,
> La douleur me torture et me fait varier,
> Attester ta justice et mes maux pallier.
> C'est, c'est moy qui l'ay fait; c'est toute ma famille,
> Las! j'ay ravy moy-mesme à moimesme ma fille:
> C'est un supplice pur, c'est le peché qui fait
> Le merité supplice, et non luy le forfait.   (IV, p. 57)

His wife Lia urges him to avenge the rape. They enter into a long debate, which Nancel added to the source, in which Jacob argues that men have no right to take vengeance, since God alone judges and punishes sinners. However, Jacob's piety comes to nothing. In the Bible Jacob criticises his sons severely for murdering the Shechemites (Genesis xxxiv 30); but Nancel wished to present the slaughter as a triumph of the faithful and omitted this scene. The play is consequently deprived of a consistent moral vision. After insisting to Lia that the Jews have no right to take vengeance, Jacob does not appear again: Nancel does not explore Jacob's reaction to his sons' flouting of his principles. Jacob's discussion with Lia has no dramatic or moral consequences: it was inserted for its value as a catechism in isolation, not for any function it might have in the play as a whole.

A similar inconsistency bedevils the treatment of Simeon and Levi. When they discuss vengeance, they debate whether or not they may break their word to the Shechemites, each taking one side in the argument and neither being persuaded by the other; but in act v both take equally zestful part in the slaughter. Nancel introduced the debate over breaking one's word with no heed for its place in the total effect, and left obscure the important question raised, namely, whether vengeance against the Shechemites is just.[45]

Yet the question of guilt was clearly important to Nancel, for he raised it several times. He introduced Hemor, Sichem's father, to give his opinion: he is ashamed of his son's conduct, principally because it violated the laws of hospitality. Sichem himself feels no guilt: his only doubt is whether circumcision is too high a price for Dina. Hemor's widow at the end of the play is convinced that Dina seduced her son and lays all the blame on her; she also blames Simeon and Levi for murdering all the male Shechemites for the crime of only one. Dina agrees that they were excessively bloodthirsty, but denies that she prostituted herself to Sichem; yet immediately after the rape she blamed only herself.

Nancel was apparently not disturbed by these loose ends and unresolved contradictions. He considered primarily the separate expressions of opinion, without heed to their relationship with each other, with the plot, or with the characters who state them. Hemor appears only once, to deliver his opinion in a monologue: he is not confronted with his son or with the Jews, and how far his revulsion at Sichem's crime might lead him to approve of their vengeance is not explored. Jacob is similarly spared confrontations with himself or others. The characters express edifying opinions on various topics, but the views stated receive no corroboration from the situation or from the other attitudes of the speaker. Nancel's interest hardly extended beyond airing a number of moral issues: he did not orchestrate the statements of opinion into a coherent account of the action into which he inserted them.

Josué too seems intended to show how God rewards virtue and punishes vice. The virtues of the Jews, and particularly of Josué, are rewarded when they take Jericho, while the vices of the inhabitants, and especially of their King, Hegemon, are punished when God orders the Jews to kill them.[46] Two virtuous inhabitants of the city are spared. In the sack, one Jew, Achan, appropriates some of the booty that should have been dedicated to God: He therefore punishes the Jews by defeat when they attack the city of Ai. The identity of the offender is revealed, and by God's order he is killed;[47] the play ends with the Jews' praise of divine justice.[48]

However, *Josué* offers incompatible interpretations of these events. The angel who delivers the opening monologue explains that God intends to send the Jews a mixture of good and bad fortune, not as just rewards for their behaviour, but because an alternation of stick and carrot keeps men in a state of virtue:

> Leur debitant ainsy d'une façon diverse,
> Les effets merveilleux que sa grandeur leur verse:
> Soit pleuvant sur leurs chefs ses biens et ses faveurs,
> Soit foudroiant sur eux ses fleaux et ses rigueurs.
> Affin qu'eux attirez par cette douce amorce,
> Affin qu'eux retirez par cette dure force,
> Ils escartent le mal par crainte qui les poinct,
> Ils suivent la vertu par amour qui les oinct.   (i, p. 96)

In the light of this, the defeat before Ai must be seen as part of the normal cycle, unrelated to any deserts in the Jews. However, in act v Josué, Epibulus (a virtuous soldier) and the High Priest maintain that the attack failed because of Achan's sin. Act iv, on the other hand, suggests yet another explanation. After the fall of Jericho, Josué decides to take Ai as well, and answers Caleb's objection that he does not have God's authority to extend the campaign by declaring that God has given him *carte blanche*:

Non Caleb, je n'ay pas une expresse parolle,
Ce n'est ici pourtant une entreprise folle,
Ainsi que de mon chef, et sans sçavoir comment,
Sans charge et sans aveu, bien que sans mandement.
J'ay la bride plus longue, et plus longue laniere,
J'ay de la part de Dieu commission planiere,
Un blan-signé de luy...   (IV, p. 147)

This suggestion of pride, however, is contradicted in the following scene, where Josué describes himself as God's 'bras', His agent, and ascribes to Him all his victories. Here Josué reveals that he fears that the Jews will neglect God in their new prosperity and so deserve some fresh punishment; this accords with the angel's warning, and Josué's interpretation is confirmed in the next scene, when Achan steals the booty and makes the Jews' defeat inevitable. Josué's discussion with Caleb has no bearing on the outcome, and his apparent pride is not developed as one of the causes of the disaster; Nancel introduced this red herring as an opportunity for a debate on an edifying theme, the limits of human discretion under God's will, but failed to realise that the discussion ran counter to the interpretation of events advanced elsewhere.

Altogether, the moral basis of the action appears confused when an attempt is made to view the play as a whole, though each strand of the plot taken in isolation illustrates clearly enough the theme of divine justice. As in *Dina*, each speech and incident illustrates the theme independently of the others. Nancel retained a firm grasp of the principle he wished to demonstrate, and contrived numerous scenes to illustrate it, but these remain discrete *exempla*: in the humanist theatre the parts could easily be greater than the whole.

Debora likewise demonstrates how sin and virtue are rewarded. The subject is the deliverance of the Jews from oppression under Jabin by the prophet Debora, and the death of Sisera, Jabin's general, at the hands of Jael (Judges iv); Nancel added Jabin's suicide.[49] *Debora* is free of the inconsistencies that mar its companion-pieces, but like them it is composed of a series of edifying scenes each conceived somewhat independently of the others. Apart from Debora herself, the characters each appear in only one or two scenes to embody or expatiate on the theme, which is that God sends tyrants to punish nations for their sins but eventually relents and punishes the tyrant in turn. Unlike *Les Juifves*, for example, *Debora* does not present God's intervention in a single event: Nancel lacked the imagination to build a whole play from one incident, and filled out his acts with repeated illustrations of the same point. It was Nancel's ill-fortune not to possess sufficient breadth of conception to notice that the parallel illustrations of his theme, each tending separately in the same direction, actually interfered with each other.

One feature of the plays gives a misleading impression of the effects Nancel sought by his chosen dramatic technique: this is the appearance of dilemmas. Three characters are given dilemmas, which they explore in monologues: Hemor hesitates to allow Sichem to marry Dina, Rahab hesitates to betray Jericho by sheltering the Jewish spies, and Jahe. hesitates to kill her sleeping guest Sisara. In each case the dilemma is quickly resolved and gives rise to no anguish or remorse: Nancel did not seek to derive the plays' substance from the characters' struggles to reach and maintain difficult decisions, as was the convention in the Classical theatre where the dilemma was such an important feature Nancel did not develop sympathy for the characters, but introduced them, usually for only one or two scenes each, to stand as examples. The plays represent a *reductio ad absurdum* of the humanist form: Nancel was frequently so intent on the instructive import of the individual speech that he admitted inconsistencies between speeches, obscuring the very religious significance of the action which he intended them to elucidate.

Where the humanist technique had arranged the extensive action so as to throw light on its cause, the growing tendency after the end of the religious wars was to focus on the action's course. This tendency was further exemplified in the *Tragedie d'Amnon, et Thamar* (Rouen 1608) of Nicolas Chrestien, who unlike Thierry did not use the subject to exemplify divine retribution but concentrated on the progress of events and the passions of the characters.

These discuss their feelings at length, in the emphatic language of the humanist manner. Amnon burns with desire for his sister, as he declares in act 1, first in a monologue and then in a dialogue with his confidant Ethay. This discussion contains many commonplace *sententiae*, but Amnon is subject to a genuine dilemma between desire and repulsion at the thought of incest. After some agonising, he resolves that he must enjoy her at any cost.

Absalon, meanwhile, is a prey to a different passion: ambition. This provides the matter of the second act, where he reveals his intention of killing Amnon so as to inherit the throne. This detail is not in the Bible or Josephus: Chrestien seems to have supplied this passion for Absalon.[50] As well as seeking the crown, Absalon wishes to wield royal power even while the old King is still alive. Requiring an accomplice, he holds discussions with Architophel and Cusay in which he suggests that David is too old to rule effectively; formal debates ensue about the relative importance of vigour and experience in a King. Architophel agrees to support his coup.

Amnon burns more than ever for Thamar: he must enjoy her or die. Jonathan, another confidant, argues sententiously that one must master passion, but when Amnon insists that the alternative to satisfaction is suicide, Jonathan decides that incest is the lesser evil and suggests a stratagem by which Amnon may enjoy his sister.

The rape occurs in the *entr'acte*, and act IV is devoted to a third passion, Thamar's desire for vengeance. She hesitates, however, to kill her own brother, and the dilemma causes her some anguish until honour effaces other considerations. She begs Absalon to avenge her. He readily agrees and kills Amnon on stage in act V, which is closed by David's lament.

Only this last speech refers to the theme around which Thierry had constructed his play on the subject, the connection between David's sins and the misfortunes of his children, and where Thierry had organised the whole play to bear on this theme Chrestien brought it in as no more than a conventional finale. Chrestien disposed his version to present three major passions, lust, ambition and vengeance. The passions are presented with the usual humanist adornments, such as formal debates, and the approach is at times quite schematic, notably in act I, where Amnon's struggle between desire and the taboo against incest, in addition to being portrayed in the character's own words, is shown symbolically in a dispute between an angel and Megere over Amnon as he lies sleeping. The three passions are treated separately in different acts, and the three characters representing them are not brought together for any confrontations: Chrestien was concerned with the progress of each passion individually, and in each case opposition to the passion comes only from within the character in a dilemma, which is speedily resolved and thereafter causes no remorse. Chrestien dissected each passion in isolation: rather in the humanist manner, his characters are examples of the harm a passion can wreak on the individual it possesses. What marks Chrestien apart from the humanist dramatists, however, is that his characters are representatives of states of mind rather than sins, and that the organising principle in the play is not illustration of a theme but the attempt to show emotions causing a chain of events. Unlike the humanist productions, this was not a *pièce à thèse* but an attempt, however schematic, to derive a dramatic structure from the process of human emotion. From our position as heirs to the Classical tradition it is tempting to hail *Amnon et Thamar* as a step in the right direction; but it is worth pondering the possibility that to a spectator accustomed to the humanist style Chrestien's approach might have seemed deficient in meaning and point.

Two other plays of this time, of which satisfactory texts do not survive, seem also to have rejected the humanist technique, though for different reasons. The posthumous volume of *Oeuvres poetiques* (Douai 1612) of Jean Loys, a lawyer of Douai, contains a summary of a play headed '*Joseph*, representé au college du roy en la ville de Douay, le XXII. de Juin M.DC.IX.' (p. 34). This apparently chronicled Joseph's life from his sale to Potiphar to the death of his father (Genesis xxxix–xlix). At about the same time the abbé Baudeville, a school-master at Ploërmel, commemorated the local patron saint in a *Tragédie de S Armel*, which survives only in a manuscript copy heavily emended in the course of later performances, from which it is impossible to reconstruct the abbé's work.[51] As it stands the text chronicles in five acts the whole of the saint's career. The old *mystères* were still being performed at this time, and plays resembling them were apparently still written.

The last year of the King who had ended the religious wars saw the appearance of the last play on an Old-Testament subject to be printed until 1622:[52] *Saül, tragedie*, by Claude Billard de Courgenay, which was published in a volume of *Tragedies* (Paris 1610) which had pre-sumably been written over the previous few years. *Saül* presents a chronicle of Saul, David and the Philistines during Saul's last hours,[53] with the usual humanist ornaments.[54] However, the play lacks one feature of humanist dramaturgy, the subordination of incident to theme. It deserves detailed analysis as an example of the disintegration of the style.

The first act consists of a monologue, in which Saül laments his misfortunes. David is in revolt; but Saül has experience of punishing rebels. He vaunts his courage, and laments at the cowardice of his troops: it is inspired by heaven, he reflects, as a punishment for his failure to kill Agag as God ordered. He justifies his clemency, and adds:

> Quay-je tant offensé? quel est mon demerite?
> Qu'il faille en pardonnant, que le pardon s'irrite
> Contre moy malheureux, que Dieu piteux à tous,
> Me soit impitoiable, et me perde en courrous.   (I, f. 115ᵛ)

Though he has repented for his sins God continues to overwhelm him with misfortune; but Saül does not fear death, and will even welcome it. The Chorus reflects that God is merciful, but not to impenitent sinners.

Billard next presents David, who also utters a long lament concerning the persecution he has endured from Saül. Nevertheless, he will never harm God's anointed King. David's Escuyer tries unsuccessfully to raise his spirits. In the following scene, Billard turns to the Philistines, among whom David is living. Achys, their King, is determined to exterminate the Jews. His Lieutenant argues that clement treatment would win their loyalty as subjects, but Achys insists on rigour. Some Philistine soldiers, forming a Chorus, do not trust David to fight alongside them against the Jews, and decide to tell Achys so; they reflect on flattery and the difficulty of giving truthful advice to Kings.

In act III this Chorus persuades Achys to expel David from the Philistine camp. David is summoned; oblivious of his previous scruples, he burns now to attack Saül, but Achys sends him away to his fief of Siceleg (i.e. Ziklag). David learns *en route* that Siceleg has been sacked and the wives and children carried off. David's followers blame their leader for always bringing disaster on them and come close to mutiny. In the next scene David encourages his men with the news that God has assured him of victory; ten lines later he congratulates them on destroying the sackers of Siceleg.[55] This incident provides a series of speeches epitomising different attitudes, but the connection between them and the method by which David regains the loyalty of his band are left obscure.

Billard now turns again to Saül, who is in despair at the cowardice of his men and expatiates on the hostility towards him of all four elements of creation. He conjures the Destins to destroy him, but realising that they will not, decides to consult the Demons to know his fate. His decision is reached thus: after realising that the Destins will not oblige him, he concludes:

> Il faut avoir recours ailleurs qu'à l'influence:
> Je veux par les Demons prendre la connoissance
> De ce qui m'est futur...   (III, f. 125ᵛ)

This is the whole motivation of Saül's fateful decision to consult the witch. Saül goes on to discourse about the powers of infernal spirits, then suddenly asks himself: 'helas! le doi-je faire?' (f. 126ʳ). Thus abruptly introduced, the dilemma is developed as follows:

> "Pourquoy non? je peux tout: et n'est rien si contraire
> "Aux Royales grandeurs, que voir rien opposé
> "Au cours de leur humeur, à ce qu'ils ont osé.
> "Mais le Ciel qui void tout deffent le sortilege:
> "N'importe en offensant, pourveu que je m'alege
> "De l'ennui qui me perd, et que par les devins
> "Je me puisse assurer quels seront mes destins.
>   Aussi bien mon erreur mon offense est si grande
> Qu'il n'y a plus de grace, et ne voit on offrande
> Pour le pauvre Saül qui puisse meriter,
> Flechir ce Dieu vengeur, si prompt à s'irriter.
>   Que sçauroy-je esperer banni de sa clemence?
> Que pourroi-je avoir pis nageant en mon offense?   (III, f. 126ʳ)

With no more ado, he knocks at the witch's door. Billard had little time for the psychological process of the decision: his purpose was to have Saül state sententiously the arguments *pro* and *contra*. The dilemma is a formality. Saül learns his fate from Samuel's ghost, and determines to die fighting. The Chorus reflects that Saül has compounded his sin; God gives the sinner time to repent, but eventually punishes the refractory.[56]

In act IV Achys anticipates victory, reflecting at length on the power of opinion and imagination, which have struck terror into Saül's troops. The Jewish Chorus too reflects on the power of imagination, which led Saül to despair; a rational man would not be deceived by Demons. Abner tries to persuade Jonatas to take command, seeing Saül is incapable; Jonatas refuses to depart from strict filial obedience. These virtuous sentiments, unlike the previous discussions of imagination and reason, do have some bearing on the plot, for if Jonatas had assumed command the Jews might have escaped defeat; but this attempt at psychological motivation of the rout is ill-placed here, since the significance of the story requires that it should be lack of God's support, not Jonatas's, that causes Saül's ruin. The Chorus of Israelite women reflects on the punishment of sin:

> "Malheureux est le peuple ou regnent les pechez:
> "Malheureux sont les Rois de vices entachez:
> "L'erreur de la commune
> "Se venge sur le Prince: et les fautes des Rois
> "Font courir mesme risque, et non moindre fortune
> "Ceux qui suivent leurs loix.
>
> (IV, f. 133ᵛ)

Jonatas attempts valiantly to rally the army in act v. Saül, wounded, wishes to die rather than fall into the hands of the Philistines, whom he is too weak to resist. He hesitates to kill himself, but quickly resolves the dilemma. To avoid the stigma of suicide, however, he asks his Squire to despatch him; the Squire refuses, so Saül kills himself, defying Hell to torment him more than this life. The Chorus describes suicide as a sin.

The play is conceived as a series of tirades in which the characters give copious and decorous expression to the passions and philosophical reflections aroused by their circumstances; the speeches epitomise stages of the action, like stills from a motion-picture, rather than forming a continuity. Since the scenes are conceived somewhat in isolation, transitions are abrupt and contradictions abound; of these the greatest occurs when David burns to attack Saül having earlier declared unequivocally his adherence to the principle of divine right.[57] To extend the subject-matter of the tirades, Billard gave large roles to figures other than the eponymous hero. After delivering the opening monologue, Saül returns to the stage only at the end of act III; he is absent again in act IV, and reappears in act V only to kill himself.[58] The whole of acts II and IV and the bulk of act III are devoted to David and the Philistines; here Billard gives detailed accounts of business with no bearing on Saül's fate. Billard was clearly not concerned to build his play around the emotions of any individual. It might appear from the inclusion of two dilemmas for Saül that Billard was interested in the King's emotional life; but these are treated so briefly that it is clear they are formalities designed to allow presentation of debates. Billard's dominant preoccupation was the poetic and sententious content of the various speeches.

Like Soret or Nancel, Billard conceived the play as a series of discrete lessons; *Saül* is not unified by the systematic reflection on a theme that was the strength of Thierry's *David* or Garnier's *Les Juifves*. Billard may have intended the play to illustrate repentance or retribution, which the Chorus mentions, but no other character refers consistently to any theme; the author did not arrange to make his theme emerge by the usual device of having his characters state it. Billard was not capable of the effort of imagination needed to unify his grandiloquent and sententious tirades so as to give a sense to the story in which they were inserted.

This indeed was the endemic weakness of the sacred plays in the humanist manner that appeared after the end of the religious wars. During the period of strife dramatists were naturally preoccupied with one theme, God's punishment of the nation's sins by such scourges as war and famine; this appeared in the doctrinal and the propaganda theatre no less than in plays on historical subjects. Among the historical plays this common preoccupation produced a remarkable unity of approach: a frequently quite extensive plot was so arranged that, while giving no very systematic account of action or emotion, its various rather separate parts all reflected on the theme, and indeed the whole was intelligible only when viewed as an extended example, while the characters expatiated explicitly on their own exemplary status. With the pacification of the country the purpose that had animated the humanist plays evaporated, and while plays were still written reproducing the elements of the humanist form they increasingly lacked any purpose to which those devices might be directed. Soret, Nancel, Billard and the unknown author of *Jeanne d'Arques* presented tirades expressing emotions and philosophical points, but these add up to no coherent interpretation of the world.

At the same time the dominance of the humanist style came to an end. The *mystères* had always continued to be performed; now a few new plays resembling them were written, notably Baudeville's *S. Armel*. Plays also began to appear that were neither medieval nor humanist in approach. These were essentially narratives of historical episodes, but differ from the narrative style of the *mystères* in not demanding faith to make sense. The new narratives abandoned the symbolic approach used in the *mystères*; they provided straightforward (indeed in cases such as La Pujade's *Jacob* decidedly pedestrian) accounts of events. This was a first step towards realism: the authors of the narratives used neither the humanist nor the medieval devices for presenting the meaning of the action through the structure of the play and the statements of the figures, but dealt with the events, the processes of life, themselves. Ouyn and Chrestien went further, in offering a degree of sympathy with the characters and some study of their emotional states: where a humanist hero stated his own exemplary significance, the focus in these plays was more on what it was like to be in the position of the various figures. Thanks perhaps to the establishment of a measure of security and prosperity in everyday life, audiences now had time to sympathise with the position of fellow men, where previously their chief preoccupation had been with seeking to understand the horrors through which they lived. The new source of interest in the theatre found its expression in a new dramatic style.

(iii) THE PROFESSIONAL STAGE

The professional theatre meanwhile was developing more rapidly in this direction. Professional troupes had been touring at least since 1550 (see p. 61 above), but it was not until the turn of the century that their existence exerted an influence on writing for the theatre. Dramatists previously had worked largely in the expectation of an amateur performance, mounted usually by a guild, the community, or a school or college. It was only in the seventeenth century that the professional theatre was so far established that playwrights aspired to see their work performed there and began to take account of the need to offer the actors an expectation of making a profit from their texts. The plays written for these conditions concentrated on exciting the spectator by the movement of the plot and by the display of the passions of the characters; such at least were the characteristics of the earliest extant professional sacred plays.[59]

A professional theatre had first emerged in the provinces. In Paris, the Confrères de la Passion had been granted a monopoly of all theatrical performances, which they used against all potential rivals, but by the latter part of the sixteenth century they had neither the ability nor the repertoire to stage successful performances themselves. Only in 1599, despairing of drawing any income from their monopoly, did they let their theatre to a professional troupe, while allowing other

troupes to play in halls other than their own Hôtel de Bourgogne
on payment of a fee; and it was not until some years later that the halls
were regularly occupied.[60] Previously, the professional companies had
prospered by touring outside Paris, as they did still in the seventeenth
century. Rouen was a major centre. The publishing business carried on
there by the Du Petit Val family was the most prolific source of plays
in France at the turn of the century.[61] Another Rouennais, Abraham
Cousturier, printed ten plays in uniform editions, including five on
sacred subjects. Only two were dated (1612 and 1614), but their companions were probably contemporary. Most were anonymous.[62] The
texts contain many errors, but these seem not to result from deficiencies
in the printing: many lines consist of carefully-set nonsense. Such
textual corruption suggests that Cousturier was working from old
actors' copies, much emended in the course of performances, which
were sold to him perhaps when a troupe disbanded or because it no
longer required the plays in its repertoire;[63] they may thus have been
first written quite some time before they were printed,[64] and certainly
they recall the preferences of the sixteenth century by the choice of
Old-Testament subjects. To what extent the ten plays are representative
of provincial taste it is impossible to say; but it is perhaps worth noting
that the presence of five sacred plays in the set of ten appears to
confirm Lebègue's conclusion[65] that the repertoire at this time commonly included a large proportion of sacred material.[66]

One of the sacred plays has not previously been analysed: I shall
describe it in some detail. This is the *Tragedie de la chaste et vertueuse
Susanne, ou l'on veoit l'innocence vaincre la malice des Juges*, dated
1614.[67]

Naman, a judge, opens the action. Despite his age he feels the grip
of love. He is ashamed of his adulterous passion, the more so since it
is his office to punish such crimes, but he is unable to master it. Seeing
his colleague Azachar approach, he disguises his feelings, but Azachar
is a prey to the same passion and quickly detects the symptoms in his
fellow. Comparing notes, they find that they both lust for Susanne.
Naman declares that he will not seduce a married woman, who in any
case would scarcely be likely to be aroused by his aged charms, but
Azachar has no such scruples and is grotesquely confident that they need
only ask Susanne to gratify them.

At the start of the second act Joachim rejoices in his happiness in
marriage. Susanne enters; they describe their mutual affection. The
scene shifts to Daniel, who laments for the sufferings of Israel. He
implores God to relent in His just anger against the Jews; but seeing
the corruption in public life he fears that Israel deserves to suffer
more yet. The judges plan to surprise Susanne while she is bathing

alone in her garden. Naman has lost his earlier scruples: he observes that if Susanne refuses them they would lose face, and suggests that they should claim in that case to have caught her in adultery; thanks to their authority, they could then punish her refusal by having her stoned. Azachar praises his sagacity.

Susanne feels a strange foreboding, but goes nevertheless to take her customary bath. She modestly dismisses her female attendant, then leaves the stage to go to the pool. Hidden in the bushes, the judges avidly describe her charms. Her bath finished, she returns to the stage; the judges step forward. She rejects their advances, at which they threaten to accuse her of adultery. Susanne reflects that she would rather die innocently than commit the sin they desire:

> qu'est-ce de la mort, a qui meurt innocent
> Un bien heureux passage ou la mort on ne sent,
> Pour la mort nous naissons et nous mourons pour vivre,
> Quand tes sentiers Seigneur nous nous forçons d'ensuivre,
> Que nous sommes trompez et que c'est a grand tort
> Que le chemin du Ciel nous appellons la mort...   (III, p. 30)

She calls her servants; the judges too shout as if chasing a fugitive, and when the servants arrive explain that they found Susanne committing adultery but could not apprehend her lover.

In act IV Joachim curses women and rues the day he married. He has Susanne brought in and despite her entreaties sends her for public trial. Daniel cannot believe her guilty, and prays for enlightenment. An angel orders him to go and prove her innocence; he praises God for protecting virtue. The judges affirm in court that they found Susanne fornicating. Being witnesses they refrain from judging her; a Chorus of Jews sentences her to be stoned. Daniel intervenes, pledging his life that she is innocent. The Chorus agrees to hear him. He has the judges separated, and asks each where he saw Susanne sinning. Their replies are contradictory; the Chorus realises that they fabricated the evidence and sentences them to be stoned in Susanne's place.

In the last act the two are led away to die. Naman is ashamed of his crime, but Azachar is too terrified at the prospect of death to think of anything else. Naman prays God to forgive him this and his other sins, for which he heartily repents; he is inspired with confidence that God will indeed pardon him and goes gladly to die. Encouraged by this example, Azachar hastens to follow. Joachim apologises to his wife for having credited the calumny, and she declares that she bears him no ill will. The Chorus reports the death of the judges, and praises God's protection of innocence.

Susanne's vindication is hailed as a triumph of divine justice at the end, but this theme hardly dominates the play. Among the characters only Daniel mentions it, in his prayer; but his comments on the Jews' sinfulness are clearly not applicable to Susanne personally.[68] The play was not constructed according to the humanist principles as an illustration of a theme; it was designed on wholly different lines, to appeal to the audience's emotions, which it effectively does by a number of means. The advance of the action by its swiftness reinforces the effect of the reverses of the plot in inducing alternating hope and anxiety in the spectator. He is enabled to feel these emotions for the characters by their being convincingly though simply drawn.[69] Joachim is a type of the uxorious husband who is so demoralised once doubts are raised about the wife on whom he depends that he is unable to think for himself in judging the accusations against her. In forgiving him for doubting her Susanne exhibits a charity no less heroic than her trust in her innocence which sustains her through her trial. Even the two judges, though they are hateful and figures of fun, are drawn with some care. Naman is the more intelligent, both in his initial scruples and in his thoroughgoing viciousness, whereas Azachar cannot think beyond immediate wants; at the end his far-sightedness saves Naman and shows Azachar the example. The play is well constructed to yield a series of contrasting moods. Susanne's steadfastness is heroic, Joachim's distrust tragic, the judges' lust comic and odious: the author calls forth all the emotional responses of the audience.

Divine justice is similarly no more than mentioned in another play in the set, the *Tragedie nouvelle de Samson le fort, contenant ses victoires et sa prise par la trahison de son Espouse Dalide, qui luy couppa ses cheveux et le livra aux Philistins, desquels il occit trois mil à son trespas.* This is a spectacular chronicle of the major events of Samson's life. In the first act he decides to burn the Philistines' crops to punish them for removing his wife. In act II a general war is averted when the Jews deliver him to the Philistines to punish his arson, but he breaks loose and in act III slaughters his captors with the jaw-bone of an ass. His exploits in Gaza are recounted. In the fourth and final act Samson is shorn of his hair by Dalide and handed over to the Philistines; but he prays for his strength to return and pulls down the palace on the banqueting Philistines and himself.

Samson's exploits are reported to his father Manué, who comments, but he provides no consistent standard. He warns Samson not to burn the Philistines' crops:

> Dieu, qui seul des humains doit chastier l'offence,
> Nous prohibe d'user contre autruy de vengeance.   (I, p. 9)

Nevertheless, when Samson slaughters the Philistines, Manué cannot refrain from rejoicing: vengeance, it seems, ceases to be a crime when

it results in a Jewish victory. When Samson prays for water, overcome
by the heat of battle, a fountain springs from the ass's jaw-bone: this
miracle seems to imply divine approval. Clearly the playwright was
not concerned with the rights and wrongs of Samson's behaviour: his
interest in the story was for its opportunities for an epic spectacle.

Equally spectacular was the *Histoire tragedienne tiree de la fureur
et tirannie de Nabuchodonozor*. This represents the events recounted
in Daniel iii and iv: the casting of the three Jewish youths into the
furnace by Nebuchadnezzar and the latter's punishment by being turned
into a wild beast. This action is summarised by Salomon in the Prologue. He emphasises that Nabuchodonozor's attempts to enforce the
cult of Jupiter offend God, and that he is punished 'Pour avoir mesprisé,
du Grand Dieu la main forte' (I, f. A3ᵛ). Salomon is followed by
Assuerus, Nabuchodonozor's son, who discusses with his squire Corbuis
the dangers endured by mariners. In act II Nabuchodonozor makes a
sacrifice to Jupiter. Assuerus and a councillor, Aula, advise the King
to destroy those who do not adore the god, and Aula remains hidden
in the Temple to catch the Jews who come to insult Jupiter's image.
In act III Nago, the Second Martyr and the Tiers Martyr insult Jupiter
as a powerless creature of men, and resolve to die if necessary in the
service of the true God. They are apprehended by Aula and led before
Nabuchodonozor, who casts them into gaol. In act IV a Magicien
conjures up snakes to torment the three. At Assuerus's suggestion,
Nabuchodonozor attempts persuasion; the three defy him, so he sends
them to be tortured. They continue in act V to defy the King, so he
has them cast into a furnace. An angel comforts them, at which
Nabuchodonozor flies into a rage: he calls on Jupiter and the furies to
kill the three, and when this fails goes mad, rampaging about the stage
like a wild beast until his son restrains him. The angel, as Epilogue,
asserts that 'Le Seigneur ta puny pour ton intime erreur' (f. D3ʳ).

Divine justice is mentioned in Prologue and Epilogue as if in
deference to a convention; the author had no idea of constructing the
play to illustrate it, unlike La Croix when he treated the same subject.
Having made his conventional gesture, the author felt free in the body
of the play to indulge his taste for exotic spectacle by means of a plot
that was only remotely connected with the biblical account. Only the
casting of the youths into the furnace and the King's madness (i.e. act
v) derive from the Book of Daniel; the sacrifice and the scene in which
the three revile Jupiter are obvious extrapolations of the source, but the
intervention of the magician and Assuerus's sympathy for mariners are
quite fanciful additions.[70] Both in his inventions and in his treatment
of the historical material, the author was clearly intent on providing an
exotic spectacle to amuse his audience.

The story of Esther was included in Cousturier's set of plays: *La Belle Hester, tragedie françoise tiree de la saincte Bible*. In this case we have the author's name, sieur Japien Marfriere, according to Lancaster a pseudonym.[71] As in the three other plays in the set considered in this chapter, the author chronicled the whole of the episode, from the banquet at which Vasthy disobeys Assuere to the fall of Aman. These events are accommodated within the space of some 1000 Alexandrines. There is none of the conventional grandiloquence and moralising with which Matthieu extended the same material to 6000 lines: this version provides a concise and vigorous account of the plot. Equally, there is little opportunity for depicting the sentiments of the characters. Mardochée suggests at the end that events were dictated by providence, but this idea is not mentioned at any other point. Marfriere did not wish to explore emotions or illustrate a theme: he presented a fast-moving version of a famous and pompous plot with a satisfying ending.

The four sacred plays in Cousturier's set considered in this chapter were well suited to be popular successes. This was partly a matter of choice of subject; all except *Samson* had a happy ending, and in *Hester* and *Susanne* the conclusion was particularly gratifying, showing the villains overthrown by the rebound against them of their own machinations. The subjects offered splendid opportunities for pomp and spectacle, calling for foreign courts, miracles, magic and devilry. In handling this material the author or authors[72] exploited these opportunities to the full. The material was disposed moreover to provide fast-moving accounts of the complex plots and to incorporate a variety of incidents and a number of reverses;[73] *La Belle Hester* is poles apart from Matthieu's handling of the subject. The principle underlying this organisation of the dramatic material was simple: the professional theatre aimed to excite the spectator's emotions by the most direct means, by involving him in a tense plot. In *Susanne* this principle was developed further when the author attempted in addition to involve the spectator in emotional sympathy with the protagonists.

A far more accomplished expression of the same objectives was achieved by another professional dramatist, Alexandre Hardy, in *Mariamne, tragedie*.[74] This is only marginally a sacred play, since although it involves a biblical figure, Herod, the action derives from Josephus and is not recorded in the Bible;[75] nevertheless it deserves some discussion as an illustration of the capabilities of the new dramatic system, which except in the work of Hardy were hardly realised in the sacred theatre until the time of Corneille.

The play opens with a soliloquy by a ghost, but his function is quite different from that of the humanist protatic monologue. He establishes the tragic inevitability of the ensuing action by recounting the history which determines the characters' emotions and actions. To secure the throne Herode killed the King and his son (the speaker) and married his daughter, Mariamne. Inevitably, she hates her husband, but Herode loves her passionately, too passionately to brook her rejection of his love without the violence in his nature asserting itself. The dénouement is inherent in the characters' pasts and personalities, and the rest of the play traces how the inevitable comes to happen. Mariamne longs to escape from Herode, and so deliberately taunts and goads him until he kills her, thus punishing him at the same time as gaining release. Herode is aware of his temper and struggles to control it; at the end he is filled with horror at the crime he has been provoked to commit and swears to spend the rest of his life in repentance.

Hardy reinforced this psychological action with similar material in the sub-plots; indeed he was capable of including for their contribution to the emotional texture scenes which were not strictly necessary to the main action, such as the episode in which the vigorous Salome brow-beats the Eschanson into making false accusations against Mariamne. The whole play was arranged to carry the spectator along in its emotional sweep.

Hardy was not content, however, with creating an enthralling action; he also endowed it with a degree of tragic significance. *Mariamne* explores the mechanisms by which the interlocked histories and personalities of the characters lead them into mutual self-destruction. There is no explicit lesson here, such as the humanists required, but by its very different technique the play offers no less clear an insight into the patterns governing men's lives.

In the sacred theatre it was the professional dramatists who first wholeheartedly and systematically adopted the principle of working on and through the spectator's emotions rather than his intellect and who organised their material to have its effect by this means. Bèze had worked by this method in *Abraham sacrifiant*, but others had not followed his example; only a few, notably Garnier, had gone some way in the direction of promoting sympathy with the characters. The abandonment of explicit didacticism and of such conventions as causing the characters to view themselves with the spectator's eyes was revolutionary: instead of stating an interpretation of events, plays in the new system offered an impression of lived experience – in the ultimate development, a slice of life – in which meaning, if any, could only be implicit. The revolution extended over several decades, however; it was not until the 1630s that the principle of requiring the spectator to identify imaginatively with the characters became the dominant theatrical style. Hardy early brought the new style to a high state of perfection, and the other professional dramatists for the most part followed the same path; but the amateur dramatists who wrote the sacred plays did not quickly adopt it, having perhaps somewhat different concerns, of which narration of the facts of sacred history was the first.

7. The renewed vogue of the sacred chronicle

Although the professional theatre grew steadily in importance from early in the new century, relatively few sacred plays were written for it before the 1630s; until then the tradition of sacred drama was carried forward almost entirely by amateurs. The amateur dramatists returned to the practice which had fallen into disuse during the religious wars: they celebrated special occasions with plays representing the careers and miracles of the appropriate saints. Sometimes the texts performed were reworkings of old *mystères*; those renovated texts that were printed were examined in Chapter 1. On other occasions new plays were written. These were divided into acts and scenes and not entitled *mystère*, but they retained the traditional approach of narrating the salient events of the subject's career: this style was exemplified in Bardon de Brun's *Sainct Jacques*. Few new saint-plays were written or printed in the years immediately following the restoration of peace in 1594; only in the reign of Louis XIII did such subjects recover some of the importance they had once had.[1]

A play celebrating the local patron saint, but entitled *Clotilde*, *tragecomedie* (Poitiers 1613), was commissioned from Jean Prevost, a lawyer of Saint-Léonard-de-Noblat,[2] by the inhabitants of the town, 'desireux de conserver leurs privileges' (Dedication, f. 41ᵛ). This was concerned only with Léonard's involvement in establishing the town's privileges and did not show his whole career. King Clovis is fighting to extend his rule and the Christian faith to the whole of France. He plans a new campaign, but does not inform his wife, Clotilde, lest, despite being eight months pregnant, she insist on accompanying him in the field, as is her habit. When Clotilde discovers the plan she is so angry that she falls ill; a doctor despairs of saving her or the child. Léonard, a hermit, learns of her illness and comes to assist at her death. By the concerted prayers of Léonard, Clovis and Clotilde herself, she is saved. Clovis discovers that the hermit is his long-lost cousin and urges him to return to the court or accept a bishopric so as to spread the Word. Léonard prefers to remain free of worldly concerns, but he does accept the gift of a tract of land where he and his disciples can live. The King arranges for them to live free of all taxes and duties, and declares that the community shall be called Noblac.

For the purpose of recounting the events leading to the granting of the town's privileges, Prevost naturally preferred the narrative form of the *mystères*. In Prevost's case it is certain that he did not make the choice out of ignorance: in three other plays he used the neo-classical form,[3] but for this subject he did not find it appropriate. However, the figures do not step out of character for the benefit of the audience, as in the *mystères*, and Léonard does more than simply name elements of doctrine when he is seeking to bolster the sick Queen's faith. Both the King and Queen experience real difficulty in sustaining their belief. Clovis is a recent convert, and when it seems that his wife will die has to be reminded by his Aumonier that God forbids suicide. The result is a heartfelt prayer of repentance and submission to the divine will:

> O Dieu qui pour ta gloire, as tousjours de coustume
> Et pour nostre salut, de mesler d'amertume
> La douceur des plaisirs, et qui n'envoyez rien
> De sinistre ou de bon, sinon pour nostre bien...
>   je suis tout prest, Seigneur de me sousmettre,
> A ta main paternelle, et tout prest de permettre.
> Que ton fleau me visite, à ta saincte bonté
> J'auray tousjours recours en mon adversité.
> Que si j'ay murmuré, si l'amour qui m'affolle
> A dans un desespoir jette mon ame folle,
> J'en sens le repentir, et t'en criant mercy,
> Te supplie, ô Seigneur, me pardonner cecy.
> Et à ta volonté juste, puissante, et saincte
> Disposer de Clovis, du fruict, et de l'enceinte.   (IV i, f. 57^{r-v})

The Queen too slips back into pagan habits of thought and is reprimanded by Léonard: she exclaims:

> Au repentir profound
> D'avoir oublié Dieu mon esprit se confond...
> Mon pere lavez moy, lavez ma conscience.
> Confessez moy mon pere; oyez ma penitence...   (IV iii, f. 63^r)

Clotilde's penitence at having forgotten God is profound and touching. Prevost combined the narrative form, best suited to his special purpose, with an insight into the characters' emotions; the other pious dramatists of the decade were rarely so ambitious.

The miraculous conversion of the same King was included as the first of five 'intermedes Heroyques à l'honneur des François' with which Nicolas Chrestien enriched *Les Amantes, ou la grande pastorelle* (Rouen 1613); the others were 'La prise de Compostelle par Charlemagne; La prise de Hierusalem par Godefroy de Boüillon; La prise de Damiette par S. Loys Roy de France; La Pucelle d'Orleans'. The interludes serve as a reminder that the new style which was evolving was not considered automatically superior: as his *Amnon et Thamar* demonstrated, Chrestien was aware of the new spirit, but here preferred a symbolic narrative in which the characters are self-consciously good or evil and the simple naming of points of doctrine is enough to persuade heathens to convert. Although the pastoral was the fashionable genre of the day, Chrestien saw no incongruity in including in it material reminiscent of the *mystères*: he saw the different dramatic forms which he cultivated as possessing equivalent status, though suitable for different purposes.

The *Tragedie de sainte Agnes* (Rouen 1615) by Pierre Troterel is not known to have been written for any particular celebration; it may on the contrary have been intended for professional performance, for Troterel had considerable experience as a secular dramatist and published in the major provincial centre of the theatre, Rouen. Certainly his play differs greatly from most of the amateur chronicles of the time: although it does in fact recount practically the whole of the legend of Agnes, it is designed to generate excitement from the movement of the plot and the feelings of the characters.

In the first scene Martian, son of the Governor of Rome, complains in the solitary forest about his hopeless love. His friend Censorin creeps up so as to discover the cause of his recent melancholy, then emerges from hiding to confront him. Martian confides his secret: his lady loves another, and a further difficulty is that his father, Simphronie, might not let him marry a commoner. Censorin's reply is pointed: 'Comment, de vostre bien prend-il donc facherie?' (1, p. 15). This is a far cry from the humanists' abstract debates about filial duty. Censorin persuades Martian to consult his father. In the following scene Martian duly tells Simphronie that he loves Agnes but conceals the fact that she loves another; seeing no impediment, Simphronie gives him permission to court her. They discuss the power of passion at length. Simphronie agrees to interview the girl's father.

The father introduces a new tone. Thus far Martian has seemed to be an ordinary tragi-comic gallant, and Simphronie an indulgent father. Agnes's father, however, describes Simphronie as a tyrant, and fears that the cause of his summons to the palace is that Simphronie has discovered that he is a Christian. He soon finds, though, that Simphronie wishes only to seek his consent to the marriage: after offering token resistance, he agrees, only to reveal once Simphronie has left that his compliance was feigned, since Agnes has dedicated her virginity to God and will never marry.

Having started in the pastoral mode, the act quickly introduces premonitions of danger; tension arises when Martian conceals the obstacle to his love from Simphronie, and is redoubled when Agnes's father conceals his faith. Apart from the discussion about the power of love, there are no conventional developments of commonplaces. Troterel did not concern himself with illustrating a theme, but created characters endowed with real existence and a plot that moved rapidly to induce anxiety.

Martian approaches his beloved with flattery, but she insists that she is already dedicated to another Husband. Martian never appreciates that her resistance is religious, not coquettish; he falls into a jealous rage against the unidentified rival. The tragi-comic device of the *quiproquo* arouses no levity here: Martian threatens to kill his rival. In the following scene Censorin finds him on his sick-bed, and encourages him by promising to discover the rival's identity; they refrain from engaging in a debate about hope and suicide in the humanist manner, and consider affairs in practical terms. Censorin next reveals the identity of the rival to Simphronie, who rejoices: he will threaten Agnes with execution unless she marries his son. Censorin considers this inexpedient; he does not engage in a debate about the proper bounds of a King's power, but points out pragmatically that Christians welcome martyrdom and to kill Agnes will scarcely help Martian. Simphronie curbs his murderous rage and agrees to attempt persuasion.

On her way to the palace at the start of act III, Agnes declares herself undaunted by the prospect of death, with such spirit that her mother finds it necessary to remind her that God forbids Christians to seek death. Simphronie urges Agnes with threats and cajolery to accept Martian; she remains adamant that her virginity is dedicated to God. This inconclusive interview drives Martian to contemplate suicide, from which Censorin dissuades him. His arguments eschew the conventional abstractions: he proposes that Martian should rape Agnes. Martian is not wholly unscrupulous: although thanks to his father's position he could use force with impunity, he prefers to win Agnes by love. Agnes is again led before the Governor, who attempts to argue against Christianity. Inspired by God, as she declares, Agnes confounds him and, far from submitting, prays God to enlighten him. Simphronie loses patience and threatens death, but she is unmoved:

> plustost je me tiendrois heureuse
> D'endurer pour Jesus une mort rigoureuse,
> Luy qui pour nos pechez et pour nous rachetter,
> Cloüé sur une croix, la voulut bien gouster.

(III, p. 60)

Simphronie makes a final offer: she may remain a virgin, but only as a
Vestal; otherwise she will be prostituted. She refuses to join the Vestals,
and is handed over to the guards.

At the start of act IV Agnes rejoices at a miracle: she was stripped
naked, but God caused her hair to grow to cover her. Her respite is
brief: a herald comes to lead her to the brothel, accompanied by a
band of Paillards who subject the maid to a torrent of jokes and insults.
Left alone briefly in the brothel, she prays God and the Virgin to
support her. Her guardian angel promises protection, at which she
praises God:

> Tyran, que tardes-tu? que tu ne me martyre,
> Fay venir tes bourreaux, applique tes tourments,
> Par eux je jouyray de tous contentements,
> Par eux je jouyray de mon amour pudique,
> Embrassant doucement mon cher amant unique,
> Amant, dont mon esprit est tellement ravy,
> Que je suis morte en moy, mais en luy je revy,
> Et luy vit en mon coeur, mais d'une façon telle
> Qu'y vivant, il me donne une vie immortelle.   (IV, p. 71)

The lyrical prayer is interrupted by the return of coarse comedy, when
Martian and Censorin join the Paillards before the brothel. Martian
learns that Agnes's virginity is still intact, because the Paillards were
driven back by a bolt of lightning; exulting, he goes in to deflower her.
After some time Censorin calls impatiently for his turn, and receiving
no reply from Martian enters, fearing Christian sorcery. He returns to
report that Martian is dead and Agnes has disappeared. The Paillards
prudently leave, while Censorin goes to inform Simphronie.

Censorin restrains Simphronie's grief and accompanies him to the
brothel to collect his son's body. There they find Agnes. She insists
that Martian was killed by the angel, not herself; to vindicate herself
she accedes to Simphronie's demand that she should bring his son back
to life. She prays that he may return to reveal the true faith; the body
comes to life and Martian admonishes the onlookers, on pain of hell,
to believe in the Christian God. At this point the priests and populace
of Rome intervene. The former insist that the Christians must be
killed, but the mob, though pagan, has been impressed by the miracle
and refuses to allow the execution. To avoid a disturbance and the
Emperor's wrath, Simphronie has Agnes imprisoned, uncertain whether
to kill her or release her secretly for his son's benefit. In the next scene
Agnes's parents learn of her death, and despite their grief rejoice at
her martyrdom:

> Le grand Dieu soit loué, le grand Dieu soit beny,
> Lequel nous a monstré son amour infiny,

Nous envoyant son fils pour nostre delivrance,
Lequel a voulu mettre Agnes en asseurance.   (v, p. 95)

The last act is perhaps the weakest. The confrontation between the
mob and the priests is a highly theatrical moment, but, unlike the
frightening comedy of act IV, it does little to intensify our feelings for
the characters. Simphronie's sympathy for Agnes likewise leads to
nothing. After his vacillation the announcement of her death comes
as a *coup de théâtre*, but this is achieved at the cost of uncertainty as
to whether she dies the victim of sexual tyranny or religious persecution:
this ambiguity demeans her martyrdom. A further new element is
introduced in the last act by the resurrection of Martian as a Christian:
it is disappointing that Troterel does not satisfy the spectator's curiosity
as to whether Martian will convert his father or Simphronie be obliged
to execute his son.[4]

Systematic illustration of a theme was clearly not Troterel's aim;
instead, the play is arranged to present an exciting account of a plot
that advances rapidly to a conclusion that is far from predetermined.
However, although the twists of the plot might be expected to encourage
the spectator to enter into the feelings of the characters as they are
submitted to new stresses, there is little in fact on which he can focus
any emotional involvement. To be sure, Martian and Simphronie are
endowed with dilemmas over whether to use force to win Agnes, but
Troterel does not enable us to sympathise with either in his indecision,
which seems to have been invented principally to keep the heroine alive
until act v. Agnes herself does not have a very compelling role. She
appears in only six scenes,[5] and in these speaks little; such taciturnity
may befit the virgin's modesty, but it is tantalising in the protagonist of
a play. She never experiences any doubt or hesitation between God and
her legitimate human inclinations. There is consequently scant religious
drama of the type Bèze found in Abraham, and indeed the characters
generally exhibit slight emotional life.

From the historical point of view what is important about *Sainte
Agnes* is precisely that such complaints are appropriate. Lamentations
about poor characterisation were not applicable to the *mystères* or the
humanist dramas; they are here. In designing the play Troterel systematically applied the principle of speaking to the spectator's emotions
through the excitement of the plot and the depiction of the characters'
feelings, though without entire success. He went further than the
unknown authors of the set of plays published by Cousturier in not
simply narrating the story but providing a genuine plot inducing contrasting moods and driven by the interactions of the characters. On the
religious level, however, *Sainte Agnes* is little different from the
mystères: it shows the saint unmoved in the midst of a scene of great

animation produced by the secondary characters and external events. Where the playwright set out to create his effects through depicting the characters' emotional states, the means to make religion dramatic within such conventions was to present the hero's religious emotion, his ecstasies, his doubts, his inner conflicts. Troterel did not make Agnes's religious feelings accessible to the spectator, nor did he endow the tensions and passions with any significance beyond themselves, as Hardy had in *Mariamne*. The dramatic principle underlying *Sainte Agnes* is radically different from that of the *mystères*, but Troterel did not apply it to expressing the religious significance of the sacred subject he had chosen.

The *mystères* continued indeed to flourish. The old texts were revised, performed and even printed still. A *mystère* in disguise was published at Douai in 1616: *Isaac, comedie*, in a collection of *Poëmes françois* by Jean Rosier, curé of Esplechin, near Tournai. This was a transcription of the *Sacrifice d'Abraham* from the *Viel Testament*,[6] which Rosier had perhaps been asked to modernise for a performance. He made some minor amendments: his version is divided into acts and scenes, he supplied a Prologue, an Epilogue and a Chorus, and he slightly shortened some of the longer speeches and exchanges. In all important respects, however, Rosier's play follows the ancient *Mistére*.

The practice of celebrating the whole of the subject's career provided Jean Boissin de Gallardon with the technique for two saint-plays, *Le Martyre de Sainct Vincent* and *Le Martyre de Saincte Catherine*, which appeared in a volume of five *Tragedies et histoires sainctes* (Lyons 1618). The careful distinction maintained between the three 'tragedies' and the two 'histoires sainctes' indicates that Boissin chose the form of his sacred plays as specially suitable for this type of material.

Sainct Vincent narrates the martyrdom of St Vincent of Saragossa. In form the play recalls *Saincte Barbe*: it consists principally of a series of torments inflicted on the saint, shown in detail. Angels intervene to encourage Vincens[7] and his death is accompanied by prodigies, but Boissin omits the conventional conversion of the *bourreau*, despite the inclusion of that feature in the legend.[8]

Unlike the *fatistes* of the *mystères*, however, Boissin provided some explanation of the events chronicled. In the first scene Saint Valere, the Bishop, feeling himself to be old and feeble, appoints the vigorous Vincens his deacon to help him discharge his duties. When they are arrested, it is Vincens who answers the Governor's attacks on Christianity; Valere, having performed the function of introducing Vincens, is quietly forgotten.

The Governor Dacian, on the other hand, is not simply an episodic figure: unlike the usual persecutor in the *mystères* he has a major role, and his character is given some development. In the first act Boissin takes care to establish that Dacian enforces the cult of the classical gods out of gratitude for the good fortune they have sent him:

> Depuis le jour qu'il pleut à la Dame Lucine
> Faire voir à mes yeux la voute cristaline
> Tirant ma liberté hors du flanc maternel,
> Où j'estois prisonnier sans estre criminel,
> Le bon heur m'a suivy...   (I, p. 210)

Although he occasionally loses his temper and has Vincens tortured, he does so regretfully; he never forgets that his aim is to encourage the cult of Jupiter, and he does not indulge in the unexplained brutality that was the common trait of the persecutors in the *mystères*. Vincens of course is quite unmoved by argument or torment.

In having Dacian appear throughout the play, Boissin seems not to have been motivated by any desire to build his intrigue from a personal clash between persecutor and victim. Dacian's role is large because it is large in the legend; had the legend said more of Vincent's early life, Boissin would have reproduced it and Dacian's role would have been proportionately smaller. Dacian emerges as an interesting figure, thanks to his reluctance to use torture, but Boissin did little otherwise to remodel the legend into a psychological drama: Vincens remains stoutly indifferent even to such a troubling argument as the suggestion that in welcoming martyrdom he is guilty of pride. The play is primarily a narrative[9] of the torments the saint endures and the prodigies that accompany his martyrdom.

Boissin's account of the martyrdom of St Catherine of Alexandria likewise concentrates on events and the prodigies accompanying her death. Most of the tortures she endured are staged, together with several miracles and angelic interventions and numerous incidents involving secondary characters.

Here too considerable interest attaches to the tyrant, the Emperor Maxence, who enforces paganism out of gratitude to the gods. When Catherine comes to tell him of the true God, he is initially more sad than angry. Only when she converts first the philosophers called to controvert her beliefs, then his own wife and a Captain, Porphirio, who in turn converts the soldiers he commands, does Maxence regretfully subject Catherine to torture and finally, in the face of her continued defiance, execute her as a danger to the state.[10]

Catherine remains unwavering throughout. Like Vincens, she is accused of pride but ignores the possibility; it is this perfect constancy that converts the Empress and Porphirio. The philosophers, on the other hand, are converted by argument. Boissin could not resist the opportunity to exhibit his erudition: act II consists of the dispute. The philosophers make their case for the classical gods by citing descriptions of them from ancient literature. Catherine offers to answer in kind, and from similar authorities cites passages criticising these deities and describing the One True God:

> Homere est le premier, dont tu soustiens la lice
> Qui charge Jupiter d'un et puis d'autre vice,
> L'appellant un menteur, un pervers, un meschant,
> Cauteleux, abuseur, trompeur, et allechant:
> Il l'outrage bien plus d'une injure vilaine
> Lui reprochant qu'il a enduré la cadene...
> A ce prime argument je ne respond plus rien,
> Le second est fondé sur le Musicien,
> Qui fut dans les enfers trouver son Euridice,
> Lequel ne sera pas vers toy gueres propice,
> Peuple retenez bien maintenant ces deux mots,
> Qu'Orphee a dit jadis à ces gens idiots,
> Vous avez la raison de folie assouvie,
> Et de stupidité envers voz Dieux sans vie:
> Cela n'est pas du mien tu le verras bien mieux
> Dans le livre appellé l'origine des dieux.
> Voila tes arguments solus à ton dommage,
> Mais escoute je veux esclarcir d'avantage
> L'erreur qui te detient, porte ton jugement
> Au discours que Sophocle a fait eloquemment,
> Les termes en sont tels: Il est un Dieu supresme,
> Lequel crea le ciel et mit au milieu mesme
> L'element terrien: apres il a fermez,
> Lez vents avec la mer l'un contre l'autre armez:
> Il loue ainsi mon Dieu...[11]   (II, pp. 298–300)

She goes on to affirm the Incarnation and the Resurrection. The philosophers find Catherine's arguments irresistible and her naming of points of doctrine compelling: they ask her for baptism.

The conversions form the bulk of the play. *Saincte Catherine* consists of a narrative of the prodigies of the martyr's brief career. Boissin's two plays, like the *mystères*, recount the whole of the legend, including all the miraculous events which the audience associated with the subject. Despite his cultivation in his secular plays of alternative styles, for hagiographic material Boissin found the simple narrative, combined with a little erudite exhibitionism, the most suitable form.

A Parisian play of the following year treated the same subject quite differently: the Parisian public seems not to have been interested in doing reverence to God through an account of the miracles He performed through the agency of the saint. E. Poytevin's *Saincte Catherine tragedie* does not treat the martyrdom at all: his brief account of the legend stops before this point, and concentrates instead on the relationship between Catherine and the Emperor, here called Maximin. The mainspring of the plot is his love for Catherine: the story of the martyr is transformed into an involved love-intrigue.

The first scene shows Maximin lamenting that life gives him no pleasure while Catherine rejects his love. His confidant suggests that by persecuting the Christians he would frighten her into accepting his addresses so as to escape death; Maximin agrees. This transforms the sense of the story: Catherine is martyred for spurning Maximin, not for her faith. Nevertheless, the following scene shows her decision to seek baptism. In act II her mother, the Queen of Egypt, in a soliloquy, regrets that Catherine rejects Maximin. Maximin prepares to offer a sacrifice, but is interrupted by Catherine, who upbraids him for persecuting the Christians and worshipping false gods. Maximin praises her beauty as if for the first time and seems to fall in love with her, the author having forgotten that he was already in that state. She rejects his advances, despite his offer to abandon his wife for her. They argue about the power of their respective gods and Maximin offers to turn Christian if she will marry him; but she spurns the bait, provoking threats of torture. The death of Catherine's mother is announced in act III: Maximin rejoices that Catherine will now be his, though the Queen had not hindered the match, and appoints the bearer of this news Governor of Spain. A messenger reports that Persia has accepted Maximin's rule, but Maximin declares that no triumph can please him without Catherine's love. Soldiers fetch her from her château by force. In act IV she again attempts to convert Maximin when he speaks to her of love; he sends her away for the philosophers to dispute with her. The Fury Alecton announces that she will ruin all happiness, and offers to serve the Empress, Faustine, who resents being abandoned by Maximin. Learning that Catherine has converted the philosophers, Maximin sends them to be martyred. The last act shows Catherine in prison, where she declares that her faith is unshakeable. An angel promises that she will be martyred and admitted to heaven.

The play is astonishingly incoherent. The plot is illogical, and many of the incidents lead to nothing. The intervention of Alecton and Faustine suggests that Maximin is to be punished for his crimes, but nothing comes of this. The role of the Queen is not exploited, and Maximin's victory over Persia is mentioned for no apparent purpose. Poytevin was intent only on presenting as much pomp and spectacle as possible in the play's brief length.

Outside Paris such sensationalism was not in order. The Belgian Denis Coppée, whose Passion-play was examined in Chapter 3, started his dramatic career with a saint-play, *La Vie de saincte Justine et de sainct Cyprien*.[12] No copy seems to have survived, but the play was probably a pious chronicle of the saints' careers, if it resembled the author's next production, *La Tres-saincte et admirable vie da madame saincte Aldegonde, patrone de Maubeuge, tragecomedie* (Liège 1622). This commemorated a local saint by chronicling her life. Encouraged by her guardian angel, Aldegonde resolves to resist her mother's desire that she should marry, since she has dedicated her virginity to God. She is supported in her resistance by her saintly sister Wautrude in act II; they also discuss charity, meditation, the trials of the elect, and other paths to heaven. In act III she resists the blandishments of her suitor, Endon, King of England. Bertille, her mother, urges her to accept Endon so as to produce an heir to whom Bertille can transmit her wealth, but Aldegonde persuades her to distribute it to the poor to save her soul. In act IV, Bertille having died, Aldegonde distributes her inheritance in alms, and is saved by a miracle from pursuit by Endon, after which she resolves to found a church. In the last act she dies, amidst miracles; Wautrude and others who had known her praise her virtue and recall those of her miracles that Coppée could not stage.

The usual features of the chronicle, the interventions of episodic figures and the plethora of prodigies, are combined with much instructive material. Every incident and phrase is made the occasion for *propos saints*: for example, when Endon declares that he loves Aldegonde for her eyes, she offers to pluck them out and give them to him, explaining that the eyes of the flesh are worthless compared to those of the soul. In addition to the edifying comments of the characters, similar material is provided by a Chorus. Thanks to Coppée's concentration on edifying commentary, narrative and physical action have perhaps less importance than in other chronicles, but the play retains the episodic construction of that style: Aldegonde alone figures throughout, while other characters appear only in individual scenes. Coppée did reverence to God by telling the story of the saint and all whose careers intersected with it.

A special occasion seems to have inspired both the theme and the treatment of another play by Coppée, *Le Beau Printemps d'hyver du grand ami de Dieu S. Francois d'Assise* (Rouen 1623). This was dedicated to the local Provincial of the Franciscans, and one of the liminary poems reveals that it was performed in the order's church in Huy in August 1622 (f. A5^v). Praise in act V of St Clare of Assisi suggests that the performance occurred on her feast, 12 August. The action is devoted principally to glorifying St Francis.

A Prologue praises S. François and begs silence. François, in the company of his confidant, rejoices that he has left the cares of the merchant's life for the path of holy poverty. The devils Belzebuth and

Asmodée are alarmed at the good he is doing, and resolve upon another attempt to lead him astray. The Chorus praises the life of abstinence. In act II François is praying when an angel announces that Christ will reward him by appearing to him. Christ offers to grant François a grace. François asks that any who pray on this spot with proper contrition, having made confession, should be absolved all sins. At the Virgin's intercession, Christ agrees, but sends François to arrange the new pardon with His plenipotentiary, the Pope. Two Swiss Guards praise Italian wine. The Chorus praises François. In act III François begs the Pope to establish the new indulgence. The Pope agrees, against the advice of a Cardinal who fears that it will reduce the trade of other places of pilgrimage. Asmodée, disguised as an angel, tries to persuade François to abandon abstinence, but François recognises him and as an exemplary mortification flings himself bodily into a thorn-bush. From it spring roses, though it is winter, whence Coppée's title. Christ confirms this to be a miracle, and tells François of the conditions under which the pardon will be granted, to which François must seek the Pope's agreement. A Chorus of angels sings the Te Deum. In act IV the Pope, impressed by the miraculous roses, gives François a bull establishing the pardon. The demons despair. The Chorus thanks the Virgin for her intercession and glorifies her as the sole route to Christ's mercy. In act V the Bishop of Assisi orders François to announce the indulgence, despite the saint's humility. The Bishop attempts to set a limitation on the pardon; miraculously, he stutters and says the opposite of what he intended. The remainder of the act is devoted to praise of Clare. A Chorus of angels praises François and his order, as does a Chorus of *bourgeois* of Assisi. Finally an Epilogue praises the saint and begs the audience's indulgence.

As in the *mystères*, the saint is quite unabashed in describing his own holiness, while the action would hardly be comprehensible without some external knowledge: the author assumes and so calls forth the spectators' belief. There are also of course traces of classicism in the division into acts, the use of choruses and the mythological allusions. Coppée, however, no doubt did not see himself as occupying a transitional place between the medieval and the neo-classical dramatic styles. His concern was simply to remind his spectators of certain familiar miracles and lead them in praise of the two saints, the Virgin, Christ and God: to this purpose his chosen style of a symbolic narrative was entirely appropriate.

Saints were the usual subjects of the sacred plays at this time, but the Bible was not entirely neglected. Some of the old *mystères* on Old-Testament subjects were still performed, and even printed in the cases of the *Patience de Job* and Rosier's revision of *Isaac*. Some new plays, such as Audibert's *Histoire des Maccabées* (1624), were written but not printed, and texts of old plays such as Garnier's *Juifves* still came off the presses. However, very few new plays on biblical subjects were written and printed: between 1610 (Billard's *Saül*) and 1637 (Vallin's *Israel affligé*) there were only those in Cousturier's set, probably written earlier, and two new productions, the anonymous *Perfidie d'Aman* (Paris 1622) and Le Francq's *Antioche* (Antwerp 1625).

Like Poytevin's *Saincte Catherine*, also published in Paris, the *Tragedie nouvelle de la perfidie d'Aman, mignon et favoris du Roy Assuerus; sa conjuration contre les Juifs, ou l'on voit nayvement representé l'Estat miserable de ceux qui se fient aux grandeurs* exploits the sacred subject principally for its opportunities for secular theatre. The play departs considerably from history.[13] There is a large comic element,[14] contributed partly by a pair of thieving servants and a demon, and to some extent by the main characters. Aman is presented in a mock-heroic light; his first speech is a pastiche of Nabuchodonozor's famous tirade in *Les Juifves* (pp. 85–6 above):

> Pareil au Roy je marche, et la vive lumiere
> De ma gloire s'estend depuis l'Aube premiere,
> Jusques dans l'Ocean...   (II, p. 14)

When Aman berates Mardochee for lack of respect, the latter asks if he is drunk, and later reflects that he is an intolerable upstart:

> Encore s'il estoit gentil homme de race:
> Je dirois qu'à bon droit il est enflé d'audace:
> Mais ce n'est qu'un coquin, ce n'est qu'un roturier,
> Son pere estoit-il pas un pauvre cousturier?[15]   (II, p. 16)

The threat to the Jews is reduced to a personal feud between Aman and Mardochee, who relies on his connections at court to protect him and in his brief role (twenty-six and a half lines) says nothing of reliance on God. Ester's role is scarcely longer, and she too hardly mentions religion. The author was not concerned to excite sympathy for the Jews as they face death for their faith, and indeed did not even establish that it is for their faith that they are in danger. The only explanation of the action is given in the Argument, which states conventionally that Aman is a victim of the mutability of fortune; this is hardly borne out in the play. But despite its deficiencies on the level of sense, *La Perfidie d'Aman* remains a lively comedy of the process by which the insufferable Aman receives his comeuppance.

Outside Paris, sacred material was not treated with such complete disregard for history and religion. Denis Coppée again exemplified the usual approach in another play celebrating a local saint, an early Bishop of Maastricht: *Tragedie de S. Lambert patron de Liege* (Liège 1624).[16]

Coppée provided a full account of the saint's career; though the action begins quite late in Lambert's life, out of deference perhaps to the unities, all the youthful miracles which consequently cannot be shown are recounted in *récit* instead. Large incidental roles are given to any-one with whom the saint was involved; indeed the action centres principally round Pepin Heristel, King of Austrasia, his concubine Alpayde and their illegitimate son Charles Martel. Lambert excom-municates Pepin until he abandons Alpayde and returns to his legit-imate wife; Alpayde is so offended that she incites her family and followers to murder the Bishop. Another major incidental figure is a second local saint, Hubert, whose path crossed Lambert's; and a further episode is provided by a battle between Lambert's brother and another Prince, which Lambert succeeds in ending, though the importance of this incident in his career is not established. As had been customary in the *mystères*, each incidental figure assumes great and independent importance for a few scenes before being forgotten.

In his last moments Lambert exhibits an impressively calm faith. Warned that Alpayde's band of murderers is approaching, he dons his episcopal robes and kneels to wait for them, after announcing:

> Si Dieu a ordonné que je fine mes jours,
> Mon vouloir ne sera jamais au sien rebours:
> Je ne dois pas douter les assassins infames,
> Qu'ainsi que sur le cors, n'ont pouvoir sur les ames.
> Si je gaigne le Ciel par le prix de mon sang,
> Des Martirs bien-heureux je me verray au rang.
> Pour mes fiers ennemis, je ne veux autres armes
> Que prier Dieu pour eux, espandant maintes larmes. (v, p. 53)

After his death an angel announces that he has, as he expected, been admitted to heaven. As in the *mystères*, Lambert's words reflect, not so much a real saint's attitudes, as the simple piety of the audience.

Despite the appearance of something akin to an intrigue in the conflict of Alpayde and Lambert, in fundamental construction the play is a chronicle of the events and prodigies associated with the saint's earthly career.[17] Coppée nevertheless divided the action into the classical five acts with choruses. The inclusion of the chorus, standard in humanist drama, had become unusual by this time: once the con-ception of the play as an *exemplum* was abandoned, the chorus, which had served to elucidate this exemplary significance, naturally fell into disuse. Of the dramatists considered in this chapter, only three besides Coppée (Rosier, Le Francq and Bello) used the chorus. Coppée seems not to have understood its utility in any case: the last chorus is devoted to the praise of Ferdinand of Bavaria, to whom the play is dedicated, and the first four, while not so wholly irrelevant, also fail to draw the significance of the action. The division into acts is similarly a meaning-less formality. Coppée used the humanist devices without appreciating their purpose; in substance his play is little different from the reverent chronicles of the *mystères*.

When Nicolas Soret, the author of *La Ceciliade*, wrote a second saint-play, he did not present all the incidents of the subject's life, having a special purpose. *L'Election divine de S. Nicolas a l'archevesché de Myre* (Rheims 1624) was written when Soret had returned from Paris to his native Rheims, where the Archbishop, Louis de Lorraine, died in 1621. The chapter elected François Brulart to succeed him, but Brulart declined. Finally William Gifford was appointed in 1622, and entered into office the following year.[18] The play was performed in the cathedral on 9 May 1624 to celebrate his installation, and its action is accordingly limited to the single episode of the election of St Nicholas to the archbishopric of Myra.

Besides Nicolas, the characters are the six Bishops of the arch-diocese, assembled as a Council to elect a new Archbishop. Their lamentations for the death of the previous incumbent open the action. The Bishops are unable to decide on a procedure for selecting a replace-ment, but an angel announces that God has already chosen the new Archbishop and he will be the first to enter the cathedral the following morning. This is Nicolas. He considers himself unworthy, but is eventually persuaded; the performance ends with his enthronement.

The action is slight; faithful to the practice of his youth, Soret constructed his play as an exhibition of eloquence and erudition, of which, being a schoolmaster, he possessed no small fund. The Bishops speak in turn, each developing some saintly proposition, which the next praises before adding his own contribution; the same order of speaking is followed throughout. Each tirade is between 30 and 300 lines long, and after praising the previous speech elaborates a single point, by means of numerous examples drawn from natural history and classical history and mythology. In total the play contains an enormous number of such examples, demonstrating Soret's reading to have been extensive. This demonstration seems indeed to have been dearer to his heart than the suitability of what is said to the situation. When Nicolas is pre-sented to the Council, not knowing that God has designated him the Archbishop, he is astonished by the respect with which he is treated. Clarius, as President, explains the reasons for it:

> Je les vous diray donc. Le fevre de Nature
> (De qui ce vuide espars est la verbe-facture)
> Pestrit l'homme mortel du boüeux element,
> Pour chef-d'oeuvre dernier parfait absolument,
> Mortel par le peché, qu'il commit, volontaire,

Rendant ainsi chacun à la mort tributaire.
Mort, implacable mort, que Dieu luy prescrivit
Sans revocation dés le moment qu'il vit.
Ayant borné ses ans, ses mois, ses jours, son heure,
Qu'il ne peut allonger tant qu'au monde il demeure.
   Religieuse foy du chrestien baptisé.
Or' qu'on prouvast cecy d'un poinct authorizé
De ceux qui ont escrit de la Philosophie:
Si que qui l'entendra faut qu'il le ratifie.
   Je consens avec eux qu'on meurt par le deffaut
Du principe vital, qu'on dit humide-chaud,
Qui journalierement dedans nous s'appetisse,
Bien que boire et manger nous fomente et nourisse.
   L'exemple est trivial. Car comme nous voyons
Une lampe lumer la-part où nous soyons
Tant que l'huile y croupit ramoitissant la mesche,
Qui luy fait flamboyer une vive flammesche.
Lampe, où si l'on mettoit à mesure autant d'eau,
Que l'huile s'amoindrit, comme en poreux vaisseau,
La liqueur jusqu'au bord s'entretiendroit de mesme:
Mais de l'huile non pas, tarissant à l'extresme:
De sorte que verser tant d'eau l'on y pourroit
Que l'huile defaillant la lampe s'esteindroit.
   Ainsi du corps humain le radical humide
Peut bien se restaurer, quand d'une faim avide.
L'on prend à temps heuré ses principaux repas.
Mais d'humide estranger qu'ils sont, ne peuvent pas
Se transmuer vrayment en celuy de Nature:
Si qu'on tire à la mort certainement future.
Car, estant consommé par le chaud naturel,
La lumiere s'esteint du vivre temporel.   (pp. 47–8)

This does not answer Nicolas's question, nor is it likely that he or the
audience needed telling that man is mortal, but Clarius continues in
the same vein for a further forty lines before informing Nicolas, very
briefly, that God has indicated him as successor to the late Archbishop.
The chief interest of the speech lay in the ingenious explanation of
death; for such a gem, irrelevance was not too high a price to pay.
Like the humanist productions, Soret's play is constructed as a series
of discrete edifying bravura passages.

   It is difficult to imagine whether Soret's dramatic technique struck
his audience as old-fashioned or fitting. Certainly the play diverges
from the taste for large and spectacular actions which was common to
both the amateur and the professional sacred theatre of the time. On
the other hand, his chosen form was well suited to his twin purposes
of celebrating the installation of the Archbishop and impressing and
delighting the chapter of Rheims with his copious erudition.

Jean-Baptiste le Francq, a Dominican of Antwerp, likewise preferred the humanist style, and he also retained the type of subject which had predominated during the religious wars, taking his plot from the Old Testament; nevertheless, the effect of his play is quite remote from what the humanists achieved. Despite the title, *Antioche, tragoedie, traittant le Martyre de septs Enfans Machabeéns* (Antwerp 1625) includes more than the martyrdom of the seven children and their mother:[19] it represents the whole of the career of Antiochus Antipater as the Bible describes it.[20] This is treated in a highly spectacular manner, with much use of dreams, flying and prodigies of every description.

Le Francq announces in the Argument that Antioche dies 'par juste vengeance de Dieu' (f. *6^r), but this is hardly substantiated in the action. In the final act Justice declares as she strikes Antioche down that he is punished for his crimes, but there is no indication that she represents divine justice: she speaks as a pagan and never refers to God's will. The action is set in motion by Megere, not an angel. The characters speak in pagan terms; even the persecuted Jews interpret their sufferings as an instance of the mutability of fortune. That God's will controls events is suggested only once, briefly, in a prayer spoken by Eleazar before he is killed for his Jewish beliefs. Rather than confining himself to the exemplary episode of Antioche's persecution of the Jews and his punishment, Le Francq included his campaign against Ptolomé; evidently he was not concerned with divine justice, but wished to show the whole of his subject's career. In proper humanist fashion there is a chorus at the end of each act and the characters philosophise about general issues, but Le Francq simply reproduced the humanist forms without appreciating their utility for endowing the action with a religious or any other significance. *Antioche* is in fact simply a pagan spectacular of the subject's career.

The technique of recounting the subject's career was combined with celebration of an individual deed of the saint in *Richecourt, tragecomedie* (Nancy 1628).[21] The play was written to be performed in the Benedictine school of Saint-Nicolas-de-Port and celebrates Nicolas, the local patron, by recalling the miracle associating him with the town; like Soret's *Election divine*, it refrains from presenting the whole of the saint's career. The miracle occurs, however, only in the last act: the bulk of the action concerns the *faits et gestes* of Richecourt, a French general, during one of the Crusades.[22] The extensive narrative includes scenes in the Turkish and Christian camps and a battle, after which the Christians are welcomed into Heaven while Alecto carries off the Turkish dead to Hell. Besides Alecto, Nemesis, Pax and Mors intervene, speaking Latin: together they govern events so as to punish men justly yet mercifully for their sins. The instructive element is reinforced by a Chorus. With this commentary the account of Richecourt's deeds provides a wealth of instruction as well as spectacle, to which the final act adds local pride and piety. The author naturally adopted as his form the loosely articulated narrative, which enabled him to combine pedagogy with celebration of the local saint.

Etienne Grandjean apparently took the more usual course of recalling the whole of the martyr's career in his *Tragédie du martyre et mort de S. Sébastien*, which was performed at Plombières on 1 May 1628 and printed that year at Nancy. Unfortunately, I have been unable to examine a copy; according to Busson[23] and Lebègue[24] the play was in five acts, with choruses, stichomythia and the other features of the humanist style. It was unusual in not showing the martyrdom on the stage, but followed custom in presenting the saint as exempt from doubt; its religious content consisted of a long sermon delivered by Sébastien and the spectacle of his miracles. Another lost saint-play from the same time seems, like *Richecourt*, to have concerned only a single miracle: *Bacqueville delivré de prison et de mort par S Julien*, performed on 26 August 1630 in the College at Ath, but never printed.[25] The principal miracles of the saint's earthly career are the subject of the *Tragicomédie de S. Rémy* written in 1631 by Jean de Fies, the curé of Huy (the home of Denis Coppée), which survives in manuscript.[26] This provides an episodic and symbolic account of the story, in which the characters stand for the audience's beliefs; roles are included for God and a chorus. The technique of the *mystère* still retained some vitality.

The comprehensive chronicle of the saintly career was chosen by Pierre Troterel for a second sacred play, *La Vie et sainte conversion de Guillaume Duc d'Aquitaine* (Rouen 1632). Since the play has not previously been described,[27] I shall summarise it at some length.

The action is opened by Asmodée, demon de concupiscence, who declares his intention of tempting Guillaume. Guillaume reflects on the power of love, which he struggles briefly to resist before resolving to discard other obligations in its pursuit. Dorotée, the wife of his brother, expresses the anxiety aroused by her husband's absence. Guillaume approaches, having been encouraged in his passion by his gentlemen, and speaks of love. When she refuses to acquiesce in adulterous incest, he drags her off, promising to use force; the Gentilshommes restrain her ladies from attempting to rescue her.[28]

In act II Valerian, a courtier, makes up his mind to take the Duke to task for raping his brother's wife. When Guillaume enters he is astonished to be criticised: he beats and banishes Valerian, who is left reflecting on the unwillingness of Princes to accept well-meant advice. Dorotée bewails her fate. Guillaume attempts to comfort her, swearing that his love is genuine and offering marriage, but she is not to be reconciled to her life as his prisoner. Valerian, in a soliloquy, rejoices to be leaving the court for rustic solitude.

In the third act the Conseil warns the Duke that he ought to recognise Innocent rather than Anaclet as Pope: Anaclet is too distant to lend military support, and Bernard has declared for Innocent. Disagreeing, Guillaume ejects the Conseil, but decides to consult Bernard out of curiosity. Saint Bernard is shown praying God to enlighten the vicious Duke. Aristarche, the Duke's brother, laments that he is powerless against Guillaume, who is in addition deaf to all appeals based on honour. However, he has hopes of releasing Dorotée, having bribed one of her gaolers, and is waiting outside the castle. They talk through a window: she asks timidly if he still loves her in her dishonoured state, and receives fervent reassurance. Realising that the bribed gaoler has not come as promised to free her, she urges Aristarche to wait for another opportunity; he, however, leads his retainers in an assault on the castle, desisting only when wounded in the skirmish. Saint Bernard rejoices that the Duke has recognised Innocent. Dorotée resolves to endure patiently. Guillaume marvels at his conversion, which he attributes to Bernard's miraculous intervention, and resolves to reform; seeing Dorotée approach, he falls to his knees and begs her forgiveness. Though astonished, she pardons him, then leaves, rejoicing, to rejoin her husband.

In act iv the Duke, having divested himself of his wealth, consults a hermit over further atoning for his sins. The hermit instructs him always to wear armour as a penance, and to make his way to Rome as a beggar to obtain absolution from the Pope. The Duke's Conseil and his Gentilshommes agree that the latter should search for their absent ruler. Asmodée fears that he is losing his victim: assuming a disguise, he offers to help the Gentilshommes in their attempt to lead Guillaume back to his worldly cares. They accept, not noticing the *double entendres* about his identity that Asmodée addresses to the audience.

Opening the last act, Guillaume rejoices that he has now lived for nine years since obtaining absolution in mortification and solitude in the Holy Land. The Gentilshommes find him and urge him to return to his responsibilities; he refuses, then in the face of their persistence promises them an answer next day, revealing in an aside that he intends to give them the slip overnight. In Italy, soldiers bemoan their lack of progress in the siege of Lucca. Guillaume decides that he has done penance long enough and offers to help them, casting aside the hair shirt he has worn under his armour; he goes blind on the instant. Recognising a divine warning he prays for forgiveness and recovers his sight; he resolves to return to solitude and mortification. Reinald decides that he will seek out Guillaume as his spiritual director. In his forest retreat Guillaume rejoices in solitude, then realising that its pleasures are a temptation redoubles his mortifications; the demons howl with disappointment. Asmodée, disguised as Guillaume's father, urges him to resume his responsibilities at home; Guillaume is not deceived by the apparition. The demons beat him, but are driven off when he prays to Christ and the Virgin; two saints, who explain that they were sent by the Virgin, heal his wounds and encourage him. He accepts Albert as a disciple. Thwarted where Guillaume is concerned, Asmodée resolves not to let the Gentilshommes escape. The demons, disguised as nymphs, attempt to seduce the knights; one succumbs, but is rescued by his companions. The demons attack again, in the guise first of giants then of a dragon, but are beaten off. The Gentilshommes disregard a voice warning them to leave the forest, recognising it as a devilish trick, and are similarly undeterred when the trees burst into flame. They press on with their quest for Guillaume in his forest retreat. Meeting Reinald, they ask for directions, mentioning that their search has lasted fourteen years; Guillaume bids him to allow the armed throng to approach, since God will overturn their purpose. On seeing Guillaume, the Gentilshommes resolve to leave the world, repenting for their sins, and live as hermits under Guillaume's guidance; the latter welcomes them and assures them that Christ will forgive them if they are truly penitent.

Guillaume d'Aquitaine recalls the earlier *mystères* both by its epic scale and by the dramatic principle at work. The play is a little more economical than the *mystères* in omitting some transitional scenes and requiring the audience to assume that certain incidents, such as Guillaume's meetings with Bernard and the Pope, have occurred without being shown on the stage; but no important character or spectacular event is neglected in the presentation of the key episodes of the saint's career. As in the *mystères*, the manner of presentation requires the spectator to possess some prior knowledge: incidental figures make their appearance without introduction, and the transitions, though eased by the system of simultaneous setting, are too swift for ready comprehension without some acquaintance with the legend.[29] The stage world is not self-sufficient, but exists as a projection of the spectators' beliefs. The human characters are scarcely less symbolic than the supernatural figures, the saints and demons; the latter are indicated only in the scenes in which they speak, but were perhaps present on the stage throughout the performance to add a commentary on the significance of every incident in pantomime. Characterisation is naturally unimportant: even the exchanges between Guillaume and Dorotée are stilted and give no impression of human feeling or personality, for this was irrelevant to Troterel's theme. Individuals are quickly forgotten once they have served their turn in the account of the prodigies of the saint's career.

In *Sainte Agnes* Troterel had attempted to create a human drama out of the martyrdom; by comparison, his choice of form for the later play seems like a backward step. Troterel, however, knew nothing of Corneille and Racine, and did not think of classicism as the inevitable way forward. Whatever subsequent history might decide, he saw no reason to discard the symbolic narrative as a method of presenting an image of the spectators' faith on the stage. By making a greater call on the spectators' participation, *Guillaume d'Aquitaine* offers a more compelling spectacle than the apparently more advanced *Sainte Agnes*. It must be recognised, however, that Troterel did not use his chosen form to the best effect. His poetry has little evocative power, and the presentation of miracles is mechanical rather than reverent. There is a considerable concentration on the mechanics of the story, and much material is included principally for its spectacular possibilities. Although there is a climactic movement as the miracles pile up in the last act and the obstacles to Guillaume's salvation are removed, there is little sense that providence is imposing a shape on events. The effect of the whole is pedestrian rather than inspirational.

The saint's career, from conversion to martyrdom, was also the subject of a *Tragedie sur la vie et martyre de S. Eustache* (Liège 1632) by Pierre Bello of Dinant. Placide, a general, is hunting when he sees a stag bearing a cross in its horns and hears a voice ordering him to be baptised: on his return home he obeys, with his wife and children, taking the name Eustache. In act II Belzebub enlists a witch to torment the convert: his livestock and servants die of plague. Ruined, Eustache decides to live abroad in obscurity, but in the third act his wife is kidnapped by the sailors who gave them passage and his two sons are carried off by a wolf and a lion. Eustache echoes Job in his lamentation. Fifteen years later, the Emperor sends messengers to find Placide, whose prowess as a general is needed to crush a revolt of the Parthians. In act IV Placide or Eustache routs the rebels. Among his troops are his two sons, who were rescued by peasants from the beasts; when they meet and exchange life-histories they recognise each other, and are overheard by their mother, who was also preserved when her ravisher was miraculously killed. She dare not make herself known, but in act V she begs the general to be allowed to accompany the army back to Rome. The general recognises his wife, who tells him that their sons are in his army: all four are reunited. They return to Rome, where the Emperor wishes to offer thanks to the gods for his victory, but

Eustache identifies himself as a Christian and refuses to participate. He and his family are thrown to the lions, but the beasts lick them affectionately. The four Christians are then martyred in a bronze bull.[30] Their bodies are untouched by the flames; the soldier who discovers this miracle is converted. An angel exhorts the audience to imitate the courage of Eustache and his family.

To celebrate his saint Bello adopted the method which had been conventional since the time of the *mystères*, a narrative of the whole of the career of the martyr, giving large roles to all the figures connected with him. Long scenes are devoted to Eustache's farm-hands and the Emperor. These are used as opportunities for airing commonplaces, in the humanist manner: the Emperor debates rigour and clemency with his court, and the peasants discuss *aurea mediocritas*. Even the Parthian general is introduced for one scene, to provide the opportunity for a tirade urging the soldiers to conquer or die. The action is divided into acts and scenes, though somewhat arbitrarily; act III contains a leap of fifteen years. It is further embellished with a Chorus, which reflects on events as instances of the mutability of fortune. However, despite these neo-classical ornaments, the play is simply conceived as a narrative celebrating the prodigies and exemplary steadfastness that composed the career of the saint.[31]

Bello's play exemplifies the common weakness of the sacred theatre of this time: despite the introduction of spectacular elements and the use of the humanist ornaments, *S. Eustache* is fundamentally a rather pedestrian and unimaginative narrative of a series of events. What is lacking is the creative reorganisation of the simple series of occurrences which would endow the story with shape and meaning. It is clearly not the case that the dramatic technique did not exist for endowing events with significance: there were indeed several such techniques available but Bello was not able to exploit them so as to make his simple story impress the audience with its own import. In this weakness of the creative imagination Bello was representative of his generation of sacred dramatists.

The two plays published in Paris in this period and apparently intended for or at least influenced by the professional theatre, the *Perfidie d'Aman* and Poytevin's *Saincte Catherine*, were rather crude and sensational affairs, in which the authors exploited the sacred material principally for exciting plots. Outside the capital, tastes were more restrained; once the interruption caused by the religious wars was over, the ancient practice was quickly resumed of doing honour to God through a chronicle of the miracles He performed by the agency of a saint, or recalling a particular miracle connected with the time or place of the performance. The seventeenth-century chronicles, however, besides differing in form from the *mystères*, being divided now into acts and sometimes featuring a chorus, though these were often meaningless formalities, differed fundamentally from those earlier narratives in not presenting the story in such a way as to be comprehensible only to the eye of faith, with the exception of Troterel's *Guillaume d'Aquitaine*. They differed similarly from the humanist plays in not requiring the participation of an analytical mind to make sense of the example. In the new chronicles the figures do not present themselves as seen by the spectator, and plot and character follow their own internal logic. In the absence of the devices used in the previous century to transmit the meaning and importance of the events shown, some of the chronicles give the impression that simply putting the saint and his deeds on the stage was *ipso facto* sufficient as an act of literary and religious significance. The chronicle plays contained little indication of why the story is important to the audience: this is something the spectator has to supply from his own religious knowledge.

The tendency towards abandoning a symbolic approach in favour of a more straightforward presentation of events was taken further by one or two authors, most notably Troterel in his *Sainte Agnes*. Troterel here combined the account of events in the plot with some impression of the characters' emotions, and explored how the interactions of passions, personalities and incidents could cause a chain of events and what these occurrences meant to those involved. In this case the emotions in question hardly included religion and the martyr remains unmoved in the eye of the storm; but this approach was capable of being highly successful as a means of injecting shape and meaning into the series of incidents. This success, however, was seen mostly in the secular theatre; the pious dramatists hardly adopted this style before 1635. The majority of the pious dramatists preferred to present chronicles of sacred history, and did not seek systematically to address the spectator's sympathetic emotions. In this they may seem backward compared to Troterel in *Sainte Agnes*, but for their purpose of recalling the miracles God had performed in history, a study of psychology would not necessarily have been the most suitable approach. It was apparently hardly possible, however, to continue to use the symbolic narrative of earlier times, thanks perhaps to the influence of the new dramatic style with its emphasis on logic of plot and character. The pious dramatists continued to present the episodes demonstrating God's benevolence, but they no longer possessed a technique for making the importance of these events for later generations clear to the audience.

8. The early Classical period

The secular theatre meanwhile had been undergoing a revolution which was hardly reflected in the sacred plays until it was almost complete. The growing interest in a drama of emotion culminated in 1634 in the performance of 'the first genuinely classical French tragedy',[1] Mairet's *Sophonisbe*. In certain aspects of form, notably the use of the unities, the new style did not differ greatly from the version of classicism developed by the humanists, but it differed completely from the earlier drama in content and intended effect. As Professor Stone has said of the humanists, 'the moral purpose, not the development of character and plot occupied the playwrights',[2] whereas for Mairet and his generation character and plot were precisely the elements on which the success of the play depended. Explicit didacticism was abandoned:[3] the performance offered emotional transport rather than material for reflection. This is the point at which I must attempt to define more closely the nature of this transformation in the conception of the play.

The dramatists of course continued to claim to provide moral edification but argued now that it derived from the realistic presentation of events and persons: for Corneille, edification derived from

la naïve peinture des vices et des vertus, qui ne manque jamais à faire son effet, quand elle est bien achevée, et que les traits en sont si reconnaissables qu'on ne les peut confondre l'un dans l'autre, ni prendre le vice pour vertu. Celle-ci se fait alors toujours aimer, quoique malheureuse, et celui-là se fait toujours haïr, bien que triomphant. Les anciens se sont fort souvent contentés de cette peinture, sans se mettre en peine de faire récompenser les bonnes actions, et punir les mauvaises.[4]

Corneille had found that a 'naïve peinture' of human behaviour without obvious condemnation of vice or praise of virtue appealed to his audience, and in claiming moral utility was perhaps seeking to rationalise a practice he favoured simply because it was successful, but he would not have appealed to moral utility had he thought his readers

would reject the argument; its apparent flimsiness indicates his confidence that his contemporaries would agree that a 'naïve' or realistic[5]
depiction of behaviour was edifying. Certainly Chapelain attributed
moral value to *vraisemblance*:

comme je tombe d'accord avec vous que le but principal de toute représentation scénique est d'émouvoir l'âme du spectateur par la force et l'évidence
avec laquelle les diverses passions sont exprimées sur le théâtre, et de la
purger par ce moyen des mauvaises habitudes qui la pourraient faire tomber
dans les mêmes inconvénients que ces passions tirent aprés soi, je ne saurais
avouer aussi que cette énergie se puisse produire sur le théâtre si elle n'est
accompagnée et soutenue de la vraisemblance...[6]

Where the humanists had subordinated everything to the illustration of
a theme, Corneille and his contemporaries felt obliged first and foremost to present a realistic account of the world. What aims the new
convention of *vraisemblance* was intended to achieve will emerge in the
next few paragraphs.

An evolution of taste towards realism occurred throughout Europe
during the Renaissance, affecting all forms of art; it triumphed particularly in the pictorial arts with the refinement of the technique of
perspective drawing, a development with important consequences in
the theatre. The origins of such an upheaval in the taste of the con-
tinent are beyond my present scope. As far as the French theatre is
concerned, scholars have shown that the new spirit manifested itself
by adopting the Italian technique of setting the action in a scene
painted in perspective,[7] and that it drew on the realistic tradition of
the neo-Latin *comoedia*,[8] but the reasons for the transfer of preference
to a realistic matter and manner have yet to be satisfactorily explained.
The fullest account is the recent attempt by Professor Stone.[9] Here I
shall be concerned principally with the symptoms and effects of the
new taste rather than its antecedents.

The preference for realism was obvious in the physical aspect of the
stage. The presentation of the *mystères* with *mansions* representing all
the locations spread across the back of the platform throughout the
performance had been far from realistic, for a set a few feet wide
would stand for a city and locations at opposite ends of the earth
would be juxtaposed; but the system possessed great flexibility and
remained in favour as long as the chronicles were performed. The
scenery of the humanist plays, improvised in college halls, was probably rudimentary and symbolic, as no doubt was that used by the
touring troupes. The professional stage-designers of the seventeenth
century, however, adopted the technique first perfected in Italy of
building scenes of foreshortened three-dimensional sets or later of
painted flats, which in the slight depth of the stage created the pictorial

illusion of streets or landscape receding into the far distance.[10] 'Pour
le théâtre néo-classique, tel qu'il s'était élaboré en Italie à l'époque
de la Renaissance, la convention fondamentale, et par où il s'opposait
au théâtre du Moyen Age ou au théâtre élisabéthain, c'est le parti pris
de réalisme illusioniste dans la représentation des choses.'[11] The ideal
now was a perfect illusion of reality.

In fact, the tableau was far from realistic. The limitation lay not so
much in the stage-designers' technique, which could produce storms,
fires and flying with sufficient realism to convince the audiences,[12] as
in the requirement placed on them to present improbable and pro-
digious events. Moreover, until the absolute unity of place was adopted
towards the middle of the century, plays frequently required several
locations. The set was not changed to show each successively: as in
the Middle Ages, each was represented by a *mansion* standing on the
stage beside the others throughout the performance.[13] The difference
was that the *mansions* were now united into a single perspective.
Locations miles apart were dragged into one composite scene:[14] this
presented the appearance of reality, but what it showed could not
possibly exist. Eventually the illusionistic technique perfected by the
Italians was applied to creating the wholly fanciful worlds of the
machine-plays: the stage presented the realistic illusion of the totally
unreal. The artifice of the designer was appreciated no less than the
illusion: 'un plaisir d'illusion parfaite et pourtant un plaisir d'art, telle
est bien, en effet, la double exigence que le spectateur du temps apporte
au théâtre'.[15] The realism of the tableau depended on convention no
less than the symbolic *mansions* of the *mystères*: by convention, the
scene in perspective was treated as real. Quite how literally it was
considered real emerges from contemporary critical opinion. Writing
in the 1640s, d'Aubignac asserted that it is

contraire à la vray-semblance, qu'une même espace et même sol, qui ne
reçoivent aucun changement, representent en même temps deux lieux differens,
par exemple la France et le Dannemarc, la Gallerie du Palais et les
Thuilleries.[16]

Since the stage is visibly one location, it cannot represent two; since the
audience observes it for three hours, the action cannot take longer.
The stage world may not deviate from the spectator's own experience
of time and space during the performance, or the illusion will be
broken:

Je sçay bien que le Theatre est une espece d'illusion, mais il faut tromper les
Spectateurs en telle sorte, qu'ils ne s'imaginent pas l'estre, encore qu'ils le
sçachent; il ne faut pas tandis qu'on les trompe, que leur esprit le connoisse;
mais seulement quand il y fait reflexion...[17]

While the artificiality of the illusion was appreciated, nothing must prevent the spectator believing in it as real.[18]

Realism was required equally in the play's substance, its plot and characters. That it is useful at all to consider these features is a measure of the distance between the humanist and Classical techniques. Schérer's assumptions in studying *La Dramaturgie classique en France*[19] reveal the new values. Considering *Polyeucte*, he remarks: 'une fois que le héros s'est procamé chrétien, la tragédie ne résulte que des heurts des volontés naturelles des personnages' (p. 89). For the humanists it was inconceivable that tragedy should originate in the clashes of men's wills: it derived from the revelation of the action of the divine will or fate, and the role of the characters was not to exercise their wills but to endure and comment. The seventeenth century, on the other hand, found tragic significance and dramatic interest in the sentiments and activities of men. Describing the use of the peripeteia, Schérer observes: 'Bien plus intéressantes seront les pièces où la péripétie demandera au héros un effort supplémentaire et permettra à l'auteur de creuser davantage la psychologie de ses personnages' (p. 90). Where the humanists arranged the plot to reveal the divine action and allow several characters to comment, Schérer's natural assumption is that the Classical dramatist disposed it so as to permit an investigation of his characters' psychology. Listing the qualities required in the hero, Schérer adds: 'Le charme des héros, pour un spectateur du XVIIe siècle, est fait d'un dernier élément: ces héros sont malheureux' (p. 22). This too would have been unthinkable earlier: Sedecie or Saül may be 'malheureux', but the desired effect was to provoke the spectator to reflection, not to charm him.

The basis of the requirement for realism was that the characters should be presented as people with whom the spectator can sympathise. Ideally, the work of playwright, stage-designer and actor converged to create the illusion of a real action involving real people in a real location. Chapelain concurred with d'Aubignac in insisting that nothing must break the illusion: the playwright should seek to 'ôter aux regardants toutes les occasions de faire réflexion sur ce qu'ils voient et de douter de sa réalité', so as to 'obliger l'esprit par toutes voies à se croire présent à un véritable événement at à vêtir par force dans le faux les mouvements que le vrai même lui eût pu donner'.[20]

Je pose donc pour fondement que l'imitation en tous poèmes doit être si parfaite qu'il ne paraisse aucune différence entre la chose imitée et celle qui imite, car le principal effet de celle-ci consiste à proposer à l'esprit, pour le purger de ses passions déréglées, les objets comme vrais et comme présents; chose qui, régnant par tous les genres de poésie, semble particulièrement encore regarder la scénique en laquelle on ne cache la personne du poète que pour mieux

surprendre l'imagination du spectateur et pour le mieux conduire sans obstacle
à la créance que l'on veut qu'il prenne en ce qui lui est représenté.[21]

The demands for a realistic set, plausible plot and profound characterisation converge on this point: ideally there should be no obstacle
to the spectator's identifying imaginatively and emotionally with the
actions and characters presented before him.[22] La Mesnardière likewise
emphasised that the dramatist's aim is to move the spectator: 'les
Troubles de l'Ame', he declared, are 'la première beauté de la Poësie
Dramatique', and 'la glorie du Poëte consiste à renverser toute une
ame par les mouvemens invincibles que son discours excite en elle'.[23] He
summed up the total effect to which the dramatic production must aim:

étant certain que le Poëte doit tendre principalement à émouvoir la Pitié, il
faut qu'il écrive des choses qui touchent extrêmement, et que l'Acteur les anime
par une expression réele de gemmissemens et de pleurs dans les endroits où
ils sont propres, s'il veut que le Spectateur le récompense par des larmes, qui
sont le plus noble salaire que demande la Tragedie.[24]

Such a recommendation that the actor should identify with his role,
which La Mesnardière extended by insisting also that the author must
share the emotions he depicts,[25] would have been quite irrelevant on
the humanist stage. La Mesnardière's principle was that 'le mouvement
des passions doit estre le premier objet de l'Ecrivain Dramatique';[26]
from this his other requirements, such as *vraisemblance*, followed.
Rapin too gave paramount importance to emotional impact: 'on ne
reconnoist la véritable poésie que par l'impression qu'elle fait sur l'âme:
elle n'est point comme il faut si elle ne va au coeur'.[27] The pleasure of
tragedy

consiste dans l'agitation de l'ame émeue par les passions. La tragédie ne
devient agréable au spectateur, que parce qu'il devient luy-mesme sensible à
tout ce qu'on luy représente, qu'il entre dans tous les différens sentimens des
acteurs, qu'il s'intéresse dans tous leurs avantures, qu'il craint, et qu'il espère,
qu'il s'afflige, et qu'il se réjouit avec eux. Le théâtre est froid et languissant,
dès qu'il cesse de produire ces mouvemens dans l'âme de ceux qui y assistent.[28]

Whereas the humanist play by its conscious artificialities encouraged
the spectator to stand back and judge the action as an *exemplum*,
things were now so arranged that he must become emotionally
involved if he was to profit from the experience. The difference in expectations has been explained by Nadal as a dereliction of the 'sacré' in
favour of the 'humain':

Ce qui me frappe dans ces trente premières années du [xviie] siècle, c'est sur
la scène la désaffection puis l'abandon du sacré; jusque-là, presque toutes les
productions de la Renaissance en étaient marquées. En même temps, un
caractère de nature entièrement différent se prononce: l'acte dramatique est

saisi au coeur même de l'homme. Certes il n'y a pas dévalorisation du mystère; mais celui-ci est autrement situé. Retiré aux forces surnaturelles, dieux ou Dieu, destin ou grâce, il fait retour à la nature humaine. Le ciel oublié, la scène s'allège de ses bontés ou de ses menaces. Dans la securité, les personnages ne parlent plus qu'à leur propre coeur; dans le péril, ils n'en appellent qu'à eux-mêmes. On voit alors succéder au lyrisme de l'immobile déploration, aux infortunes illustres broyées dans le poing de l'Inexorable, les modèles d'un tragique ou d'un comique, fondés sur une dynamique et une politique purement humaines.[29]

This is not to say, of course, that there were suddenly no more religious plays, but the focus of interest had shifted away from what the action taught about metaphysics and onto what it felt like to be in the position of the hero: the spectator did not wish now to be instructed but to be moved, and he sought drama and tragic significance, not in the relationship between the human and the divine, but in the tensions between men and within them. Accordingly, the method of constructing the play changed. For the spectator of the Classical period the essence of the plot, in distinction to the humanist practice, was that it should advance rapidly and inexorably, precipitating the characters to their ruin; by the pressure of the approaching disaster the dramatists encouraged identification with the characters' emotions and circumstances. For the same reason they limited the action to the catastrophe and the moment immediately preceding, and cultivated sudden reverses and the dilemma. The plot was no longer conceived as an example, but designed to reveal the characters' emotions and give the spectator the thrill of vicarious experience.

   Corneille, Chapelain, d'Aubignac and La Mesnardière asserted that the purpose of *vraisemblance* was moral improvement, since it enabled the spectator to purge himself of the passions he witnessed, but at the extreme development of the concern with real emotions, 'representation of the surfaces of life is seen as desirable in itself':[30] the difficulty in such a system was to impart significance to the action. Its principles required the spectator to surrender himself to the play and abandon his capacity to reflect on it, as d'Aubignac and Chapelain both insisted. It was all too easy for tragedy founded on the play of emotions to slip into sentimentality devoid of significance. La Bruyère seems to have been thinking of this danger when he explained how tragedy should stir the emotions:

Le poëme tragique vous serre le coeur dès son commencement, vous laisse à peine dans tout son progrès la liberté de respirer et le temps de vous remettre, ou s'il vous donne quelque relâche, c'est pour vous replonger dans de nouveaux abîmes et dans de nouvelles alarmes. Il vous conduit à la terreur par la pitié, ou réciproquement à la pitié par le terrible, vous mène par les larmes, par les sanglots, par l'incertitude, par l'esperance, par la crainte, par les surprises et par l'horreur jusqu'à la catastrophe. Ce n'est donc pas un tissu de jolis sentiments, de déclarations tendres, de portraits agréables, de mots *doucereux*, ou quelquefois assez plaisants pour faire rire, suivi à la vérité d'une dernière scène où les mutins n'entendent aucune raison, et où, par bienséance, il y a enfin du sang répandu, et quelque malheureux à qui il en coûte la vie.[31]

The facile sentimentality of which La Bruyère complained was one direction in which the Classical style had been capable of developing from the beginning. Denied explicit didacticism, the dramatist had to convey his insight into the way men provoke disaster by suggestion; it was easy in this system to create exciting plots, striking characters, strong emotions, without a glimpse of the universal laws animating the whole. Saint-Evremond shared La Bruyère's distaste for an undemanding drama of sentiments. In a spirited defence of Corneille, he pretended to renounce his previous conception of tragedy, and ironically declared himself to have been mistaken when

J'ai soûtenu que pour faire une belle Comédie, il faloit choisir un beau sujet, le bien disposer, le bien suivre, et le mener naturellement à sa fin; qu'il faloit faire entrer les Caractéres dans les sujets, et non pas former la constitution des sujets après celle des Caractéres; que nos actions devoient précéder nos qualités et nos humeurs; qu'il faloit remettre à la Philosophie de nous faire connoître ce que sont les hommes, et à la Comédie de nous faire voir ce qu'ils font; et qu'enfin ce n'est pas tant la nature humaine qu'il faut expliquer, que la condition humaine qu'il faut représenter sur le Théatre.[32]

With the same irony, he denounced the old fashion: 'il y a eu des tems où il faloit choisir de beaux sujets, et les bien traiter; il ne faut plus aujourd'hui que des Caractéres'.[33] Thinking principally of Racine, his complaint was that tragedy had been reduced to character-drawing instead of containing a 'sujet'; sentiment (only a part of the total effect) had taken precedence over construction. His complaint is perhaps not totally remote from Artaud's desire, expressed in his manifesto for the theatre of cruelty, to escape from portraying 'l'homme psychologique'.[34]

In the last quarter of the seventeenth century, La Bruyère and Saint-Evremond concurred in regretting that French Classical tragedy had degenerated into providing facile emotions and character-portraits; but this tendency had been inherent from the beginning of the genre's existence. A recent study has offered a definition of 'la tragédie classique',

telle qu'elle est, et telle que l'ont voulue les dramaturges habités par un authentique instinct du théâtre: des pièces passionantes par leurs intrigues, impressionantes par leurs acteurs, émouvantes par leurs drames d'amour, et, de plus, largement politiques.[35]

The definition is significant for what it omits: any notion that these exciting elements might provide some contact with the metaphysical or anything else beyond the immediate thrill.

The sacred theatre had long been neglected in Paris, or at least, no record survives of performances; towards the end of the 1630s the genre suddenly returned. Given that the sacred theatre had remained popular elsewhere, an explanation must be sought for its ever having been neglected rather than for its return to the capital. One reason was that the Parisian theatre was by now a professional theatre, and while in Paris the professional troupes apparently did not regale their audiences with sacred plays, fearing no doubt to lose money; if any such plays were performed, they did not find their way into print.[36] The texts which have reached us from the early part of Louis XIII's reign were composed for amateur performances in the provinces, where the tradition continued of celebrating feast-days with sacred plays; in Paris the feasts were apparently not marked in this way, following the prohibition of the *mystères* which had been used for such festivities. As soon as the professional actors were shown that a sacred play could yield a profit in Paris, they adopted the national custom of performing them and plays were speedily written and printed satisfying this new demand.[37]

The trail to success in the emerging fashionable theatre was blazed at the Marais in 1636 by a play concerning the ancient Jews: Tristan l'Hermite's *Mariane, tragedie*.[38] Tristan explained that he was attracted to the subject by its combination of passions which seemed especially suited to the stage:

j'ay seulement voulu descrire avec un peu de bien-seance, les divers sentiments d'un Tyran courageux et spirituel, les artifices d'une femme envieuse et vindicative, et la constance d'une reine dont la vertu meritoit un plus favorable destin: Et j'ay dépeint tout cela de la manière que j'ay creu pouvoir mieux reüssir dans la perspective du Theatre...   (Advertissement, ll. 19–26)

Unlike the dramatists of the previous generation, he said nothing of the play's exemplifying divine justice. Tristan concentrated on the emotions of his characters, and gave considerable space to figures and events strictly superfluous to the main action, such as Salome's plotting against Mariane, so as to add scenes of conflict and enhance the emotional richness of the play. The action is psychological: Tristan traces the process by which Hérode's frustration at Mariane's defiant refusal to return his love is goaded by her into a murderous rage which he instantly repents. Hérode finally attains the tragic appreciation of his own role in provoking the disaster and of his wife's innocence of the crime for which he imagined he was punishing her. The characters' emotions are not simply the opportunity for vivid speeches, as in many

works of the beginning of the century: they are the very substance of
the play, which centres on the tragic insight into the way men destroy
their own happiness by pursuing it blindly. Few of the sacred plays
which followed Tristan's masterpiece succeeded to a similar degree in
endowing the emotions that they explored with larger significance or
even with such intensity.

Mariane was not strictly a sacred play, since the subject derived
from Josephus rather than the Bible, and in any case Tristan treated
it like any other historical material; but once he had shown that a
piece on such a subject could succeed others were quick to follow with
sacred dramas. Balthazar Baro, as the author of the last books of the
Astrée, an *habitué* of the salons and an Académicien, was the first
writer of any consequence in the world to produce a sacred play since
the courtier Billard. He consecrated the restored social acceptability of
the genre with *Sainct Eustache martyr, Poeme dramatique* (Paris 1649),
which was probably first performed in 1637.[39] This was the first saint-
play produced by the capital since the publication there of Poytevin's
Saincte Catherine in 1619.

Baro preferred the traditional method of presenting the saint: he
recounted the major episodes of his career from conversion to martyrdom.[40] He did something to reduce the subject to the unities by neglecting to mention that legend places much of the action in Egypt and by
setting it all in the environs of Rome. The result was still far from
regular, as Baro confessed:

Cher Lecteur, Je ne te donne pas ce Poëme comme une piece de Theatre où
toutes les regles seroient observées. Le sujet ne s'y pouvant accommoder, c'est
sans doute que je n'y aurois point travaillé si je n'y avois esté forcé par une
autorité souveraine.
                                        (Advertissement, f. ã4r)

But for the insistence of the same 'authorité',[41] he would not have
dared publish. By 1649 Baro had become ashamed of his play for its
irregularity but, despite his claimed lack of enthusiasm, there had been
much romantic material in the subject to attract the disciple of d'Urfé.

Throughout the vicissitudes of his life Eustache demonstrates perfect
steadfastness. When he is ruined, his wife complains that they have
done nothing to deserve God's wrath. Eustache explains patiently:

Ma chere Teopiste il faut que je confesse
Que je plains moins encor ton mal que ta foiblesse,
Tu murmures à tort, et resistes en vain
Aux decrets merveilleux d'un Juge souverain,
Si le coupable rit, et l'innocent souspire,
Si l'un monte aux honneurs quand l'autre s'en retire,
Si l'un a dans sa gloire autant d'adorateurs
Que l'autre dans sa honte a de persecuteurs,

> Dieu pour authoriser ces effects admirables
> Se forme des raisons qui sont impenetrables,
> Nous trouvans donc reduits aux termes d'endurer,
> Nous devons obeïr, et non pas murmurer.   (ii ii, pp. 23–4)

This faith that all God's actions are just sustains Eustache after the loss of his wife and children. He briefly wishes that death would release him, but quickly recollects that

> Dieu seul me peut donner quelque soulagement,
> Et qui cherche ailleurs manque de jugement.   (ii iii, p. 31)

God does indeed console Eustache when he retreats into rustic calm. At the end, Eustache welcomes martyrdom as the path to Heaven; watching his wife and children cast themselves into the burning bull, his only reaction is envy while he waits for his turn.

Teopiste has more difficulty in sustaining her faith, and on occasion needs Eustache's support. Even at the end she urges him to abandon his creed so as to escape martyrdom; but grace shows her her error, and she embraces God's will gladly:

> Juste Dieu c'en est fait, je cede, je me rends,
> La foiblesse du sexe a fait ma resistance,
> Pardonne à mes defauts ce defaut de constance,
> Pour estouffer l'ennuy qui me vient devorer,
> C'est ta seule bonté que je dois implorer,
> Vien donc à mon secours, c'est en toy que j'espere,
> Quitte le nom de Juge, et prends celuy de pere
> Et donne-moy la gloire avecque le plaisir,
> De seconder Placide dans son juste desir.   (v iv, p. 83)

She shows Eustache the example by casting herself first into the bull.

Thanks to her struggle to welcome God's will, Teopiste attracts more sympathy than her husband. The attention Baro gave to such episodes as the reuniting of the family, which occupies the whole of act iv, indicates that he wrote in accordance with the Classical taste, which valued a play principally for the emotions it contained and induced. He clearly thought it unseemly, however, to endow the saint with any great anguish. Baro fell into a trap which the Classical system offered to dramatists with a simple piety: if the saint was to be as nearly as possible impassive, dramatic interest would inevitably centre on some figure other than the supposed protagonist.

In any case, while Baro sought his dramatic effects through the emotional life of the characters, he constructed his play by the traditional technique: as in the earlier chronicles, the action is so laden with incidents and secondary figures that there is little opportunity to develop the protagonists' psychology. By his fidelity to the traditional form, Baro denied his play the emotional impact he clearly sought.

However, the play is not a reverent chronicle of the saint's acts. Baro omitted a number of miracles recorded in the legend,[42] while emphasising its spectacular content. Eustache's sons are carried off by wild beasts and his wife's ravisher is struck by lightning on the stage. There is a great variety of mood and incident; even comedy intervenes when two courtiers fail to recognise the former general in his peasant garb. Baro's handling of the subject was perhaps directed less by piety than by a desire to extract a sensational and romantic plot.

While the Parisian theatre tended to seek secular sensation in sacred material, events in Switzerland inspired a play which returned to preoccupations familiar during the French religious wars. The fighting in the Grisons during the Thirty Years War[43] provoked a schoolmaster, Jean Vallin, to meditate on God's punishment of the nation's sins in *Israel affligé, ou tragecomedie sur la peste advenue du temps de David* (Geneva 1637). Vallin took no side in the quarrel: as he declared in a sonnet to the bourgeois of Neuchâtel (f. A4^r), he conceived the play as a thank-offering to God for sparing the town when other localities were ravaged by the fighting.

To express his relief, Vallin took the story of God's anger when David took a census: He punished Israel with plague, but eventually relented (II Samuel xxiv; I Chronicles xxi). The first act is spoken by the fury, Alecton, who warns that Israel will be punished; the remaining four follow the biblical narrative closely.[44] The scenes are simply constructed: they consist mostly of long speeches delivered by one or two characters, and there is nothing resembling the dialogue of Classical tragedy. Motivation is similarly unimportant. When the prophet Nathan vilifies David for having disobeyed God, David is not present to hear this criticism: Vallin was not interested in individuals' emotions, only in the correct theological interpretation of the case. Various other characters are introduced, like Nathan, for one scene only, to deliver edifying comment, and a Chorus too provides instructive reflections. None of these is personally involved in the action of David's error and repentance: Vallin did not seek to write a psychological drama about those concerned, but used his story to illustrate divine justice with the utmost clarity.[45] Whatever the movements in Parisian vogues, the humanist form was still the most appropriate for certain purposes, at least in the opinion of Vallin and his audience.

In Paris at about this time a play appeared which made a wholly secular use of religious material: *L'Athénaïs, tragi-comedie*, written by Jean Mairet probably in 1637-8,[46] following Caussin's edifying compilation, *La Cour sainte*.[47] This concerns the marriage of the Emperor

Theodose to Athénaïs, who is persuaded to accept him by the end of the third act. This left two acts to fill by raising obstacles: one is the discovery that Athénaïs is a pagan, resolved when some divines convert her. The religious interlude, which is carefully kept off the stage, is no more than one of the obligatory incidents of the tragi-comic plot.[48]

Pierre du Ryer's *Saul, tragedie* (Paris 1642), probably first performed in 1640,[49] also achieved a predominantly secular effect. At first sight Du Ryer's treatment of the famous episode of Saul's death is somewhat oddly constructed: Saül's consultation of the witch and his death occupy only the last three acts, while the first two are taken up with his feud with the absent David. In fact these acts do not infringe the unity of action; like the rest of the play they bear on the theme of Saül's reprobation. Saül is clear from the start that he is the object of God's 'equitable courroux' (l. 7). He is demoralised by the loss of God's favour, but Jonathas argues encouragingly that if God were angry He would have incited Saül's subjects to reject his rule; at once the news comes of the revolt of Jerusalem. This incident, invented by Du Ryer, provides evidence of Saül's reprobation and a touching scene in which Saül hesitates to expose his son to danger by sending him to quell the revolt but is overruled by Jonathas's insistence on doing his duty. Michol consolingly reminds her father that he can still rely on her husband, David; but, as soon as Saül is persuaded despite his mistrust to believe in David's loyalty, news comes that he is marching with the Philistines. Saül believes him a traitor without further proof. Michol argues that the report may be false: Phalti, who brought it, loves her and so has a motive for seeking to get rid of her husband. Michol ends the act with a soliloquy grieving at David's apparent treachery. The situation is as complex as in any of Corneille's political tragedies: no character has access to the truth, but can only guess at it by analysing others' motives for what they say. Where La Taille had concentrated on Saül's guilt, Du Ryer combined this with an interest in the motives and emotions of the secondary characters, from which he drew considerable drama and pathos: the play consequently possesses a richness of emotional texture quite alien to the effects which La Taille sought.

Act II further evidences Saül's reprobation. Devastating though the revolts of Jerusalem and David may be, Saül is more alarmed by God's silence and determines to consult a witch in his anxiety to know the future:

> Ce dessein est un crime,
> Mais la necessité le rendra legitime,
> C'est le dernier espoir d'un Prince malheureux,
> A soy-mesme aujourd'huy cruel et dangereux,
> A qui dans les douleurs, dont son esprit abonde,

Du Ciel ou de l'enfer n'importe qui responde;
Plus accablé d'ennuis qu'un esclave de fers,
Si je n'esmeus les Cieux, j'esmouveray les enfers.   (ll. 358–65)

Michol brings evidence that David is not with the Philistines, but Saül
refuses to trust him. Without grace, Saül has lost his judgement; he
obstinately rejects the one person who could help him defeat the
Philistines. Michol repeats her imputations against Phalti, at which
Saül angrily declares David no longer fit to be his son-in-law and gives
Michol to Phalti instead. This terrible insult to Michol is one of the
most intense moments of the play. However, nothing is made of it later:
Phalti never hints at any desire for Michol and she continues to be
treated by all, including Saül, as David's wife. Du Ryer could not
resist the opportunity for a confrontation but did not integrate it with
the rest of his play. As soon as Saül has thus brutally severed relations
with David, Jonathas returns to report that the revolt of Jerusalem
was caused by a rumour that Saül was hostile to David, so he calmed
the citizens easily by assuring them that it was untrue. On learning that
Saül has indeed rejected David, Jonathas urges him to relent; Saül
refuses, preferring to owe victory to his son rather than David. Jonathas
accepts the responsibility, at which Saül, touched by his bravery, agrees
to send for David; but the following act reveals that he again changes
his mind.

The first two acts, though mainly concerned with the question of
David's loyalty, through this present evidence of Saül's reprobation
and also provide pathetic and noble scenes. Having lost God's favour,
Saül is deprived of wisdom and rejects help and advice. Jonathas and
Michol exhibit heroic filial loyalty in not abandoning Saül to the
disaster he seems set on provoking. The combination in the children
of *générosité* in serving the crown and grief at their father's derange-
ment provides Du Ryer with much affecting material.

In the remaining acts Saül commits his greatest sin in consulting the
witch, and dies bravely fighting the Philistines. He continues to suffer
principally as a father, a factor neither La Taille nor Billard had
sought to exploit. Saül is undismayed when Samuel warns him of
dethronement and death, but when Samuel adds that his sons must die
Saül exclaims: 'Hélas! voylà le coup dont l'atteinte me tuë' (l. 1041).
He explains later to his suite:

J'esprouve icy qu'un Pere a beaucoup de foiblesse.
O Nature, Nature, outrageuse à ton tour,
N'as-tu mis dans ce coeur une si forte amour,
Que pour estre toy-mesme, impitoyable Mere,
Le supplice eternel d'un Monarque, et d'un Pere?
Ha! la haine du Ciel mon ennemy fatal,

> En m'ostant mes grandeurs me feroit peu de mal,
> Si pour rendre ce mal plus grand et plus funeste,
> La nature n'aidoit à la haine Celeste. (ll. 1086–94)

His first concern is to protect his children. In doing so he may be guilty
of resisting God's will, but he reasons that

> Le Ciel punit souvent par la seule menace,
> Et ne defend jamais en Tyran insensé,
> Qu'on tâche à se sauver quand il a menacé. (ll. 1146–8)

He sends Michol to Jerusalem to await her husband, calling him the
future King. She protests that David has no designs on his throne, but
Saül replies that it is God's will:

> Tout ce que veut le Ciel est juste et legitime:
> Mais il soulagera le fardeau de mes fers
> S'il te laisse une part des grandeurs que je perds.
> Va donc attendre ailleurs le bien qu'il te destine,
> Mes maux seront moins grands, s'ils en sont l'origine.
> Que David regne en paix... (ll. 1218–23)

This scene of paternal concern is followed by a heroic episode, in which
Jonathas refuses to be deprived by his protective father of the honour
of fighting the Philistines, though he knows of Samuel's prophecy. He
urges his father rather to spare himself, but Saül is no less insistent on
sharing the honour of a valiant death. The competition in *générosité*
ends when father and son go to fight together. In the last scenes pathos
naturally predominates: Saül watches Jonathas die by the bodies of
his brothers, then, being too disabled by his wounds to die fighting, begs
his squire to kill him lest he fall prisoner; at the squire's refusal, the
King is reduced to falling on his sword.

In defining Saül's offence, Du Ryer departed from his source. In the
Bible Samuel states that God is angry because Saul spared His enemies
the Amalekites (I Samuel xxviii 18), but in the play Samuel charges
Saül with disobedience to God in general, and mentions one specific
crime: 'Pense à ce peuple saint par tes Lois égorgé' (l. 991). Whereas
in the Bible Saul is punished for showing mercy, for Du Ryer his sin
is murder of the innocent.

Partly because his fate is more obviously just in this play than in
other versions, Du Ryer's Saül does not follow the precedents of rebellion against God.[50] He is tempted to rebel only once, watching his
son dying, but Jonathas reminds him not to blaspheme. Although Saül
considers the killing of his innocent sons in expiation of his guilt an
'Espouventable Arrest du Ciel inexorable' (l. 1641), he does not rail
against God's justice; his first lines showed him submissive to the divine
will, and he remains so throughout.

He finds difficulty only in accepting that his children should die: he is more concerned at his loss as a father than at his own reprobation. In this Du Ryer's hero differs from La Taille's Saül, whose consciousness of God's wrath drives him mad, causes him to reject any possibility of divine mercy and so ensures his damnation: Du Ryer's version was not a study in the process of reprobation. He also differs from Garnier's Sedecie, another reprobate, who devotes his energies principally to the attempt to accept that God is just in ordaining the deaths of his children. Du Ryer's Saül is more preoccupied by his paternal feelings and less exercised by any religious consciousness; his grief is consequently perhaps more accessible, but the sentiment is secular rather than religious. Indeed, Saül's moral growth as the play proceeds is close to contradicting any religious interpretation. Once assured of his fate he recovers the decision and wisdom that make him worthy to be a King, and accepts his destiny to the extent of welcoming David as his successor; yet he is not cowed or exasperated by Samuel's prophecy and calmly takes such precautions as human prudence allows to protect his children, while resigning himself to God's will. The tragic irony is that he begins to show himself a worthy King only once his earlier rejection of help and advice have assured his ruin; this is the usual irony of tragedy, but has little to do with divine justice. The other dramatic and emotional effects are also predominantly secular. Although the first two acts do bear on a religious theme, their interest derives principally from the feelings of Jonathas, Michol and Phalti, besides the protagonist. Subsequently Du Ryer continues to exploit the uplifting effect of Jonathas's *générosité* and the passions of the other characters, who are frequently brought into conflict. Du Ryer vigorously evokes and combines a variety of emotions, paternal grief, heroism, love; but among the *ressorts* of the play religious consciousness hardly figures. He was bound by his source to show Saül's reprobation, but he sought the play's impact elsewhere than in the King's awareness of his sin.

When the Classical dramatic technique, by now quite well developed, was first applied to sacred subjects, the playwrights were able at once to satisfy the taste for a strong emotional impact produced by sympathetic and vivid characterisation, and a tense and complex plot; but they did not endow their plays with any great religious sense. In the Classical system both drama and a religious sense were to be found in the hero's religious emotion, his consciousness of God's will and his struggle to obey it, but the Parisian dramatists did not exploit this, perhaps out of a certain squeamishness: Eustache obeyed God with a minimum of difficulty, and Saül's anguish arose from his paternity rather than awareness of God. Vallin, meanwhile, retained a technique akin to the humanists': his play had abundant religious import, but lacked drama of the sort Parisian audiences demanded. The playwrights did not rapidly find a way to express the religious sense of the subjects they chose in the new dramatic language.

(ii) THE REDUCTION OF THE SAINT-PLAY TO THE 'CRISE'

Baro presented the whole of his saint's career, whereas Du Ryer limited himself to Saül's last hours. Since the time of Bèze it had been common in biblical plays to show only the *crise*, but this had yet to be attempted in a saint-play. The standard procedure was to stage all that history or legend told of the saint's career from conversion to martyrdom, except where the audience had a special interest in only one incident, as in Soret's treatment of the election of St Nicholas. Even those like Prevost who used the restricted action in dramatising other material preferred the extended chronicle when treating a saint. In the 1640s for the first time plays appeared which were limited to a concentrated account of the saint's last hours.

The first to write such a play was Jean Puget de la Serre if, as seems likely, his *Thomas Morus, ou le triomphe de la foy, et de la constance, tragedie en prose* (Paris 1642)[51] was first performed in 1640.[52] This traces only More's final quarrel with Henry and his martyrdom,[53] which seems all to occur within twenty-four hours. In this appear the King himself, Catherine of Aragon and Anne Boleyn: it is a complex court drama involving several powerful figures. These are skilfully brought into conflict, but the result is remarkably dull and obscure; indeed, the play is interesting principally for La Serre's unintelligent application of the Classical formula, which affords an insight into the workings of that dramatic style.[54]

The first scene confronts Morus and Sofoc (Suffolk), the former insisting that the King's plans must be resisted, the latter urging complaisance. It is not made clear to what Morus objects, La Serre expecting the audience to know: the scene consists of a series of ringing retorts which afford scant insight into the basis of the argument. The following scenes similarly present disputes between the Queen and her confidante, and between the King and Arthenice (Anne Boleyn). The situation remains unchanged in act II – Arthenice continues to rebuff Henry – but La Serre introduces variety by confronting different pairs of characters: Arthenice and her mother, Henry and his confidant, the confidant and Arthenice. The confrontations continue in act III: Henry with his confidant again, and Henry with the Queen. The fourth scene at last introduces a change in the situation: Arthenice suddenly agrees to marry Henry if he repudiates Catherine. The origin of this change of heart is unclear, for Arthenice has spoken only in vigorous retorts and we know little of her feelings or character: she simply announces her decision, quite unexpectedly. The result is a fresh round of confrontations, between Arthenice and the Queen, Arthenice and the King, the King and the Queen.

Having extracted all the possible confrontations from the situation, La Serre returns in act IV to Morus, who denounces the King for repudiating Catherine and is consigned to prison. Catherine has a brief scene in which she puts a brave face on her rejection, and Morus is visited in gaol by his daughter, Clorimene, whom he persuades not to pity him since he is dying for his principles. In the last act Arthenice is crowned. Clorimene fails to obtain her father's pardon from Henry, but he is given a chance to recant; he stands firm and is sent off to execution. The last scenes show Arthenice's realisation that her ascent has not brought her happiness, and Clorimene's grief, in which she rejects Henry's attempts to console her.

From the exhausting series of retorts of which the play consists it is impossible to gauge Morus's religious sentiments. His criticism of Henry seems a gratuitous act of defiance. There are no moments of reflection in which La Serre might explore Morus's feelings in following his principles to the death. Even the interview between Morus and Clorimene in gaol, in which some personal tenderness might be expected, is couched in the prose equivalent of stichomythia:

MORUS: Que je sorte de prison, dites-vous, ma fille, à quelque prix que ce soit! Le Roy a beau le permettre: ma conscience me le deffend: si mes amis le desirent, mon devoir ne veut pas que je l'espere. En fin vous m'en priez, mais Dieu me commande de rejetter vos prieres, et d'estre sourd à vos plaintes, aussi bien qu'aveugle à vos larmes.

CLORIMENE: Monsieur, si vous considerez le déplorable estat où vostre infortune m'a desja reduite, vous aurez plus de pieté que de raison.

MORUS: La Vertu n'est jamais malheureuse: que craignez vous avec elle?

CLORIMENE: J'apprehende de vous perdre.

MORUS: Dans le port où je suis, il n'y a point de peril de naufrage.

CLORIMENE: Si prevoy-je pourtant que la Mort sera vostre escueil.

MORUS: Cette prevoyance me menace d'un bon-heur, qui me fait souspirer d'impatience en son attente.

CLORIMENE: Mais vous ne considerez pas, Monsieur, qu'en mourant vous m'entrainez dans la sepulture.

MORUS: Ne seriez vous pas heureuse de mourir pour la gloire du Ciel, avec celuy qui vous a fait naistre?

(IV iv, pp. 84–5)

That La Serre troubled to bring the two together for this scene shows that psychological drama was his goal, but the cold periods repel any sympathy. It is as if La Serre knew that clashes between characters are the material of Classical tragedy but did not understand that the purpose of the clashes is to create emotions with which the spectator may sympathise, so consistently does his play fail to arouse any feelings. La Serre applied some skill to extracting the maximum of confrontations, but these are without interest because the characters lack life. The author uncomprehendingly used a form intended to move by its emotional impact; by this standard the characters' lifelessness is unpardonable. Adherence to the forms and rules of Classical dramaturgy was certainly no guarantee of producing a superior play.

Such psychological drama as there is does not centre in Morus, who does his duty without hesitation. As in the *mystères*, a large part of the action concerns incidental figures. *Thomas Morus* differs from those chronicles principally thanks to a formal trick: La Serre subordinated the activities of the court to Morus's destiny by giving Morus himself the first scene and so turning the scenes concerning the court, which make up the bulk of the action, into a parenthesis, albeit long, in the *crise* of Morus. But La Serre could not make Morus's tribulations interesting in themselves: he had therefore to rely on the long account of the doings of the court for the play's substance.

The importance of limiting the action of the saint-play to the crisis was well understood by the abbé d'Aubignac, as one would expect of that guardian of the unities, and in *La Pucelle d'Orleans, tragedie en prose, selon la verité de l'histoire et les rigueurs du Theatre* (Paris 1642)[55] he dealt more resolutely than La Serre in reshaping an intractable subject. In a Preface, d'Aubignac conceded that Joan's exploits provided material better suited to epic than dramatic treatment; the early stages of her career offered much of interest, but the rules of tragedy required of course that the action should be limited to her last day, and 'dans ce jour il n'y a rien de notable que son innocence, et la cruauté de ses Juges' (f. $\tilde{e}^r$). His solution was to place her trial on the day of her execution, and to have her exploits recounted as evidence. The trial presented difficulties of its own:

cette histoire oblige à faire des Conseils sur le Theatre, qui jusqu'icy n'ont guere bien reüssy, les Juges estants tous mauvais Acteurs, mal vestus, portants d'ordinaire une image ridicule de Juges de village et ne paroissans que pour mal dire deux mauvais vers.   (f. $\tilde{e}^{r-v}$)

The solution was to avoid judges by turning the trial into a court-martial, and to introduce variety by dividing it into two sessions. Nevertheless, with the Maid's trial, the accounts of her exploits and her death, d'Aubignac still felt he lacked an intrigue to drive the action. The solution was to involve the Pucelle in a love-triangle:

Pour y mettre une intrigue qui donnast le moyen de faire jouër le Theatre, j'ay supposé que le Comte de Warwick en estoit amoureux, et sa femme jalouse: car bien que l'histoire n'en parle point, elle ne dit rien au contraire; de sorte que cela vray-semblablement a peu estre...

(f. ẽ2^{r–v})

To derive the play's motive power from Warwick's love instead of from the heroine herself was a considerable infringement of the unity of action and of the proprieties, to say nothing of history; but d'Aubignac well knew that his contemporaries relished a romantic plot above all.

The Preface explains what effects d'Aubignac sought by thus improving on history: he had arranged the action

De sorte que la Pucelle paroist innocente en sa vie et genereuse en sa mort, ses ennemis coupables et chastiez, et le Theatre soustenu de diverses passions et violences, comme sont l'amour et le desespoir du Comte, la jalousie et la fureur de sa femme, la rage et la terreur des Anglois, et la constance de la Pucelle.

(f. ẽ3^{r–v})

It is notable that most of the emotions by which the Classical playwright seeks to move his audience are centred in characters other than the Pucelle herself.

The play begins spectacularly: 'Le Ciel s'ouvre par un grand esclair, et l'Ange paroist sur une Machine eslevée' (stage direction i i, p. 1). The angel has freed the Pucelle from her cell[56] so as to warn her of the martyrdom she must face; she is impatient to die. After the angel's departure she is found by her gaoler, Warwick, who offers her freedom if she will reciprocate his love; she refuses and is returned to her cell. In an interview with Sommerset, Warwick is told that she must be condemned and that he must sign her sentence with the other judges if he is to avoid disgrace. Warwick laments, and in a desperate attempt to save his beloved arranges for her to be carried off to Scotland. In act ii Warwick's wife, jealous of the Pucelle, incites the judges against her; they need no encouragement, save Talbot, who suspects that she is truly supported by God. Warwick rejoices to think that she is speeding to safety in Scotland and anticipates that she will accept his love in gratitude when the Pucelle herself bursts in, having disarmed her kidnappers: she declares that she prefers death to the dishonour Warwick intended and returns voluntarily to gaol. The fencing between Warwick and the powerful Sommerset continues in act iii. Their interview is a tense scene, as each invokes lofty principles as a colour for his love or hatred of the Pucelle, and it derives added piquancy from the fact that each is aware of the other's true motive but still hopes to disguise his own. The trial follows, but the Pucelle, who confides that she is inspired by God, accuses her judges and predicts the disasters that will befall the English collectively and her judges individually. They adjourn in confusion. Before the trial resumes, Warwick's wife vents her jealousy to her husband. In the courtroom in act iv the Pucelle repudiates the charges, but when Talbot opines that she is innocent he provokes a public uproar which Sommerset is quick to exploit to force Warvick and Talbot to concur with the more obedient judges in condemning her. Warvick's wife bursts in, maddened by remorse, and urges them to spare the Pucelle, whom she now declares innocent. In the last act the Pucelle rejoices as she is led away to the stake. Warvick reflects that if he had loved her genuinely, he would have freed her unconditionally instead of provoking her to refuse his help by requiring her in return to satisfy his lust. His self-reproach is deepened by the madness of his wife. Sommerset returns to the stage to banish one of the judges who tried to interrupt the Pucelle's execu- tion, proclaiming her innocent; his punishment fulfils one of her earlier prophecies. Warvick and his wife desire to make restitution to her, but Talbot brings an account of her death and the accompanying miracles. The following scenes detail the accomplishment of the Pucelle's other prophecies as the judges are mysteriously struck down. At the end Warvick describes the agonies of his conscience.

Warvick it is who suffers the torments of love and responsibility for his beloved's death; his interviews with his fellow judges and with his wife provide the most vivid scenes; and the principal action is nothing done by the Pucelle but concerns whether her judges will reconcile their differences sufficiently to condemn her. The Pucelle endures no psycho- logical struggle. When the angel shows her a vision of her fate at the stake, she voices an absolute indifference to suffering, which she recalls in her last speech as she waits to be led away to be burnt:

Je touche enfin l'heureux moment d'une entiere liberté, puis que je sors de prison pour sortir du monde; et mes chaisnes commencent d'estre legeres à mon corps, comme elles l'ont tousjours esté à mon âme. Apres avoir esté glorieuse à la guerre, et malheureuse dans mon captivité, je suis attenduë dans une paix de gloire, et une felicité tousjours libre: Et je sens bien que le Conducteur de ma vie, est encore alentour de moy. Cette esperance qui m'éleve au Ciel, et ce mespris absolu qui me separe des choses terrestres, en sont des preuves sensibles à ma foiblesse. Non, Seigneur, sans le secours de vostre Ministre je ne verrois pas allumer les flâmes de mon tourment avec la mesme indifference que j'en ay veu l'Image; sans luy, je serois morte de frayeur à la peinture du feu qui me va devorer: et sans luy, que deviendrois-je aux approches d'un embrasement veritable? mes yeux se fermeroient, mes pieds deviendroient immobiles, et tous mes sens espouvantez laisseroient eschapper mon ame avant le temps: Mais faites, ô Dieu Tout-puissant, que cette victime qui vous est immolé par l'injustice et la haine devienne une victime de satisfaction et d'humilité: que je sois l'offrande de moy-mesme...

(v i, pp. 136–8)

Whatever dismay she feels is effectively destroyed by d'Aubignac's prose, though in fairness to the author we must remember that he was sufficiently aware of his limitations to ask someone else to put his play into verse before presenting it in the public theatre. The historical Joan endured considerable anguish arising from uncertainty as to the divine inspiration of her mission, and was even persuaded so far to doubt herself as to recant;[57] but d'Aubignac allowed his Pucelle no such hesitations. For religious action he was content to exhibit a few minor miracles. He sought the psychological action outside the Pucelle, in Warvick and the love-plot. To these elements he added a large patriotic component and many insults to the English.[58] For interest in his dramatisation of Joan's death, d'Aubignac relied on love and politics. The play is correctly constructed according to the lights of Classical dramaturgy, with a complex intrigue inducing intense and varied emotions, but the focus is not the anguish of the heroine herself: despite the use of the Classical form, *La Pucelle* is not a Classical drama about the Maid but relies like the *mystères* on the episodic elements of love and politics.

A similar discrepancy between form and content arises in another prose play concerning a medieval saint, La Calprenède's *Hermenigilde, tragedie* (Paris 1643). The subject was the execution of Hermenigildus as an orthodox Christian by his Arian father, King Leovigildus.[59] By placing the details of Hermenigilde's conversion and rebellion in *récit* and omitting any mention of the passage of time, La Calprenède fitted the story into the prescribed twenty-four hours. There are few events; Hermenigilde's death is determined from the beginning of act ii but the sentence is not carried out until act v. La Calprenède thus provided himself with four acts to fill with psychological action. This consists of a series of attempts by various characters to persuade Hermenigilde or his father to yield; since both are inflexible and the situation remains unchanged, what we have is really psychological inaction.

Nevertheless, there are many confrontations and moral dilemmas. Hermenigilde has rebelled and is besieged by his father when his younger brother, Recarède, comes to offer a pardon. Hermenigilde declares that he rebelled because his stepmother, Goisinthe, was cruel towards Indegonde, his wife; when Indegonde urges him to forgive Goisinthe as she does, Hermenigilde, who has already suffered pangs of conscience, quickly agrees to submit to his father. He yields with no great confidence, however, since he suspects that under Goisinthe's influence Levigilde will play him false; with *généreux* disregard of his own safety he goes to meet his father, murmuring 'courons à la mort' (i iii, p. 18).

This situation, quickly established in the first act, furnishes dilemmas for the remainder of the play. Recarède is ashamed to discover that the promise of pardon he made on his father's behalf was a trick, and confronts Levigilde to urge him to honour his word. The King replies that 'aucune parolle ne peut engager un souverain à ses sujets' (II i, p. 22). Recarède considers himself responsible for betraying his brother; when his attempt to save him fails, in a pathetic scene in Hermenigilde's cell he begs his brother to kill him (Hermenigilde of course exonerates him), and at the end declares that he will never mount the throne to which his brother's death makes him heir.[60]

Levigilde endures no such anguish. At times he relents briefly: after deciding to condemn Hermenigilde he considers pardoning him:

il vaut mieux hazarder la perte de ton Sceptre que pancher à celle de ton fils, les considerations de la Commune sont legeres, si tu les balances contre celles de la nature.   (II ii, p. 27)

This is his closest approach to paternal affection. When Levigilde gives his son opportunities to recant, he is visibly prompted principally by the need to keep the execution for act v.

Levigilde promises to pardon Hermenigilde if he will return to Arianism. This produces repeated scenes in which Recarède[61] (III i), Levigilde himself (IV i), and a courtier (V ii) in turn urge him to comply. Hermenigilde is of course unmoved, and receives support from Indegonde in III ii, repeated in V i. He grieves at the separation from his wife that martyrdom will entail:

Ah! ma chere Princesse, mon ame est accablée de sa douleur, et quelque consolation que je reçoive du ciel, ma constance s'esvanoüit au souvenir de ma chere Indegonde. Je ne crains point la mort pour la deffence de ma foy, et je l'affronteray avec tant d'asseurance que vous n'aurez point honte des beaux sentimens que vous m'avez inspirez: mais ô Dieu! comment me resoudray-je à nostre separation? comment quitteray-je mon Indegonde pour jamais? et comment pourray-je songer à ses malheurs et à ses desplaisirs, sans prevenir par une mort causee de ma douleur celle que Levigilde me prepare?
                                                      (III ii, p. 54)

It is no surprise that such an insipid passion does not deflect Hermenigilde from his duty. After he goes to his death, Indegonde desires to follow, but of course may not kill herself; she prays God to release her from life and miraculously weakens and dies.

The plot provides much potentially affecting material: the calm self-immolation of Hermenigilde, Levigilde's harshness, Goisinthe's venom, Recarède's remorse, Indegonde's miracle-working grief. It is skilfully constructed to create moments in which the characters' emotions might play on each other. However, the potential for psychological drama is not realised, because the confrontations produce no new decisions, while the cold prose denies the emotions any impact. Such anguish as there is does not stem from the characters' religion: Hermenigilde's adherence to his faith costs him little. La Calprenède exercised considerable skill in devising the plot for a psychological and religious drama, but failed to fill it with psychological or religious action.

To follow *Thomas Morus* La Serre took a more conventional subject and form. *Le Martyre de sainte Caterine, Tragedie en Prose* (Paris 1643) is a faithful chronicle of as much as legend records of the career of the early martyr; but the legend was adapted to modern taste by the addition of a love-plot.[62] The miracles associated with the saint receive considerable attention. There are numerous conversions. Porphire, the Emperor's favourite, is sent to Catherine in prison to urge her to reject Christianity and accept his master's hand and throne. Porphire suddenly abandons the arguments and departs, explaining in an aside: 'Fuyons promptement, je sens ma foiblesse comme si mon coeur tenoit déja son party' (III iv, p. 50). In the following act he declares himself a Christian. The conversion of the Empress is better prepared, since she announced a sympathy for the Christians in the opening scene. She follows Porphire to Catherine's cell to upbraid her for stealing the affection of her husband. Inspired, Catherine answers that they will indeed share a husband: Christ. The Empress replies:

Ha Divine Catherine! vos paroles toutes de lumiere et de feu en illuminant mon esprit, enflamment tellement mon coeur de l'amour de ce celeste Epoux dont vous me faites esperer la joüissance, que je soûpireray sans cesse du regret de son éloignement. Allons, allons donc au devant de la mort, je ne voy plus le jour qu'à regret en l'attente de ce beau Soleil qui doit éclairer nos ames d'une lumiere eternelle. Et toutes les grandeurs qui m'environnent me sont si fort à mépris, que je n'en sçaurois souffrir la pensée, bien loin d'en supporter l'éclat.   (III v, p. 54)

In act IV the philosopher Lucius is ordered to dispute with Catherine, and he too is rapidly converted. He, the Empress and Porphire announce their new faith to the Emperor, and are sent to execution. The sequence of prodigies is completed in the last act, when courtiers recount their brave deaths and Catherine's escape from the wheel. The Emperor orders her to be beheaded; further miracles are reported, and finally he has a vision of singing angels burying her body on Sinai, at which he is converted.

The conversions and other prodigies occur with mechanical ease and rapidity; the converts seem to leap instantaneously from one faith to the other, and immediately conceive an ardent desire to endure martyrdom. Catherine herself, when she learns of the edict of persecution, desires only to defy the Emperor and die:

Que cét Edict qu'on a fait contre les Chrestiens me paroist doux et cruel tout à la fois. Il est doux en menassant de nous oster une vie toute remplie de miseres, pour nous en donner une autre toute pleine de felicitez! Et il est cruel

en voulant effacer du milieu de nos coeurs ou par le fer, ou par la flame, les
sacrez caracteres de nostre Religion. Le silence et la crainte en cette rencontre
me rendroient malheureuse et criminelle. Je veux plaider la cause des
Chrestiens, puis je suis également interessée et dans le gain, et dans la perte
qu'ils en feront.   (II ii, pp. 15–16)

Her friends and relations suggest that she is motivated by pride, but
she ignores the possibility: like the other martyrs, she wishes only to
win glory in Heaven and escape the vanity of the world, and says
nothing of serving God. This is the extent of their religious life.

However, *Sainte Caterine* is not simply a naïve catalogue in the
manner of the *mystères* of prodigies associated with the saint. La Serre
took care to provide an intrigue, in the form of the Emperor's love,
which, however, is born as unexpectedly as the converts' faith and is
as insipid in its expression. He and Catherine are confronted in several
scenes, though the paradoxes they exchange do more to display the
author's skill than to explain their feelings. Other confrontations are
also arranged. La Serre used the devices which were popular on the
Parisian stage, but without endowing them with the life required to
give them interest; and he combined the technique of psychological
drama with a matter to which it was not suited, the chronicle of the
saint's miracles.

Another play chronicling a saint's career was published in the same
year: Desfontaines's *Le Martyr de St Eustache, Tragedie* (Paris 1643).
Like Baro (whose *Sainct Eustache* had not yet been printed), Desfontaines presented the greater part of the legend, starting only slightly
later, from Placide's[63] conversion, and ending with his martyrdom.[64]
The miracle by which Placide was converted is not enacted, the play
opening to reveal Placide praying immediately after his encounter with
the stag; otherwise Desfontaines had no hesitation over staging prodigies. Trajane, Placide's wife, is carried off by pirates in II ii, and in the
next scene his two sons are carried off by a wolf and a lion as he is
attempting to ford a river. III i occurs on board the pirate ship: the
captain attempts to ravish Trajane but is struck by lightning in response
to her prayer. At the end Placide, Trajane and their sons are martyred
in the burning bull, still on the stage; in the last scene 'L'Ange tenant
des palmes, et des couronnes sur l'ouverture du Taureau brûlant chante
l'air ensuivant' to welcome the martyrs to Heaven, then 'Il remonte
au Ciel en chantant'.[65] There are also scenes in the Emperor's palace
in Rome, in rustic isolation, and in the camp of the army in Egypt.

The incidents of their eventful lives incite the characters to express
their emotions with the utmost vigour; but frequently their words are
belied in the following line, without the speaker betraying any awareness of the contradiction. Desfontaines attached more importance to

giving vivid expression to delicate feelings than to their consistency.
This makes it difficult to gauge Placide's state of mind. When deprived
of wife and children he laments vehemently, then immediately expresses perfect submission to God's will:

> je suis prest, Seigneur, à perdre la clarté,
> Si pour l'extréme erreur où j'ay passé mon aage,
> Vostre justice encor veut ce dernier hommage,
> Ou si ce que je souffre est trop peu pour mes maux,
> Rendez du moins ma force esgale à mes travaux,
> Et ne permettez pas que parmy ma souffrance,
> Us triste desespoir abatte ma constance.   (ii iv, p. 28)

This self-abnegation costs Placide no visible effort; his faith is perfectly
steadfast in the face of all trials. Indeed, to judge from his words, his
faith consists principally of steadfastness: he regards life as a trial of
endurance. He does not regret the loss of his fortune:

> Je ne m'esbranle point pour un si foible orage,
> Le Ciel me laisse assez, me laissant mon courage.   (i iv, p. 12)

He is indifferent to the vanities of the world, and when he enters
rustic seclusion extols the simple life at length. He accepts the summons
back to public life to quell the rebellion as a new trial. Although in the
last act he exhibits true zeal in refusing to sacrifice to pagan gods, in
the bulk of the play his Christianity consists only of Stoic indifference
to worldly goods and the blows of fortune. When he is martyred, his
wife and children follow; a son echoes his sentiments:

> La mort est tousjours belle et tousjours honorable
> Quand on meurt innocent, et non pas en coupable;
> Les Tombeaux aux grands coeurs sont bien indifferens,
> Les plus beaux sont affreux aux esprits des Tyrans.   (v vi, p. 82)

Placide and his family die gladly, it seems, not because they are serving
God, but because the 'grand coeur' (as opposed to the worldly 'Tyran')
is indifferent to death.

Desfontaines's play is primarily a romance in which the various
characters express laudable sentiments: friendship, loyalty, constancy,
patriotism, self-sacrifice, disdain of the world. The Christian sentiments
which occur are simply part of the pattern of noble feeling with which
the romance is filled; that the hero is a saint and martyr is almost
incidental, and never provides the dramatic impulse.

In the first years of the 1640s the Parisian audiences were treated
to saint-plays which depended for their interest on secular elements:
love, politics, spectacular effects and prodigies. In this spirit Du Ryer
followed the success of *Saul* with a second biblical play on a famous

subject, *Esther, tragedie* (Paris 1644). Of this material he made a
remarkably tense and complex court drama. The play has been
criticised, indeed, as excessively complex.[66] Du Ryer was aware of the
difficulty, but considered that the complications served a purpose. In
a Preface he conceded that the play was perhaps wrongly entitled
Esther, since it contains much unrelated to the heroine, and suggested
that a better title would be *La Délivrance des Juifs*, for

En effet toutes choses y contribuënt au salut, et à la conservation de ce peuple,
l'Orgueil de Vasthi, la Beauté d'Esther, l'Amour d'Assuerus, ou d'Artaxerce
Roy de Perse, les Injustices d'Haman, et les soins de Mardochée. Enfin la
Délivrance des Juifs est le but et comme la principale action de cette
Tragedie...   (f. ã2ʳ)

Du Ryer's claim is somewhat disingenuous. The 'délivrance des Juifs'
was less a theme than an excuse for a play in which he could exploit
Orgueil, Beauté, Amour, Injustice and *Soins*, and the complexity of
the plot, both separately and in combination.

The action occurs on the day set for Esther's coronation. According
to the Bible Vashti had already been dismissed from the court while
Haman had yet to appear there,[67] but Du Ryer was not prepared to
deny himself the clashes between these vivid personalities and so
arranged for all three to be present at once.[68] To make the confrontations more bitter, he further arranged for the eunuchs' plot (which
occurs after Esther's coronation in the Bible) to have been discovered
by Mardochée and to have been secretly instigated by Haman, who
hoped by it to seize the throne.[69] A second motive for Haman to hate
Mardochée and all his race is a further invention of the author's:
Haman loves Esther, and cannot forgive Mardochée for marrying her
to the King.

In the first three acts Vasthi, Haman and Mardochée manoeuvre in
the attempt to thwart or confirm Esther's elevation. The wrathful
Haman and the proud, vindictive Vasthi are both defeated by Esther's
calm humility. Vasthi is far from reconciled to disgrace and is insulted
by the King's choice of a commoner to replace her. She browbeats
Haman to urge Assuerus to change his mind; Haman agrees, not out
of any regard for Vasthi, but in hope of winning Esther himself
if Assuerus drops her. Haman's blandishments fail and he is obliged
to his great annoyance to lead Esther up to the throne for her coronation. Vasthi bursts in on the ceremony and challenges the King to
justify having repudiated her. Esther intercedes spontaneously on her
behalf, but when the King leaves to deliberate Vasthi rounds on her
and savagely rejects her help, declaring that she does not wish to owe
her throne to the intervention of a slave. Haman optimistically tells

Esther that the King has chosen Vasthi; Esther hears the news with equanimity, but to Haman's discomfiture word comes that Esther is confirmed Queen.

By his rewriting of history Du Ryer created in these three acts a series of vivid confrontations. Vigorous personalities are brought into conflict by their opposed interests, producing tense scenes as they struggle to outwit each other. The atmosphere is maintained in the historical portion. Haman decides to put into effect the scheme against the Jews that he was meditating at the beginning, hoping to ruin Mardochée and Esther, since he suspects a connection between the Jews and her. He is humiliated, however, when Assuerus forces him to honour Mardochée. When a rumour of Haman's plan is brought to Esther, she confronts him to discover if it is true. She easily outwits him by simulating hostility to the Jews: he is so besotted that he loses his presence of mind and reveals his plans against her nation in the hope of pleasing her. Esther approaches the King and declares that the Jews are loyal subjects and do not deserve to be slaughtered; as proof she reveals that they have apprehended a man involved in the eunuchs' plot and produces a letter he was carrying, which implicates Haman. Finally, she reveals her own religion. Assuerus orders Haman's execution. Here Du Ryer simplified history, omitting Esther's days of prayer and suppressing the banquets. As in the unhistorical acts, he arranged events skilfully to yield a series of tense confrontations.

That the material for his court drama derived from the Bible did not inspire Du Ryer to treat it in a religious manner. The only religious action is a transformation which overtakes Esther in the first act. The thought of the danger to which she will be exposed on a throne fills her with terror. Mardochée urges her to accept the crown to protect her nation, and she replies:

> Soit que par vos raisons ma raison se r'appelle,
> Soit que le Ciel m'inspire une force nouvelle,
> Je sens que dans mon coeur autrefois abbatu
> Succéde à la foiblesse une masle Vertu.
> Et par cette Vertu que le Ciel me suggere,
> Je sens bien qu'il nous aime, et qu'il veut que j'espere.   (i ii, p. 12)

Thereafter she acts with perfect assurance and decision. God, it seems, has removed her timidity; but even here Du Ryer leaves room for a secular explanation by suggesting alternatively that she has taken heart from Mardochée's reasoning. Du Ryer used the sacred subject for the vivid confrontations it allowed. Where the humanists introduced debates for their own sake with scant regard for their relevance, Du Ryer created personal clashes. The result may lack the extreme coherence of a Racinian tragedy, by which standard Lichtenstein criticised it, but it is one of the most vivid productions of the decade.

Reducing the saint-play to the *crise* did not produce any concentration on the saint's religious emotion. *Thomas Morus, La Pucelle* and *Hermenigilde* showed only the saint's last hours, and were arranged to satisfy the taste for powerful emotional impact by using complex and tense plots to produce vivid confrontations between strongly delineated characters, but they derived little of their effect from the emotions and dilemmas a Christian might be supposed to experience when threatened with death for his faith; in each case dramatic interest was principally sustained instead by the persecutors and their conflicts. Two plays, La Serre's *Sainte Caterine* and Desfontaines's *Saint Eustache*, retained the Classical devices for producing a psychological drama but applied them to narrating the whole of the saint's career: here any concern for his religious emotions was all the slighter. Indeed, these plays are remarkable for the thoughtlessness with which the Classical devices were applied to sacred subjects. The principal importance of figures such as Eustace or Esther was religious, yet the playwrights did not apply the Classical devices to making this part of their material significant according to the Classical dramatic values: to transmit the religious importance of the sacred subject they relied on nothing more than the simple presence of the saint on the stage. Even with the reduction of the action to the *crise* (and *a fortiori* in the more extensive chronicles), interest in the first Classical sacred plays centred as in the *mystères* in the episodic elements – love, politics, spectacle – rather than in the saint's decision to sacrifice his life for his beliefs; but where the *mystères* had demanded the spectator's faith in order to be comprehensible, the Classical plays did not express religion in the ways of which that system was capable. If the Classical dramatists of this period sought to express the importance of the material they chose, they were apparently content that the simple act of putting the saint on the stage contained its own religious significance; they did not make the meaning of the existence of the saint or patriarch accessible within the new conventions.

(iii) 'POLYEUCTE'

It is no exaggeration to say that Corneille was the first to solve – dare one say the first to think about? – the problem of conveying the religious significance of sacred material in the Classical form. In *Polyeucte martyre, tragedie*, probably first presented in the winter of 1642–3, he limited the action to the martyr's final hours. His death is provoked by a tense intrigue combining political and amatory interests, yet important though they are, these elements do not provide the principal interest of the play: they are subordinated to the major action, which concerns the martyr's decision to lay down his life. The play's emotional effect and psychological action depend, not on secondary figures nor on the amorous intrigue, but on his struggle to reach and perfect a state of faith. *Polyeucte* produces the Classical effect on the emotions through a religious action.

Corneille never loses sight of the religious import of his subject. He does not show Polyeucte in prison or present torments and martyrdom or the smashing of idols, though such was the ordinary stuff of saint-plays at the time; equally, he did not write scenes of confrontation for confrontation's sake. Not unlike the humanist dramas, *Polyeucte* was constructed so that each scene should contribute to reflection on a major theme: the individual's acquisition of a fully humane and fully Christian understanding of life and death.

It has been suggested recently, notably by Serge Doubrovsky, that Polyeucte is no Christian: his Christianity ignores God and serves only to sanction his proud urge to attain heroic status. Comparing Polyeucte to Horace, Doubrovsky remarks:

La 'religion' a ici remplacé le 'patriotisme' et Dieu Rome, comme prétexte, ou plutôt comme contexte de l'héroïsme, mais le projet fondamental de Maîtrise, les conduites qui s'y rattachent et les moyens qui le réalisent sont strictement les mêmes, dans cette tragédie chrétienne et dans les tragédies païennes.

La 'palme' de Polyeucte, ce sont les 'trophées' d'Horace, mais avec une garantie éternelle. En mourant pour son Dieu, Polyeucte meurt donc exclusivement pour lui-même.[70]

That Polyeucte is more concerned with 'gloire' than serving God is undoubtedly true in the first scenes of the play, but it cannot be maintained that he is so throughout without ignoring the change brought about in him by the evolution of his relationship with Pauline. This may seem paradoxical, since Polyeucte and Pauline scarcely speak to each other before act IV:[71] in fact it is precisely this lack of communication that reveals the falsity of Polyeucte's initial conception of Christianity.

Once his faith has been confirmed by baptism, Polyeucte exhibits its true nature by proposing a public act of defiance:

> Allons, mon cher Néarque, allons aux yeux des hommes
> Braver l'idolâtrie, et montrer qui nous sommes.   (ll. 645–6)

Polyeucte seems to be motivated by exhibitionism, as Doubrovsky points out: 'Ostentation, bravade, égolâtrie, tous les motifs héroïques se retrouvent et se conjuguent pour célébrer le culte orgueilleux du Moi.'[72]

The next account of his faith comes from Stratonice, who reports to
Pauline his words as he attacked the pagan images: Polyeucte pro-
claimed that God

> De la terre et du ciel est l'absolu monarque,
> Seul être indépendant, seul maître du destin,
> Seul principe éternel, et souveraine fin...
> Lui seul tient en sa main le succès des combats...
> Sa bonté, son pouvoir, sa justice est immense;
> C'est lui seul qui punit, lui seul qui récompense.
> Vous adorez en vain des monstres impuissants.   (ll. 842-51)

What Polyeucte adores above all in God is His omnipotence. Such a
conception was scarcely uncommon, especially in the wars of religion
when the two camps often viewed God as the ultimate deterrent, but to
a France where François de Sales had preached it must have seemed
incomplete. Polyeucte reveals the quality of his Christianity again
later, when he is warned by his guards that Pauline is coming to urge
him to abandon his faith. He sets about strengthening himself against
her charms:

> Source délicieuse, en misères féconde,
> Que voulez-vous de moi, flatteuses voluptés?
> Honteux attachements de la chair et du monde,
> Que ne me quittez-vous, quand je vous ai quittés?
> Allez, honneurs, plaisirs, qui me livrez la guerre:
>   Toute votre félicité,
>   Sujette à l'instabilité,
>   En moins de rien tombe par terre;
>   Et comme elle a l'éclat du verre,
>   Elle en a la fragilité.   (ll. 1105-14)

Of course Polyeucte is trying here to detach himself from Pauline
rather than offering a complete exposition of his faith; nevertheless, it
is noteworthy that he ignores love of God and gives as his only reason
for aspiring to Heaven disgust with the vanity of worldly pleasures.
This is combined with a defiance of his enemies to do their worst which
is more Stoic than Christian:

> Que cependant Félix m'immole à ta [Décie] colère;
> Qu'un rival plus puissant éblouisse ses yeux;
> Qu'aux dépens de ma vie il s'en fasse beau-père,
> Et qu'à titre d'esclave il commande en ces lieux:
> Je consens, ou plutôt j'aspire à ma ruine.
>   Monde, pour moi tu n'as plus rien:
>   Je porte en mon coeur tout chrétien
>   Une flamme toute divine;
>   Et je ne regarde Pauline
>   Que comme un obstacle à mon bien.   (ll. 1135-44)

Having persuaded himself to ignore his love for Pauline, he awaits her
with indifference.

But when Pauline appears, Polyeucte is unable to disregard his love.
His Christianity based on rejection of the world collapses in the face of
his love for his wife. He discovers thanks to his passion that he was
wrong in predicating his idea of Christianity on inhumanity, and
undergoes a 'second conversion'[73] to a Christianity in which love is
not denied.

That Polyeucte's Christianity is misconceived has been demonstrated
throughout the play, but he discovers this himself only in act IV when
he is forced to take account of Pauline because, being no longer at
liberty, he cannot continue to evade her. In the first three acts, when
brought into contact with Pauline, Polyeucte strives to end the interviews as soon as possible: he tells her nothing of his conversion and
even when he returns from receiving baptism says nothing of his new
faith and delivers instead only insipid declarations of love (ll. 621–6).
By these evasions Polyeucte spares himself the pain of conflict with his
wife. In the absence of Pauline, on the other hand, he is all zeal: he
tells Néarque when summoned to the temple that he intends to smash
the idols and that his love for his wife is no impediment (l. 587).
Polyeucte evades the conflict between his duties to God and to Pauline:
he is alternately a loving husband and a zealous Christian, but he does
not face up to the need to be both at once.

Polyeucte's neglect of the claims of affection stems from Néarque's
advice that he should look on Pauline as an agent of the devil when it
appears that she will prevent his baptism (ll. 53–68). Polyeucte succeeds
all too well. As a new convert he feels that his dedication to God must
be absolute and exclusive, lest he slide back. In fact there is no suggestion of his being too weak: the worst danger is rather that he will
become another Horace, excluding all humane considerations in blind
obedience to his ideal. From this he is saved by the very emotion he
thinks he should shun, his love for Pauline.

Polyeucte's initial inability to reconcile his love with the service of
God is contrasted with the behaviour of Pauline and Sévère. Polyeucte's
first flight from his wife is followed by Pauline's resolute confrontation
of exactly the sort of emotional conflict which he fears. She accepts
that she cannot avoid a meeting with Sévère, painful though it must
be, and when she sees him immediately declares that he must abandon
his passion for her. Polyeucte has not this courage: although he does
not shrink from the physical pain of martyrdom, he evades conflict with
those he loves. Only when he ceases to use his Christianity as an excuse
for avoiding suffering in his relations with Pauline will he become
fully Christian. Pauline and Sévère do not evade such suffering, but

confront it deliberately. Their triumph over it, however, is incomplete: they agree not to see each other again. Polyeucte has to learn, not to avoid Pauline, but to find room for her in his conception of Christianity.

After Polyeucte's conversion, Pauline's confidante and her father both urge her to forget him. She arouses the wrath of Félix by refusing to deny him: unlike Polyeucte she will not shirk the commitment of marriage. At this point Corneille keeps Polyeucte off the stage. His continued absence epitomises his evasiveness: he remains aloof and unhurt by refusing to face choices such as that made by Pauline.

Before the crucial interview with Pauline, then, Polyeucte's Christianity has three unworthy motives, made apparent to the audience partly by the contrast between him and the surrounding characters. In addition to the selfish desire for 'gloire' diagnosed by Doubrovsky, these are disgust with the world and, more unexpectedly, cowardice: like Horace in the service of Rome, he uses Christianity as an excuse for evading emotional dilemmas.[74] Pauline's confrontation with him is thus the encounter of the man who evades human responsibilities on the excuse of Christianity with the pagan who deals sincerely with others at no matter what cost to herself. Pauline attempts first to persuade him to abandon his faith by describing the power, wealth and 'gloire' that would be his as a Prince, but Polyeucte is not tempted by such vain inducements. Exasperated, she appeals to his love. Polyeucte is enlightened. He weeps, not for himself, but for Pauline. For the first time he grieves at her loss rather than his own at his death: Pauline has at last punctured his 'égolâtrie'. As a Christian he regrets above all that he will leave her a pagan, and prays for her enlightenment. He now sees martyrdom less as an opportunity to win Heaven than as an opportunity to lead Pauline there: 'Je vous aime', he tells her, 'Beaucoup moins que mon Dieu, mais bien plus que moi-même' (ll. 1279–80); 'C'est peu d'aller au ciel, je vous y veux conduire' (l. 1284). Pauline is outraged that he should wish her a Christian, but he avoids arguing, not, this time, evading conflict, but realising that until she is converted she will not recognise his wish as proof of his love, and fearing that a futile argument could harden her against the enlightenment he trusts God to send.[75]

Thanks to his wife Polyeucte emerges in the last act as a complete and completely human Christian. When Félix asks why he seeks death, he replies:

> Je ne hais point la vie et j'en aime l'usage,
> Mais sans attachement qui sente l'esclavage,
> Toujours prêt à la rendre au Dieu dont je la tiens:
> La raison me l'ordonne, et la loi des chrétiens;

Et je vous montre à tous par là comme il faut vivre,
Si vous avez le coeur assez bon pour me suivre.   (ll. 1515-20)

This contradicts his earlier disgust with life: his Christianity no longer
depends on arrogant rejection of the world. His new concern for
Pauline emerges when he tries to ensure her happiness after his death
by entrusting her to Sévère; the attempt may be clumsy, but at least
he no longer evades painful emotional problems. Indeed, this is his
greatest trial, because Pauline can only regard the instruction to seek
consolation with Sévère as an insult, and his determination not to avoid
martyrdom as 'égolâtrie'. It is painful to Polyeucte that his actions are
misunderstood by his wife when they are motivated by love of her
almost as much as love of God; but he is not dismayed and his per-
severance in this trial of incomprehension is rewarded when she is
converted.

Polyeucte conceives Christianity and martyrdom initially as a means
of attaining a heroic status which the mutability of the world cannot
tarnish. He attempts, like Rodrigue and Horace, to cut by violent action
the knot of contradictory emotional and moral claims that might impede
his ascent, but Pauline's example teaches him that heroism does not
consist of evasion of difficulties: the true hero, like Curiace or Sertorius,
follows his path without inhumanly eradicating other considerations and
in full consciousness of the cost of his choice. The true Christian, he
discovers simultaneously, cannot pretend to have no worldly attach-
ments: such seeming heroism would be mere escapism. When he lays
down his life he no longer seeks mere self-aggrandisement but hopes
to enlighten the pagans. In martyrdom he is allowed the apotheosis
that was denied to Horace, who was not rescued from the belief that
the eradication of all humane sentiments is the condition of heroism.
That Polyeucte's new faith is valid is shown by its ability to produce
miracles, the conversions of Pauline and Félix.[76]

A curious feature of the play's construction is that Polyeucte knows
nothing of the criticism of his initial notion of Christianity that is
suggested in his absence by the behaviour of the other characters.
Being absent, Polyeucte of course learns nothing from the scenes
showing the emotional honesty of Pauline and Sévère, but these are
essential to the audience's understanding of the play because they
establish what Polyeucte's Christianity lacks. It is the spectator rather
than the protagonist who transfers to Polyeucte the lessons suggested
by Pauline and Sévère, who are according to the strict canons of
Classical orthodoxy irrelevant to the principal action. Corneille in-
fringed the unity of action in order to make the intellectual movement
of his play clear, and in requiring the spectator to apply lessons from
one scene in another came oddly close to the humanist practice. He

differed from his contemporaries in arranging his scenes as a contribution to an argument and not simply for immediate emotional impact,
though this of course is far from lacking; but had it been the only
effect he sought he would have arranged more confrontations between
Polyeucte and Sévère, for example, or Polyeucte and Pauline. The last
scenes, however, – act v and the last two scenes of act iv – seem to
exhibit a change of purpose. Having invented Sévère to contrast with
Polyeucte's evasiveness, Corneille was unable to resist exploiting the
emotional impact of the love-triangle he had created. In fact Sévère
has inclined to this function throughout the play: while Pauline has
been struggling against Polyeucte's inhumanity, Sévère has been winning sympathy from the audience by lamenting and showing himself
to be noble. In the last scenes this aspect predominates. In act v
Polyeucte renounces his love for Pauline and attempts to give her to
his rival, but she renounces her old passion and Sévère too renounces
his former hopes. This chain of *généreux* renunciations draws the play
briefly towards the lachrymose. While Corneille constructed *Polyeucte*
primarily as a reflection on the nature and motivation of faith, he was
not above abandoning his theme to achieve emotional effects.

Polyeucte traces a religious crisis in the life of a saint. The dramatic
content and impact of the play thus derive from a religious action,
and not, as in much contemporary sacred theatre, from love, politics,
or the activities of pagans, though these make their own contribution.
The emotional response elicited is not to be enjoyed for itself only: the
various uplifting or pathetic scenes all contribute to an intellectual
argument. On the other hand, *Polyeucte* differs from the cerebral productions of the humanists in encouraging the emotional identification
and release they did not seek. Corneille produced a drama involving
the spectators in the personal anguish of the Christian's religious crisis;
no other playwright considered here achieved such a combination of
significance and power.

(iv) PROFESSIONAL SACRED DRAMAS

Polyeucte stands apart from the other productions for the Parisian
professional theatre by the imaginative coherence with which the
usual expedients of love, politics, confrontations and a tense intrigue
are drawn together to suggest an insight into the laws governing men's
lives. The other playwrights who presented sacred plays to the same
audience did not match Corneille in intellectual strength.

Desfontaines, a professional actor as well as an author,[77] gave a
second saint-play to his printer in 1644: *L'Illustre Olympie ou le St
Alexis, tragedie*. It followed the tradition of staging the whole of the

saint's career, though this is compressed in deference to the unities.[78]
In other respects Desfontaines embroidered the legend. He made
Alexis's bride, Olympie, a ward of the Emperor Honorius and also
the object of his affection. When Honorius promises to reward the
services of Alexis's father, the latter asks him to give Olympie to Alexis
in marriage. Realising that Olympie and Alexis love each other,
Honorius nobly sacrifices his own interest in his ward. At once two
other victorious generals arrive at court, each demanding the hand of
Olympie as his reward; being unable to satisfy them, Honorius instead
offers his own throne to one and to the other the province he has just
conquered, but with equal *générosité* they decline. Olympie's three
frustrated suitors allow their hopes to revive when it is discovered that
Alexis has abandoned her, and her resistance to their blandishments
provides several affecting scenes; Desfontaines's invention of the love-
plot thus yielded a variety of passions and moods. Pathetic scenes are
also devoted to Olympie's desolation following Alexis's unprovoked
desertion and her heroic loyalty. As a result Olympie rather than Alexis
is the centre of interest in all acts but the fourth.

When Alexis returns home incognito, Desfontaines confronts him
with Olympie, who does not recognise him.[79] When she asks the beggar
if in the course of his travels he has met her husband, Alexis replies
ambiguously:

> Quand du ciel irrité la rigueur est extréme,
> A peine un malheureux se connoit-il soy-mesme.   (iv vii, p. 84)

The characters' behaviour is difficult to understand: it is astonishing
that Olympie does not follow up Alexis's broad hints, and quite incomprehensible that he should drop them while disguising his identity,
unless his object is to amuse himself at his wife's expense. Desfontaines
sacrificed logic of character and sentiment to a rather crude dramatic
irony.

In concentrating on such effects, Desfontaines neglected the religious
sense of Alexis's self-denial. Alexis scarcely explains why he abandons
his bride on their wedding night: as a result his behaviour seems simply
inhuman rather than Christian. However, Desfontaines was concerned
above all to exploit the sensational possibilities of his material: act iii
includes a shipwreck, and act v presents a flight of angels. The play is
irregular: it requires several locations, and the time, despite the author's
careful silence, must exceed twenty-four hours, while some characters
are superfluous to the action. Desfontaines packed all he could into his
play to provide the maximum of spectacles and emotions, without great
concern for their congruence.

The desire to exploit the devices which would immediately thrill the audience is also apparent in Desfontaines's *L'Illustre Comedien, ou le martyre de sainct Genest, Tragedie* (Paris 1645), which probably preceded Rotrou's more famous dramatisation of the subject.[80] Desfontaines offers an unusually refined example of the fashionable device of the play within a play, in which Genest presents for the court a dramatisation of his own youth. This is a piquant variation on the device, for the illusion presented in the inner play is thus as real as the outer play.[81]

The court's reaction to Genest's performance illustrates the extent to which audiences liked to think of the theatrical illusion as real. Genest is ordered to present a play mocking Christianity, which as a good pagan he gladly does; the subject he chooses is his own youthful rejection of his parents' Christian faith. When the performance of his rejection of Christianity is interrupted by his real conversion, the royal spectators only slowly realise that his praise of Christianity is not part of the show; but finally Diocletian sends Genest to be tortured, then rounds on the other actors. In their roles in the play they were attempting to convert Genest: now Diocletian holds them responsible for his real conversion, and proposes to have them tortured too. Only after some argument is he persuaded that the actors are not really Christians. Diocletian does not distinguish between the theatrical illusion and reality.

Both the inner play and the lives of the actors are embellished with love-plots. The actress playing Genest's beloved in the inner play, Pamphilie, is his beloved in real life. After his conversion, she is detailed to use her influence to persuade him to return to paganism. The result is a scene recalling the interview of Polyeucte and Pauline. Pamphilie accuses him of betraying and abandoning her by his conversion. Genest insists that he loves her 'bien plus que moy-mesme' (p. 61) and is prepared to endure martyrdom in the hope of converting her. Thanks to his prayers she is enlightened, and in the last act a *récit* tells us how they encouraged each other as they were martyred together.

These deaths so grieve another actor, Aristide, that his lady suspects him of secretly loving Pamphilie and throws herself into the Tiber in despair; on learning this Aristide follows her, dragging with him another actor who attempts to restrain him. This makes a contrast between pagan and Christian values: while these three meet a futile end caused by a lovers' misunderstanding, Genest and Pamphilie die for God and in death (the *récit* quotes their words) find perfect union. However, Desfontaines did not choose to draw attention to this contrast: it seems that he added the extra deaths to the martyrdoms simply because two bodies were not enough to end a tragedy.

The final scene adds the motif of madness, when Diocletian falls prey to remorse for his cruelty. He has a vision of the martyrs in heaven and begs their forgiveness; he ends the play hoping death may come soon.[82] The conclusion is conventional and satisfying. Desfontaines managed to combine a number of devices – the inner play, the love-plot, madness – whose recurrence in the plays of the time evidences their popularity. In dramatising the saint's life he did not look beyond its theatrical possibilities to its sense.

Rotrou's treatment of the subject was even more embroiled. In *Le Veritable St Genest, tragedie* (Paris 1647)[83] much play is made with illusion and reality and no less than three actions are traced. Rotrou did not entirely escape the danger that the subordinate elements would be more interesting than the religious action. The device of framing the major action in the *fiançailles* of Valerie and Maximin, while providing unity of time and place, subverts the more important unity of action by giving the impression that the play about the martyrdom of Adrian and the real martyrdom of Genest are no more than inter-ludes in the tale of the happiness of the royal couple. A second element tending to distract attention from Genest is Rotrou's interest in the actors' professional business: this seems to correspond more to a fascination with the techniques and life of the stage than to any concern to explain Genest's conversion.[84]

In fact the activities of the court and the actors do have some bearing on this process. The play opens as a banal tragi-comedy. As daughter of the Emperor Diocletian, Valérie is horrified by a dream portending that she will marry a shepherd; but her fears are resolved in the happiest possible way when it transpires that Maximin, to whom Diocletian decides to marry her (and for whom she falls on sight), was a shepherd before rising to be co-Emperor and thus a suitable match. Genest naturally subscribes to the values of this frivolous world, as he shows by his alacrity in approving Diocletian's taste in plays; but the values he expresses in his role as Adrian are radically different. Rotrou emphasises the contrast between worldly and Christian values through ironic verbal parallelisms between the two systems. When Maximin is accepted by Valérie, he kisses her hand and exclaims:

> O favorable arrest, qui me comble de gloire,
> Et fait de ma prison ma plus digne victoire!   (ll. 197–8)

For Genest or Adrian, imprisonment is indeed the way to eternal glory; like Maximin, they are willing prisoners, but of God, not Cupid. Maximin's enslavement to love is constantly belittled by juxtaposition with the self-sacrifice of the martyrs. Genest makes the contrast explicit after his conversion, when he rejects service of the court and its vain preoccupations:

> Aujourd'huy je veux plaire à l'Empereur des Cieux;
> Je vous ay diverti, j'ay chanté vos loüanges,
> Il est temps maintenant de réjoüir les Anges;
> Il est temps de pretendre à des prix immortels...   (ll. 1366–9)

The continuous presence of the court on the stage serves to keep the opposition between the two sets of values constantly before the audience. The courtiers offer uncomprehending comments on Genest's performance as Adrian, and remain unmoved by the conversion they have witnessed and provoked. Maximin sums up the spirit of the court when he delivers the flippant last word: all he sees in Genest's martyrdom is the opportunity for a joke as he declares that he is not to be pitied because

> il a bien voulu, par son impieté,
> D'une feinte, en mourant, faire une verité.   (ll. 1749–50)

The scenes concerning the court exhibit a vain world, severely judged by Genest's rejection of it.[85]

The green-room scenes too have their relevance, for it is through his acting that Genest discovers the true values. When Genest and Diocletian first discuss the actor's craft, although they take the plausibility of the illusion as the goal, they are careful always to describe acting in such terms as 'feinte' and 'figurer'. This awareness that the production of an illusion depends on artifice is amplified when the Décorateur points out to Genest that the set, which looks false seen from the stage, will look real from the auditorium. Speaking of his own part in the illusion, Genest encapsulates the principle: 'Il s'agit d'imiter, et non de devenir' (l. 420). Identification by the actor with his role spoils the illusion. When Genest permits the fusion of his personality with that of Adrian, his performance ends; but his failure as an actor is his triumph as a Christian. By identifying with his role Genest grasps the truth contained in the illusory world of the theatre, and sees that the real world of the court is vain. The work of artifice gives access to true values, and having discovered them Genest can return to reality to suffer martyrdom and attain glory in his own person rather than in the figure of Adrian.[86]

The apparently incongruous worlds of the court and the theatre are thus closely connected with Genest's conversion: the court exemplifies the vanity the Christian rejects, and the concern with the theatrical illusion illustrates the paradoxical nature of Christianity which, though insubstantial, contains greater truths than the so-called real world. However, these links are abstract: between Genest and the court there is not the emotional connection which binds Pauline into Polyeucte's martyrdom. The intellectual movement of the play does not impose itself on the audience by the emotional charge that the Classical theatre required. Despite his professional experience as a playwright,[87] Rotrou did not endow the play with the dominant protagonist and the emotional impact which were popular on the Parisian stage: the concern we might feel for Genest is dissipated by his appearing in three identities, courtier, actor and martyr. In a performance, the play would be most readily appreciated for the separate interests which its constituent parts provide.

A similar dispersal of interest was perhaps the cause of the relative failure of Corneille's *Théodore, vierge et martyre, tragédie chrestienne* (Paris 1646) when it was first presented, probably in 1645.[88] Here the major dramatic effects are produced by the clashes of characters other than the saint. Corneille exercised great skill in arranging the confrontations of the secondary figures, and indeed when he reflected on the play's failure he could find nothing wrong with its construction and attributed it to the subject, which he assumed Parisian audiences found distasteful.[89] This was no doubt a factor, but the play's major flaw was one Corneille was not well placed to perceive, since it lay in what ought to have constituted its strength, the author's success in constructing an exciting and moving plot.

The two *Lives* of Theodora[90] told only that she was rescued from enforced prostitution by Didymus, with whom she was later martyred. The Italian play on the subject which Corneille may have known added little.[91] Corneille was given only the basis of the fourth and fifth acts; the rest he supplied from his own imagination, principally by adding a love-plot, to which he attached even more importance than in *Polyeucte*. In these inventions Corneille sought strong emotions deriving from the situations of the characters, and tension and surprise arising from the plot. This emerges from his *Examen* of the play:

Je ne veux pas toutefois me flatter jusqu'à dire que cette fâcheuse idée [prostitution] aye été le seul défaut de ce poëme. A le bien examiner, s'il y a quelques caractères vigoureux et animés, comme ceux de Placide et de Marcelle, il y en a de traînant, qui ne peuvent avoir grand charme ni grand feu sur le théâtre. Celui de Théodore est entièrement froid: elle n'a aucune passion qui l'agite...   (p. 12)

The success of a play depends apparently on the vigour, animation and fire exhibited by the characters in their passion, and Corneille regrets only that he did not seek such qualities sufficiently consistently. A similar opinion was voiced by d'Aubignac, who maintained that *Théodore* was Corneille's masterpiece thanks to the emotions induced by the variety and number of unexpected (but plausible) twists in the plot.[92] Critic and dramatist agreed in seeking the play's excellence in the thrills provided by the *coups de théâtre* and the passions, rather than in any significance these might have; and it was according to this principle that *Théodore* was constructed. In thinking first of the play's emotional impact Corneille strayed from his usual concern with serious reflection on moral issues,[93] but perhaps moved closer to contemporary habits.

Corneille's concentration on emotional impact appears particularly in act IV, where Théodore's escape from the brothel is recounted to Placide in such a way that he several times gains the wrong impression; the audience, while suspecting the worst, knows little more than Placide and so shares his shock, anxiety and suspense. When Placide finds Théodore missing from her gaol and realises that Marcelle's confidante has been detailed to delay him, we pity him as he slowly discovers the deception, but not knowing what Marcelle intends we share his alarmed uncertainty. However, a second servant confirms that Théodore is missing simply because she has been freed, not taken to the brothel; Placide is only too willing to believe this and begins chiding himself for mistrusting Marcelle, while we have no sound reason for not sharing his optimism. Placide continues to praise Marcelle at the entry of Théodore's guard, Paulin, to the latter's astonishment; only after some confusion does Placide understand that Théodore has indeed been sent to the brothel. Following his hopes, his anger and grief are intense. Paulin reports that Didyme followed Théodore into the brothel. Placide has long suspected her of preferring Didyme to himself, and jealous rage is added to his other feelings. Paulin continues that, after Didyme left, the next to go in was Cléobule, a friend to Placide and related to Théodore; Placide is disgusted at this treachery, despite Paulin's assertion that Cléobule intended to rescue Théodore. When Cléobule now enters, Placide praises him sarcastically for his role in the escape. Though surprised, Cléobule supposes he has already learned of her disappearance; only after this misunderstanding is resolved does Placide learn that she escaped by changing clothes with Didyme. Placide has been wrought to such a pitch of emotion that when Didyme is now led in under arrest, he might be expected to kill his rival on the spot. He masters himself, but accuses Didyme of taking advantage of Théodore in the brothel. Didyme insists that he simply exchanged clothes with her to allow her to flee. Placide admires Didyme's *générosité* in risking his life for Théodore's honour and is ashamed that his own love did not inspire him similarly; with heroic renunciation, he promises to protect Didyme and arrange for him to live safely abroad with Théodore.

In five scenes Placide is driven three times from hope to despair, and three times returns from despair to hope. By having Paulin leave his vantage point before Théodore's escape is discovered, Corneille engineered several poignant misunderstandings before Placide learns the truth.[94] Placide's emotions are further complicated by outrage at Marcelle's treachery, and by jealousy. The act extracts the maximum of emotional turmoil from the simple fact of Théodore's escape.

In the other acts, however, Placide is not the centre of attention; Corneille concentrated at each stage on whichever figure would provide a vivid display of emotions. This insouciance appears particularly in his treatment of the fate of Placide: he stabs himself, but we never learn if the wound is fatal. For the exploration of Placide's emotional state there was no need to go beyond the stabbing since this was a sufficient expression of despair, but if Corneille had wished to establish a pattern of divine justice Placide's end would not have been so unimportant. Corneille was less concerned with the significance of the action than with the amount of pathos it would provide.

Nevertheless, *Théodore* raises intellectual and moral problems no less difficult than those in *Polyeucte*; but here Corneille ignores them. Two difficulties arise in the interview between Théodore and Placide. The latter offers to save the maid from prostitution and suggests that in marriage she would convert him (ll. 850–6). Théodore does not hesitate: she has dedicated her virginity to God and there can be no question of marrying, even to save a pagan. There is here none of the questioning of the hero's unwavering adherence to possibly flawed principles that animated such plays as *Horace*, *Cinna* or *Polyeucte*. Théodore proposes to escape defilement by suicide, which she justifies:

> Ma loi me le défend, mais mon Dieu me l'inspire:
> Il parle, et j'obéis à son secret empire;
> Et contre l'ordre exprès de son commandement,
> Je sens que c'est de lui que vient ce mouvement. (ll. 911–14)

Again, there is no exploration of the problem raised by her supposing herself dispensed by a special revelation from the divine prohibition of suicide.[95] Corneille invented her desire to kill herself for its pathetic effect (redoubled when Placide offers to kill himself instead) and then threw together this flimsy excuse for her without regard to its heretical implications. Equally unsatisfactory is her reason for allowing Didyme to take her place in the brothel, risking his life for her honour. According to Didyme's subsequent account she resisted at first:

> Je m'apprête à l'échange, elle à la mort s'apprête;
> Je lui tends mes habits, elle m'offre sa tête,
> Et demande à sauver un si précieux bien
> Aux dépens de son sang, plutôt qu'au prix du mien;
> Mais Dieu la persuade, et notre combat cesse. (ll. 1447–51)

God apparently persuades her to let Didyme die for her. However, when Didyme is consequently to be executed, she returns to court, intending to save him by dying herself. She explains that she could allow Didyme to die to save her honour, but now that the threat she faces is only death rather than prostitution she cannot let him sacrifice his life for hers, and concludes:

> Rends, Didyme, rends-moi le seul bien où j'aspire:
> C'est le droit de mourir, c'est l'honneur du martyre.
> A quel titre peux-tu me retenir mon bien?   (ll. 1623–5)

Not without justification, Didyme retorts, 'A quel droit voulez-vous vous emparer du mien?' (l. 1626). Corneille sought a pathetic effect from the competition for martyrdom, but the result is only that Théodore seems selfish. There is not in *Théodore* the unflinching confrontation of problems that is Corneille's hallmark: although the maid's impulses are at least as suspect as the initial motivation of Polyeucte's Christianity, their value is not questioned.

The weakness of *Théodore* does not lie in any failure of technique; in fact Corneille seldom displayed greater skill in disposing the action to create tension and subject the characters and audience to powerful emotions. The difficulty is that the technique is not directed to any purpose beyond itself: the actions and emotions do not form any pattern which would invest them with significance as an interpretation of human or Christian experience. There is no sense that it is right that Placide dies (if he does). On some occasions the devices used to arouse pathos positively create moral and intellectual problems, which are ignored. The play is, in short, a melodrama.

It is noteworthy that these three dramatists, all with long experience of their Parisian audiences, saw fit to prepare their hagiographic material for the stage by adding a love-interest. In *Théodore* this motivates the action and provides the major confrontations, but these mostly involve figures other than the saint herself; in the other plays the love-plot is less important, but the role of spectacle and other theatrical devices was correspondingly greater. Only in Rotrou's *Saint-Genest* was the saint's struggle for faith dramatically important, but even here it was overwhelmed by the wealth of other business. The successful professional playwrights seem to have sought the dramatic interest of their saint-plays anywhere but in the saint and his saintliness; the result is like trying to write a play about Lear without mentioning that he was a King.

(v) THE ABSORPTION OF THE CLASSICAL TECHNIQUE IN THE AMATEUR SACRED THEATRE

These plays mark the effective end of the Parisian vogue of the sacred theatre: between 1645 and Racine's *Esther* (1689) only one sacred play was written by an established Parisian dramatist.[96] The Parisian audiences lost their taste for sacred subjects, partly perhaps because of unease at the use of this material to produce predominantly secular entertainments.[97] However, sacred plays continued to be written and performed by amateurs in the provinces; in fact the tradition had continued unabated outside the capital, but during the Parisian vogue of the genre these texts are not known to have been printed.

The provincial taste, as represented by the plays which began again in the mid 1640s to be printed, continued the tradition of providing extensive chronicles of events; and the plays printed in Paris after 1645 also reverted to this form. All, however, showed in various degrees a concern with characterisation, confrontations and tension. The pious dramatists settled to a form containing the matter traditional since the time of the *mystères* (though now more compressed) with something akin to the Classical preference for direct emotional impact. This style remained substantially unchanged while the sacred theatre survived; I shall not pursue its individual manifestations beyond 1650.[98]

In 1645 Jean d'Ennetieres, a former mayor of Tournai,[99] published *Ste. Aldegonde, comedie*, celebrating the traditional subject, a local saint, in the traditional form, a chronicle of her career. Having dedicated herself to God, Aldegonde refuses her parents' wish that she should marry. However, she knows that disobeying her parents is a sin, and is sufficiently humble to doubt that she should trust her own divine inspiration against this rule; the promptings may actually be a demonic temptation. She takes this problem to her spiritual director, Sobin, who assures her that her humility guarantees that her inspiration is genuine.[100] He warns her sternly against the pride that such direct contact with God might arouse. She tells him of a period when God abandoned her, and Sobin explains that He often tries His favourites with severe suffering. Perfectly submissive to His will, she accepts this suffering gladly and without pride at this evidence of divine favour.

In these first two acts d'Ennetieres exercised some skill to rearrange the source[101] to yield a vigorous clash between Aldegonde and her parents and a serious religious dilemma in the saint herself. However, drama of emotions was not the author's main concern: the remainder of the play is devoted to the events of Aldegonde's subsequent saintly career. Acts III and IV concern the romantic and miraculous incidents

of her flight through the forest from her suitor, and the last act provides a summary chronicle of the miracles associated with her cloistral
career. By comparison with the source the space occupied by the love-
plot is expanded, while that devoted to miracles is reduced. D'Ennetieres
modified the traditional chronicle of the saint's career with something
of the Parisian preference for romantic subject-matter, but stopped
short of adopting the Classical method of seeking the spectators'
sympathetic participation.

An author who identified himself only as D.L.T.[102] went further in
combining Classical elements with the matter of the *mystère*, in
Josaphat ou le triomphe de la foy sur les Chaldéens, Tragicomedie
(Toulouse 1646). This play was thought lost after the dispersal of
Soleinne's collection,[103] and no coherent account exists of what it
contains:[104] I shall analyse it in some detail.

D.L.T. omits Josaphat's youth: his subject was only the crisis
provoked by his conversion. This, however, is treated at length, starting
with the conversion itself, in the midst of which the play opens. A
pedlar promises the solitary prince Josaphat a panacea for his
melancholy, that can be acquired simply by desiring it: he proffers
a Bible, with a prayer for his conversion. Josaphat reads and declares:

> C'en est fait je me rends sans avoir combatu,
> Je ne puis resister, succombez ma vertu,
> Contre tant de puissance il faut baisser les armes,
> On ne sçauroit manquer en adorant ses charmes,
> Et puisque c'est un Dieu qui veut être vainqueur
> Bien loin de reculer, offrons luy nôtre coeur.   (1 ii. p. 7)

To justify this sudden conversion Josaphat reveals that he has long
had doubts about paganism, and that his father, King Abenner, has
imprisoned him from infancy in his solitary palace so as to shield him
from any contact with Christians, because astrologers had predicted
his conversion. It also emerges that the pedlar is really a hermit,
Barlaam. Josaphat's *gouverneur*, Zardan, overhears the conversion
from 'derrière la tapisserie en avançant la teste' (stage direction, 1 ii,
p. 6) and is placed in a dilemma when the arrival of Abenner is
unexpectedly announced: he ought to warn the King of Josaphat's
conversion, but fears the consequences for his pupil. Abenner explains
that he thinks Josaphat old enough to be exposed to the world, and
arranges for his *début* at court. In the first act D.L.T. shows some skill
in rearranging the source[105] to provide a precipitate opening, a dilemma,
and a note of tension at the end.

In act II, Zardan has betrayed Josaphat, who persuades Barlaam to
flee despite his disregard for his own safety. Josaphat tells his sister,
Géronde (added by D.L.T. to the legend), that he is being punished

for his excess of virtue. He is summoned to the King, leaving Géronde dismayed by his obscure hints, the more so since she has had a dream portending disaster. Abenner enters, having interviewed his son, and vents his rage at his conversion; men are sent to find Barlaam. His favourite, Arachés, proposes a remedy: Nacor shall impersonate Barlaam, whom he closely resembles, and shall pretend to be convinced in public debate by pagan philosophers that Christianity is an error; seeing his mentor confuted, Josaphat will have to recant. Abenner browbeats his son, but seeing that he is making no impression proposes that Barlaam should sustain his faith in public debate. Knowing Barlaam to be safe, Josaphat agrees, but to his dismay Abenner announces that he has been caught. However, Zardan makes amends for his earlier betrayal by revealing to Josaphat that Barlaam has not been found and will be impersonated by Nacor.[106]

Act III begins with an interview between Géronde and Arachés, her *amant*; to his disappointment she is too anxious for Josaphat to speak of love. Abenner enters and reproaches them for dallying at such a time; Arachés hastens to declare that they were not. Nacor is brought in disguised as Barlaam, and reminded by the King of the role he must play. When Josaphat enters he similarly tells 'Barlaam' that if the debate reveals Christianity to be an error, he will kill him for having misled him. Nacor reflects unhappily that Abenner will kill him if Christianity wins the debate and Josaphat if it loses; but he feels a divine inspiration and decides to refute paganism no matter what the danger. Overhearing his soliloquy, Géronde reflects that the Christian God must have real power. It is reported that Nacor has converted the pagan philosophers (the Chaldéens of the title); Abenner resolves to execute them.

In act IV Josaphat thanks God for the victory. Nacor and Zardan declare themselves to be Christians and are arrested; Josaphat envies them. He is next confronted with his sister, an interview he fears, but she reveals that she has been converted by the example of his endurance of persecution. Hearing Abenner approach, she persuades Josaphat to avoid his wrath; it soon emerges that she sent him away so as to enjoy alone the glory of defying the King, to whom she announces her conversion. Dismayed at losing both his children, Abenner sends Géronde off under arrest. Arachés wonders whether he should remain loyal to Géronde or Abenner. Abenner threatens Nacor with torture, but he is undismayed; Zardan is threatened more gently, and sent to prison. Nacor's martyrdom is recounted. Arachés attempts to defend Géronde, but Abenner silences him. A courtier, Theudas, suggests a new scheme for reconverting Josaphat: his *valets* shall be replaced with female servants, who will seduce him and so be able to cajole him into returning to paganism. At this stage in St John's narrative Abenner himself seems on the point of conversion; D.L.T.'s King gives no sign of wavering.

In act v the Princess Emadule, a captive of war, is promised that if she seduces and reconverts Josaphat she will be freed and shall marry him. Josaphat refuses even to look at her, and when she turns the conversation to love speaks only of love of God. Emadule fears Abenner's wrath when he learns of her failure, but when he enters he does not rage: he hears the voice of God:

> Ce secret mouvement dont mon ame est navrée
> Est-il de ton secours une marque asseurée?
> Et cette vive ardeur dont je me sens brusler
> Est-ce ta voix enfin qui me vient appeller?
> Non, tu veux m'espreuver, il faut que ma constance
> Contre ce feint assaut use de resistance,
> Ton effort sera vain comme dissimulé,
> Et mon coeur ne peut être aisement ébranlé.
> Mais d'ou vient malgré moi que tant plus je resiste,
> Ce mouvement me force, et céte ardeur persiste?
> Que mon coeur dechiré par ces deux passions
> De fuïr ou d'ecouter tes inspirations,
> Encline à celle-cy par un noeud qui l'attache,
> Et devienne pour l'autre et si féble et si lâche?
> Ha c'est trop là dessus consulter ma raison!
> Mes doutes éclaircis ne sont plus de saison;
> Je vois bien que tu veux surmonter ma malice
> Par tes rares bontez, et non par ta justice,
> Et que pour effacer les crimes que j'ay faits
> Tu ne me veux punir qu'à force de bienfaits.   (v iv, pp. 94–5)

He decides to announce his conversion to the whole court; meanwhile Emadule declares herself to be converted by his example. Josaphat, Géronde and Zardan enter and rejoice at his announcement; Arachés, declaring that Kings are never wrong, is also converted, as is Theudas. Abenner resigns his crown to his son, who refuses it, having no interest in the world; at his father's insistence he accepts, but only to resign in favour of Arachés, declaring that he intends to leave the court. Abenner begs him not to abandon him in his old age, but Josaphat explains that 'C'est le Ciel qui m'inspire' (v v, p. 102); Abenner resigns himself to his departure, and does what he can to reconcile Géronde to it by marrying her to Arachés. In the final scene Josaphat is left alone to thank God for his triumph and announce his intention of becoming a hermit.[107]

D.L.T. omitted Joasaph's pious end as he had omitted his youth, retaining only the crucial episode of his conversion and near-martyr-dom. This he treated as a complex psychological intrigue, in which the action is driven by the conflicting interests and passions – sexual, paternal and sisterly love, faith and *raison d'état* – of closely connected characters. The secondary figures (excepting Barlaam and Emadule) do not appear in one episode only, as in the *mystères*: they are treated as characters in their own right, so that their interventions in the action may have their full force and the spectator may develop some attachment to their interests. Above all, D.L.T. invented Géronde, a liberty which the printer explained in the Preface:

Il y [à l'histoire] a ajoûté le personnage d'une soeur afin de la rendre plus agreable par ce nouvel incident, et de mêler un peu de guerre et un peu d'amour avec beaucoup d'artifice et beaucoup de constance.   (f. B2ᵛ)

Géronde's feelings towards her brother and her father and her love for Arachés contribute greatly towards the variety and complexity of interests at work. The psychological drama is combined, however, with features derived from the tradition of the *mystères*: the story is narrated *in extenso* and miracles abound.[108] Once converted, the Christians never waver: the psychological drama does not concern their belief. D.L.T. produced a rather successful combination of the pious chronicle of the saint's *acta* with psychological drama; but religion and drama remain separate, for the anguish endured by the characters does not involve their faith.

A second play on the subject appeared in the following year.[109] *Josaphat, tragicomedie* was written by an established Parisian dramatist, Jean Magnon,[110] but it provided as extensive an account of the legend as D.L.T.'s version, from Josaphat's conversion (here placed after his return to court) to his triumph over his father.[111] The major sources of interest are a love-triangle, involving the saint himself, and suspense over Josaphat's fate. This material is skilfully handled to produce a variety of emotions and moods, and many vicissitudes to excite our concern for the characters; but these are too superficially drawn to sustain much sympathy. Each is endowed with a dilemma, but in each case it is expressed by the character's contradicting in one line what he said in the last: it is resolved when he lights on one option or the other, but there seems often no good reason why the choice should not have gone the other way. In consequence the characters appear unstable rather than torn. Some care is taken to motivate their conversions, but their Christianity consists only of an urgent desire to be martyred; they express no other consciousness of man's relationship with God. For religious content Magnon exhibited a series of miraculous conversions, as in the *mystères*, rather than showing a *crise*; on the other hand the play followed the Parisian vogue in deriving its interest principally from amorous complications

and matters of state. Magnon combined provincial and Parisian techniques on the professional stage: the two tastes were converging.

Parisian tastes did not affect Pierre Mouffle, a legal officer of Saint-
Clair-sur-Epte,[112] who turned to the theatre with the traditional
intention of celebrating the local patron saint. As he put it in the
Avant-parler, his desire was to

redire
Les Heroiques Faicts, les Combats, le Martyre,
Et les rares Vertus du Glorieux Sainct CLAIR...   (pp. 9–10)

Le Fils exilé, ou le martyre de sainct Clair, Tragi-comedie chrestienne
(Paris 1647) conscientiously transcribes the whole of the legend,[113]
omitting only Clair's childhood. Clair is determined to serve God
exclusively, so he leaves England, where his father is King, to avoid
being married. In France he becomes a hermit and effects several
miraculous cures until he enters a monastery to escape his growing fame
as a healer. In the fourth and final act he refuses to lie with a Dame
Impudique who desires him: she is so offended that she has him beheaded by her servants. Clair performs one last miracle: 'Il lave sa
teste dans la fontaine, et la porte jusqu'à l'Eglise' (stage direction, IV
iv, p. 66). Three choirs of angels welcome his soul to Heaven.

Mouffle gives large roles to the incidental figures, who appear in one
episode only before being forgotten as the narrative moves on. Only
Clair figures throughout, but his personality is not developed; his only
characteristic is a wonderful humility, displayed on every occasion.
Having resolved to abandon bride and succession in the service of God,
he knows no further anguish and goes through the vicissitudes of his
life with perfect calm. Like the plays performed a hundred years
earlier, *Sainct Clair* celebrates the local saint in a pious chronicle of
his exemplary words and deeds.

An even greater respect for the source was exhibited by Antoine
Girard Bouvot of Langres in *Judith, ou l'amour de la patrie, tragoedie*
(Paris 1649). In the Dedication he declared that he had used no artifice
in composing the play, but 's'est licencié à suivre et à s'abandonner de
rendre conforme le François au sens litteral du Latin' (f. ã2ᵛ): *Judith*
is as close as possible to a literal translation of the Vulgate. We observe
Nebuchadnezzar's anger against the Jews, the raising of an army for
the campaign, the Jews' preparations for war, the quarrel between
Holofernes and Achior, and Judith's intervention in the siege of
Bethulia; after Holofernes's death, Bouvot shows the rejoicings in the
town and the rout of Holofernes's army.[114] For this epic Bouvot used
the simultaneous setting and allowed himself six acts.

Bouvot's fidelity to his source was so absolute that on two occasions, where the Bible marks a division between chapters, he indicated a division between scenes and an exit, heedless that the result was to break an interview in the middle only to have it resume in the following scene. Bouvot did not appreciate that the formal division into scenes served a dramatic purpose. On the other hand he was capable of adding a comic scene to his source: two captains stagger drunkenly away from Holofernes's tent after the banquet and hope that wine has not incapacitated the general for pleasure with Judith.

A more significant addition is a scene in which Judith, having gained entry into Holofernes's camp, wonders how she is to kill him; the plan is finally suggested by her servant. God apparently inspires her to go to the camp but does not tell her what to do there, and instead inspires the servant. In the Bible Judith is uniquely favoured by God for her virtues; Bouvot changed this so as to give the *confidante* something to do, but the result was only to rob Judith of her special status. Bouvot did not seek to explore the significance of the story as an example of the operation of providence, like the humanists, nor did he explore the impact of the events on the faith of the individuals involved: his respect for the Bible was such that he felt that simply reproducing it was an act of sufficient religious significance. It is unfortunate that his few concessions to dramatic technique were so ill-judged as positively to interfere with the ostensible purpose of staging the story, its religious import.

Bouvot was unusual in modifying his source so little. A more conventional freedom was taken by the unknown author[115] of *Le Martyre de sainte Catherine, tragedie* (Caen and Lyons 1649), who presented Catherine's last hours as an involved intrigue of love and politics.[116] The major action centres in Maximin and concerns his amorous hesitation to execute Catherine. He is not a simple tyrant: he is conscientious in serving the gods, and in realising that his love for Catherine does not allow him to exempt her from the general persecution. In this dilemma he attracts considerable sympathy. Another dilemma confronts Vallerie, the Empress, who was brought up a Christian but has disguised her faith: inspired by Catherine's example she now wishes to end her hypocrisy. With the greatest difficulty, encouraged by Catherine, she finds the necessary courage and defies her husband, provoking him to martyr her. The third major source of interest is a political sub-plot, in which two favourites give Maximin contradictory advice in his dilemma, then in his absence reveal that their declarations about *raison d'état* were motivated by personal interest.[117]

Catherine herself is relatively unimportant as a source of interest. She announces in act I that she is proof against all threats and temptations:

> mon coeur sçait des-ja ce qu'il doit devenir:
> Il ne va pas combattre, il vosle à la victoire . . .   (1 ii, p. 11)

She is indeed spared all combats, and in the few scenes in which she is put under pressure remains perfectly steadfast; only Vallerie, whose role is longer than Catherine's, experiences a struggle for faith. The events around the nominal heroine are handled with skill to yield a tense and interesting drama of love, politics and the feelings of those involved, but the saint and her saintliness contribute little to this effect.

A similar approach was taken by Gaspard Olivier in his *Hermenigilde, tragedie* (Auxerre 1650), though he did not interweave quite so many strands in his *crise*.[118] Personal interest and *raison d'état* produce a tense drama of discord in the Spanish royal family.[119] Moving situations arise when Levigilde, having promised to pardon Hermenigilde, determines after all to execute him. Recarede considers himself responsible for his brother's fate, since he was instrumental in obtaining his submission, and reproaches Levigilde severely; when he remains unmoved, Recarede begs him to kill him as well as his brother. Such scenes of noble feeling and family strife abound, and are even provided at the expense of consistency: thus in act 1 Hermenigilde tells his followers that he is ready to end his rebellion, but in the following scene argues against laying down his arms when Recarede brings Levigilde's offer of a pardon, so that there may be a clash between the brothers.

Olivier's care to arrange confrontations of some emotional intensity is quite undermined by the prose in which the characters lengthily describe their emotions. Although the audience witnesses the meeting of Hermenigilde and Recarede which ends the rebellion, Recarede later describes it in detail, for the benefit of his father:

J'ai vû . . . mais non pas sans horreur, ce Prince de tous les hommes le plus accomply, ensevely dans le düeil, tout pasle de tristesse, dans cet affligeant et aymable desordre, ou la beauté languissoit avec la pitié, la douleur paroissoit dans son Triomphe: mais cependant, il estoit si fort changé de vostre Hermenigilde, qu'il n'estoit connoissable que par les marques de ce grand coeur, d'estre si affligé et de n'en mourir point; aussi eut-on pris son corps pour son ombre, tant il estoit deffait. . . . il ne m'a pas si tost apperçû, qu'il a couru m'embrasser; j'ay reçû par des tendresses son affection, qu'il m'a rendües avec usure, et dans ces ravissantes caresses qu'il m'a faits, nos ames se sont insensiblement colées comme nos corps, aux yeux de tous les Soldats, et comme s'il m'eut transmis la sienne, son esprit est demeuré extasié, et le mien suspendu, et peu apres revenant il a donné a ses l'armes la liberté qu'une insensible sensibilité leur avoit disputée; il les a confondues avec les miennes, et par ces mutuels et cent fois redoublés mouvemens de sang, on nous a vû solemniser la force et la proximité de celuy que nous avons l'honneur de tenir commun avec vous.   (11 iii, pp. 26–7)

This precious language, for all its sentimentality, is remarkably im-
precise in indicating the nature and course of the emotions stated: thus
although Goisuinthe rages at length against Hermenigilde, the spectator
who does not know the story in advance has to wait till act IV to
discover that the reason for her hatred is that she is his stepmother.

That Hermenigilde is a Christian does not emerge until act III,
when Goisuinthe produces forged letters implicating him in a Christian
intrigue against the King.[120] She could as well calumniate him with
some other offence; his faith is only an accident of the plot. Hermenigilde speaks mainly of filial loyalty, not service of God. The principal
effects of the play depend on the relations between father, sons and
stepmother, and on the self-reproach of Recarede and of Levigilde
when he discovers too late that the letters were forged; dramatically
the saint counts for little.

Barbe de Saint-Balmon, the warrior countess,[121] sought interest like
Olivier in the agitations of those surrounding the martyrs. Marc and
Marcellin, the heroes of *Les Jumeaux Martyrs, Tragedie* (Paris 1650),
are already in gaol at the start of the action, which consists largely
of the attempts of family and friends to save them.[122] First their two
friends urge them to save themselves by abandoning Christianity or at
least pretending to. When this fails, their two parents appeal to them
similarly, with equal effect: when their mother begs them to dissimulate,
the cold reply is

> Trahir la verité pour complaire à l'erreur,
> Seroit pour des Chrestiens avoir trop peu de coeur.
> Le Dieu que nous servons se plaist à la franchise,
> Et n'aime pas un coeur que la langue déguise;
> Sa grandeur, son pouvoir, nous le font admirer,
> Son amour, sa douceur, nous le font adorer.   (IV iii, p. 108)

Only when the twins' two wives join the two friends and two parents in
a combined appeal do they feel themselves waver; they pray for
strength. They do not have to find the solution to their dilemma in
themselves: their prayer is answered by the appearance of Sebastien,[123]
who delivers a sermon which converts all the friends and relations, who
thereupon join the twins in seeking martyrdom.

A similar series of appeals is made simultaneously to Cromace, the
judge. He would like to spare the twins, being a friend of their father,
but dare not because he is about to retire and fears the wrath of his
designated successor, Fabian, if it were found that he had favoured
Christians. Eventually he screws up courage to compromise himself
on behalf of the twins, and appeals to the cruel Fabian (to whom the
two friends and the father also appeal); he is threatened with execution

as a Christian. In the last act Cromace is converted by Sebastien's sermon and martyred.

There are two twins, two friends, two wives, two parents. These figures usually appear in pairs, and speak alternately: the effect is most mechanical, especially in interviews between two pairs.[124] Equally mechanical are the conversions in the last act. The series of appeals to the twins and to Cromace by characters with successively stronger moral claims on them produces increasingly severe dilemmas and mounting anguish, but this is not expressed. The author appreciated well how to arrange the action to create mounting pressure, but was quite unable to fill it with the emotions for which she had devised the opportunity.

Even more involved were the interests and relationships in Marthe Cosnard's *Les Chastes Martirs, tragedie chrestienne* (Paris 1650).[125] Three Christians – Philargirippe (an old priest), Agathon and Tryphine – have been wrecked off Sicily. The Prefect, Pompone, holds them under arrest, and falls in love with Tryphine, while his wife conceives a passion for Agathon. Discovering that Agathon is Tryphine's *amant*, Pompone decides to execute his rival on a charge of Christianity; his wife determines to punish him by obliging him to execute Tryphine as well. Meanwhile the Prefet de Mer, also captivated by Tryphine, argues that she falls into his jurisdiction since she was shipwrecked: the Prefects squabble. Tryphine's mother and brother arrive to rescue her, but are converted. Before the five can be martyred, Pompone's wife declares herself a Christian: the Prefet de Mer orders her execution, but the account of the six martyrdoms converts him in turn; he then is executed. Finally the Prefet, converted by a vision of his wife, becomes the eighth martyr.[126]

Conversion consists simply of a sudden announcement of the character's desire to endure martyrdom; the last act recalls the automatic conversions of the *mystères*. On the other hand, much space is given to the material of which psychological drama is made: the love-intrigues, the clashes between Pompone and his wife, the quarrel with the Prefet de Mer. Only the religious element is not handled by the Classical method: here the author turned to the traditional pious chronicle of prodigies, with no study of the characters' religious struggles. The result in an otherwise Classical play is that the religious basis of the story takes second place to its romantic content.

Although the vogue of the Classical sacred theatre was brief and confined to the professional stage in Paris, it exerted a considerable influence on the genre as it continued to be practised by amateur authors throughout France. They adhered to two venerable traditions, some, like Sainct André and Jacquemin (considered in Chapter 3), presenting matters of doctrine with the minimum of adornment, and others presenting chronicles of the saint's career and associated prodigies. Of those who took the latter course, Mouffle and Bouvot preferred to offer a plain narrative of the story, but the others exercised considerable ingenuity and technical skill in rearranging history or legend in order to satisfy the Classical taste for emotional impact by providing tense intrigues in which personal interest (provided by a love-plot) and *raison d'état* combine to produce vigorous conflicts between the characters. These features are the principal sources of interest; though *Polyeucte* had shown that religion could provide the motive power of a saint-play, these authors did not seek dramatic interest in the saint's faith and his struggle to maintain it, although the reason for choosing a saint rather than any other hero as subject was his religious significance. The amateurs no doubt selected sacred subjects with pious intentions, but were unable to get to the real heart of their material: because they adopted the fashionable form developed in the professional theatre without making the adjustment of concentrating on the hero's faith rather than his passions, they could not help but produce plays in which interest centred outside the ostensible subject, the saint and his religious life.

*   *   *

The devices of the Classical style were designed to yield a drama which achieved its effects by allowing the spectator to participate in the emotional states and crises of the characters. Incident was omitted and the action was restricted to the moments immediately leading to the disaster, which was provoked by a complex intrigue involving the conflicting interests of the characters: the effect was to intensify the pressures on these and on the sympathetic spectator. The characters were required to behave unselfconsciously, as if no audience were present, and although many artifices were in fact employed, the stage world was by convention considered to be real, so that no obstacle of artificiality should prevent the spectator from identifying with the heroes. The effect sought, however, was not simply emotional exaltation and release for the spectator: the best dramatists also arranged the action to suggest how the pressures of events, principles, passions and personalities converged in a number of interdependent figures to provoke the catastrophe. The result was both to transport the spectator, and to offer an insight into the mechanism of disaster which seems to suggest an explanation of human suffering by showing it to conform to intelligible patterns.

It is a matter of some surprise that among the early Classical dramatists who took sacred subjects only Corneille fully exploited the capacity of this style to express the religious significance of such material. In *Polyeucte* the spectator shares the saint's anguish as he struggles to maintain and purify his faith: the dramatic and religious actions of the play are one. In the other Classical plays on sacred subjects the dramatists seem to have depended for interest on almost any element other than the hero's faith: love, politics, the tensions and shocks of the intrigue, vivid confrontations, spectacle. These were essentially means, but the dramatists took them as ends in their own right; among the pious playwrights Corneille alone was completely successful in *Polyeucte* in harnessing these components of the drama-tist's armoury of effects to yield an account of his sacred subject that while moving the spectator offered him also some experience of the operation of universal truths in individuals' lives.

Few of Corneille's contemporaries seem to have possessed a profound understanding of the Classical system which they used: they had grasped its superficial requirements, and duly produced confrontations and dilemmas in plenty, but they had not appreciated its capacity for significance. In La Calprenède's *Hermenigilde*, for instance, or La Serre's *Thomas Morus*, the vigorous exchanges carefully arranged between the characters do not produce any change in the situation or in their perception of it: the characters are brought together, not to afford an insight into how the coming together of people provokes the catastrophe, nor to learn and to explain to the audience their own responsibility for it, but to produce emotional fireworks which are appreciated for their own sake. The fireworks are not directed towards illuminating the human condition; the varied emotional shocks enjoyed by the spectator do not offer a glimpse of how the emotions paraded may be understood and accepted as part of the human lot and of God's just design. This was not the result of any incapacity in the Classical dramatic system to illuminate such questions: it is a result of an in-adequacy of creative imagination in the playwrights, a failure to look beyond immediate excitements and arrange the action so that it should offer some explanation of itself.

Conclusion

In the century between 1550 and 1650 the French theatre underwent a transformation in the relationships between author, actor, character and spectator. At the end of the period the author was no longer transparently visible in his creation. In the *mystères* and the humanist plays the authorial presence was strong, as plot and character were manipulated to symbolise the spectator's belief or illustrate a theme. In the chronicle plays of the early seventeenth century the manipulative presence of the author was less apparent, but the handling of the story depended more on the audience's prior knowledge, as in the *mystères*, than on inner logic: the stage world was still subject to external control. In the Classical theatre, on the other hand, this element of external direction was removed: as Chapelain pointed out at the time, the author was 'hidden'[1] and did not speak with his own voice. The requirement was that the spectator should not see the play as a deliberate human creation, but approach it like the other experiences that life offers, sharing the concerns of the characters as if his reactions had not been pre-ordained by the poet.

A parallel transformation overtook the position of the actor. It seems indispensable to us that the actor should first identify with his role if his performance is to be convincing, but such a requirement had not existed before the advent of the Classical style; it was then quickly identified by the critics.[2] Previously the actor's duty had been to exhibit the significance of his character in the symbolic pattern and to draw attention, in the humanist theatre at least, to the fine lines the poet had provided; on the Classical stage, by contrast, his duty was to assist the spectator to experience how it felt to be in the position of the protagonist, for which the actor had first to experience these emotions himself. Notoriously it was Molière who was responsible for instituting a natural style of acting, in which the performer interposed his own personality as little as possible between the character and the spectator;

but the need for such a style had been implicit in the Classical theatre from its beginning.

The position of the character was similarly transformed. In the *mystères* and the later chronicles he was a projection of the audience's expectations and beliefs rather than a person in his own right. In the propaganda and the humanist theatre the character was a symbol: the Pharaohs of Chantelouve or Heyns were tyrants rather than individuals, important principally as elements in the exemplary patterns. In either case the character's behaviour was governed by requirements from the other side of the footlights. On the Classical stage, on the other hand, the character was required to behave as if no audience were present, to pretend that his actions were not directed towards affecting the spectator but were dictated by his own inner imperatives. By seeming to be engaged in his own unique and autonomous life, the character allowed the spectator to believe in him and identify with him in a way that was not intended with the self-consciously symbolic or exemplary figures used in the earlier theatre.

The sum effect of these changes on the position of the spectator was, perhaps, to make him into a spectator where previously he had been something of a collaborator. The *mystères*, the later chronicles and the doctrinal plays required him to contribute his religious knowledge and his belief if the action, which was otherwise deliberately implausible, was to make sense. The humanist and the propaganda dramas required the spectator to apply his judgement to the various more or less discrete episodes so as to synthesise them into exemplary patterns. The Classical theatre, by contrast, required the spectator to open his heart and absorb into his own being the human experience that was offered. Full appreciation of the Classical play required, of course, the active application of intelligence and sensibility, but not quite the positive collaboration that was needed earlier if the play was to mean anything: where previously the spectator had almost to create the theatrical experience himself out of the symbolic materials the author offered, the Classical work transmitted some thrill even when the spectator was lazy or inattentive.

On first meeting the Classical theatre one is inevitably impressed by its artificialities, its ornateness and its remoteness from everyday life, but despite the apparent distance of the style from the plays of our own day its fundamental principle is the same as has continued to inform the theatre until recently: to move the spectator by sympathy with the protagonists. The Classical theatre was far from offering a slice of life, but in this principle it did not differ from the work of Chekhov. In this sense the Romantic revolution was less momentous than the transformation that overtook the theatre on the advent of Classicism. Before that date, the play had presented a symbol; after it, a vicarious experience. The latter style has dominated our expectations of the theatre (which, after all, is why we call it Classical); but now, with the benefit of the experiments with which the name of Brecht is principally associated, we are in a position once again to give due value to the earlier approaches which disdained verisimilitude in the interests of representing the poet's apprehension of the meaning of life.

I promised at the beginning of this book to attempt to say a little about the tragic status of these plays and whether indeed such a thing as religious tragedy can exist. Following an examination of many examples of plays that were described as religious tragedies by their authors, this seems to be the point at which to return to the question. The general opinion has been that a religious action can hardly provide material for drama, still less for tragedy, since the conclusion is predetermined and the hero is rewarded for his trials with eternal bliss at the end; but on these grounds Sophocles too would be disqualified. Tragedy, I believe, is not wholly negative in its conclusion, nor does it consist only of sharing the hero's misery, while Christianity allows the saint more sufferings than a squeamish piety might admit. The trials that figures such as Polyeucte and Abraham endure as they struggle to do what they know to be right despite the world and their own inclinations seem to me eminently dramatic, and tragic too not only in the portrait of individual anguish but also in the suggestion of a redeeming order beyond the apparent chaos of human life. The majority of the plays of the period considered here did not use the individual sympathetic hero and were not tragic in this sense, though some, such as Garnier's *Les Juifves*, at least approached tragedy of this kind; but of the plays in other styles a respectable number offered at least something akin to the tragic insight into the sense of human suffering.

By this I mean that tragedy requires, not only that the victim should endure a frightful destiny, against which in the name of humanity he puts up a heroic but pathetically unavailing resistance, but in addition that his suffering should be accepted by the audience at least as in some way right and fitting; while it is unjust according to human notions of equity, it is sensed to be appropriate according to a supernatural order, which tragedy allows the spectator mysteriously to apprehend without necessarily making it articulate. Catharsis is the recognition that the universe contains laws which surpass human understanding, and that a fate which seems cruel in men's judgement may nevertheless be just according to this superior pattern of right. It is not enough for a tragedy to show a man nobly undergoing a harsh fate: this would be merely outrageous and senseless, not tragic. The full tragic emotion requires that the play should give some sense of the fitness of things which governs the hero's horrible doom. It requires, in other words, something like a religious confidence that the seemingly arbitrary disasters of human life can be shown to make sense. For the ancient Greeks, the fitness of the tragic fate was guaranteed by the gods.[3] For modern audiences, without any firm belief in a deity, the sense of appropriateness is provided by the conviction that things could not have been otherwise which is generated by the patterns and rhythms of the plot, that is, by the play's aesthetic rigour and coherence. This aesthetic assurance of the rightness of the tragic fate also existed, of course, for the Greeks. For the Renaissance too the mysterious justice of tragedy was guaranteed by the aesthetic sense of appropriateness, and by belief in a God defined as Just.

Such a view of tragedy is no doubt a twentieth-century or at least a post-Classical one, for it requires a degree of sympathy with the hero in his apparently unwarranted anguish and so seems to exclude the humanist plays, in which the exercise of judgement rather than sympathy was usually required of the spectator. Sympathetic identification with the hero was called for uniquely in the outstanding masterpiece of the humanist sacred theatre, *Les Juifves*. Sedecie's struggle to accept his sufferings as just simultaneously excites pity and provides an insight into the workings of the supernatural order: here we do attain something akin to the tragic insight as I have attempted to define it. In La Taille's *Saül* too we share the hero's anxieties, but any sense in the spectator of reconciliation to Saül's anxieties is at best confused. These two plays, however, were not typical of the humanist theatre: the authors in the main did not aim at a tragedy based on empathy, but sought to provide historical or even, in the case of Grezin, allegorical examples of divine justice. They found drama and a significance similar to that which we find in tragedy in the establishment of a pattern which stood as an archetype of good and evil, chaos and the divine order. The destruction of persecutors such as Haman or Pharaoh, no less than that of more amiable figures, was a reminder of the mutability of fortune to which all men are subject, and of the divine plan governing this apparent disorder. It is perhaps difficult for us, accustomed to giving our attention to the individual human figure, Lear or Oedipus, to find much power in a conflict which can take place only in the spectator's mind because the representatives of good and evil never meet on the stage; but the humanist spectator looked beyond the immediate subject-matter of the play to see symbolised in it a compelling picture of his own fate.

Much in the humanists' writing, however, was calculated to prevent the spectator's seeing beyond the surface of the text. The preoccupation with stylistic ornaments was allied in many authors with an inability to look beyond the individual line or incident to create a larger pattern of experience informing the whole action. Moreover, the imagination of many of the poets was not only short-winded, but fundamentally prosaic: their plays said little that could not have been expressed in expository prose as well or better. Matthieu was perhaps the worst offender in this respect, though others such as Nancel were hardly behindhand. Few possessed the power of imagination to create and sustain consistently the exemplary pattern that the humanist spectator sought. Only Garnier succeeded completely, while Thierry and Rivaudeau achieved at least the necessary coherence of vision; a few others, among them notably Chantelouve, succeeded in creating the intellectual framework for an illustration of God's purpose, but filled it out with irrelevant or even contradictory material. Many apparently hardly saw the need to fuse their piecemeal offerings of instruction and rhetoric by thematic and poetic patterns into coherent works of art. The weakness of much of the humanist sacred theatre must be attributed, not to any inherent incapacity of the style to present a vision of the world, but in large part to the imaginative poverty of many of the practitioners of the genre.

The authors of the *mystères* and the doctrinal plays of course did not aspire to write tragedy. Here there is never any ambiguity as to how the hero may win the divinity's favour, nor doubt that right will prevail: the tragic exploration of the injustice of the world and the apparent cruelty of the gods is lacking. However, in celebrating God's triumph these plays, and also the works of propaganda, set up a nervous dialogue between the spectator and the stage world: the latter shows God saving the archetypal heroes of the Bible or hagiography, but the spectator is left wondering whether this applies equally to himself, whether he is capable of imitating the example and whether God really died for him too. By their symbolic action the plays demand the spectator's faith, yet at the same time they awaken his doubt. As in the humanist theatre, the most important dialogue in the performance is not that among the characters but that between the spectator and the stage: here the theatrical world was not self-contained, as it was in the Classical system. However, not all the playwrights were successful in thus awakening the spectator to anxiety and awe in the face of the inscrutability of the divinity's intentions towards himself. In the *mystères* as they survived at this time, the accretion of comic and sensational material inhibited any such reaction. The propagandists were often preoccupied with giving more immediate and robust encouragement. Even some of the authors of the doctrinal plays, such as Gaulché and Moucque, allowed themselves to be diverted from their ostensible purpose by considerations of fashion. Nevertheless, in the hands of a competent author such as Buschey, this manner of writing for the theatre was capable not only of recalling the divinity's actions but also of exploring the mysteriousness of His purpose.

The chronicle-plays of the first third of the seventeenth century lacked this capacity to penetrate beneath the surfaces of history. They did not place such demands on the spectator's faith as the *mystères* did, since they presented actions that were at least relatively logical and self-explanatory. The straightforward accounts of events did not hint at greater significance. Here too there were exceptions: Hardy most notably combined a presentation of events and human feelings that invites involvement with some suggestion of the processes by which men destroy their own happiness. Once again, the weakness of many of the plays in this style seems to reflect the incapacity of many of its practitioners more than any inability of the style itself to explore the conditions of human life.

Of the various theatrical styles considered here, the Classical is the only one that has been commonly recognised today as being capable of producing tragedy, though I hope I have shown that the others at least had potential in that direction. The Classical style was peculiarly adapted to exciting the spectator's sympathy for the hero in his anguish. Moreover, by its concentration on what was individual rather than typical in the hero and his fate, it was capable of giving to the theme that the dramatist wished to express an almost corporeal reality. The play had its effect by inviting the spectator to incorporate into his own experience the sensation that it offered of what it feels like to be in the place of the hero: this was a most potent method for the author to share with the spectator his sense of the patterns that life contains. However, the method worked strictly by suggestion: it did not allow any authorial intervention to make the moral plain, either through the self-conscious statements of the figures or through visibly symbolic manipulation of plot and character. In *Polyeucte*, the course of the action and the personalities and sentiments of the characters suggest a rich meditation on the nature of heroism and Christianity which is nowhere explicitly articulated. Few other poets were capable of the sustained effort of creative imagination that such a method of dramatic writing required: they were not able to shape the spectator's responses in such a way that a significant pattern is sensed as emerging, and many, one suspects, were not even conscious of the need so to prompt the spectator throughout the length of the play. In the main the Classical dramatists attended to the devices of the style – confrontations, dilemmas, tension, vivid and varied passions and personalities – without bending these to their end, which was to produce a pattern of ex-

perience. It was all too easy for a Classical play to contain nothing
more than a selection of extraordinary sentiments, as in the work of
La Calprenède or La Serre. The dramatists had perhaps no very
profound understanding of the genre they were using and of the
capacity for significance available in the presentation of the hero's
emotional states. Here the difficulty was not exactly a failure of
imagination (a d'Aubignac or a Saint-Balmon had no difficulty in
inventing innumerable conflicts and pressures); it was rather an absence
in their imagination of breadth and organising power, an inability
to arrange their imaginings into a significant whole, or, in the cases
where a pattern was present, a failure to flesh out the mechanical
armature of conflicts with living characters.

I am conscious that throughout this study I have allowed myself to
adopt a simplification – necessary if its length was to be kept within
bounds – in treating the various dramatic styles as if they existed
almost independently of their users and creators. This separation of
style and practitioner seems justified in any case by the work of the
playwrights themselves. There is no escaping the impression that for
many of the poets studied here the dramatic style prevalent among
their generation dictated their vision, determined their insights and
perceptions no less than the forms they used to express them. No doubt
the perceptions of Bèze, Garnier, Hardy and Corneille were also con-
ditioned to a degree by what the prevailing orthodoxies allowed them
to see, but for them the style adopted was the servant of the vision,
and they recreated the conventions they inherited to make them suitable vehicles for what they had to express. Such creative independence
amounts to genius, and is rare in any age. There is no contradiction,
I think, between this judgement of the bulk of these plays and the
argument that I have been advancing throughout this study, that
allowance should be made for the possibility that those who did not
write Classical dramas had positive reasons for attempting to write
other kinds of play; there is a large step between observing that they
did not always succeed in fulfilling these objectives and condemning
them as failures for not having satisfied the Classical standard. I would
share the opinion of previous scholars that the sacred theatre contained many poor plays, but without accepting their ground for this
assessment, which was that the non-Classical styles were inherently
inferior; in my view the disappointing quality of much of the sacred
theatre must be attributed to the failure of the playwrights to understand or fully realise the expressive capacity of the conventions they
adopted. Used with creative imagination, the dramatic styles of the
mystère and the chronicle, the doctrinal, the propaganda and the
humanist plays, were no less capable than the Classical system of

producing coherent and compelling accounts of the world and man's place within it; but such creative imagination was no more commonplace at that time than at any other.

It may reasonably be asked why I have studied these plays at length if in my view so few of them were of the highest quality. My answer is the one that I gave at the beginning: that aside from any inherent interest, these plays are of value to us in offering an insight into the nature and purpose of the conventions that were current, and are likely to be more representative in these respects than the unique masterpieces of the day. A large part of my intention has been to use the sacred plays as a vehicle for an attempt to define the various dramatic styles and the ways they were designed to work on an audience. It is my hope that the result is to provide, not only a better understanding of the pre-Classical styles, but also a firmer foundation for appreciation of the triumphs of the French Classical theatre.

Chronology of the
French sacred theatre, 1550–1650

I have listed here in chronological order all the editions known to me of French sacred plays made between 1550 and 1650, together with details of performances and dates of composition. Only plays in French are listed, though it is possible that some of the performances of lost texts in the schools, of which the subject was recorded in French, were in fact given in Latin. For the sake of completeness, certain plays on subjects that were only marginally sacred, and were consequently excluded from detailed discussion in the previous chapters, are included here.

No list of performances can claim to be exhaustive. Often it is known that a sacred play was performed at a certain location on a particular date, but the subject of the play is not recorded. Undoubtedly sacred plays were frequently performed by the touring troupes, but it is not known when and where they gave the sacred plays in their repertoires. Similarly, religious fraternities in many towns performed sacred plays every year, but what subjects they chose is no longer known. It has not seemed useful to reproduce such incomplete information; I have listed here only the performances about which we possess the minimum of necessary information: date, location, and title or at least subject. Even with this restriction, some 400 performances are listed; and in evaluating the popularity of the sacred theatre at this time it should be remembered that this impressive total probably represents only a small proportion of the real number of performances.

Fuller information about the editions of the texts is given in the Catalogue. Where I have listed an edition of which I have not seen a copy, the source of my information is mentioned in parentheses.

The composition of a play is mentioned only where this is known to have preceded the first performance or edition by some time, or where a play is known, thanks to some contemporary source, to have been written, but is not known to have been printed or staged. I have not ventured to estimate dates of composition for every play recorded.

Unless it is specified otherwise, references are to the first edition listed in the Catalogue of the play in question. The following abbreviations are also used, in addition to those listed on pp. ix–x:

Actes Raymond Lebègue, *Le Mystère des Actes des apôtres: contribution à l'étude de l'humanisme et du protestantisme au XVIe siècle*, Paris 1929

Brunet Jacques-Charles Brunet, *Manuel du libraire et de l'amateur de livres*, 6 vols, Paris 1860–5, and *Supplément*, 2 vols, Paris 1878–80

Bulard Marcel Bulard, 'Un Manuscrit du Mystère de la Passion découvert en Savoie', *Mélanges de la Société toulousaine d'études classiques* i (1946), pp. 245–63

Busson Henri Busson, *La Pensée religieuse française de Charron à Pascal*, Paris 1933

Dainville François de Dainville, S. J., *Les Jésuites et l'éducation de la société française*, vol. ii, *La Naissance de l'humanisme moderne*, Paris 1940

Dauphiné Jacques Chocheyras, *Le Théâtre religieux en Dauphiné du moyen âge au XVIIIe siècle (domaine français et provençal)*, Geneva 1975

Du Ryer H. C. Lancaster, *Pierre Du Ryer, Dramatist*, Washington 1912

Etudes Raymond Lebègue, *Etudes sur le théâtre français*, vol. i, Paris 1977

'Fêtes' Raymond Lebègue, 'Fêtes religieuses dramatiques en France sous la monarchie absolue', *Maske und Kothurn* x (1964), pp. 217–24

Gofflot L.-V. Gofflot, *Le Théâtre au collège du moyen âge à nos jours*, Paris 1907

Hérelle G. Hérelle, *Les Théâtres ruraux en France (langue d'oc et langue d'oïl) depuis le XIVe siècle jusqu'à nos jours*, Paris 1930 (offprint from *Bulletin de la Société des sciences, lettres, arts et d'études régionales de Bayonne*)

Jonker G. D. Jonker, *Le Protestantisme et le théâtre de langue française au XVIe siècle*, Groningen 1939

Lanson Gustave Lanson, 'Etudes sur les origines de la tragédie classique en France', *RHLF* x (1903), pp. 177–231, 413–36

McGowan Margaret M. McGowan, *L'Art du ballet de cour en France, 1581–1643*, Paris 1963

'Noël Georges' Raymond Lebègue, 'Noël Georges et le théâtre rural en Haute-Bretagne', *Mélanges d'histoire littéraire offerts à Daniel Mornet*, Paris 1951

'Nord' Raymond Lebègue, 'L'Evolution du théâtre dans les provinces du Nord', *La Renaissance dans les provinces du Nord*, ed. F. Lesure, Paris 1956, pp. 117–26

'Notes' Raymond Lebègue, 'Notes sur la tragédie française', *BHR* ix (1947), pp. 190–4

Poupé 1899 Edmond Poupé, 'Les Représentations scéniques à Cuers à la fin du XVIe siècle et au commencement du XVIIe', *Bulletin historique et philologique du Comité des travaux historiques et scientifiques*, 1899, pp. 53–7

Poupé 1900 idem, 'Documents relatifs à des représentations scéniques

	à Correns, au xvie et au xviie siècle', *Bull. hist. et phil.*, 1900, pp. 95–7
Poupé 1903	idem, 'Documents relatifs à des représentations scéniques en Provence au xvie et au xviie siècle', *Bull. hist. et phil.*, 1903, pp. 26–39
Poupé 1904	idem, 'Documents relatifs à des représentations scéniques en Provence du xve au xviie siècle', *Bull. hist. et phil.*, 1904, pp. 13–28
Poupé 1906	idem, 'Documents relatifs à des représentations scéniques en Provence du xvie au xviiie siècle', *Bull. hist. et phil.*, 1906, pp. 33–42
Poupé 1920	idem, 'Documents relatifs à des représentations scéniques en Provence du xve au xviie siècle', *Bull. hist. et phil.*, 1920, pp. 145–58
'Répertoire'	Raymond Lebègue, 'Le Répertoire d'une troupe française à la fin du xvie siècle', *RHT* i (1948), pp. 9–24
Rey-Flaud	Henri Rey-Flaud, *Le Cercle magique: essai sur le théâtre en rond à la fin du moyen âge*, Paris 1973
Savoie	Jacques Chocheyras, *Le Théâtre religieux en Savoie au XVIe siècle*, Geneva 1971
'Tableau comédie'	Raymond Lebègue, 'Tableau de la comédie française de la Renaissance', *BHR* viii (1946), pp. 271–344
'Tableau tragédie'	Raymond Lebègue, 'Tableau de la tragédie française de 1573 à 1610', *BHR* v (1944), pp. 375–93
Théâtre comique	Louis Petit de Julleville, *Histoire du théâtre en France: répertoire du théâtre comique en France au moyen âge*, Paris 1886
'Une Tragédie archaïsante'	Raymond Lebègue, 'Une Tragédie archaïsante à Plombières en 1628', *Annales de l'Est*, sixième série, ix (1958), pp. 187–94

A question mark preceding an entry indicates that the date is approximate.

Performance	Edition	Composition

1550

Histoire d'Abraham, Barjols
  (Poupé 1920, 145)
Actes des apôtres and *Apocalypse*,
  Amiens (*Actes* 30)
Bèze, *Abraham sacrifiant*, Lausanne
  (*TR* 295)
Jugement dernier, Orléans
  (*Mystères* ii 157)
Passion, Amiens ('Nord' 119)
Passion, Rouen, an annual event
  (*Mystères* ii 157)
? *Ste Susanne*, Vitray-en-Beauce
  (*Mystères* ii 157)

Bèze, *Abraham sacrifiant*,
  Geneva

Performance	Edition	Composition
1551		
Sacrifice d'Abraham, Rumilly (*Savoie* 35)	Coignac, *Déconfiture de Goliath*, Geneva; and 2	
S. Etienne, Beaulieu (Hérelle 9)	satires (Brunet)	
Baptême de Jésus-Christ and *S. Jean-Baptiste* (from *Passion*), Draguignan (*Mystères* II 158)		
Patience de Job, Barjols (ed. Meiller, 17)		
Passion, Auxerre (*Mystères* II 158)		
Passion, Champ-le-Blanc (*Dauphiné* 73)		
1552		Barran, *Homme justifié par Foi* (Preface)
1553		
S. Laurent, Lanslevillard (*Savoie* 54)	Bèze, *Abraham sacrifiant*, Geneva	
Notre-Dame de Liesse, Soissons (*TR* 71)		
Vengeance de Notre-Seigneur, Le-Puy-S-Pierre (*Dauphiné* 73)		
Passion, 3 *journées*, Bessans (*Savoie* 12)		
1554		
Prison de réformation, Collège at Clairac (*TR* 150)	Barran, *Homme justifié par Foi*, Geneva	
1555		
Miracle de la Vierge, S.-Omer ('Nord' 124)		
1556		
Patience de Job, Rouen (ed. Meiller 169)		
Passion, Le Puy (Lanson 196)		
Passion, Seillans (Hérelle 13)		
Ste Susanne, Barjols (Poupé 1920, 145)		
Conception de la très-sainte Vierge, Le Mans (*Mystères* II 159)		

Performance	Edition	Composition

1557
Sacrifice d'Abraham and *Vendition de Joseph*, Nancy (*Mystères* II 161)
L'Assomption, Jesuit College, Billom (Dainville 187)
Création des premiers parents and other sections of *VT*, Draguignan (*Mystères* II 160)
S. Etienne, Jesuit College, Billom (Dainville 187)
L'Eucharistie, Jesuit College, Billom (Dainville 187)

1558

Abel et Caïn, Jesuit College, Billom (Dainville 188)	Naogeorgus, *Marchand converti*, trans. Crespin, Geneva (*Soleinne* 294)	
Jugement et finiment du monde, Barjols (Poupé 1906, 35)		
Malingre, *Maladie de chrétienté*, La Rochelle (Lanson 197)		
Défloration de Thamar, Douai ('Nord' 120)		

1559

Joseph le juste, Draguignan (*Mystères* II 161)	*La Vérité cachée*, Geneva	

1560

Apocalypse, Amiens (*Mystères* II 162)		Buchanan, *Jephthé*, trans. Vesel (Privilège)
Ste Appollonie, Astillé (Hérelle 9)		

1561

Badius, *Pape malade*, Geneva (ed. Shaw)	Badius, *Pape malade*, Geneva	
Cousin, *L'Homme affligé*, Lyons (Jonker 71)	Bèze, *Abraham sacrifiant*, Geneva	
	Cousin, *L'Homme affligé*, Lyons (summary only: La Vallière I 162)	
	La Croix, *3 Enfants dans la fornaise*, location unknown	
	Naogeorgus, *Marchand converti*, trans. Crespin, Geneva, 2 eds (Brunet)	

Performance	Edition	Composition
1562		
Sacrifice d'Abraham, Collège at S-Jean-de-Maurienne (*Savoie* 35) *Vie de Mgr S. Eloi*, Béthune ('Nord' 124)	Badius, *Pape malade*, Geneva Foxe, *Triomphe de Jésus-Christ*, trans. Bienvenu, Geneva	? La Taille, *Saül* (ed. Forsyth xv)
1563		
Vengeance de N.-S. Jésus-Christ, Champ-le-Blanc (Hérelle 12) *Veau d'or*, Mouveaux (*Théâtre comique* 395)	Desmasures, *David* trilogy, Geneva (*TR* 338) F.D.B.P., Eglogues sacrées, Lyons (La Vallière I 171) *Timothée chrestien*, Lyons	? La Taille, *Famine* (ed. Hall & Smith 2)
1564		
? *Passion*, Albiez-le-Vieux (Bulard 262)	Macropedius, *Joseph*, trans. Tiron, Antwerp (Approbation 1563)	
1565		
Conversion de Ste Catherine, Draguignan (*Mystères* II 163) *S. Martin*, S-Martin-la-Porte (*Savoie* 59) *Passion*, Argentan (*Mystères* II 163) *S. Sébastien*, Albiez-le-Vieux (*Savoie* 48) *S. Sébastien*, Beaune (*Savoie* 47) *Susannah* in French, German, Greek and Latin, Lausanne (*VT* v lxxvii)	Bèze, *Abraham sacrifiant*, Geneva Grezin, *Advertissements faits à l'homme*, Angoulême	
1566		
Ste Scholastique, Cambrai ('Fêtes' 223)	Buchanan, *Jephthé*, trans. Vesel, Paris (Privilège 1560) Demasures, *David* trilogy and *Bergerie spirituelle*, Geneva Philone, *Josias*, Geneva Rivaudeau, *Aman*, Poitiers	

Performance	Edition	Composition

1567
S. *Jacques*, S-Quentin, annually   Buchanan, *Jephté*, trans. F.
('Nord' 124)   Chrestian, Orléans

Passion, Argentan (*Mystères* II
165)
S. *Sébastien*, Lanslevillard
(*Savoie* 29)

1568
Bienvenu, *Monde malade*, Geneva Bienvenu, *Monde malade*,
(author's Preface)   Geneva
Passion, Argentan (*Mystères* II
165)

1569
Décollation de S. Jean-Baptiste,
Auriol (*Mystères* II 165)

1570
S. *Donat*, Fayence (*Dauphiné*   ? *Mystère de S. Martin*,
161)   location unknown (*TR* 60)
Ste Scholastique, Cambrai
('Fêtes' 223)
Ste Susanne, and *Trois Rois*,
Signes (Poupé 1906, 35)

1571
Abel et Caïn (from *VT*),   ? *Ste Barbe*, Paris, between
Parthenay (*Mystères* II 166)   1571 and 1593
Actes des apôtres, Argentan   ? *Patience de Job*, Paris,
(*Actes* 31)   between 1571 and 1593

1572
Ste Catherine, Jesuit College,   La Taille, *Saül*, Paris
Avignon (Pascoe 115)
Histoire du monde, Aix-en-
Provence (*Dauphiné* 163)
Jugement de Dieu, Modane
(Bulard 262)
Catherine de Parthenay,
Holoferne, La Rochelle
(Lanson 203)
Tiraqueau and Sainte-Marthe,
Job, Poitiers (Lanson 202)
? Vivre, *Abraham et Agar*,
Cologne (author's preface)

Performance	Edition	Composition

1573
Passion et résurrection, S-Jean-de-   Buchanan, *Jephté*, trans.

Maurienne, 4 *journées*   F. Chrestian, Paris
(*Savoie* 5)   La Taille, *La Famine*, Paris
1574
Judith, Collège de la Trinité,   La Taille, *La Famine*, ed. of
Lyons ('Notes' 191)   1573 reissued dated 1574
Jugement de Dieu, Modane
(Bulard 262)

1575
David et Golias, Le Puy, 3   Chantelouve, *Colligny*, Paris
journées, (*VT* IV lxviii)   (approbation 1574)
Histoire du monde, Draguignan
(Lanson 203)
Job, Le Val (Poupé 1920, 146)
Ste Scholastique, Cambrai
('Fêtes' 223)

1576
Abraham, Correns (Poupé 1900,   Bèze, *Abraham sacrifiant*,
94)   Geneva
Histoire de monde, Forcalquier
(Lanson 204)

1577
Calvin, Jesuit College, Pont-à-   Chantelouve, *Pharaon*, Paris
Mousson (Lanson 204)   (Preface dated 1576)
Ste Christine, Cuers (Poupé
1899, 53)
Job, Barjols (*Dauphiné* 156)

1578
S. Jean l'Evangéliste, Jesuit
College, Pont-à-Mousson
(Lanson 204)

1579
Bordesins, *Julien l'apostat*, Jesuit   Des Roches, *Tobie*, Paris
College, Pont-à-Mousson   *Patience de Job*, Paris
(Lanson 206)
Elisée, Achab et Jézabel, Soissons
('Fêtes' 219)
Job, Bargemont (Poupé 1906, 35)
Passion, Montsurs (Hérelle 9)

Performance	Edition	Composition

1580

*Mystère de l'Antéchrist et du
  Jugement*, Modane, 3 *journées*
  (*Savoie* 20)

Fronton du Duc, *Julien l'apostat*,
  Jesuit College, Pont-à-
  Mousson ('Tableau tragédie'
  385)

Fronton du Duc, *Pucelle
  d'Orléans*, Jesuit College,
  Pont-à-Mousson (Preface)

Jugement dernier, S-Jean-de-
  Maurienne (*S. Sébastien*, ed. F.
  Rabut, introduction)

D'Amboise, *Holoferne*, Paris

Bèze, *Abraham sacrifiant*,
  Antwerp

Le Coq, *Caïn et Abel*, Paris

? *Vie de Mme Ste Marguerite*,
  Paris?

Vivre, *Abraham et Agar*,
  Antwerp

1581

Tobie (from *VT*), Amiens
  (*Mystères* II 169)

Buchanan, *Jephté*, trans.
  F. Chrestian, Geneva

Fronton du Duc, *Pucelle
  d'Orléans*, Nancy

? *Patience de Job*, Lyons,
  between 1581 and 1592

1582

Abel, Seillans (Poupé 1903, 27)

Heyns, *Holoferne et Judith*,
  Antwerp (p. 91)

Patience de Job, Seillans (Poupé
  1903, 27)

Conversion de Ste Marie Madeleine,
  S-Maximin (Poupé 1904, 13)

Ste Susanne, Lorgues (Poupé
  1904, 13)

Bèze, *Abraham sacrifiant*,
  Geneva

Chantelouve, *Pharaon*,
  Lyons (Brunet)

Desmasures, *David* trilogy,
  Antwerp

Naogeorgus, *Marchand
  converti*, trans. Crespin,
  Geneva

1583

Matthieu, *Esther*, College at
  Verceil (Lanson 208)

Passion, Bessans, 3 *journées*
  (*Savoie* 12)

Passion, Fayence (Poupé 1904,
  13)

Desmasures, *David* trilogy
  and *Bergerie spirituelle*,
  Geneva

Garnier, *Les Juifves*, Paris

Philone, *Josias*,
  Geneva

Performance	Edition	Composition

1584

S. *André*, La Cadière (Poupé 1920, 146)

Crocus, *Joseph*, trans. Cahaignes, Caen ('Tableau comédie' 295)

Histoire du monde, Cuers (Poupé 1899, 53)

Histoire du monde, Seillans (Poupé 1903, 27)

Ste Marguerite, Bargemont (Hérelle 13)

Passion, Bargemont (Poupé, 35)

Saül furieux (by La Taille?), Amiens (*TR* 435)

Badius, *Pape malade*, Geneva

Du Monin, *Peste de la Peste*, Paris

? Buchanan, *Jephté*, trans. Le Digne, before 1584 (La Croix du Maine II 154)

? Le Duchat, *Tragédie de Susanne*, before 1584 (La Croix du Maine I 216)

1585

La Mort d'Olofernes, Le Puy, 2 journées (Lanson 210)

? *Passion*, Fontcouvert (*Savoie* 15)

Garnier, *Tragédies* (containing *Les Juifves*), Paris

Matthieu, *Esther*, Lyons

Naogeorgus, *Marchand converti*, trans. Crespin, Geneva

1586

Buschey, *L'Incarnation*, in church at Bastogne (Dedication)

Philone, *Adonias*, Lausanne

1587

Du Monin, *Peste de la Peste*, Collège de Nazareth, Brussels ('Tableau tragédie' 386)

Judith, Grenoble (*Dauphiné* 63)

Buchanan, *Jephté*, trans. F. Chrestian, with Desmasures, *David* trilogy, Paris

Buschey, *L'Incarnation*, Antwerp

1588

George, *Tentations d'Abraham*, Montbéliard (Lanson 211)

Les Innocents, College at Besançon ('Tableau tragédie' 375)

Siège de Jérusalem, Jesuit College, Pont-à-Mousson (Gofflot 299)

Garnier, *Tragédies*, Toulouse

1589

Bienvenu, *Frère Fecisti*, Nîmes

Buchanan, *Baptiste*, trans. Brisset, Tours (some copies dated 1590)

Performance	Edition	Composition
	Garnier, *Tragédies*, Niort	
	Matthieu, *Aman* and *Vasthi*, Lyons	
	Matthieu, *La Guisiade*, Lyons, 3 eds	
	Perrin, *Sichem*, Paris	
	Poncet, *Colloque chrétien*, Paris	
	Vivre, *Abraham et Agar*, Rotterdam	

1590
Julien l'apostat, Jesuit College, Lyons ('Notes' 191)
Passion, Lille (*TR* 48)

1591
Patience de Job, Paris ('Noël Georges' 30)

Naogeorgus, *Marchand converti*, trans. Crespin, with Badius, *Pape malade*, Geneva

1592
Belyard, *Le Guysien*, Troyes (Dedication)

Belyard, *Charlot* and *Le Guysien*, Troyes
Bèze, *Abraham sacrifiant*, Geneva
Garnier, *Tragédies*, Antwerp
Garnier, *Tragédies*, Lyons
? *Patience de Job*, Lyons, between 1592 and 1603

1593
Siège de Jérusalem, Jesuit College, Pont-à-Mousson (McGowan 206)

1594
Bèze, *Abraham sacrifiant*, Leyden (*TR* 312)
Garnier, *Les Juifves*, Arras (*Etudes* 260)
Jugement de Salomon, Louvain (Rey-Flaud 216)

Bèze, *Abraham sacrifiant*, Geneva
Naogeorgus, *Marchand converti*, trans. Crespin, Geneva

1595
Bèze, *Abraham sacrifiant*, Leyden ('Répertoire' 14)

Bèze, *Abraham sacrifiant*, Geneva

Performance	Edition	Composition
Siège de Jérusalem, Jesuit College, Pont-à-Mousson (Lanson 214) *Passion*, Seillans (Poupé 1903, 27)	Desmasures, *David* trilogy, ed. of 1587 reissued dated 1595 (Brunet) Garnier, *Tragédies*, Lyons, 3 eds Vivre, *Abraham et Agar*, Antwerp	

1596

Bardon de Brun, *S. Jacques*, Limoges (title-page) *Tobie*, Seillans (Poupé 1903, 27) *Histoire des Maccabées ards* (by Virey?), Aix-en-Provence (*Dauphiné* 157)	Bardon de Brun, *S. Jacques*, Limoges Garnier, *Tragédies*, Rouen, 2 eds Heyns, *Holoferne et Judith*, Amsterdam Laudun d'Aigaliers, *Diocletian*, Paris Virey, *La Machabée*, Rouen	

1597

Ste Barbe, Bargemont (Poupé 1906, 35) *Ste Barbe*, Fréjus (Poupé 1904, 14) *Joseph*, Seillans (Poupé 1903, 27) *Mystère de S. Joseph*, Amiens ('Nord' 124) ? *Passion*, Aime (*Savoie* 15)	Garnier, *Tragédies*, Lyons Heyns, *Comédies et tragédies* (containing *Jokebed*, and *Holoferne et Judith* ed. of 1596), Amsterdam	

1598

Behourt, *Esaü*, Collège des Bons-Enfants, Rouen (title-page) *Ste Catherine*, Collège de l'Arc, Dôle ('Tableau tragédie' 387) *Le Chevalier désespéré* (a *Miracle de N-D*), Barjols (*Dauphiné* 162) *Patience de Job*, Callas (ed. Meiller 170) *Ste Julienne*, Nuillé-sur-Vicoin (*Mystères* II 171) *Vie et passion de S. Pierre*, Jarriers (Bulard 262)	Behourt, *Esaü*, Rouen (some copies dated 1599) Bèze, *Abraham sacrifiant*, Geneva Garnier, *Tragédies*, Niort La Taille, *Saül* ed. of 1572, and *La Famine* ed. of 1573, reissued dated 1598 Virey, *La Machabée*, Rouen (some copies dated 1599)	

Performance	Edition	Composition

1599

Passion de Mgr S. Barthélemy, Béthune ('Nord' 124)
Garnier, *Tragédies*, Paris, 3 eds, and Rouen, 2 eds

Vendition de Joseph, Bréal ('Noël Georges' 31)
Heudon, *S. Clouaud*, Rouen

Noces de Cana, Jesuit College, Pont-à-Mousson (Gofflot 299)
Anthology, *Diverses tragédies de plusieurs auteurs de ce temps*, Rouen (contains

Saül furieux (by La Taille?), Jesuit College, Pont-à-Mousson (Lanson 216)
Behourt, *Esaü* (1599); Heudon, *S. Clouaud* (1599);

Virey, *La Machabée*, Vallognes (Lanson 215)
Virey, *La Machabée* (1598))

1600

Abraham, Signes (Poupé 1906, 35)
Fonteny, *Cléophon*, Paris

? Garnier, *Les Juifves*, Angoumois (Lanson 217)
Garnier, *Tragédies*, Lyons
? *Patience de Job*, Rouen

S. Jean-Baptiste, Salbertrand (*Dauphiné* 124)
Thierry, *David*, Pontoise
Virey, *Victoire des Machabées*,

Jézabel, Collège de l'Arc, Dôle ('Tableau tragédie' 387)
Rouen

S. Laurent, Barjols (Poupé 1920, 145)

? *Conversion de Ste Marie-Madeleine*, Grasse (*Mystères* II 171)

? Mauger, *Lavement des pieds*, Rouen (ed. Le Verdier)

Mondot, *Le Petit Joseph*, Le Puy, 3 *journées* (Lanson 218)

Rivier, *S. Paulin de Nôle*, Jesuit College, Pont-à-Mousson (Lanson 218)

S. Romaric, Remiremont (*Mystères* II 172)

Verdier, *L'Histoire de Jonas*, College at Arles (*RHT* II (1950) 194)

1601

Tragédie des Gabaonites (by La Taille?), Béthune (Lanson 218)
Buchanan, *Jephté*, trans. Mage de Fiefmelin, Poitiers

Histoire de la vie et patience de Job, Cuers (Poupé 1899, 53)
Garnier, *Tragédies*, Lyons
Gaulché, *L' Amour divin*, Troyes

Performance	Edition	Composition
S. Julien, Jesuit College, Lille (Lanson 218)	La Taille, *Saül*, Rouen	
	Marcé, *Achab*, Paris	
Ste Marguerite, Malestroit (*Mystères* II 173)	Montchrestien, *Tragédies* (containing *Aman* and *David*) Rouen	
Montreux, Joseph le chaste, Montafié household (Prologue)	Montreux, *Joseph le chaste*, Rouen	
Nativité, Marseilles, 3 *journées*, (*Mystères* II 173)		
S. Paulin, Jesuit College, Pont-à-Mousson ('Tableau tragédie' 385)		
S. Sigismond, Collège de l'Arc, Dôle ('Tableau tragédie' 387)		

1602

S. Alexis, in Latin and French, Jesuit College, Pont-à-Mousson (Lanson 219)	*Ste Barbe*, Lyons	
	Garnier, *Tragédies*, Lyons	
	Garnier, *Tragédies*, Saumur	
Passion, Signes (Poupé 1906, 35)	La Taille, *La Famine*, Rouen	
Résurrection, Bargemont (Poupé 1906, 35)	La Taille, *Saül* ed. of 1572, and *La Famine* ed. of 1573, reissued dated 1602	
L'Usurier (a *Miracle de N-D*), Draguignan (*Dauphiné* 162)	Moucque, *L'Amour desplumé*, Paris	
	Vivre, *Abraham et Agar*, Antwerp	

1603

Vendition de Joseph, Remiremont (*Mystères* II 174)	*Patience de Job*, Lyons	
S. Laurent, Fayence (Poupé 1904, 14)	Montchrestien, *Tragédies*, Rouen	
S. Laurent, Rians (Poupé 1903, 27)	Virey, *La Machabée*, Rouen	
Passion, S-Michel-de-Maurienne (*Savoie* 16)		
Histoire de S. Pons, Draguignan (*Mystères* II 173)		
vow to perform *S. Sébastien*, S-Jean-de-Maurienne (*Savoie* 50)		

1604

? Bèze, *Abraham sacrifiant*,	Des Roches, *Tobie*, Rouen (Soleinne 789)	

erformance	Edition	Composition
Leyden ('Tableau tragédie' 388)	Garnier, *Tragédies*, Rouen 3 eds	
ustache victorieux des Daces, Jesuit College, Rouen (Gofflot 307)	La Pujade, *Jacob*, Bordeaux Le Doux, *Tobie*, Cassel (*VT* v xix)	
arnier, *Les Juifves*, Barjols (Poupé 1920, 145)	Montchrestien, *Tragédies*, Rouen	
Jean-Baptiste, Signes (Poupé 1906, 35)		
a Pujade, *Jacob*, Marguerite's court (Prologue)		
e Doux, *Tobie*, Cassel (Lanson 220)		
. Perrin, *Julien l'apostat*, Jesuit College, Pont-à-Mousson (Lanson 220)		
Mystère de S. Pierre, Jarriers (*Savoie* 65)		
eu de S. Pierre et de S. Paul, S-Martin-la-Porte (*Savoie* 65)		
eu de S. Roch, S-Martin-de-la-Chambre (*Savoie* 65)		
Tropez, S-Tropez (Poupé 1903, 27)		

505

Etienne, Jesuit College, Mons (Lanson 220)	Garnier, *Tragédies*, Rouen, 2 eds	? Hardy, *Mariamne*
eu de S. Rémy, S-Rémy (*Savoie* 65)	Lancel, *Les Quatre Etats*, The Hague	
eu de S. Roch, S-Martin-de-la-Chambre (Bulard 262)	*Marie Magdaleine*, Lyons	

506

Mystère de l'Antechrist et du Jugement, Modane (*Savoie* 20)	Behourt, *Esaü*, Rouen	
arberon, *Mystère des 3 martyres*, Valence (*Dauphiné* 50)	Bèze, *Abraham sacrifiant*, Geneva	
èze, Abraham sacrifiant, for William of Orange's widow (*TR* 312)	Bèze, *Abraham sacrifiant*, Saumur	
estruction de Jérusalem, Fréjus (Poupé 1904, 13)	Garnier, *Tragédies*, Lyons	
	Heudon, *S. Clouaud*, Rouen	
	Jeanne d'Arques, Rouen	
	Montchrestien, *Tragédies*, Rouen	
	Ouyn, *Thobie*, Rouen	
	Perrin, *Sichem*, Rouen	

Performance	Edition	Composition
	Soret, *La Céciliade*, Paris	
	Anthology, *Diverses tragédies saintes*, Rouen (contains Behourt, *Esaü* (1606); La Taille, *Saül* (1601); La Taille, *La Famine* (1602); Montreux, *Joseph le chaste* (1601); Ouyn, *Thobie* (1606); Perrin, *Sichem* (1606); Virey, *La Machabée* (1603))	
	Anthology, *Théâtre des tragédies françoises*, Rouen (contains Heudon, *S. Clouaud* (1606); *Jeanne d'Arques* (1606))	

1607

Performance	Edition	Composition
S. Fiacre, Béthune (Lanson 221)	Garnier, *Tragédies*, Paris	
Décollation de S. Jean, College at Chabeuil (*Etudes* 69)	2 eds, and one at Lyons	
Jour du Jugement, Collège de la Trinité, Lyons, 3 *journées* (*Savoie* 23)	Nancel, *Théâtre sacré*, Paris	
Nancel, *Debora, Dina, Josué*, Douai (Maine-et-Loire) (Preface)		
Jugement de Salomon, Pignans (Poupé 1903, 27)		

1608

Performance	Edition	Composition
S. Alexis, Le Puy (Lanson 221)	N. Chrestien, *Amnon et Thamar*, Rouen	
Histoire de S. Antoine, Jarrier (*Savoie* 65)	Garnier, *Tragédies*, Paris	
Occision des Innocents, La Garde-Freinet (Poupé 1903, 27)	Garnier, *Tragédies*, Lyons	
S. Tropez, S-Tropez ('Fêtes' 223)		

1609

Performance	Edition	Composition
S. Blaise, Le Val (Poupé 1920, 146)	Garnier, *Tragédies*, Rouen	
George, *Tentations d'Abraham*, Montbéliard (Lanson 222)	George, *Tentations d'Abraham*, Montbéliard	
Jacob ou l'antidolatrie, Jesuit College, Brussels (Lanson 223)		

Performance	Edition	Composition
Histoire de la destruction de Jérusalem par Vespasien et Titus and *L'Invention de la sainte croix*, S-Jean-d'Arves (Bulard 262)		
Loys, *Joseph*, Collège du Roi, Douai (text p. 34)		
Mondot, *Daniel*, Le Puy, 3 *journées* (Lanson 222)		

1610

Action de la conversion d'Ignace Loyola, Jesuit College, Liège (Lanson 223)	Billard, *Tragédies* (contains *Saül*), Paris	
? *Histoire de Ste Susanne*, Auray ('Noël Georges' 31)	Garnier, *Tragédies*, Rouen	

1611

? Baudeville, *S. Armel*, annually until 1780, Ploërmel ('Fêtes' 220)	Garnier, *Tragédies*, Rouen, 2 eds	
Conversion de Ste Catherine, Tourves (Poupé 1906, 35)	*Jeanne d'Arques*, Rouen (Brunet)	
S. Georges, Le Val (Hérelle 13)	Virey, *La Machabée* and *La Victoire des Machabées*, Rouen	
Virey, *La Machabée*, Six-Fours (Poupé 1906, 35)		

1612

Buchanan, *Jephté*, at court (Stone 44)	Billard, *Tragédies*, ed. of 1610 reissued dated 1612	
S. Eustache, Barjols (Poupé 1920, 145)	Garnier, *Tragédies*, Rouen, 2 eds	
	Patience de Job, Lyons	
	Loys, *Joseph*, Douai (some copies dated 1613)	
	Moucque, *L'Amour desplumé*, Paris	

1613

S. Eustache, Barjols (Poupé 1920, 145)	Billard, *Tragédies*, ed. of 1610 reissued dated 1613	
S. Jacques en Galicie, Remiremont (*Mystères* II 174)	Buchanan, *Baptiste*, trans. Brinon, Rouen	
Prévost, *Clotilde*, S-Léonard (Lanson 224)	? Marfrière, *La Belle Hester*, Rouen	
La Purification du temple de	? *Nabuchodonozor*, Rouen	

Performance	Edition	Composition
Jérusalem, Jesuit College, Valenciennes (Lanson 225) *S. Terentin*, College at Douai, ('Fêtes' 223)	Prévost, *Clotilde*, Poitiers ? *Samson le fort*, Rouen ? Ville-Toustain, *Creation*, Rouen	
1614 *S. Guillaume*, Jesuit College, Brussels (Lanson 226)	Buchanan, *Jephté*, trans. Brinon, Rouen *La Chaste et Vertueuse Susanne*, Rouen	
1615 *Histoire de S. Cyr*, La Cadière (Poupé 1920, 146)	Garnier, *Tragédies*, Lyons *Patience de Job*, Lyons Troterel, *Ste Agnés*, Rouen	
1616 *Tragédie du martyr de 5 Japonnais*, Jesuit College, Namur (Lanson 226)	Garnier, *Tragédies*, Rouen Rosier, *Isaac*, Douai	
1617 *Joseph le juste*, S-Maximin (Poupé 1904, 14) *Ste Madeleine*, S-Maximin ('Fêtes' 222) *S. Pierre et S. Paul*, Barnabite College, Annecy (*Savoie* 76)	Bèze, *Abraham sacrifiant*, Geneva; perhaps also an ed. at Paris	
1618 Candide, *Daphnis, célébrant l'Ascension du Christ*, Barnabite College, Annecy (Lanson 227) *Histoire de la Reine Esther*, Cuers (Poupé 1899, 53) *S. Ferréol*, Lorgues ('Fêtes' 221) *Ste Madeleine*, S-Maximin ('Fêtes' 22)	Boissin de Gallardon, *Ste Catherine* and *S. Vincent*, Lyons Garnier, *Tragédies*, Rouen, 6 eds	
1619 *S. Amatre*, Langres ('Fêtes' 220) *Histoire de Judith*, Cuers (Poupé 1899, 53) *Sédécias prisonnier* (by Garnier?) Barnabite College, Annecy (*Savoie* 76)	Garnier, *Tragédies*, Rouen Poytevin, *Ste Catherine*, Paris	

Performance	Edition	Composition

1620

S. Ferréol, Langres ('Fêtes' 220) ? Garnier, *Tragédies*, Paris

S. Jean-Baptiste, Solliès-Pont ? Heudon, *S. Clouaud*, Rouen
  (Poupé 1906, 35) Anthology, *Théâtre des
    tragédies françaises*, Rouen
    (contains Troterel, *Ste
    Agnés* (1615); Virey,
    Victoire des Machabées
    (1611))

1621

La Révolte d'Absalon, Seillans Coppée, *La Vie de Ste Justine
  (Poupé 1903, 27)   et de S. Cyprien*, Liège
La Vie de S. Alexis, Jesuit   (*History* 1 198)
  College, Béthune (Lanson *Patience de Job*, Troyes
  229)
David et Goliath, Langres
  ('Fêtes' 220)
S. Georges, Le Val (Poupé 1920,
  146)
Nativité, Bois-David ('Noël
  Georges' 31)

1622

Perfidie d'Aman, Hôtel de *Perfidie d'Aman*, Paris
  Bourgogne, Paris (Lanson P.D.B., *Tragédie des rebelles*,
  229)   Paris
Ste Catherine, Le Beausset Coppée, *Ste Aldegonde*, Liège
  (Poupé 1920, 146)
Coppée, *S. François*, Franciscan
  church, Huy (f. A5ᵛ)
S. Eustache, Barjols (*Dauphiné*
  161)
*Pastorelle sur les victoires de la
  Pucelle d'Orléans*, Jesuit
  College, Lyons (McGowan
  212)

1623

S. Ferréol, Lorgues (*Dauphiné* ? Bèze, *Abraham sacrifiant*,
  161)   Sedan
Conversion de S. Ignace, Jesuit Coppée, *S. François*, Rouen
  College, Pont-à-Mousson
  (Lanson 230)
S. Sébastien, Cotignac (Poupé
  1904, 14)

Performance	Edition	Composition

1624
Audibert, *Histoire des Maccabées*, Draguignan (*Mystères* I 452)
S. *Elisabeth*, Jesuit College, Nivelle (Lanson 231)
Histoire de Samson, Le Luc (Poupé 1904, 14)
Soret, *L'Election de S. Nicolas*, Rheims (text p. 75)

Coppée, *Tragédie de N-S Jésus-Christ* and S. *Lambert*, Liège
Soret, *L'Election de S. Nicolas*, Rheims

1625
N. Bello, *Sacrifice d'Abraham*, Dinant (*VT* II xii)
Comte and Hyeure, *Judith*, Barnabite College, Annecy (*Savoie* 77)
Nativité, Le Beausset (Poupé 1920, 146)

Hardy, *Théâtre* vol. II (contains *Mariamne*), Paris
? *Patience de Job*, Troyes
Le Francq, *Antioche*, Antwerp

1626
Abraham revenant de combattre les 5 Rois et le sacrifice de Melchisédech, Barnabite College, Annecy (*Savoie* 77)

Bèze, *Abraham sacrifiant*, Sedan
Garnier, *Tragédies*, Rouen
Jeanne d'Arques, Troyes

1627
Desmasures, *David combattant*, Montbéliard (Lanson 231)
S. *Maurice*, Jesuit College, Rheims (Lanson 231)
S. *Norbert*, Jesuit College, Antwerp (Lanson 231)
S. *Sébastien*, Barjols (Poupé 1920, 145)

Montchrestien, *Tragédies*, Rouen

1628
Grandjean, S. *Sébastien*, Plombières (Busson 547)
Richecourt, Benedictine College, S-Nicolas-de-Port (title-page)
S. *Sébastien*, Jesuit College, Pont-à-Mousson (Lanson 231)

Bèze, *Abraham sacrifiant*, Hainault
Grandjean, S. *Sébastien*, Nancy ('Une Tragédie archaïsante')
Richecourt, S-Nicolas-de-Port

Performance	Edition	Composition

1629
? Garnier, *Les Juifves*, Briançon   P. M., *La Rocheloise*, Troyes
  ('Répertoire' 18)

1630
Bacqueville délivré de prison et de
  mort par S. Julien, College at
  Ath (*History* I 679)
Le Coq, *Caïn et Abel*, Rouen
  (*Mystères* I 450)
Arsaces, Collège de Clermont,
  Paris (Gofflot 285)

1631
Martyre de S. Etienne, Sollières   J. de Fies,
  (*TR* 4)   S. Rémy

1632

                      P. Bello, *S. Eustache*, Liège
                      Hardy, *Théâtre* vol. II, Paris
                      Troterel, *Vie et sainte*
                          conversion de Guillaume duc
                          d'Aquitaine, Rouen

1633
C. Borella, *Le Retour des 3 Mages*
  après l'adoration du Christ,
  Barnabite College, Annecy
  (*Savoie* 77)
Histoire de Ste Catherine, Fréjus
  (Poupé 1904, 14)
A. Comte, *L'Hystoire de*
  Matthatias, Annecy (*Savoie* 77)

1634
Bello, *Procès de la justice et*   *Ste Barbe*, Troyes (Brunet)
  miséricorde divine au parquet de   *Ste Susanne*, Troyes
  Dieu sur la rédemption du genre
  humain, Dinant (*Etudes* 67)

1635

                      Croock, *S. Sébastien*, Ghent
                        (programme only:
                        Pascoe 23)
                      Hersent, *La Pastorale sainte*,
                        Paris (La Vallière II 505)

Performance	Edition	Composition

1636
Tristan, *Mariane*, Paris (*History*
  II 50)

1637
? Baro, *S. Eustache*, Paris   Bèze, *Abraham sacrifiant*,
  (Loukovitch 142)   Sedan
                                          Tristan, *Mariane*, Paris,
                                            3 eds
                                          Vallin, *Israel affligé*, Geneva

1638
? La Calprenède, *La Mort des*   Bèze, *Abraham sacrifiant*,
  enfants d'Hérode, Paris   Geneva
  (*History* II 188)

1639
La Piété polonaise, Jesuit College,   La Calprenède, *La Mort des*
  Rouen (Gofflot 307)   *enfants d'Hérode*, Paris
                                          Tristan, *Mariane*, Paris

1640
? D'Aubignac, *La Pucelle*, Paris
  (*History* II 357)
? Du Ryer, *Saül*, Paris (*Du Ryer*
  96)
Jézabel, Jesuit College, Rouen
  (Gofflot 307)
? La Serre, *Thomas Morus*, Paris
  (*History* II 361)
Passion, Le Beausset (Poupé
  1920, 146)

1641
S. Blaise, La Garde-Freinet
  (Poupé 1903, 27)
L'Immolation d'Isaac, Jesuit
  College, Pont-à-Mousson
  (Gofflot 300)
? La Calprenède, *Herménigilde*,
  Paris (*History* II 354)
? *Passion*, Briançon (Hérelle 12)
Passion, Huy (*Etudes* 92)

1642
? Corneille, *Polyeucte*, Paris   D'Aubignac, *La Pucelle*,
  (*History* II 320)   Paris, in prose and verse
                                            eds

Performance	Edition	Composition
? Desfontaines, *S. Eustache*, Paris (*History* II 779)	Du Ryer, *Saül*, Paris	
? Du Ryer, *Esther*, Paris (*Du Ryer* 106)	La Serre, *Thomas Morus*, Paris	
? La Serre, *Ste Caterine*, Paris (*History* II 779)		
Histoire de S. Vincent, La Garde-Freinet (Poupé 1903, 27)		

1643

? Desfontaines, *S. Alexis*, Paris (*History* II 780)	Corneille, *Polyeucte*, Paris	
	Desfontaines, *S. Eustache*, Paris	
	La Calprenède, *Herménigilde*, Paris	
	La Serre, *Ste Caterine*, Paris	
	Picou, *Le Déluge universel*, Paris	

1644

S. Alexis, Le Val (Hérelle 13)	Bèze, *Abraham sacrifiant*, Paris	
? Desfontaines, *S. Genest*, Paris (*History* II 538)	Corneille, *Polyeucte*, Paris, and pirate ed. Leyden; some copies of latter bound in pirate *Théâtre*, Leyden 1644	
	Desfontaines, *S. Eustache*, Paris, 2 eds	
	Du Ryer, *Esther*, Paris	
	Saint-André, *Nativité*, Béziers	
	Tristan, *Mariane*, Paris, 2 eds	

1645

? Corneille, *Théodore*, Paris (*History* II 516)	Corneille, *Polyeucte*, pirate	
S. Donat, Callian (Poupé 1904, 14)	Desfontaines, *S. Alexis*, Paris ed. Caen?	
S. Eustache, S-Maximin (Poupé 1904, 14)	Desfontaines, *S. Genest*, Paris	
Passion, Correns (Poupé 1900, 94)	D'Ennetières, *Ste Aldegonde*, Tournai	
? Rotrou, *S. Genest*, Paris (ed. Dubois 11)	Tristan, *Mariane*, Paris	

Performance	Edition	Composition

1646
Ste Catherine, La Cadière
  (Poupé 1920, 146)

Corneille, *Théodore*, Paris,
  2 eds (some copies dated
  1647)
Desfontaines, *S. Genest*, Paris
Jaquemin, *Triomphe des
  bergers*, Lyons
D.L.T., *Josaphat*, Toulouse

1647
Mermillod, *Conversion de Celse
  enfant*, Barnabite College,
  Annecy (*Savoie* 77)

Coppée, *Miracle de N-D de
  Cambron*, Namur (*History*
  I 198)
Corneille, *Polyeucte* ed. Paris
  1644 and *Théodore* ed.
  Paris 1646 reissued in
  Oeuvres, Paris
Corneille, *Théodore*, location
  unknown, pirate ed.
Magnon, *Josaphat*, Paris
  (Privilège 1646)
Mouffle, *S. Clair*, Paris
Rotrou, *S. Genest*, Paris

1648
S. Victor, La Garde-Freinet
  (Poupé 1903, 27)

Corneille, *Polyeucte*, Paris,
  2 eds (some copies in
  Oeuvres, Paris); also
  pirate ed. Leyden
Desfontaines, *S. Alexis*,
  Paris
Rotrou, *S. Genest*, Paris

1649
S. Ustache, Nantes (*History*
  II 365)

Baro, *S. Eustache*, Paris
Bouvot, *Judith*, Paris
Le Martyre de Ste Catherine,
  Lyons
Le Martyre de Ste Catherine,
  Caen
Chevillard, *La Mort de
  Théandre*, Orléans
  (*Soleinne* 1246)
Corneille, *Théodore*, pirate
  ed. Caen?

Performance	Edition	Composition

1650
Histoire des saints apôtres
  Pierre et Paul, Exilles
  (*Dauphiné* 136)

Le Martyre de Ste Catherine,
  Caen
Cosnard, *Les Chastes Martyrs*,
  Paris
Olivier, *Herménigilde*,
  Auxerre
Saint-Balmon, *Les Jumeaux
  Martyrs*, Paris

Catalogue of editions of
French sacred plays, 1550–1650

I have attempted to describe here all the known editions of French sacred
plays printed between 1550 and 1650. Most of these have long been known to
bibliographers, but only in a very few cases have satisfactory descriptions
appeared: all too often previous bibliographers have presented transcriptions
of the title-pages in which the use of upper-case and italic letters has been
standardised, and have given little indication of the arrangement of the contents of the volumes. My transcriptions of the title-pages are, I hope, faithful
to the originals (save in respect of the long s, which I have been unable to
reproduce as such, and the hyphen, which, where it has been contributed by
the modern printer and does not appear in the original, is shown by a
swung dash, ~), and I have provided collations of the contents of the
volumes. This last may seem a superfluous refinement, but the printers of the
day were quite capable of issuing the text of one edition with the title-page
of another; by studying both I have found in some cases that what appeared to
be a new edition was in fact a reissue of an old one adorned with a new title-
page, and in other cases that the same title-page could cover different states of
the text.

The descriptions, then, are the fruits of my own researches. In some cases,
however, I have been unable to trace editions mentioned by earlier bibliographers: here I have reproduced the information they provide, with a note of
the source. Where I have seen several copies of a particular edition I have
described only one, habitually that held in the Bibliothèque nationale; other
copies are mentioned only where they show variations. I have not described
the editions of plays which are available in modern critical editions, seeing no
profit in duplicating information easily accessible elsewhere; I have thus been
able to avoid burdening the reader with descriptions of, for example, the
several dozen editions of *Abraham sacrifiant* made in this period. Naturally the
places and dates of publication of texts not described here are listed in the
Chronology.

I have not drawn attention to the places where other bibliographies seem
to contain errors.

The Catalogue contains only the editions of sacred plays made between
1550 and 1650, and modern critical editions of them. For other editions of
sacred plays, and for non-sacred plays, reference should be made to the
Bibliography. Plays are listed in alphabetical order by the name of the

author. Anonymous works are entered in the same order, by the name of the principal character: thus the *Tragédie de la perfidie d'Aman* appears under Aman. Where an author identified himself only by initials, the play is entered under the last initial, on the assumption that this was the initial of the author's surname.

I wish to thank Kevin Cook for providing me with collations of three volumes which I omitted to make on my own visit to Geneva: nos 5(iii), 16, and 41(v).

The following abbreviations, in addition to those listed on pages ix–x, are used here:

Ars	Bibliothèque de l'Arsenal
Baudrier	Henri-Louis Baudrier, *Bibliographie lyonnaise*, 12 vols, Lyons 1895–1921
BL	British Library
BN	Bibliothèque nationale
BPU	Bibliothèque publique et universitaire, Geneva
Brunet	Jacques-Charles Brunet, *Manuel du libraire et de l'amateur de livres*, 6 vols, Paris 1860–5, and *Supplément*, 2 vols, Paris 1878–80
Brussels	Bibliothèque royale, Brussels
Heitz	Paul Heitz, *Genfer Buchdrucker- und Verlagerzeichen in XV., XVI., und XVII. Jahrhundert*, Strasbourg 1908
Lepreux (*Normandie*)	G. Lepreux, *Gallia typographica*, Série départementale part 3, *Province de Normandie*, 2 vols, Paris 1912
Marques des P-B	*Marques typographiques des imprimeurs et libraires qui ont exercé dans les Pays-Bas*, 2 vols, Ghent 1894
Parfaict	F. and C. Parfaict, *Histoire du théâtre françois depuis son origine jusqu'à présent*, 15 vols, Paris 1734–49
Renouard	Philippe Renouard, *Répertoire des imprimeurs parisiens, libraires, fondeurs de caractères et correcteurs d'imprimerie depuis l'introduction de l'imprimerie à Paris jusqu'à la fin du XVIe siècle*, 2nd ed., Paris 1965
Renouard *Marques*	Philippe Renouard, *Les Marques typographiques parisiens du XVe et XVIe siècles*, Paris 1926
Silvestre	Louis-Catherine Silvestre, *Marques typographiques*, Paris 1853–67
Van Havre	G. van Havre, *Marques typographiques des imprimeurs et libraires anversois*, 2 vols, Antwerp and Ghent 1883–4

1. *La Perfidie d'Aman*

TRAGEDIE / NOVVELLE DE LA / PERFIDIE D'AMAN, / MIGNON ET FAVORIS / DV ROY ASSVERVS. / Sa coniuration contre les Iuifs, / *Ou l'on voit nayuement representé l'Estat miserable de / ceux qui se fient aux grandeurs. / Le tout tiré & extraict de l'Ancien testament / du liure d'Esther. / Auec vne farce plaisante & recreative, tiree d'vn des / plus gentils esprits de ce temps. / [orn] / A PARIS, / Chez la veufue Ducarroy, ruë des Carmes. / à l'enseigne de la Trinité. / M. DC. XXII.*

4°: A^v blank; A2^r 3 Argument; A2^v 4 list of Entreparleurs; A3^r–D2^r 5–27 text; D2^v–4^v 28–32 the farce.

BN Yf 6536

> Parfaict (vol. III, pp. 264–8) and La Vallière (vol. I, p. 473) mention an ed. of 1617, but Lancaster opines (*History* I, p. 186) that they imagined it to corroborate the theory that the play refers to the fall of d'Ancre, and that there was only this ed.

2. D'Amboise, *Holoferne*

HOLOFERNE / TRAGEDIE / SACREE EXTRAITE / DE L'HISTOIRE DE / IVDITH. / *Par. A. d'Am. Par.* / [orn] / A PARIS, / Pour Abel l'Angelier, tenant sa boutique / au premier pillier de la grand / salle du Palais. / M. D. LXXX.

8°: A^v Latin epigraph by S.S.T.; A2^r–3^r 2^r–3^r Dedication to Mme de Broon; A3^r 3^r list of characters; A3^v–D6^v 3^v–30^v text; D7^r–8^v 31^r–32^v Ode to dedicatee, signed Adr. d'Amboyse.

BN Rés Yf 4261

3. D'Aubignac, *La Pucelle d'Orleans*

LA / PVCELLE / D'ORLEANS, / *TRAGEDIE EN PROSE.* / Selon la verité de l'histoire & les / rigueurs du Theatre. / [orn] / A PARIS, / Chez FRANÇOIS TARGA, / au premier pillier de la grand' / Salle du Palais, au / Soleil d'or. 1642. / *Auec priuilege du Roy.*

12°, signatures by 6: ã^v blank; ã2^r–5^v Le Libraire au lecteur; ã6^r–v, ẽr–4^r Preface; ẽ4^v blank; ẽ5^r–v Privilège, 10 March 1642, and Achevé, 11 March 1642; ẽ6^r blank; ẽ6^v list of Acteurs; A^r–16^v 1–108, K^r–K6^v 107–118, L^r–O6^r 121–167 text; O6^v blank.

BN Rés Yf 3955

> Also issued in a versified text:

LA / PVCELLE / DORLEANS. / TRAGEDIE. / [orn] / A PARIS,

Chez { ANTHOINE DE SOMMAVILLE, en la Ga- / lerie des Merciers, à l'Escu de France, / & / AVGVSTIN COVRBE', en la mesme Gale- / rie, à la Palme. } Au Palais.

M. DC. XXXXII. / *AVEC PRIVILEGE DV ROY.*

4°: π^v blank; π2^r Privilège in Courbé's name, 8 April 1642, and note associating Sommaville in it, and Achevé, 15 May 1642; π2^v list of Personnages; A^r–N^v 1–98 text; N2 blank.

BN Rés Yf 374

The probable identity of the versifier is discussed in *History* II, p. 360.

4. P.D.B., *La Tragedie des rebelles*

LA / TRAGEDIE / DES REBELLES, / *Ou sont les noms feints, on* *void leurs conspirations,* / *machines, monopoles, assemblees, prattiques* / *& rebellions descouuertes.* / DEDIEE A LA REYNE. / [orn] / A PARIS, / Chez la veufue Ducarroy, ruë des Car- / mes, à l'enseigne de la Trinité. / M. DC. XXII.

4°: A^v blank; A2^r 3 Dedication, signed P.D.B. Parisien; A2^v 4 list of Personnages; A3^r–4^v 5–8 Argument; B^r–D4^r 9–31 text; D4^v blank.

BN Yf 12023

5. Badius, *Comedie du pape malade*

(ia) *COMEDIE* / DV PAPE MALADE ET / tirant à la fin: Où ses regrets, & complain- / tes sont au vif exprimees, & les entrepri- / ses & machinations qu'il fait auec Sa- / tan & ses suppots pour maintenir / son siege Apostatique, & em- / pescher le cours de l'E- / uangile, sont cathe- / goriquement / descouuer- / tes. / *Traduite de vulgaire Arabic* *en bon Romman &* [obliterated] / [obliterated] *ar Thrasibule Phenice.* / A ROVEN. / 1561.

8°: A^v blank; A2^r–3^v 3–6 Au lecteur; A4^r–v 7–8 Argument; A5^r–6^r 9–11 Prologue; A6^r 11 list of Personnages; A6^v–E5^v 12–74 text; E6^r–8^r La Truye au foin (a coq à l'âne); E8^v blank.

BN Rés Yf 4120.

Shaw, in her ed. of the play, points out that the imprint Rouen is fictitious: this ed. was made in Geneva.

(ib) The ed. by Gustave Revilliod, Geneva 1859, reproduces what seems to be a different ed. of 1561, of which I have not seen the original: COMEDIE DV / PAPE MALADE ET / tirant à la fin: / Où ses regrets, & complaintes sont au vif / exprimees, & les entreprises & machina- / tions qu'il fait auec Satan & ses suppots / pour maintenir son siege Apostolique, & / empescher le cours de l'Euangile, sont ca- / thegoriquement descouuertes. / Traduite de vulgaire Arabic en bon Romman / & intelligible, par Thrasibule Phenice. / AVEC PRIVILEGE. / M. D. LXI.

8°: A^v blank; A2^r–4^r 3–7 Au lecteur; A4^v–5^r 8–9 Argument; A5^v–6^r 10–11 Prologue; A6^v–E4^v text.

(ii) 1562, 8°, 72 pp. (Shaw ed., p. 68).

(iii) COMEDIE DV / PAPE MALADE, / ET TIRANT A / LA FIN. / Où ses regrets, & complaintes sont au / vif exprimees, & les entreprises & / machinations qu'il fait auec Satan / & ses suppots pour maintenir son / siege Apostatique, & empescher le / cours de l'Euangile, sont cathego- / riquement descouuertes. / *Traduite du vulgaire Arabic en* *bon* / *Roman & intelligible, par Thrasibu-* / *le Phenice.* / POVR GLAVDE D'AVGY. / M. D. LXXXIIII.

8°: a^v Sonnet, L'excuse de Maillard, absent du Colloque de Poissy;

a2^r–4^v 3–8 Au lecteur; a5^{r-v} 9–10 Argument; a6^r–7^r 11–13 Prologue; a7^r 13 list of Personnages; a7^v–e7^r 14–77 text; e7^v blank.

BPU Rés Hf 4945

Bound with Crespin's *Marchand converti*, no. 41 (v).

(iv) COMEDIE / DV PAPE / malade. / Où ses regrets & complaintes sont au vif ex- / primees, & les entreprises & machinations / qu'il fai auec Satan & ses supposts pour / maintenir son siege Apostolique & empes- / cher le cours de l'Euangile, sont cathegori- / quemen descouuertes. / *Traduite de vulgaire Arabic en bon Roman & / intelligible, par Thrasibule Phenice.* / [orn] / Par François Forest. / *M. D. XCI.*

8°: M7^r title; M7^v L'excuse de Maillard; M8^r–N^v Au lecteur; N^v–2 Argument; N2^v–3^v Prologue; N3^v list of Personnages; N3^v–R2^v text [36 ff]

Although this play has its own title page, it was printed in the same volume as Crespin's *Marchand converti*, no. 41 (vi), the signatures running continuously through both texts.

BN Rés Yf. 4121, this play alone.
BN Rés Yf. 4568, with *Marchand*.

Ars Rf. 1317 ⎱
BPU Bc. 3191 ⎰ with *Marchand*; author's name written Phoenice.

Crit. ed. by Helen A. Shaw, *Conrad Badius and the Comédie du Pape malade*, Philadelphia 1934. She was not aware of the distinction between (ia) and (ib), nor of the existence of (iv).

6. *Saincte Barbe*

(i) LA Vie de Mada= / me saincte Barbe / par personnages. / Auec plusieurs de ses Miracles. Le tout represente par quarante per= / sonnages, desquelz les noms sont en la page suiuante. / Nouuellemen reueue & mise en son entier, & corrigee / tant au sens que a la rithme viii Ca. / [large woodcut, showing Barbe and her emblems, and scenes of her martyrdom] / A PARIS. / Par Simon Caluarin, rue Sainct Jacques a lenseigne / de la Rose blanche couronnee.

4°: A^v list of Personnages; A2^r–G6^r text; G6^v woodcut as on title-page [30 ff].

Gothic letters, two columns.

BN Rés Yf. 1651

Calvarin used this address from 1571 until his death in 1593 (Renouard).

(ii) *LA VIE /* DE MADAME / SAINCTE / BARBE. / *PAR PERSON~ NAGES.* / [woodcut showing Barbe with a palm, and a tower behind] / *A LYON,* / PAR PIERRE RIGAVD.

8°: A^v list of Personnages; A2^r–4^r 2^r–4^r Prologue; A4^v–K7^v 4^v–79^v text; K7^v 79^v colophon: Cy finist la vie et martyre de madame saincte Barbe par personnages, nouvellement imprimée à Lyon, 1602; K8 blank.

BN Rés Yf. 4688

(iii) *La Vie de Madame Saincte-Barbe*, Troyes, Nicolas Oudot, 1634, 16⁰.
(M. Corrard de Breban, *Recherches sur l'établissement et l'exercise de
l'imprimerie à Troyes*, 3rd ed., Paris 1873, p. 148; Parfaict vol. III, p. 36;
Brunet.)

7. Bardon de Brun, *Sainct Jacques*

SAINCT / IACQVES, / TRAGOEDIE, / REPRÆSENTEE PVBLI~
QVEMENT / A LYMOGES PAR LES CONFRERES / Pelerins
dudict Sainct, en l'Année / 1596. Le Iour & Feste Sainct / IACQVES
25. Iuillet. / Par B. BARDON, De Brun. / [mark: Silvestre 1242 (lacks
motto)] / *A LYMOGES*, / Par HVGVES BARBOV. / 1596. / *Auec
permission.*

8⁰: ã^v Approbation, 10 September 1596, and image of James; ã2^r–5^r
Dedication to James; ã5^r–v Au lecteur; ã5^v–6^r Argument; ã6^v–7^r verses
by Bardon addressed to his book; ã7^v–8^v, ẽ^r–4^r encomiastic verses; ẽ4^v
list of Personnages; A–E8 1–80, F–K8, LI–4, MI 91–178 text.

BN Rés Yf 3908

8. Baro, *Sainct Eustache*

SAINCT / EVSTACHE / MARTYR. / POËME DRAMATIQVE /
DE BARO. / [Sommaville's mark] / A PARIS, / Chez ANTOINE DE
SOMMAVILLE, au Palais, / dans la petite Salle, à l'Escu de France. /
M. DC. XLIX. / *Auec Priuilege du Roy.*

4⁰: ã^v blank; ã2^r–3^v Dedication to Henriette-Marie, fille de France; ã4^r
Advertissement; ã4^v list of Acteurs; A–M [misprinted N] 3^v 1–94 text;
M4^r Privilège, 24 November 1648, and Achevé, 1 July 1649; M4^v blank.

BN Yf 479

9. Barran, *L'Homme justifié par Foy*

TRAGIQVE / COMEDIE / FRANCOISE / de l'homme iustifié /
par Foy. / * / GALAT. III. / Auez-vous receu l'Esprit par les oeuures
de / la Loy, ou par la predication de la Foy? [woodcut, hand-coloured,
of arabesques; in centre a shield, reading] Hebr. 10. g. LE IVSTE
VIVRA DE FOY. [and in space at foot] Composé Par M. Henry de
Barran. / [below woodcut] 1554.

8⁰: a^v list of Personnages; a2^r–3^r Au lecteur; a3^v–f7^v text; f8 blank [48 ff].

BN Rés Yf 4064

10. Behourt, *Esau*

(i) ESAV / OV / LE CHASSEVR, / EN FORME DE / TRA~
GOEDIE, / *Nouuellement representee au College* / *des Bons Enfans de
Rouen,* / *le 2. d'Aoust,* 1598. / [Du Petit Val's mark, without motto] /
A ROVEN, / DE L'IMPRIMERIE / De Raphaël du Petit Val,
Libraire & / Imprimeur du Roy, deuant la / grand' porte du Palais, /
à l'Ange Raphaël. / 1598. / *Auec Priuilege de sa Majesté.*

12°: A^v blank; A2^{r-v} 3–4 Dedication to Montpensier, signed J. Behourt; A3^r 5 Aux lecteurs and list of Personnages; A3^v 6 sonnet rejoicing at peace; A4^r–CIO^v 7–68 text; CII^r Privilège, 4 February 1597; CII^v–12^v blank.

BL 241.c.41.(2).

> Several copies bear the date 1599, and are bound into Du Petit Val's anthology, *Diverses tragedies de plusieurs autheurs de ce temps,* Rouen 1599: see no. 57 (ii).
>
> BN Yf 4741
> Ars 8° BL 14160, lacks CII, 12
> Ars 8° BL 14161
>
> The Privilège is unusual in not specifying the text to which it applies: Du Petit Val possessed a general Privilège, by virtue perhaps of his position as Imprimeur du Roi, which he was able to apply to any text at discretion (see Arbour, 'R. du Petit Val', p. 91). The presence of this Privilège thus gives no indication of the date of composition of the text which it accompanies. Other sacred plays for which Du Petit Val used his general Privilège are nos 10 (ii), 57 (ii), 57 (iiia), 95, 125 (ii), 125 (iii).

(ii) ESAV / OV / LE CHASSEVR, / EN FORME DE / TRAGEDIE, / *Nouuellement representee au College / des Bons Enfans de Rouen.* / [Du Petit Val's mark, without motto] / *A ROVEN,* / DE L'IMPRI~ MERIE, / De Raphaël du Petit Val, Libraire & Im- / primeur du Roy, deuant la grand porte / du Palais, à l'Ange Raphaël. / 1606. / *Auec Priuilege de sa Maiesté.*

12°: A^v blank; A2^{r-v} 3–4 Dedication to Montpensier, signed J. Behourt; A3^r 5 Aux lecteurs and list of characters; A3^v 6 Sonnet rejoicing at peace; A4^r–CIO^v 7–68 text; CII^r Privilège, 4 February 1597; CII^v–12^v blank.

BN Yf 9221

> Some copies, e.g. BN Rés Yf. 2903, bound in Du Petit Val's anthology, *Diverses tragedies sainctes,* Rouen 1606: see no. 97 (ii).

11. Bello, *S. Eustache*

I have seen only the ed. by H. Helbig, Liège 1865 (publications of the Société des bibliophiles Liégeois no. 3), which reproduces the title page in semi-facsimile:
TRAGÉDIE / SUR LA VIE / ET MARTYRE / DE S. EUSTACHE, / COMPOSÉE / PAR M. PIERRE BELLO, DINANTOIS, / RECTEUR DE LA CHAPELLE DE / S. LAURENT A DINANT. / [orn] / à LIÉGE, / DE L'IMPRIMERIE DE JEAN OUWERX, IMP. JURÉ / de S. Altesse, à la Corne du Cerf. / 1632.

12. Belyard, *Charlot*

CHARLOT / EGLOGVE PASTORELLE / sur les miseres de la France, & sur / la tresheureuse & miraculeuse deliurance / de tresmag~ nanime & tresillustre Prince / Monseigneur le Duc de GVYSE / A / *Venerable & discrete personne, Messire* IEAN / DEHAVLT *grand*

*vicaire de Monsieur de / Troyes & grand Archidiacre en l'Eglise /
Cathedrale de sainct Pierre / Par* SIMON BELYARD, *Vallegeois.* /
In otio negotium. / Pasquin du Psalme 116: Dirupisti vincula &c. /
*Tu m'as de prison retiré, / Seigneur; je t'en presenteré / Vne tresagreable
hostie, / Te sacrifiant l'heresie: / Puis ton saint nom ie chanteré* /
A TROYES. / De l'imprimerie de Iean Moreau, / M. Imprimeur du
Roy. / *Auec permission.* / M. D. LXXXXII.

4⁰: A^v–3^v Dedication; A3^v–4^v sonnets to dedicatee; A4^v Latin and French
encomiastic verses; B^r–D3^v 1–22 text; D4^r–E4^v 23–32 Latin and French
verses and anagrams.

BL 243.f.7.(2.)

13. Belyard, *Le Guysien*

LE GVYSIEN / OV / PERFIDIE TYRANNIQVE / commise par
Henry de Valois es personnes / des illusstriss. reuerendiss. & tres~
genereux / Princes Loys de Loraine Cardinal, & Ar- / cheuesque de
Rheims, & Henry de Loraine / Duc de Guise, grand Maistre de France. /
A / Tresvertueux & honorable homme NICOLAS / DEHAVLT
President des Tresoriers, & / Maire de la ville de Troyes. / Par SIMON
BELYARD, *Vallegeois.* / In otio negotium. / *Il n'est besoin, liuret; il
n'est besoin de dire / Que tu as esté fait en quinze, ou seize iours. /
Assez-tot le verra l'enuieux, qui tousiours / De l'aymable vertu ne cherche
qu'a médire.* / Preciosa in conspectu domini mors sancto- / rum eius.
Psal. 116. / A TROYES. / De l'imprimerie de Iean Moreau, /
M. Imprimeur du Roy. / *Auec permission.* / M. D. LXXXXII.

4⁰ (prelims 8⁰): A^v Au lecteur and errata; A2^r–3^v Dedication; A4^r–6^v
Latin and French verses by Belyard; A7^r–8^v encomiastic verses; B^r Au
lecteur catholique, sonnet en forme de Prologue; B^v list of Personnages;
B2^r–K4^r 1–69 text; K4^v–L4^v 70–78 Latin and French epigrams.

BL 243.f.7.(1.)

14. Bèze, *Abraham sacrifiant*

Crit. ed. by Keith Cameron, Kathleen M. Hall and Francis Higman,
Geneva and Paris 1967 (TLF 135).
See also Frédéric Gardy, *Bibliographie des oeuvres théologiques,
littéraires, et juridiques de Théodore de Bèze,* Geneva 1960 (THR XLI).

15. Bienvenu, *Le Triomphe de Jesus Christ*

LE TRIOMPHE DE / IESVS CHRIST: / Comedie Apocalyptique,
traduite du Latin de Iean / Foxus Anglois, en rithme Françoise, &
augmentee / d'vn petit discours de la maladie de la Messe, / Par
Iacques Bienuenu citoyen de Geneue. / [mark: Heitz 18, without sur-
round] / A GENEVE. / Par Iean Bonnefoy, pour Iaques Bienuenu. /
M. D. LXII.

4⁰: A^v blank; A2^r Sonnet; A2^v list of Personnes; A3^r–4^r Advertissement;
A4^v blank; B^r–T5^r text; T5^v–6^r music; T6^v blank [78 ff].

BL c.47.e.17.

16. Bienvenu, *Comedie du monde malade*

POESIE DE / *L'ALLIANCE* / PERPETVELLE ENTRE / deux nobles & Chrestiennes villes fran / ches, BERNE & GENEVE, faite l'an / M. D. LVIII. / ITEM / *VNE COMEDIE DV MON-* / de malade & mal pensé, recitee au renouuelle- / ment desdites alliances à Geneue le deuxieme / iour de May M. D. LXVIII. / [mark: Heitz 45] / *M. D. LXVIII.*

8⁰: aᵛ blank; a2ʳ–4ʳ Devis entre Volonté divine, Verité, Paix, Mensonge, et Guerre; a4ᵛ–5ᵛ Sentence de Volonté divine; a6ʳ–bʳ Cantique; b2ʳ title of Comedie du monde malade; and list of Personnes; b2ᵛ–3ʳ Epistre to municipalities of Geneva and Berne by Jaques Bienvenu; b3ᵛ–d8ʳ Comedie; d8ᵛ blank [32 ff].

BPU Rés Hf. 2204

Bound with other works, including a copy of no. 17.

17. Bienvenu, *Comedie du voyage de Frere Fecisti*

COMEDIE / FACETIEVSE ET TRESPLAISANTE, / DV VOYAGE DE FRERE / Fecisti en Prouuence, vers / Nostradamus: / *POVR SAVOIR CERTAI-* / nes nouuelles des clefs de Paradis & / d'enfer, que le Pape / auoit perdues. / Imprimé à Nismes. / 1589.

8⁰: aᵛ blank; a2ʳ–b4ʳ 3–23 text; b4ᵛ blank.

BPU Rés Hf. 2204.

Bound with other works, including a copy of no. 16.

18. Billard, *Saül*

(ia) TRAGEDIES / FRANCOISES / DE / CLAVDE BILLARD / Seigneur de Courgenay, Bourbonnois. / AV / *TRES-CHRESTIEN, TRES-* / grand, & tres-victorieux Roy de France / & de Navarre. / [mark] / A PARIS, / Chez DENYS LANGLOIS, ruë saint Iacques, pres / l'image saint Iean. / M. DC. X. / *Auec priuilege du Roy.*

8⁰: ãᵛ blank; ã2ʳ⁻ᵛ Dedication; ã3ʳ–6ʳ encomiastic verses; ã6ᵛ blank; ã7ʳ Latin epigraphs; ã7ᵛ Privilège in Billard's name, 27 February 1610, and statement that Billard has permitted Langlois to print the plays, 9 March 1610; ã8ʳ–9ᵛ Au lecteur; ã10ʳ Dedication of *Polyxene* to Mme de Conty; ã10ᵛ Argument and list of Entre-parleurs; Aʳ–D2ʳ 1ʳ–26ʳ *Polyxene*; D2ᵛ title, *Guaston de Foy*; D3ʳ 27ʳ Dedication; D3ᵛ Argument; D4ʳ 28ʳ list of Entre-parleurs; D4ᵛ–H2ʳ 28ᵛ–58ʳ *Guaston de Foix*; H2ᵛ title, *Merovee*; H3ʳ⁻ᵛ 59 Dedication; H4ʳ 60ʳ Argument; H4ᵛ list of Entre-parleurs; H5ʳ–L5ᵛ 61ʳ–85ᵛ *Merovee*; L6ʳ 86ʳ Dedication of *Panthee*; L6ᵛ Argument; L7ʳ 87ʳ list of Entre-parleurs; L7ᵛ–08ᵛ 87ᵛ–112ᵛ *Panthee*; Pʳ 113ʳ Dedication of *Saül*; Pᵛ Argument; P2ʳ 114ʳ list of Entre-parleurs; P2ᵛ–R8ʳ 114ᵛ–[136ʳ] *Saül*; R8ᵛ [136ᵛ] title of *Albouin*; Sʳ 137ʳ Dedication; Sᵛ–S2ʳ 137ᵛ–138ʳ Argument; S2ʳ 138ʳ list of Acteurs; S2ᵛ–X2ᵛ 138ᵛ–162ᵛ *Albouin*; X3ʳ⁻ᵛ 163 Dedication of *Genevre*; X3ᵛ 163ᵛ list of Entre-parleurs; X4ʳ⁻ᵛ 164 Argument; X5ʳ–Aa5ʳ 165ʳ–189ʳ *Genevre*; Aa5ᵛ–7ᵛ verses; Aa8 blank.

BN Yf 2074

(ib) TRAGEDIES / FRANCOISES DE / CLAVDE BILLARD / SEIGNEVR DE / COVRGENAY / Bourbonnois. / *AV TRES-CHRESTIEN, TRES-* / *grand, & tres-victorieux Roy de France* / *& de Nauarre.* / [mark] / A PARIS, / Chez DENYS LANGLOIS, ruë saint Iacques, pres / l'image saint Iean. / M. DC. X. / *Auec priuilege du Roy.*

Another state of the title-page; in other respects identical to (ia).

Ars Rf 5499

(ic) TRAGEDIES / DE CLAVDE BILLARD / SIEVR DE COVRGE~ NAY, / Bourbonnois. / *DEDIEES* / *A TRES-GRANDE ET* / *TRES-GENEREVSE PRINCESSE* / *la Reine Regente en France.* / [orn] / A PARIS. / De l'Imprimerie de FRANÇOIS HVBY, ruë sainct / Iacques au soufflet vert. Et en sa bouticque au / Palais en la gallerie des Prisoniers. / M. DC. XII. / *Auec Priuilege du Roy.*

The same as (ia), but with *Henry le grand*, 4°, added at the beginning: **v list of contents; *2r-v Dedication; *3r-v Argument; *3v list of characters; *4r, *–*********4v, ********2r text; ********2v blank [42 ff]. Followed by the other plays, as in (ia), but with the first gathering amended: ã, the title-page of (ia), is omitted; the rest are unchanged, save ã4 and ã7, which are a cancel, bearing the same material as in (ia) but reset, and with the note after the Privilège on ã7v amended to record that Billard has given Huby the right to print his plays.

BL C.39.c.61

> In some copies of (ic), the first gathering of (ia) was incorrectly assembled:
> BN Rés Yf 2972 has ã2, ã3, ã5, ã4, ã7, ã6, ã8, ã9, ã10
> Ars 8° BL 12633 lacks ã4–7
> Ars 8° BL 12634 retains ã, the title-page of (ia), and on ã7v retains the Privilège of (ia); ã5, ã6 bound after ã10.

(id) Identical to (ic), but with the date M. DC. XIII at the foot of the title-page.

BN Yf 2075 (contains an error in the reassembling of the prelims from (ia): ã7, reset as in (ic), is followed by ã7 as in (ia)).

Although the *Tragedies* appeared with four title-pages, there was only one ed., made in 1610, with two slightly different title-pages; unsold sheets of this were reissued in 1612, with a new title-page and *Henry le grand* added at the front, and the original preliminary material emended to show the name of the new printer (this gathering, now in the middle of the volume, was frequently assembled incorrectly); some copies of the composite volume of 1612 were dated 1613.

19. Boissin de Gallardon, *Sainct Vincent* and *Saincte Catherine*

(ia) LES / TRAGEDIES / ET HISTOIRES / SAINCTES DE IEAN / BOISSIN DE / Gallardon. / *La I. contenant la deliurance d'Andromede & les malheurs* / *de Phinee.* / *La II. la fatalité de Meleager & le desespoir d'Althee sa mere.* / *La III. les Vrnes viuantes ou les amours de Phelidon &* / *Polibelle.* / *La IV. le martyre de Sainct Vincent.* / *La V.*

le martyre de Saincte Catherine. / [mark: Silvestre 470] / *A LYON,* /
De l'Imprimerie de SIMON RIGAVD, / Marchand Libraire en ruë
Merciere. / *MDC XVIII.* / Auec priuilege du Roy.

12⁰: A^v blank; A2^(r–v) Aux lecteurs; A3^r–5^v encomiastic verses; A6^r–7^r
Dedication of *La Perseenne*; A7^v list of Acteurs; A8^r–D6^v 1–70 *La
Perseenne*; D7^r–8^r 71–73 Dedication of *La Fatalle*; D8^v 74 list of Acteurs;
D9^r–G6^v 75–142 *La Fatalle*; G7^(r–v) 143–144 Dedication of *Les Urnes
vivantes*; G8^r 145 list of Acteurs; G8^v–1 11^v 146–200 *Les Urnes vivantes*;
1 12^r–K^r 201–203 Dedication of *S. Vincent*; K^v 204 list of Acteurs; K2^r–
MII^r 205–271 [printed 281] *S. Vincent*; MII^v–12^v 272–274 Dedication of
Ste Catherine; N^r 275 list of Acteurs; N^v–P12^r 276–345 *Ste Catherine*;
P12^v blank.

Ars 8⁰ BL 12645

(ib) The same, but with a different title-page, a cancel:
LES / TRAGEDIES / ET HISTOIRES / SAINCTES DE JEAN /
BOISSIN DE / Gallardon. / *La I contenant la deliurance d'Andromede
& les malheurs / de Phinee.* / *La II. la fatalité de Meleager & le
desespoir d'Althee sa mere.* / *La III. les Vrnes viuantes ou les amours de
Phelidon & / Polibelle.* / *La IV. le martyre de Sainct Vincent.* / *La V. le
martyre de Saincte Catherine.* / [orn] / A Lyon, chez SIMON
RIGAVD. / 1618.

BL 240.a.16

It is not obvious why this was substituted for the earlier title-page.

20. Bouvot, *Judith*

IVDITH, / OV L'AMOVR / DE LA PATRIE, / TRAGOEDIE. /
Par Noble ANTOINE GIRARD–BOVVOT, *Langrois.* / [orn] / A
PARIS, / Chez CLAVDE BOVDEVILLE, ruë des Carmes / au Lys
Fleurissant. / M. DC. XLIX. / *AVEC PRIVILEGE DV ROY.*

4⁰, sigs by 2: ã^v blank; ã2^(r–v) Dedication to Jacqueline Pascal; A^r half-title:
IVDITH, / OV L'AMOVR / DE / LA PATRIE, / TRAGOEDIE.;
A^v list of Acteurs; A2^r–O2^v 3–56 text.

BN Yf 305

21. Brinon, *Baptiste*

(i) BAPTISTE, / OV LA CALOMNIE, / TRAGEDIE. / *TRADVITTE
DV LATIN* / *de Buchanan.* / [mark: Silvestre 1254] / *A ROVEN,* /
Chez IEAN OSMONT, dans / la Court de Palais. / 1613.

12⁰, sigs by 8 and 4: A^v blank; A2^r 3 Au lecteur; A2^v 4 list of Personnages;
A3^r–8^v, BI–4, CI–8, DI–4^r 5–47 text; D4^v blank.

BN Rés p. Yc 1556

(ii) *Baptiste*, Rouen, Jean Osmont, 1614, 12⁰, 3 & 46 pp. (Brunet).

22. Brinon, *Jephté*

IEPHTE' / OV LE VOEV / TRAGEDIE. / Traduitte du Latin de
Buchanan par P. de / Brinon Conseiller du Roy en sa Cour / de

Parlement de Normandie. / *Risus dolore miscebitur, & extrema gaudij* / *Luctus occupat.* Prouerb. 14. / [mark: Silvestre 1254] / *A ROVEN,* / Chez IEAN OSMONT, dans / la Court du Palais. / 1614.

12°, sigs by 8 and 4: A^v blank; A2^r–v Dedication to Brinon's father; A3^r Latin encomiastic verses; A3^v Argument and list of Personnages; A4^r–8, B1–4, C1–8, D1–4, E1–2^v 1–46 text; E3^r–v Latin encomiastic verses.

Ars 8° BL 14110

23. Brisset, *Baptiste*

LE / PREMIER LIVRE / DV THEATRE / TRAGIQVE / DE / *ROLAND BRISSET,* / *GENTIL-HOMME TOVRANGEAV.* / [orn] / A TOVRS, / Par CLAVDE DE MONTR'OEIL, / & IEAN RICHER. / M. D. LXXXIX. / AVEC PRIVILEGE DV ROY.

4°: ã^v blank; ã2^r–4^v, ẽ^r–2^r Aux lecteurs; ẽ2^r Advertissement; ẽ2^v–4^v, ĩ^r–2^r encomiastic verses; ĩ2^v Privilège, 15 July 1589; A^r–v 1–2 Argument of *Hercule furieux;* A^v 2 list of Personnages; A2^r–K^v 3–74 *Hercule furieux*; K2^r–v 75–76 Argument of *Thyeste;* K2^v 76 list of Personnages; K3^r–R3^v 77–134 *Thyeste;* R4^r–v 135–136 Argument of *Agamemnon;* R4^v 136 list of Personnages; s^r–Aa2^v 137–188 *Agamemnon;* Aa3^r–4^r 189–191 Argument of *Octavie;* Aa4^r 191 list of Personnages; Aa4^v–Hh2^r 192–243 *Octavie;* Hh2^v–3^r 244–245 Argument of *Baptiste;* Hh3^r 245 list of Personnages; Hh3^v–Qq4^r 246–311 *Baptiste;* Qq4^v errata.

Ars 4° BL 3427

Some copies dated M. D. XC.:
BN Rés Yf 129
Ars 4° BL 3429

24. Buschey, *Mystere de l'Incarnation*

LE / MYSTERE / de la saincte / INCARNATION / de nostre redempteur & sauueur / IESVS-CHRIST: / *Par personnages.* / Accommodé sur certains passages con- / tenus au vieil & nouueau Testament: / *Par Frere Henri Buschey, de l'Ordre* / *de S. François de l'Obseruance.* / [mark: Van Havre: Plantin 34] / A ANVERS, / De l'Im~ primerie de Christofle Plantin. / Imprimeur du Roy. / M. D. LXXXVII.

8°: A^v woodcut of Annunciation; A2^r–8^v 3–16 Dedication to Père Jean Balla, abbé of S-Hubert; A8^v 16 list of Personnages; B^r–E5^v 17–74 text; E5^v–H2^v 74–116 Actions de grâce and prayers; H3^r Approbation, 17 December 1586; H3^v Privilège, 18 October 1586, confirmed 21 April 1587.

BL C.39.a.28

25. *Sainte Catherine*

(i) *Le Martyre de Sainte Catherine*, Lyons, P. Compagnon, 1649 (*History* II, p. 668; *Soleinne* no. 1190).

(ii) LE / MARTYRE / DE Ste CATHERINE. / TRAGEDIE. / [orn] / A CAEN, / Chez ELEAZAR MANGEANT, ruë / Saint Iean, au

Parc le Roy, / proche le Pont S. Pierre. / M. DC. XLIX.

4°: A^v blank; A2^r blank; A2^v list of Acteurs; A3^r–M4^v text.

BN Yf 4836

> It is strange that Compagnon allowed a rival to bring out an ed. within months of his own, and the lack of a Privilège in (ii) is doubly suspicious. A number of plays was printed in the same format, using the same ornaments, but bearing the names of several printers, who in each case had been responsible for the first ed. of the play: see nos 42 (iii), 43 (ii), 44 (ii), and a 1651 ed. of Mme de Saint-Balmon's *Jumeaux martyrs*. These were probably pirate eds. It is possible that in the case of *Ste Catherine* the printer forgot to give the name of the original printer, but wrote his own: Mangeant may have been responsible for the pirate eds.

(iii) LE / MARTYRE / DE S^TE CATHERINE. / TRAGEDIE / [orn] / *Sur la copie Imprimée à Caën,* / Chez ELEAZAR MANGEANT, ruë Sainct / Iean, au Parc le Roy, proche le Pont S. Pierre. / M. DC. L.

4°: π^v list of Acteurs; A^r–Q^v 1–122 text.

BN Rés Yf 240

> Apparently an unauthorised copy of the ed. by Mangeant, itself perhaps pirated.

> The play is attributed in the BN Catalogue to both d'Aubignac and Marthe Cosnard, and by Parfaict (vol. vi, p. 305) to Saint-Germain; Lancaster (*History* ii, p. 668) dismisses all these attributions, and concludes that the author is unknown.

26. Chantelouve, *Gaspard de Colligny*

   Crit. ed. by Keith Cameron, Exeter 1971.

27. Chantelouve, *Pharaon*

(i) TRAGEDIE / DE PHARAON ET AVTRES / OEVVRES POETIQVES CONTENANT / Hymnes, diuers Sonnets & chansons. / *Par François de Chantelouue Gentilhomme bourde-* / *lois Cheualier de l'ordre de Sainct Iean* / *de Ierusalem.* / DEDIEE, / A treshaut, tresmag~ nanime & Catholique Prince / Charles de Lorraine Duc de Mene, Marquis / de Villars, Viconte de Castillon. / [mark: Silvestre 126] / A PARIS, / Par Nicolas Bonfons, demeurant en la rue neu- / ue nostre Dame, à l'enseigne S. Nicolas. / 1577.

8°: ã^v blank; ã2^r–3^r Dedication; ã3^v–4^r letter, by Frère G. Vigerius, dated 30 September 1576, stating that he has seen through the press work Chantelouve was too modest to publish; ã4^v encomiastic verses; A^r–D4^r text; D4^v–H8^v Hymns, sonnets, etc. [68 ff].

BN Rés Yf 4340 *bis*

> The lower half of the date on the title-page has been cut off in binding, but enough remains to distinguish 1577.

(ii) Lyons, Pierre Rigaud, 1582 (Brunet)

28. Chevillard, *La Mort de Théandre*

Soleinne no. 1246 describes the first ed., Orléans, G. Hotot, 1649, 8°, 4 ff
and 72 pp. I have been unable to trace this. Other eds date from after
1650. I have used BN Rés Yf 4556 (undated).

29. Florent Chrestian, *Jephte*

(i) [border] *JEPHTE, OV LE VEV,* / Tragedie tiree du Latin de Geor- /
GE BVCHANAN, PRINCE / DES POETES DE NOSTRE /
SIECLE. / *Par Florent Chrestian.* / [mark: Silvestre 426] / *A
ORLEANS,* / *De l'Imprimerie de Loys Rabier.* / *M. D. LXVII.*

4°: A^v blank; A2^r sonnet to Cardinal Châtillon; A2^v Argument and list of
Personnages; A3^r–K^v text; K2^v–4^v translation of lamentations of Jerome;
K4^v errata [40 ff].

BN Rés m. Yc 885

(ii) IEPHTE', / TRAGEDIE / TRADVICTE DV / LATIN DE
GEORGE / Buchanan Escossois. / PAR FL. CH. / [mark: Renouard
Marques 304] / A PARIS, / De l'Imprimerie de Robert Estienne. /
M. D. LXXIII. / AVEC PRIVILEGE.

4°: A^v Argument and list of Personnages; A2^r–H3^r 1^r–32^r text; H3^v blank.
BN Rés Yf 3901

(iii) IEPHTE', / TRAGEDIE / TRADVICTE / DV LATIN DE /
GEORGE BUCHA- / nan Escossois. / [orn] / Par Florent Chrestien. /
[mark: Heitz 3] / Par Pierre de Sainct André. / *M. D. LXXXI.*

4°: A^v Argument and list of Personnages; A2^r–F4^v 3–48, G^r–H4^r 41–55
text; H4^v blank.

BL 1070.e.8

Sainct André is listed by Heitz as having worked in Geneva.

(iv) IEPHTE', / OV / LE VEOV, TRAGEDIE / TRADVITE DV
LATIN / de George Buchanan, / Escossois. / PAR / FLORENT
CHRESTIAN. / [mark: Renouard *Marques* 296] / A PARIS, / Par
Mamert Patisson Imprimeur du Roy, / au logis de Robert Estienne. /
1587.

12°: A^v Argument and list of Personnages; A2^r–c6^r 2^r–30^r text; c6^v blank.
Followed by the *David* trilogy of Desmasures, which is not given an
independent title-page, but of which the signatures and pagination are
not continuous with *Jephté*: see no. 45 (iv).

BN Rés p. Yc 1199(1)

The mark used belonged to Estienne rather than Patisson.

30. Nicolas Chrestien, *Amnon et Thamar*

TRAGEDIE / D'AMNON, ET / THAMAR. / [mark: Silvestre 899] /
A ROVEN, / Chez THEODORE REINSART, / pres le Palais, à
l'Homme Armé. / 1608.

12⁰: A^v blank; ã^r–2^v (a cancel of 2 ff.) encomiastic verses; A2^r Sujet de la Tragedie; A2^v list of Acteurs; A3^r–E8^r 1–107 text; E8^v blank.

BL 163.b.13

BN Rés Yf 2963
Ars 8⁰ BL 12631 } lack the supplementary leaves in the preliminaries.

31. Coignac, *La Desconfiture de Goliath*

LA / DESCON- / FITVRE DE / GOLIATH, / [orn] / Tragedie. / Par M. Ioachim de-Coignac. / I. SAMVEL 17. / *Sachent tous les habitans de la terre, / que Dieu est en Israel.* / [mark: Heitz 133, with motto in Roman] / A GENEVE, / *Par Adam & Iean Riueriz, freres.* / 1551.

8⁰: A^v 2 dizain by Jacques Bourgeois; A2^r–6^v 3–12 Dedication to Edward VI of England; A7^r 13 note: L'hystoire de la presente Tragedie, est contenue au 17. chap. du premier livre de Samuel; A7^v 14 list of Personnages; A8^r–E4^r 15–71 text; E4^v blank.

BL C.65.c.11

32. Coignac, *Satires*

Two satires, on the subjects of the Pope and the Papacy, are reported by Brunet to have been published by Coignac, Geneva 1551; also *Soleinne* II Supplément 322.

33. Coppée, *La Vie de saincte Justine et de sainct Cyprien*

Liège 1621 (*History* I, p. 198).

34. Coppée, *Saincte Aldegonde*
LA / TRES-SAINCTE ET / ADMIRABLE VIE DE MA- / DAME SAINCTE / ALDEGONDE / PATRONE DE / MAVBEVGE. / Tragecomedie. / *Par DENYS COPPEE, NATIF* / de Huy païs de Liege. / [orn] / A LIEGE, / Chez Christian Ouvverx le jeune, / demeurant proche S. Denis / à la Patience. / L'an M. DC. XXII.

4⁰: A^v blank; A2^r–3^r Dedication to Mont-Joye; A3^v anagram to same; A4^r Sujet de la tragecomedie, and list of Entreparleurs; A4^v Prologue; B^r–G4^v 1–48 text; H^r prayer to Aldegonde; H^v sonnet and errata; H2^r–v prayer.

Brussels II 61800 L.P.

35. Coppée, *S. François*

LE BEAV / PRINTEMPS / D'HYVER, DV / GRAND AMI DE DIEV / S. FRANCOIS D'ASSISE. / TRAGECOMEDIE PAR / DENIS COPPEE DE HVY / Pays de Liege. / [orn] / A ROVEN. / Chez Raphael du petit Val, libraire Impri- / meur ordinaire du Roy. / L'an M. DC. XXIII.

8⁰: A^v blank; A2^r–3^v Dedication to Fr Jean du Rieu, Provincial of the Franciscans at Liège; A3^v–5^v verses, including some to Arnoul de

Waresme, aged about 16, who played François in the church of the
Franciscans at Huy, August 1622; A6^{r-v} Prologue, spoken by Martin
Coppée, aged about 7; A7^r–E3^v text; E4^r sonnet in praise of St Francis;
E4^v prayer to same [36 ff].

Bonn University Library 1: an Fc 198/2

This description is derived from a photocopy.

36. Coppée, *S. Lambert*

TRAGEDIE / DE / S. LAMBERT / PATRON DE / LIEGE. /
Dediée à Son ALTEZE *Serenissime,* / *par* Denis Coppee *Huitois.* /
[small woodcut, showing a bishop (Lambert?) in front of a church] /
A LIEGE, / Par Leonard Streel, Imprimeur iuré. / M. DC. XXIIII. /
Auec permission des Superieurs.

8°: A^v blank; between A and A2 a large sheet, unsigned, which folds out,
bearing acrostic poem to Ferdinand de Bavière; A2^r–4^v 3–8 Epitre
declamee par l'un des petits Fils de l'Auteur, presentant ladite Tragedie
au prince Serenissime Ferdinand...Archevesque de Cologne; A5^r 9
sonnet to Duc de Bavière; A5^v–6^v 10–12 anagram of Ferdinand de Bavière
and ode; A6^v 12 list of Entreparleurs; A7^r–D4^v 13–56 text.

BN Yf 6691

37. Coppée, *Passion*

LA SANGLANTE / ET PITOYABLE / TRAGEDIE / DE NOSTRE
SAVVEVR / ET REDEMPTEVR / IESVS-CHRIST, / Poëme mêlangé
de deuotes meditatiõs, / figures, complaintes de la glorieuse / Vierge,
de la Magdalene, & de / Sainct Pierre. / Auec quinze Sonnets en
memoire des quinze / Effusions de nôtre Sauueur. / *Par* DENIS COPEE
Bourgeois de Huy. / [orn] / A LIEGE, / Chez LEONARD STREEL,
Imprimeur iuré. / M. DC. XXIIII. / *Auec Permission des Superieurs.*

8°: A^v blank; A2^r–3^r 3–5 Dedication to Anne Jaymaert, Abbesse du Val
Nostre Dame; A3^v–4^v 6–8 Ode to same by Du Chasteau; A5^r 9 sonnet,
anagram and acrostic to same by Coppée; A5^v 10 ode to Josine de Blehen,
by Coppée; A6^r 11 Au lecteur; A6^{r-v} 11–12 Prologue; A7^r–L2^v 13–164
text; L3^r–8^r 165–175 sonnets; L8^v–M4^v 176–184 Table; M4^v 184 errata.

Brussels II 61803 L.P.

38. Corneille, *Polyeucte*

Crit. ed. by Charles Marty-Laveaux, Paris 1862 (vol. III of *Oeuvres*,
12 vols, Paris 1862–8 (GEF)). See also Emile Picot, *Bibliographie
cornélienne*, Paris 1876.

39. Corneille, *Théodore*

Crit. ed. by Marty-Laveaux, Paris 1862 (vol. IV of *Oeuvres*); see also
Picot, *Bibliographie cornélienne.*

40. Cosnard, *Les Chastes Martirs*

(ia) LES CHASTES / MARTIRS, / TRAGEDIE / CHRESTIENNE. /

Par MADEMOISELLE COSNARD. / [orn] / A PARIS, / Chez
NICOLAS & IEAN de la COSTE, au mont S. Hilaire, à / l'Escu de
Bretagne: Et en leur boutique à la petire porte du Palais, / qui regarde
le Quay des Augustins. / M. DC. L. / *AVEC PRIVILEGE DV ROY.*

4°: ã^v blank; ã3^r–4^r Au lecteur; ã4^v list of Acteurs; A–M4^r 1–95 text; M4^v
blank.

BN Rés Yf 239

> The lacking leaf in the prelims is supplied in the ed. by L. de la
> Sicotière, Rouen 1888 (Soc. des bibliophiles normands 48): it bore a
> Dedication to the Regent, and encomiastic verses by Corneille and
> S-Nicolas. I have not seen a copy of the original ed. with this leaf.

(ib) LES CHASTES / MARTIRS, / TRAGEDIE / CHRESTIENNE. /
Par MADEMOISELLE COSNARD. / [Courbé's mark] / A PARIS, /
Chez AVGVSTIN COVRBE', dans la petite Salle / du Palais, à la
Palme. / M. DC. L. / *AVEC PRIVILEGE DV ROY.*

> Contents as in (ia): one printer sold his sheets to the other, who added
> a new title-page; there is no Privilège naming the printer.

Ars Rf 5832

41. Crespin, *Le Marchant converti*

(i) Geneva, Jean Crespin, 1558, 8°, 4 ff. & 168 pp. (*Soleinne* 294).

(ii) Geneva, Jean Crespin, 1561, 8°, 171 pp. (Brunet, s.v. Naogeorgus;
Soleinne 3725).

(iii) Geneva, 1561, 16°, 175 pp. (Brunet, s.v. Naogeorgus)

(iv) *LE* / MARCHANT / CONVERTI. / [orn] / TRAGEDIE EXCEL- /
LENTE. / En laquelle la vraye & fausse religion, au / parangon l'vne
de l'autre, sont au vif / representees: pour entendre quelle est / leur
vertu & effort au combat de la / conscience, & quelle doit estre leur
issue / au dernier iugement de Dieu. / [mark: Heitz 24, without
surround] / PAR GABRIEL CARTIER. / M. D. LXXXII.

8°: A^v blank; A2^{r-v} Aux fidèles; A3^r–4^r Prologue; A4^r list of characters;
A4^v Advertissement; A5^r–M6^v text [94 ff].
BPU Rés Hf 4641

> Cartier is listed by Heitz as having worked in Geneva.

(v) *LE* / MARCHANT / CONVERTI. / TRAGEDIE EXCEL- /
LENTE. / En laquelle la vraye & fausse reli- / gion, au parangon l'vne
de l'autre, & / sont au vif representees: pour en- / tendre quelle est leur
vertu & / effort au combat de la conscien- / ce, & quelle doit estre leur
issuë / au dernier iugement de Dieu. / *Item suit apres la Comedie du
Pape / malade, & tirant à la fin.* / POVR CLAVDE D'AVGY. / M. D.
LXXXV.

8°: A^v blank; A2^{r-v} Aux fidèles; A3^r–4^r Prologue; A4^r Les noms de ceux qui sont introduits en ceste Tragedie; A4^v Advertissement; A5^r–M8^v text [96 ff].

BPU Rés Hf 4945

Bound with Badius's *Pape malade*, Augy 1584, which nevertheless has its own title-page, signatures and pagination (no. 5 (iii)).

(vi) [border] LE / MARCHANT / CONVERTI. / [orn] / *Tragedie excellente.* / En laquelle la vraye & fausse Reli- / gion, au parangon l'vne de l'autre, / sont au vif representees: pour en- / tendre quelle est leur vertu et ef- / fort au combat de la conscience, / & quelle doit estre leur issuë au / dernier iugement de Dieu. / *Item suit apres la Comedie du Pape mala-* / *de, & tirant à la fin.* / [orn] A GENEVE. / PAR François Forest. / *M. D. XCI.*

8°: A^v blank; A2^{r-v} Aux fidèles; A3^r–4^r Prologue; A4^r list of characters; A4^v Advertissement; A5^r–M6^v text [94 ff]; remainder of volume occupied by Badius's *Pape malade*, Forest 1591 (no. 5 (iv)).

BN Rés Yf 4568

Ars Rf 1317 ⎫
BL 163.b.59 ⎬ lack address on title-page, A GENEVE.

BPU Hf 5123 has address on title-page in lower case, à Genéue.

(vii) LE / MARCHAND / CONVERTI, / Tragedie excellente: / En laquelle la vray & fausse religion, au / parangon l'vne de l'autre, sont au vif / representees; pour entendre quelle / est leur vertu & effort au combat de la conscience, & quelle doit estre leur / issue au dernier iugement de Dieu. / [mark] / Pour Iaques Chouët. / M. D. XCIIII.

8°: A^v blank; A2^r–3^r L'Imprimeur aux lecteurs; A3^v–4^v Prologue; A4^v list of Personnages; A5^r–M5^r I^r–89^r text; M5^v–6^v 89^v–90^v Aux fidèles.

BPU Rés S 18940

42. Desfontaines, *St Eustache*

(i) LE / MARTYRE / DE / S^T EVSTACHE. / TRAGEDIE. / [Sommaville's mark] / A PARIS, /

Chez TOVSSAINCT QVINET, ⎫
ET ⎬ au Palais.
NICOLAS DE SERCY, ⎭

M. DC. XXXXIII. / *AVEC PRIVILEGE DV ROY.*

4°: π^v blank; π2^r Privilège in Quinet's name, 13 January 1643, note associating De Sercy in it, and achevé, 20 July 1643; π2^v list of Personnages; A–L4^v I–88 text.

Ars Rf 5991

(ii) LE / MARTYRE / DE S^T EVSTACHE. / TRAGEDIE. / [orn] / A PARIS, /

⎧ TOVSSAINCT QVINET. ⎫
Chez ⎨ & ⎬ Au Palais.
⎩ NICOLAS DE SERCY. ⎭

M. DC. XLIV. / *AVEC PRIVILEGE DV ROY.*

4°: π^v blank; $\pi 2^r$ Privilège in Quinet's name, 13 January 1643, note associating De Sercy in it, and achevé pour la seconde fois, 30 December 1644; $\pi 2^v$ list of Acteurs; A–L4^v 1–88 text.

BN Rés Yf 221

(iii) LE / MARTYRE / DE S^T EVSTACHE. / TRAGEDIE. / [orn] / *Sur l'imprimé.* / A PARIS. /
Chez TOVSSAINCT QVINET.
ET
NICOLAS DE SERCY, } au Palais.

M. DC. XLIIII.

4°: A^v blank; A2^r blank; A2^v 4 list of Personnages; A3^r–L3^v 5–86 text; L4 blank.

BN Yf 4835

The absence of a Privilège is suspicious: this may be a pirate ed.: see no. 25 (ii).

43. Desfontaines, *St Alexis*

(i) L'ILLVSTRE / OLYMPIE / OV LE / S^T ALEXIS. / TRAGEDIE. / *Par le Sieur DESFONTAINES.* / [mark] / A PARIS, / Chez PIERRE LAMY, en la Grand' / Salle du Palais, au second Pillier. / M. DC. XXXXV. /*AVEC PRIVILEGE DV ROY.*

4°: π^v blank; $\pi 2^r$–3^r Dedication to Mme de Talmant; $\pi 3^v$ Privilège, 7 May 1644, and achevé, 4 December 1644; $\pi 4^r$ epigram to Mme de Talmant; $\pi 4^v$ list of Personnages; A–O2^r 1–107 text; O2^v blank.

BN Rés Yf 262

(ii) L'ILLVSTRE / OLYMPIE / OV LE / S^T ALEXIS / TRAGEDIE / *Par le Sieur DESFONTAINES.* / [orn] *Sur l'imprimé* / A PARIS, / Chez PIERRE LAMY, en la Grande. / Salle du Palais, au second Pillier. / M. DC. XLVIII.

4°: π^v blank; $\pi 2^r$–3^v Dedication to Mme de Talmant; $\pi 4^r$ epigram to same; $\pi 4^v$ list of Personnages; A–L4^v 1–88 text.

BN Yf 4838

The absence of a Privilège is suspicious: this may be a pirate ed.: see no. 25 (ii).

44. Desfontaines, *Sainct Genest*

(i) L'ILLVSTRE / COMEDIEN, / OV / LE MARTYRE / DE / SAINCT GENEST. / TRAGEDIE. / [mark] / A PARIS, / Chez CARDIN BESOGNE, au Palais, / au haut de la Montée de la saincte Chapelle, / aux Roses Vermeilles. / M. DC. XLV. / *AVEC PRIVILEGE DV ROY.*

4°, sigs by 2: π^v blank; $\pi 2^r$ Advis, and Privilège, 30 April 1645, and achevé, 8 May 1645; $\pi 2^v$ list of Acteurs; A–Y2^r 1–87 text; Y2^v blank.

BN Rés Yf 539

(ii) L'ILLVSTRE / COMEDIEN / OV / LE MATYRE / DE S. GENEST. / TRAGEDIE. / [orn] *Sur l'imprimé.* / A PARIS. / Chez CARDIN BESOGNE, au Palais, / au haut de la Montée de la saincte Chap- / pelle, aux Roses vermeilles. / M. DC. XL.VI.

4°: A^v blank; A2^r 3 Advis; A2^v 4 list of Acteurs; A3^r–L^v 5–82 text; L2 blank.

BN Yf 4833

The absence of a Privilège is suspicious: this may be a pirate ed.: see no 25 (ii).

45. Desmasures, *Tragedies sainctes (David combattant, David triomphant, David fugitif)*

(i) TRAGEDIES / *SAINCTES.* / Dauid combattant. / Dauid triom~ phant. / Dauid fugitif. / *Par Louïs Des-Masures Tournisien.* / [mark: Heitz 126, without motto] / *A GENEVE,* / De l'Imprimerie de François Perrin. / *M. D. LXVI.*

8°: a^v epigraph; a2^r–6^r 3–11 Epistle to Le Brun; a6^v 12 Au lecteur; a7^r half-title, *David combattant*; a7^v 14 list of Personnages; a8^r–g2^r 15–99 *David combattant*; g2^v half-title, *David triomphant*; g3^r 101 list of Personnages; g3^v–m^v 102–178 *David triomphant*; m2^r half-title, *David fugitif*; m2^v 180 list of Personnages; m3^r–r8^v 181–272 *David fugitif*. Includes music for the choruses.

Ars 8° BL 13906

(ii) TRAGEDIES / *SAINCTES.* / Dauid combattant. / Dauid triom~ phant. / Dauid fugitif. / *Par Louïs Des-Masures Tournisien.* / [mark: variant of Silvestre 359] / *A ANVERS* / Par Nicolas Soolmans, / au Lion d'or. / *M. D. LXXXII.*

8°: A^v epigraph; A2^r6^r 3–11 Epistle to Le Brun; A6^v Au lecteur; A7^r half-title, *David combattant*; A7^v 14 list of Personnages; A8^r–F8^v 15–96 *David combattant*; G^r 97 half-title, *David triomphant*; G^v 98 list of Personnages; G2^r–L8^v 99–176 *David triomphant*; M^r 177 half-title, *David fugitif*; M^v 178 list of Personnages; M2^r–R7^v 179–270 *David fugitif*; R8 blank. Includes music for the choruses.

Ars Rf 1209

(iii) TRAGEDIES / SAINCTES. / Dauid combattant. / Dauid triom~ phant. / Dauid fugitif. / Bergerie Spirituelle. / Eclogue Spirituelle. / *Par Louys Des-Masures Tournisien.* / [mark: Heitz 24] / PAR GABRIEL CARTIER. / Pour Claude D'Augy. / 1583.

8°: A^v blank; A2^r–5^v 3–10 Epistle to Le Brun; A5^v 10 Au lecteur; A6^r 11 list of Personnages of *David combattant*; A6^v–F6^v 12–92 *David combattant*; F7^r 93 list of Personnages of *David triomphant*; F7^v–L6^r 94–171 *David triomphant*; L6^v 172 list of Personnages of *David fugitif*; L7^r–R4^r 173–263 *David fugitif*; R4^v 264 list of Personnages of the *Bergerie spirituelle*; R5^r–v2^r 265–307 *Bergerie spirituelle*; v2^v–8^r 308–319 *Eclogue spirituelle*; v8^v blank. Includes music for the choruses.

Ars Rf 1210

(iv) Following Christian's *Jepthé*, Paris, Patisson, 1587 (no. 29 (iv))
Desmasures's trilogy, though apparently printed separately, because it
has independent signatures and pagination, was not intended to be sold
alone, because it has no title-page, only a half-title:
Dauid combattant. / Dauid triomphant. / Dauid fugitif. / *Tragedie
sainctes*. / PAR / Loys Des-Masures Tournisien.

12°: aᵛ list of Personnages of *David combattant*; a2ʳ–c11ʳ 2ʳ–35ʳ *David
combattant*; c11ᵛ list of Personnages of *David triomphant*; c12ʳ–e11
36ʳ–59ʳ, e12ʳ–f11ᵛ 66ʳ–77ᵛ *David triomphant*; f12ʳ 78ʳ list of Personnages of *David fugitif*; f12ᵛ–k4ᵛ 72ᵛ–112ᵛ *David fugitif*.

BN Rés p. Yc 1199

The crit. ed. by Charles Comte, Paris 1907 (STFM) appeared without
the introduction or apparatus.

46. Desmasures, *Bergerie spirituelle*

(i) BERGERIE / spirituelle. / [orn] / Par Louïs Des-Masures Tour~
nisien. / *EZECH. XXXIIII.* / *Je sauueray mon trouppeau (dit le
Seigneur) & ne sera / plus en rapine: & iugeray entre une brebis
& l'autre.* / [mark: Heitz 126, without motto] / *A GENEVE*, / De
l'Imprimerie de François Perrin. / *M. D. LXVI.*

8°: Aᵛ, A2ʳ epigraph; A2ᵛ list of Personnages; A3ʳ–C7ᵛ 5–46 text; c8 blank
Includes music.

Ars 8° BL 13906

(ii) Included in Desmasures's trilogy, Geneva 1583 (no. 45 (iii)).

Ars Rf 1210

47. Du Monin, *La Peste de la peste*

LE QVAREME / DE IAN EDOVARD / DV MONIN, [ornamented
initials] PP, / Diuisé en trois parties. / PREMIERE. / *Le triple Amour
ou l'Amour de Dieu, du Monde / Angelique, & du Monde Humain.* /
SECONDE. / *La Peste de la Peste, ou Iugement diuin, Tragedie.* /
TROISIEME. / La Consuiuance du Quaréme. / *A son Mecenas, Messe*
Ἰῶ, τὸν οὐχ οἶδα, / ἦ τῷ Θυασιμόδῳ. / Tome cinquiéme. / [mark: Renouard
Marques 867] / *A PARIS*, / Chez Iean Parent, rue sainct Iacques. /
Auec priuilege du Roi. / 1584.

4°: ãᵛ Hebrew, Greek and Latin epigraphs; ã2ʳ–4ʳ Dedication; ã4ʳ
verses: ã4ᵛ portrait of the author; Aʳ–T4ʳ 1–151 *Le Triple Amour*; T4ᵛ–
Ll4ʳ 152–271 *La Peste de la peste*; Ll4ʳ–yy3ʳ 271–357 *Consuivance du
Quaréme*; yy3ʳ 357 Privilège, undated; yy3ᵛ–4ᵛ Sommaire des matieres
yy4ᵛ errata.

BL 164.e.16

Ars Rf 1230 'Tome cinquiéme' on the title-page appears to have been
rubbed out.

48. Du Ryer, *Saül*

SAVL, / TRAGEDIE / DE / M^R DV RYER. / [Sommaville's mark] /
A PARIS, /

Chez {
ANTOINE DE SOMMAVILLE,
en la petite salle, à l'Escu de France.
ET
AVGVSTIN COVRBE', en la
mesme salle, à la Palme.
} au
Palais.

M. DC. XXXXII. / *Auec priuilege du Roy.*

4º: ã engraved frontispiece; ã^v blank; ã2^r title-page; ã2^v blank; ã3^r–4^r
Dedication to the public; ã4^v list of Acteurs; A–O3^v 1–110 text; O4^r
Privilege, 8 April 1642, and achevé 31 May 1642; O4^v blank.

BN Rés Yf 533

Also ed. by H. C. Lancaster, Baltimore 1931 (Johns Hopkins Studies
in Romance Literatures and Languages, 17).

49. Du Ryer, *Esther*

ESTHER, / TRAGEDIE. / De P. DV RYER. / [Sommaville's mark] /
A PARIS, /

Chez {
ANTOINE DE SOMMAVILLE, en la Salle
des Merciers, à l'Escu de France.
&
AVGVSTIN COVRBE', Libraire & Imprimeur de Monseigneur le Duc d'Orleans,
à la mesme Salle, à la Palme.
} au Pa-
lais.

M. DC. XXXXIV. / *AVEC PRIVILEGE DV ROY.*

4º: ã^v blank; ã2^r Preface; ã2^v list of Personnages; A–Q^v 1–122 text; Q2^r
Privilège, in names of both Sommaville and Courbé, 15 July 1643, and
achevé, 30 March 1644; Q2^v blank.

BN Rés Yf 537

50. D'Ennetieres, *Ste Aldegonde*

Ste. ALDEGONDE / COMEDIE. / Par Messire IEAN D'ENNE~
TIERES Che- / ualier, Seigneur de Beaumé. / [mark: *Marques des P-B*,
Tournai, Quinqué 2] / A TOVRNAY, / Chez ADRIEN QVINQVE'. /
M. DC. XLV.

8º: A^v blank; A2^{r–v} Dedication to Louise de Lorraine; A3^r Approbation,
4 April 1645; A3^v list of Acteurs; A4^r–5^v 1–4 Prologue; A6^r–G7^r 5–103
text; G7^v blank.

BN Rés Yf 4408

51. Fonteny, *Cleophon*

CLEOPHON. / Tragedie. / *Conforme & semblable à celles que* / *la*
France a veues durant les / *Guerres Ciuilles.* / Par I.D.F. / [orn] /
A PARIS, / Chez FRANÇOIS IACQVIN Imprimeur, / demeurant ruë
des Poires, vis à vis / la porte de Sorbonne. / cIɔ Ic c.

4°: πv blank; $\pi 2^r$ Dedication to François Miron; $\pi 2^v$ list of Personnages; A^r–$F3^v$ 1–46 text; $F4^r$ anagram and sonnet to Miron; $F4^v$ blank.

BN Rés Yf 3888

Author identified in *Soleinne* 884.

52. Fronton-du-Duc, *La Pucelle de Dom-Remy*

L'HISTOIRE / TRAGIQVE / De la Pucelle de Dom-Remy, / aultre~ ment / D'ORLEANS. / Nouuellement departie par Actes, / & representée par / Personnages. / [mark: Silvestre 990 with added ornamental surround] / A NANCY, / Par la vefue Iean Ianson pour son filz / Imprimeur de son ALTESSE. 1581.

4°: A^v blank; $A2^r$–4^r Dedication to Comte de Salm, 26 May 1581, signed Jean Barnet; $A4^v$, B^r verses by Barnet to same; B^v–2^r list of Personnages; $B2^v$ blank; $B3^r$–4^v Avant-jeu; C^r–$O2^r$ 1^r–46^r text; $O2^v$ sonnet; $O3^{r-v}$ errata. BN Rés Ye 468

Lacks gathering L; complete text available in ed. by Durand de Lanson, Pont-à-Mousson 1859, where the author is identified.

53. Garnier, *Les Juifves*

Crit. ed. by Raymond Labègue, Paris 1949 (Les Textes français). See also the list of eds in Forsyth, pp. 437–9.

54. Gaulché, *L'Amour divin*

L'AMOVR DIVIN / TRAGECOMEDIE. / *Contenant vn bref discour des Saincts & / sacrés mysteres de la Redemption de / l'humaine nature.* / Par IEAN GAVLCHE'. / [large woodcut, showing the six characters] / A Troyes, Chez Claude Briden.

8°: A^v repeats woodcut on title page with list of Acteurs; $A2^r$–3^r Dedication to Jean Angenoust; $A3^r$ device containing laurels, palms, fleurs de lis and initials L; $A3^v$ Aux lecteurs; $A4^{r-v}$ Argument; $A4^v$ device containing 3 crowns, crossed sceptres, sword, and initials L; $A5^r$–$C4^r$ text; $C4^v$ Approbation, 26 July and 15 September 1601.

Ars 8° BL 14090

The initial L combined with crowns and sceptres in the devices on ff. $A3^r$ and $A4^v$ may suggest that the play was printed in the reign of Louis XIII, despite the date of the Approbation.

55. George, *Les Tentations d'Abraham*

TRAGIQVE COME- / DIE AVGMENTEE, / *En laquelle l'histoire d deux tresgriefues / tentations, desquelles le S Patriarche Abra- / ham esté exercé, ascauoir (lors qu'il fut con / traint de chasser hors de s maison son fils / Ismaël: & puis fut tout prest de sacrifier son / fils Isaac, est representee: / Pour l'instruction & consolation de tous fi- / deles lesquels sont aussi souuent visitez & / esprouuez par diuerses tentations*

& tribulations. / *Nouuellement augmentee.* / [orn] / A MONT~
BELIARD, / Par IAQVES FOILLET. / M. DC. IX.

8º: a^v blank; a2^r–4^v Dedication to Guillaume Vessaux, signed Jean
George Maistre d'Eschole à S. Julien; a5^r Aux lecteurs; a5^v Aux pères;
a6^{r–v} encomiastic verses; a7^{r–v} Cantique de l'esperance et ferme
asseurance du fidele; a8^r list of personnages, and Argument; a8^v Epigraphs; a9^{r–v} (numbered 1 on recto only) Prologue; a10^{r,v}, unnumbered,
text starts; b^r–e7^r 17–77 text; e7^v, e8, blank.

Musée Condé, Chantilly, V B 50

56. Grezin, *Advertissements faicts à l'homme*

[orn] ADVERTIS- / SEMENTS FAICTS A L'HOM- / me par les
fleaux de nostre Seigneur, / de la punition à lui deuë par son /
peché, comme est aduenu / depuis trois ans / en ça. / [orn] / PAR
IACQVES GREZIN / Curé de Condac, Vicaire general de Reue- /
rendissime Cardinal de la Bordaizie- / re, Euesque d'Angoulesme. /
A ANGOVLESME. / PAR IEAN DE MINIERES. / Mil. D. LXV.

4º: a^v Au lecteur, by printer; a2^{r–v} Ode to M. de Hauteclaire; a2^v Latin
distich, and Rondeau à l'homme pescheur; a3^{r–v} Au lecteur, dated 1 May
1565; a4^r–d2^v text; d3^r–4^r pious verses; d4^v blank [24 ff].

BN Rés Ye 429

57. Heudon, *S. Clouaud*

(i) S. CLOVAVD, / ROY D'ORLEANS, / *Tragedie auec des Choeurs,* /
Par I. HEVDON. / [orn] / A ROVEN, / Chez RAPHAEL DV PETIT
VAL, / 1599.

8º: a^v blank; b^r–e2^v 17–68 *S. Clouaud* (lacks c8); cancel title-page of
Pyrrhe; e3^r half-title of *Pyrrhe;* e3^v list of Entreparleurs; e4^r–I 10^r 71–147
Pyrrhe (lacks h3, h6); I 10^v blank; a2^r–7^r 3–14 Avant-Propos (a8 lacks).

Ars 8º BL 12621

I have not seen a less mutilated copy of this ed.

(ii) Issued as the first play in Du Petit Val's anthology, *Diverses tragedies,*
Rouen 1599; *S. Clouaud* has no title-page of its own, but the title-page of
the anthology:

DIVERSES / TRAGEDIES / DE PLVSIEVRS / AVTHEVRS / de
ce temps. / *Recueillies par Raphael* / *du Petit Val.* / [Du Petit Val's
mark, without motto] / *A ROVEN,* / DE L'IMPRIMERIE / Dudit
DV PETIT VAL, Libraire & / Imprimeur ordinaire du Roy. / 1599. /
Auec Priuilege de sa Majesté.

12º: a^v blank; a2^r–4^v Argument of *S. Clouaud;* a4^v list of plays in the
anthology: *S. Clouaud, Pyrrhe,* La Péruse's *Medee,* Virey's *Machabee*
(no. 125 (ii)), Le Breton's *Adonis,* Behourt's *Polyxene* and *Esau* (no.
10 (i)); a5^r–8^v 9–16 Avant-Propos; a8^v list of Personnages of *S. Clouaud;*
a9^r–c9^v 17–66 *S. Clouaud;* c10^r Privilège, 4 February 1597; c10^v orn;
c11, c12 blank.

BN Yf 4735

Although the other plays are listed on f. A4ᵛ, they were printed separately, each with its own title-page, signatures and pagination: the anthology was made up of spare copies of the other plays. Only *S. Clouaud*, which contains material relating to the anthology as a whole, could not be sold separately.

(iiia) SAINCT / CLOVAVD / TRAGEDIE. / *De Iean Heudon Parisien.* / [Du Petit Val's mark, without motto] / *A ROVEN,* / DE L'IMPRIMERIE, / De Raphaël du Petit Val, Libraire & Im- / primeur du Roy, deuant la grandporte / du Palais, à l'Ange Raphaël. / 1606. / *Auec Priuilege de sa Maiesté.*

12°: Aᵛ blank; A2ʳ–5ʳ 3–9 Argument; A5ᵛ blank; A6ʳ–9ᵛ 11–18 Avant-propos; A9ᵛ 18 list of Personnages; A10ʳ–C10ᵛ 19–68 text; C11ʳ Privilège, 4 February 1597; C11ᵛ orn.

BL 163.b.23

(iiib) Copies of (iiia) were issued in an anthology, with the title-page removed and replaced with:
LE / THEATRE / DES TRAGE- / DIES FRAN- / ÇOISES. / *Nouuellement mis en lumiere.* / [Du Patit Val's mark without motto] / *A ROVEN,* / DE L'IMPRIMERIE, / De Raphaël du Petit Val, Libraire & Im- / primeur du Roy, deuant la grand porte / du Palais, à l'Ange Raphaël. / 1606. / *Auec Priuilege de sa Maiesté.*

Contents as in (iiia), save that A5ᵛ lists contents of the volume: *S. Clouaud, Priam, Pyrrhe, Medee, Adonis, La Pucelle d'Orléans* (no. 61 (i)), *Acoubar, Sophonisbe, Hypsicratée,* and *César.* These were all printed separately, and lack in the present volume.

BN Rés Yf 3762

(iv) Another ed. lacks the title-page:
A2ʳ–5ʳ 3–9 Argument of *S. Clouaud*; A5ᵛ list of contents of the volume: *S. Clouaud, Pyrrhe, Pryam, Adonis, Cyrus, Les Corrivaux, Gillette, Iris, Le Martire des Macabées* (no. 125?), *La Victoire des Macabées* (no. 126?); A6ʳ–9ᵛ 11–18 Avant-propos; A9ᵛ 18 list of Personnages; A10ʳ–C11ʳ 19–69 *S. Clouaud*; C11ᵛ blank.

Ars 8° BL 12620

Although the pagination is the same as in (iii), it is visibly a different printing.
Bound with Heudon's *Pyrrhe,* separately printed. A MS note on the fly-leaf declares this to be a copy of Heudon's *Theatre, c.* 1602–3; but the inclusion in the list on f. A5ᵛ of works by other authors which were printed by Du Petit Val makes this seem improbable: it is more probably one of his anthologies, though the other plays promised lack.

58. Heyns, *Holoferne et Judith*

LE / MIROIR DES / VEFVES. / Tragedie sacrée d'Holoferne & / Iudith. / *Representant, parmi les troubles de ce monde, / la pieté d'une vraye Vefue, & la cu- / riosité d'une follastre.* / Exhibée & mise en lumiere par M. PIERRE / HEYNS, au Laurier. / [mark: *Marques des*

P-B Amsterdam, Heyns 5] / Imprimé à Harlem, par Gilles Romain, / Pour ZACHARIE HEYNS, Libraire à l'enseigne / des trois Vertus, à AMSTERDAM, 1596.

8⁰: A^v Epigraph, I Tim. v 5; A2^{r-v} 3–4 Dedication to Mlle van Nispen; A3^r 5 Aux lectrices; A3^v 6 list of Personnages; A4^r–F3^v 7–86 text; F3^v–6^r 86–91 Application; F6^v 91 note, Joüée et representée en Anvers, l'An 1582. le 1. et 2. de Juillet; F6^v–7^v 92–94 Translation of Judith's canticle; F8^r 95 Emblem of Daphne and laurel; F8^v blank.

BL 11737.aaa.4

BN Rés Yf 4471 lacks f. F8; bound with Heyns's other plays into one vol. with the collective title:

LES / COMEDIES / ET TRAGEDIES / DV LAVRIER.

La { Iokebed / Susanne / Iudith } Miroire des { Meres. / Mesnageres. / Vefves.

Representans l'estat des femmes, tant mariées, qu'à / marier. Fort utiles & propres pour le sexe / feminin.

This collected ed. was presumably made in 1597, when *Jokebed* appeared (no. 59), by binding with it unsold copies of no. 58 and *Susanne* (1595).

59. Heyns, *Jokebed*

IOKEBED. / MIROIR DES / VRAYES MERES. / Tragi-comedie de l'enfance de / Moyse. Exod. 2. / *Representant les afflictions que les enfans de Dieu ont à / souffrir avant que parvenir à salut.* / Exhibée & mise en lumiere par M. PIERRE / HEYNS, au Laurier. / Luc. 17.33. / *Celuy qui perd sa vie en Christ, la sauvera, / Mais qui garder la veut, la mort n'eschappera.* / [mark: *Marques des P-B* Amsterdam, Heyns 5] / Imprimé à Harlem, par Gilles Romain, / Pour ZACHARIE HEYNS, Libraire à l'Enseigne des / trois Vertus, à AMSTERDAM, sur l'eau. L'An 1597.

8⁰: verso of title-page, blank; a3^{r-v} Dedication to Mme van der Meulen; a4^r Aux fideles meres, et a leurs enfans; a4^v list of Personnages; A^r–E8^v 1–80 text; F^r–2^v 81–84 Conclusion; F3^r–4^r Dutch poem; F4^v blank.

BL 11736.a.23

The first gathering lacks one leaf, probably the collective title (see no. 58), which would have preceded the title of this play.

BN Rés Yf 4471 has the collective title, but lacks the title of this play.

60. Jaquemin, *Le Triomphe des bergers*

Crit. ed. by Georges Couton, Saint-Etienne 1971 (Centre interuniversitaire d'éditions et de rééditions of the Universités de la région des Alpes, Images et Témoins de l'âge classique no. 1).

61. *Jeanne d'Arques*

(i) TRAGEDIE / DE / IEANNE D'ARQVES, / DITE LA PVCELLE / d'Orleans, / *Natiue du village d'Emprenne, pres* /

Voucouleurs en Lorraine. / [mark: Silvestre 445] / *A ROVEN,* / DE L'IMPRIMERIE, / De Raphaël du Petit Val, Libraire & Im- / primeur du Roy, deuant la grand porte / du Palais, à l'Ange Raphaël. / 1606. / *Auec Priuilege de sa Maiesté.*

12º: A^v blank; A2^r–3^v Au lecteur;   A4^r–5^r Prologue; A5^v list of Entre-parleurs; A6^r–B12^v 11–48 text.

BN Rés Yf 3954

Arbour, 'R. Du Petit Val', p. 110, attributes this to François Berthrand d'Orléans and dates it 1600.

(ii) A slightly mutilated copy in the BL has a MS title-page: TRAGEDIE / DE / IEANNE DARQVES / DITE LA PVCELLE / d'Orleans / *Natiue du Village d'Emprenne* / *Prés Voucouleurs en Lorraine* / *Par Simon FAVCONIER* [crossed out, and the name le Pasteur Calianthe substituted] / A ROÜEN / DE L'IMPRIMERIE / de Raphael de Petitual libraire / et imprimeur du Roy deuant la / grande Porte du Palais à lange. / Raphael / 1606 [crossed out, and the date 1611 substituted]

contents as in (i); ff. A1, A2, A6 supplied in MS.

BL 163.b.57

It is difficult to know if this is genuinely a new ed. of 1611; the volume is remarkably similar to (i) (of which the BL does not possess a copy for comparison), but La Vallière, vol. 1, p. 362, and Brunet, record an ed. of 1611.

(iii) TRAGEDIE / DE IEANNE / D'ARQVES, DITE / LA PVCELLE / D'ORLEANS. / *Natiue du village d'Epernay, pres Vaucouleurs / en Lorraine.* / [woodcut of battle scene] / A TROYES, / Chez NICOLAS OVDOT, demeurant en la ruë / nostre Dame, au Chappon d'Or / Couronné. / M. DC. XXVI.

8º: A^v blank; A2^{r-v} Au lecteur; A3^r–4^r Prologue; A4^v list of Personnages; A5^r–c8^v text [24 ff].

Ars 8º BL 13962

62. *La Patience de Job*

Crit ed. by A. Meiller, Paris 1971 (Biliothèque française et romane, Series B, vol. XI)

63. La Calprenède, *Hermenigilde*

HERMENIGILDE. / TRAGEDIE. / De MR de la CALPRENEDE. / [Sommaville's mark] / A PARIS, /

Chez { ANTOINE DE SOMMAVILLE, en la Salle des Merciers à l'Escu de France. & AVGVSTIN COVRBE', Libraire & Imprimeur de Monsieur Frere du Roy, à la mesme Salle, à la Palme. } au Palais

M. DC. XXXXIII. / *AVEC PRIVILEGE DV ROY.*

4º: πᵛ blank; π2ʳ Privilège in Sommaville's name, 6 February 1643, note associating Courbé in it, and achevé, 10 September 1643; π2ᵛ list of Acteurs; A–M4ᵛ 1–96 text.

BN Rés Yf 225

64. La Croix, *Les Enfans dans la fornaise*

Tragi-comedie. / L'ARGUMENT PRIS / DVTROISIEME CHA- / pitre de Daniel: auec le Can- / tique des trois enfans, / chanté en la / fornaise. / MATTH. 10. / *Ne craignez point ceux qui tuent les corps,* / *& ne peuuët tuer l'ame: mais plustost crai-* / *gnez celuy qui peult perdre* *l'ame & le* / *corps en la gehenne: & mesme les cheueux* / *de vostre teste* *sont tous comptez.*

8º: Aᵛ blank; A2ʳ⁻ᵛ Dedication to Queen of Navarre, dated Paris, 9 August 1561, signed A.D.L.C.; A3ʳ–5ʳ Ode to same; A5ᵛ Sonnet du S.D.S. à A.D.L.C.; A6ʳ–8ᵛ Argument; A8ᵛ list of Personnages; Bʳ–G2ᵛ text; G3ʳ–4ᵛ Ode to author by B. de Monmeia [52 ff].

BN Rés p. Yc 1198(2)

The omission of the name of author or printer, date, mark or location suggests a clandestine ed. inside France. Du Verdier (vol. III, p. 111) suggests Paris. Author identified in *TR*, p. 320.

65. Lancel, *Commedie des quatre estats*

[border] COMMEDIE. / EN LAQVELLE / SE REPRESENTE LES / QVATRE ESTATS DV / Monde. Leurs disputes & / leurs fins en outre le triom- / phe de la Charité & / de la Iustice. / *Nouvellement* *mise en lumiere.* / *Par.* / ANTOINE LANCEL. / [orn] / Celui pour vrai qui examinera, / Ce sens moral sans doute il trouvera / Ce que chacun voit par experience, / Donc sans blamer gardons la con~ sequence. / A LA HAYE. / Chez Hillebrand Iaques. / ANNO 1605.

8º: Aᵛ blank; A2ʳ Dedication to municipality of The Hague; A2ᵛ Sonnet to his pupils; A3ʳ Au lecteur; A3ᵛ list of Personnages; A4ʳ–D3ᵛ text [27 ff].

BL 11737.aa.10

66. La Pujade, *Jacob*

IACOB. / HISTOIRE SACRE'E / EN FORME DE TRAGI- / comedie retirée des sacrés / feuillets de la Bible, du com- / mandement de la Royne MAR- / GVERITE Duchesse de Valois. / *Par* ANTHOINE DE LA PVIADE *Conseil-* / *ler & Secretaire des finances de sa* *Majesté.* / A Monsieur DVSAVLT Conseiller & Aduo- / cat general pour le Roy en la Court de / Parlement de Bourdeaus, chef du / conseil de ladicte Dame Royne / en Guyenne. / [orn] / *A BOVRDEAVS,* / Par SIMON MILLANGES Imprimeur / ordinaire du Roy. 1604.

Although *Jacob* has its own title-page, it is printed in a volume of pious verses, *La Mariade*:

LA MARIADE, / CONTENANT LES LOVAN- / GES DE LA TRES- SAINCTE ET / très-sacrée Vierge Marie. / *Par* ANTHOINE DE LA

PVIADE *Conseil-* / *ler & Secretaire des finances de sa Majesté.* /
A très-haute très-puissante & très-illustre / Princesse MARGVERITE
Royne Duchesse / de Valois. / [orn] / *A BOVRDEAVS,* / Par SIMON
MILLANGES Imprimeur / ordinaire du Roy. 1604.

12°: ã^v blank; ã2^r–3^r Dedication to Marguerite; ã3^r Au lecteur; ã3^v–6^v
encomiastic verses; A–D6^r 1–83 *La Mariade*; D6^v blank; D7^r title-page of
Jacob; D7^v blank; D8^r–9^v 87–90 Dedication to Dusault; D10^r–12^v 91–96
encomiastic verses; E^r–E5^r 97–105 Prologue; E5^v 106 list of Personnages
entreparleurs; E6^r–K3^r 107–221 text; K3^v blank.

Ars 8° BL 10434 Rés

67. La Serre, *Thomas Morus*

(i) THOMAS MORVS, / OV / LE TRIOMPHE / DE LA FOY, ET /
DE LA CONSTANCE. / *TRAGEDIE EN PROSE.* / Dédiée à Madame
la Duchesse D'ESGVILLON, / PAR MONSIEVR DE LA SERRE. /
[Courbé's mark] / A PARIS, / Chez AVGVSTIN COVRBE', Libraire &
Imprimeur de Monsieur / Frere du Roy, dans la petite Salle du Palais, /
à la Palme. / M. DC. XXXXII. / *AVEC PRIVILEGE DV ROY.*

4°: engraved frontispiece (cancel), dated 1641; ã^r title; ã^v blank;
engraving of Mme d'Aiguillon (cancel); ã2^r–3^v Dedication; ã4^r blank;
ã4^v list of Acteurs; A–O^v 1–106 text; O2^{r-v} Privilège in author's name,
26 October 1641, note appointing Courbé the printer, and achevé,
2 January 1642.

BN Rés Yf 1534

(iia) THOMAS MORVS, / OV / LE TRIOMPHE / DE LA FOY,
ET / DE LA CONSTANCE. / *TRAGEDIE EN PROSE.* / Dediée à
Madame la Duchesse d'ESGVILLON, / PAR MONSIEVR DE LA
SEERE. / [Courbé's mark] / A PARIS, / Chez AVGVSTIN COVRBE',
Libraire & Imprimeur de Monsieur / Frere du Roy, dans la petite Salle
du Palais, / à la Palme. / M. DC. XXXXII. / *AVEC PRIVILEGE
DV ROY.*

4°: engraved frontispiece (cancel), dated 1642; ã^r title; ã^v blank; ã2^r–3^v
Dedication; ã4^r blank; ã4^v list of Acteurs; A–P4^r 1–119 text; P4^v Privilège
and note as in (i), and achevé pour la première fois, 4 January 1642.

Ars 4° BL 3455

(iib) Title as in (iia).
Contents as in (iia), save that ff. 12 and 13 have been removed and
replaced with four ff. signed †12, †2, †3, and one unsigned: these contain
new material transforming the first scene of act IV.

BN Rés Yf 488

(iic) Title as in (i).
Contents a compilation: sheets of (i) up to f. L4^v; from M^r it follows (iia).

BN Yf 511

La Serre apparently decided to extend the last act of the play almost
as soon as it had been printed: the new version (iia), still called the

first ed., was issued two days after the first. Later he decided to amend act IV: this improvement was carried out in the new, longer version (producing (iib)), but not in the earlier version (i), of which the sheets had mostly left the shop. In the resulting confusion of states, some sheets remaining from the first version (i) were issued with the final gatherings of the second version (iia), incorporating the additions to act V but without the amendments to IV i, yielding (iic). The version with all the additions seems to represent La Serre's final intention: (iib) is the definitive text.

68. La Serre, *Sainte Caterine*

(ia) LE / MARTYRE / DE SAINTE / CATERINE / *Tragedie en Prose.* / DEDIEE / A MADAME LA CHANCELIERE. / *Par Monsieur DE LA SERRE.* / [orn] / A PARIS, / Chez ANTHOINE DE SOMMAVILLE, à l'Escu de France, / dans la salle des Merciers, / ET / AVGVSTIN COVRBE' Lib. & Impr. de Monsieur Frere du / Roy, à la Palme, en la mesme Salle, au Palais. / M. DC. XXXXIII.

4°: π^v list of Acteurs; A–L3^v 1–86 text, with engravings before acts II, III, IV, and V; L4 blank.

Ars 4° BL 3456

(ib) LE / MARTYRE / DE SAINTE / CATERINE. / *Tragedie en Prose.* / DEDIEE / A MADAME LA CHANCELLIERE. / *Par Monsieur DE LA SERRE.* / [orn] / A PARIS, / Chez ANTOINE DE SOMMAVILLE, à l'Escu de France, / dans la Salle des Merciers. / ET / AVGVSTIN COVRBE', Libraire & Imprimeur de Monsei- / gneur / Frere du Roy, à la Palme, en la mesme Salle. / M. DC. XXXXIII. / *Auec Approbation, & Priuilege du Roy.*

4°: π^r engraved frontispiece, dated 1643; π^v blank; π2^r title; π2^v blank; π3^r–4^v Dedication; ẽ^r Aux Esprits forts; ẽ^v Privilège in author's name, 22 February 1643, note appointing Sommaville and Courbé the printers, and achevé pour la première fois, 20 March 1643; ẽ2^r list of Acteurs; ẽ2^v engraving; A–L4 as in (i).

BL 87.c.11(1)

The ed. was apparently made up in two versions, one having only a title-page, the other containing a full set of preliminary material; the text is the same in either case.

69. La Taille, *Saül le furieux* and *La Famine*

Crit. ed. by Kathleen M. Hall and C.N. Smith, London 1972; see also their 'The Early Editions of the Tragedies of Jean de la Taille', *Kentucky Romance Quarterly* XX (1973), pp. 75–88.

70. Laudun d'Aigaliers, *Diocletian*

LES / POESIES DE / PIERRE DE LAVDVN / DAIGALIERS. / *CONTENANS* / *Deux Tragedies, la Diane, Meslanges,* / *& Acro~ stiches.* / Oeuure autant docte & plein de Moralité, / que les matieres y traictées sont belles / & recreatiues. / [orn] / A PARIS, / Par DAVID LE CLERC Imprimeur, / demeurant ruë Frementel, à / l'Estoille d'Or. / CIƆ IƆ XCVI.

12º: A^v blank; A2^r Au lecteur; A2^v portrait of author, and verses by S.D.; A3^r–6^r 1^r–4^r encomiastic verses; A6^v–7^v 4^v–5^v Epistle to Duc d'Uzès; A7^v–8^r 5^v–6^r Argument of *Diocletian;* E8^v 6^v list of Acteurs; B^r–CI2^v 7^r–30^v *Diocletian*; D^r–2^v 31^r–32^v encomiastic verses; D3^{r–v} 33 Dedication of *Horace* to Joyeuse; D4^r 34^r Sonnet to same; D4^v–5^r 34^v–35^r Argument; D5^v 35^v list of Acteurs; D6^r–H3^r 36^r–81^r *Horace*; H3^v blank; H4^r– 1 6^r 82^r–96^r *La Diane*; 1 6^v blank; 1 7^r–L7^v 97^r–121^r *Meslanges*; L8^r–12^v 122^r–126^v, M^r–M4^r 123^r–126^r *Acrostiches*; M4^v blank.

BN Rés Ye 4284

71. Le Coq, *Cain et Abel*

TRAGEDIE / REPRESENTANT L'O- / DIEVS ET SANGLANT MEVRTRE / commis par le maudit Cain, à l'en- / contre de son frere Abel: ex- / traicte du 4. chap. / de Genese. / [mark: Silvestre 126] / A PARIS, / Par Nicolas Bonfons ruë neuue nostre / Dame, à l'enseigne S. Nicolas.

8º: A^v list of characters; A2^v–C4^v text [20 ff].

BN Rés Yf 4340 *bis*

La Croix du Maine, vol. II, p. 433, identifies the author and dates the ed. 1580.

72. Le Doux, *Tobie*

Catherin le Doux, *Tobie, comedie, en laquelle on void comme les mariages sont faicts au ciel: et qu'il n'y a rien qui eschappe la providence de Dieu*, Cassel, Guillaume Wessel, 1604, 12º, 76 ff. (*VT* vol. v, pp. xix–xx).

73. Le Francq, *Antioche*

ANTIOCHE / TRAGOEDIE. / *Traittant le Martyre de septs Enfans / Machabeéns.* / Dedieé a Monsr ADAM LERMANS Re- / ceueur General de la ville / d'ANVERS. / [mark: Van Havre, Verdussen 6] / A ANVERS. / *Chez HIEROSME VERDVSSEN* / M. DC. XXV.

8º: *^r half-title: ANTIOCHE / TRAGOEDIE.; *^v blank; *2^r title; *2^v blank; *3^r–4^v Dedication, signed Religieux Fr. Jean Baptiste le Francq; *5^r Sonnet to Mlle Josine de la Croix; *5^v–6^v Argument; *7^r–8^r list of personnages representez; *8^v blank; A–F5^v text; F6^r Approbation, Prid. Calend. April, M.DC.XXV.; F6^v note: Antwerpiae. Typis Hieronymis Verdussii. Anno 1625 [54 ff].

BN Rés Yf 4521

74. Loys, *Joseph*

LES / OEVVRES POETIQVES / DE / IEAN LOYS / DOVYSIEN, / LICENTIE' E'S DROICTS. / *Diuisées en IIII. Liures, comme on*

pourra / veoir en la page suyuante. / [orn] / A DOVAY, / De
l'Imprimerie de PIERRE AVROY, au Pelican d'or, M. DC. XII. /
AVEC PRIVILEGE.

8º: *ᵛ table of contents; *2ʳ half-title: LES / OEVVRES POETIQVES /
DE IEAN / ET / IACQVES LOYS / PERE, ET FILS, /
DOVYSIENS; *2ᵛ Privilège, 5 March 1612, and Approbation, 14 February 1612: *3ʳ (mis-signed *4)–ᵛ Au lecteur; *3ᵛ sonnet au lecteur; *4ʳ⁻ᵛ
Dedication to Bishop of Tournai, 9 October 1612, signed Nicolas
Philippes Loys; A–F8ʳ 1–95 Livre I, *Poésies sacrées,* including Cᵛ–C4ᵛ
34–40 summary of *Joseph;* F8ᵛ orn; Gʳ–17ᵛ 97–142 Livre II, *Epithalames;*
18ʳ–L8ᵛ 143–176 Livre III *Epitaphes;* Mʳ–Q2ʳ 177–243 Livre IV, *Chants
congratulatoires;* Q2ᵛ–4ᵛ Table; Q4ᵛ errata.

BL 11475.a.28

BN Rés Ye 4341 ⎫
Ars 8º BL 9014 ⎭ dated M. DC. XIII.

75. P.M., *La Rocheloise*

LA / ROCHELOISE / TRAGEDIE. / Où se voit les heureux succez &
Glorieu- / ses Victoires du Roy Tres Chrestien / LOVYS XIII. depuis
l'aduenement / de sa Majesté à la Couronne de / France, jusques à
present. / *Par P.M.* / [orn] / A TROYES, / Chez IEAN IACQVARD. /
Iouxte la copie Imprimée à Rouen. / M. DC. XXIX. / *Auec Permission.*

4º: Aᵛ list of Acteurs; A2ʳ–C3ᵛ 3–22 text.

BN Yf 11465

Soleinne no. 1038 suggests that the author was Pierre Matthieu;
Brunet considers this 'fort hazardé'.
I have found no trace of any ed. of Rouen.

76. Mage de Fiefmelin, *Jephté*

LES / OEVVRES / DV SIEVR DE / FIEFMELIN. / *Diuisées en
deux parties, contenuës en / la page suyante.* / [woodcut of printing shop,
with a pelican perched on top of the press] / A POICTIERS, /
A l'Imprimerie du Pelican, Par / IEAN DE-MARNEF, / Imprimeur &
Libraire du Roy. / MD. CI.

12º (mostly): Aᵛ blank; A2ʳ table of contents; A2ᵛ blank; A3ʳ title of
Polymnie; A3ᵛ epigraph; A4ʳ half-title; A4ᵛ blank; A5ʳ–6ᵛ Dedication;
Bʳ–B4ᵛ 5ʳ–8ᵛ Eclogue; B5ʳ title of *Accueil poétique;* B5ᵛ list of Person-
nages; B6ʳ⁻ᵛ Argument; Dʳ–D8ᵛ 10ʳ–17ᵛ *Accueil poétique;* Eʳ–E8ᵛ, Fʳ⁻ᵛ
18ʳ–26ᵛ *Le Triomphe d'amour;* F2ʳ–11ᵛ 27ʳ–36ᵛ *Alcide;* F12ʳ title of
Aymée; F12ᵛ blank; Gʳ–G12ᵛ, Hʳ–H6ʳ 38ʳ–55ʳ *Aymée;* H6ᵛ–8ʳ 55ᵛ–57ʳ
verses; H8ᵛ blank; Iʳ half-title of *Jephté;* Iᵛ blank; I 2ʳ–I 12ᵛ, Kʳ–12ᵛ, Lʳ–12ᵛ,
Mʳ–M12ʳ 59ʳ–105ʳ *Jephté;* M12ᵛ blank; Nʳ half-title of second part of
Meslanges; Nᵛ blank; N2ʳ–4ʳ prelims; N4ᵛ blank; N5ʳ–12ᵛ, Oʳ–O12ᵛ, Pʳ–P12ᵛ,
Qʳ–Q12ᵛ, Rʳ–R12ᵛ, Sʳ–S12ᵛ 1ʳ–67ᵛ, Tʳ⁻ᵛ unnumbered, T2ʳ–4ᵛ 68ʳ–70ᵛ
miscellany of poems; AAʳ title, *L'Image d'un mage;* AAᵛ blank; AA2ʳ
epigraph; AA2ᵛ Au lecteur; AA3ʳ–6ᵛ 70ʳ–73ᵛ, AA7ʳ–9ᵛ 73ʳ–75ᵛ prelims;

AA10^r half-title of *Prières*; AA10^v blank; AA11^r–xx6^v 77^r–312^v spiritual verses; xx7$^{r–v}$ prayer; xx8 blank.

Ars 8° BL 8991

77. Magnon, *Josaphat*

(ia) IOSAPHAT, / TRAGICOMEDIE. / *De Mr Magnon.* / [Sommaville's mark] / A PARIS, / Chez ANTOINE DE SOMMAVILLE, au Palais, / dans la Salle des Merciers, à l'Escu de France. / M. DC. XLVII. / *AVEC PRIVILEGE DV ROY.*

4°: ã^v blank; ã2^r–3^v Dedication to d'Epernon; ã4^r Privilège in Sommaville's name, 31 August 1646, note associating Quinet in it, and achevé, 12 October 1646; ã4^v list of Personnages; A–O2^r 1–107 text; O2^v blank.

BN Rés Yf 383

(ib) IOSAPHAT, / TRAGICOMEDIE. / *De Mr Magnon.* / [orn] / A PARIS, / Chez TOVSSAINCT QVINET, au Palais, dans la / petite Salle, sous la montée de la Cour des Aydes. / M. DC. XLVII. / *AVEC PRIVILEGE DV ROY.*

Contents as in (ia).

Ars Rf 6480

78. Marcé, *Achab*

ACHAB / TRAGEDIE. / Composée, par Rolland de Marcé Escuyer / Conseiller du Roy, lieutenant general / en la Seneschaussée, siege & res- / sort de Baugé. / *Dediée à Monseigneur Forget Conseiller du Roy en / ses conseils d'Estat & priué, President en sa / Cour de Parlement à Paris.* / [mark: Renouard *Marques* 460] / A PARIS, / Par FRANÇOIS HVBY, ruë sainct Iacques / à l'enseigne du soufflet vert. / M. DCI.

4°: ã^v blank; ã2^r–3^r Dedication; ã3^v Sonnet by L. de la Barre; ã4^r Argument; A4^v list of Entre-parleurs; A–L4^v 1^r–44^v, M$^{r–v}$ 46$^{r–v}$ text.

Ars Rf 1369

79. Marfriere, *La Belle Hester*

LA BELLE / HESTER: / TRAGEDIE FRANÇOISE / tiree de la saincte Bible. / De l'inuention du S$^r·$ IAPIEN MARFRIERE. / [large woodcut of Esther kneeling before Ahasuerus, who holds his sceptre over her, with Haman hanging in the background] / *A ROVEN,* / Chez ABRAHAM COVSTVRIER, ruë de la / grosse Orloge, deuant les Cycoignes.

8°: A^v Argument and list of Acteurs; A2^r–B8^v text.

BN Rés Yf 3889

Lancaster (*History* I, p. 75) points out that Iapien Marfriere is an anagram of Pierre Mainfray, whom he identifies as the author. He dates the ed. *c.* 1612–14.

80. *La Vie de madame saincte Marguerite*

This is the running title: the only copy I have seen has no title-page.

8°: A lacking; A2ʳ–H8ᵛ 1–128, 1 –M7ᵛ 127–197 text.

BN Rés Yf 4690

Soleinne no. 581 and Brunet suggest Paris, Nicolas Bonfons, 1579.

81. *La Vie de Marie Magdaleine*

LA VIE DE / MARIE MAGDA- / LEINE. / CONTENANT PLVSIEVRS / beaux miracles, comment elle, son / frere le Lazare, & Marthe sa soeur / vindrent à Marseille, & comme elle / conuertit le Duc & la Duchesse. / *ET EST A XXII. PERSON-* / *nages, dont les noms s'ensuiuent en la* / *page cy apres.* / [small woodcut] / *A LYON,* / PAR PIERRE DELAYE, / *M. DCV.*

12°: Aᵛ list of Personnages; A2ʳ–DI1ʳ 1–91 text; DI1ᵛ, DI2 blank.

BN Rés Yf 2914

82. *Mystere de la vie et hystoire de sainct Martin*

I have been informed by the Librarian of the Bibliothèque municipale of Chartres that the original ed. was destroyed by fire in 1944; according to the ed. by Doublet de Boisthibault (Paris 1841) this was the only surviving copy of the original. Confusingly, his reproduction, though it has the appearance of a facsimile, does not correspond to the descriptions of the original made by Brunet and Petit de Julleville (*Mystères*, vol. II, pp. 535–8). Both declared that on the title-page and in a colophon the printer was named as veuve Jean Bonfons of Paris (active 1568–72: Renouard); in Doublet de Boisthibault's reproduction the printer is not named. Either Brunet and Petit de Julleville were not referring to the text reproduced by Doublet de Boisthibault, or the latter's ed. is unfaithful. The summary of the action given by Petit de Julleville corresponds well to the plot in Doublet de Boisthibault's text, so one is driven to conclude that it is not a faithful copy of the original. However, a doubt remains: it is impossible to understand why in reproducing the original Doublet de Boisthibault should have suppressed the two mentions of the printer's name. It is consequently impossible to be certain that the identity of the printer supplied by Brunet and Petit de Julleville applies to the text reproduced by Doublet de Boisthibault, and so impossible to ascribe a date to this text.

83. Matthieu, *Esther*

ESTHER / TRAGEDIE / DE PIERRE / MATTHIEV, / Histoire tragique en laquelle est representée la / condition des Rois & Princes sur le theatre de / fortune, la prudence de leur Conseil, les desa- / stres qui surviennēt par l'orgueil, l'ambition, / l'enuie & trahison, combien est odieuse la de- / sobeissance des femmes, finablement cōme les / Roynes doibuēt amollir le courroux des Rois / endurciz, sur l'oppression de leurs subiects. / [mark: Baudrier, vol. II, p. 384] / *A LYON,* / Pour Iean Stratius a la Bible d'or. / *M. D. LXXXV.*

12°, sigs by 8 and 4: *ᵛ blank; *2ʳ–5ʳ Dedication to Mme de Villeneuve; *5ᵛ–6ᵛ verses to same; *7ʳ–8ᵛ, **ʳ–**3ᵛ encomiastic verses; **3ᵛ–4ᵛ, ***ʳ–ᵛ Prologue; ***2ʳ errata; ***2ᵛ list of Entre-parleurs; aʳ–s2ʳ 1–211 text; s2ᵛ–x4ʳ 212–247 verses; x4ᵛ 248 Approbation, Cal. Jun. 1584.

BN Rés Yf 3890

84. Matthieu, *Vasthi*

VASTHI / PREMIERE / TRAG EDIE DE / Pierre Matthieu / Docteur és / droicts. / En laquelle, outre les tristes effects de l'orgueil / & desobeissance, est monstree la louange / d'vne Monarchie bien ordonnee, l'office / d'vn bon Prince, pour heureusement com- / mander, sa puissance, son ornement, son / exercise, eloigné du luxe & dissolution, & la / belle harmonie d'vn mariage bien accordé. / Auec un petit Abregé de l'histoire / des Roys de Perse. / *Au serenissime Prince Monseigneur le Duc de / Nemours & Geneuois, Gouuerneur / de Lyon.* / [mark: Baudrier, vol. III, p. 457, no. 10] / *A LYON,* / PAR BENOIST RIGAVD. / M. D. LXXXIX.

12°: *ᵛ blank; *2ʳ–4ʳ Dedication; *4ʳ–ᵛ ode to Nemours; *5ʳ–6ᵛ encomiastic verses: *7ʳ–ᵛ Latin dialogue between Matthieu and Tragedy; *8ʳ Latin poem on utility of tragedy; *8ᵛ–11ʳ Abregé de l'histoire des Roys de Perse; *11ᵛ–12ʳ encomiastic verses; *12ᵛ list of Entreparleurs; A–E4ʳ 1–103 text; E4ᵛ errata.

BN Yf 2057

85. Matthieu, *Aman*

AMAN / SECONDE / TRAGEDIE DE / PIERRE MATTHIEV / Docteur és droits. / De la perfidie & trahison. Des pernicieux / effects de l'ambition & enuie. De la grace / & bien-vueillance des Roys dangereuse à / ceux qui en abusent, de leur liberalité / & recompense mesuree au merite non à / l'affection. De la protection de Dieu sur / son peuple qu'il garentit des coniurations / & oppressions des meschans. / *Au Prudent, noble & graue Consulat / de la ville de Lyon.* / [orn: arms of Lyons, identified by Baudrier, vol. III, p. 414] / *A LYON,* / PAR BENOIST RIGAVD. / M. D. LXXXIX.

12°: †ᵛ blank; †2ʳ–3ᵛ Dedication; †4ʳ verses; †4ᵛ list of Entre-parleurs; AAʳ–FF8ʳ 1–135 text; FF8ᵛ blank; FF9ʳ–12ʳ 137–142 Eglogue de l'ingrat exercise de la poësie; FF12ᵛ errata.

BN Yf 2058

86. Matthieu, *Guisiade*

(i) GVISIADE, / TRAGEDIE / NOVVELLE. / [orn] / En laquelle au vray & sans passion, est / representé le massacre du Duc / de Guise. / DEDIEE / *Au Treschrestien & tresgenereux Prince, Charles / de Lorraine, Lieutenant general de l'Estat / & Coronne de France.* / [orn] / *A LYON,* / L'an mil cinq cents quatre vingts & neuf. / *Auec permission.*

4°: Aᵛ blank; A2ʳ–4ʳ Dedication, signed I.R.D.L.; A4ᵛ–B4ʳ Argument; B4ᵛ list of Entreparleurs; c^r–n^v 9–90 text; n2^{r-v} Advertissement au lecteur sur la continuation de ceste tragedie; n3^r Distichum chronicum on death of Guises; n3^v errata; n4 blank.

Ars Rf 1403

(ii) *TROISIESME EDITION* / DE LA / GVISIADE, / TRAGEDIE / NOVVELLE, / *En laquelle au vray, & sans passion, est representé / le massacre du Duc de Guise.* / Reueuë, augmentee, & dediee / *Au tres-Catholique & tres-genereux Prince, Charles de / Lorraine, protecteur et Lieutenant general de / la Coronne pour le Roy tres-Chrestien, / Charles X. par la grace de Dieu / Roy de France.* / Par PIERRE MATTHIEV, Docteur és Droicts, / & Aduocat à Lyon. / [orn] / *A LYON,* / PAR IAQVES ROVSSIN. / *M. D. LXXXIX.*

4°: a^v blank; a2^r–4^r Dedication; a4^v–b3^r Discours sur le sujet de ceste tragedie; b3^v–4^r encomiastic verses; b4^v list of Entre-parleurs; c^r–k4^v 1–64, l^r–o3^r 61–89 text; o3^v Distichum numerale; o4^r Advertissement au lecteur sur la continuation de ceste Tragedie; o4^v blank.

Ars Rf 1404

The second ed., if it ever existed, has escaped detection.
There are considerable differences in detail between the two versions.

87. Montchrestien, *Aman*

Crit. ed. by George Otto Seiver, Philadelphia 1939.

88. Montchrestien, *David*

Crit. ed. by Lancaster E. Dabney, Austin 1963.

89. Montreux, *Joseph le chaste*

IOSEPH / LE / CHASTE, / COMEDIE: / PAR / Le Sieur du Mont-sacré, Gentil- / homme du Maine. / [Du Petit Val's mark, without motto] / *A ROVEN,* / DE L'IMPRIMERIE, / De Raphaël du Petit Val, Libraire & / Imprimeur ordinaire du Roy. / 1601. / *Auec Priuilege de sa Majesté.*

12°: a^v blank; a2^{r-v} 3–5 Dedication to Mlle de Lucé; a3^r 5 Argument; a3^v 6 list of Acteurs; a4^r–d11^v 7–94, d12^r–e8^v 99–116 text; e9^r–12^r Quatrains; e12^v blank.

Ars 8° BL 14592, lacks ff. e10–12.

BN Rés Yf 2906, in Du Petit Val's anthology, *Diverses Tragedies sainctes*, Rouen 1606, no. 97 (ii).

Ollénix de Mont-Sacré was the usual pseudonym of Nicolas de Montreux: see Daele, *Nicolas de Montreux.*

90. Moucque, *L'Amour desplumé*

L'AMOVR DESPLUME', / OV / LA VICTOIRE / DE L'AMOVR DIVIN. / *Pastorelle Chrestienne.* / De l'inuention de I. M. Boulenois. /

[orn] / A PARIS, / De l'Imprimerie de Charles Chappellain. / M. DC. XII.

4°: A⁵ blank; A2ʳ Au lecteur and encomiastic verses; A2ᵛ encomiastic verses; A3ʳ (misprinted A2) 1 Argument of act 1; A3ᵛ 4 list of Acteurs; A4ʳ–Lʳ 7–81 text; Lʳ 81 anagram of author's name: I. M. Ou manque-je [Jean Mouque]; Lᵛ errata.

Ars 8° BL 14583

This copy has an apparently autograph inscription on the title-page, signed J. Moucque.

91. Mouffle, *Sainct Clair*

LE / FILS EXILE', / OV LE / MARTYRE / DE / SAINCT CLAIR. / *TRAGI-COMEDIE CHRESTIENNE.* / PAR Mᴿ PIERRE MOVFFLE, / *Conseiller du Roy, Lieutenant Particulier de / Magny, & Bailly de Sainct Clair.* / [mark] / A PARIS, / De l'Imprimerie de CHARLES CHENAVLT, / Au bout du Pont Sainct Michel, à l'entrée de la / rue de la Huchette. 1647.

4°: A⁵ 2 list of Acteurs; A2ʳ–3ᵛ 3–6 Ode to Archbishop of Rouen; A4ʳ 7 epigram to Prior of S-Clair; A4ᵛ 8 epigram to Curé of Gisors; Bʳ–3ᵛ 9–14 summary of life of St Clair; B4ʳ–12ᵛ 15–68 text; 1 2ᵛ 68 permission d'imprimer, 31 January 1647.

Ars 4° BL 3665, margins cut off in binding.
Ars Rf 6600, parts MS; between title-page and f. A2, has a cancel, the Au lecteur.

92. *Nabuchodonozor*

HISTOIRE / TRAGEDIENNE, TIREE / DE LA FVREVR ET TIRANNIE / de Nabuchodonozor. / [large woodcut of turbaned princes] / *A ROVEN,* / Chez ABRAHAM COVSTVRIER, Libraire / tenant sa boutique au bas de la / ruë Escuyere.

4°: A⁵ blank; A2ʳ Argument and list of Acteurs; A2ᵛ blank; A3ʳ–D4ʳ text; D4ᵛ blank [16 ff].

BN Rés Yf 3922

Lancaster (*History* I, p. 74) dates the ed. *c.* 1612–14.

93. Nancel, *Dina, Josué* and *Debora*

LE / THEATRE SACRE'. / DINA, / OV / LE RAVISSEMENT. / IOSVE', / OV / LE SAC DE IERICHO. / DEBORA, / OV / LA DELIVRANCE. / *AV ROY.* / [orn] / A PARIS, / Chez CLAVDE MOREL, ruë Sainct / Iacques, à la Fontaine. / M. DCVII.

8°: ã⁵ blank; ã2ʳ–3ʳ Dedication, signed Pierre de Nancel; ã3ᵛ blank; ã4ʳ–5ᵛ Aux lecteurs; ã6ʳ Sonnet, le théâtre au lecteur; ã6ᵛ blank; Aʳ–3ʳ Recit pour l'entrée des jeux; A3ᵛ Argument of *Dina* and list of Entreparleurs; A4ʳ–G2ʳ 1–91, *Dina*; G2ᵛ–3ʳ 92–3 Argument of *Josué*; G3ʳ 93 list of Acteurs; G3ᵛ–M8ᵛ 94–186 *Josué*; aʳ⁻ᵛ 1–2 Argument of *Debora*; aᵛ 2 list of Acteurs; a2ʳ–g2ʳ 3–99 *Debora*; g2ᵛ blank.

BN Rés Yf 2060–2061 (1 vol)

> Although the signatures and pagination of *Debora* are independent of the rest of the volume, there is no indication that the play was intended to be sold separately: there is no sign that a title-page has been removed from the first gathering, which is complete as it stands.

4. Olivier, *Hermenigilde*

HERMENIGILDE, / TRAGEDIE. / [orn] / A AVXERRE, / Chez NICOLAS BILLIARD, Imprimeur du ROY, / demeurant en la ruë sainct Simeon. / *Auec Permission.* / M. DC. L.

4°: πᵛ blank; π2ʳ–3ʳ Dedication to S. Zamet, Bishop of Langres, signed Gaspar Olivier, Doct. en Theol. C.D.M.; π3ᵛ blank; π4ʳ Au lecteur; π4ᵛ list of Acteurs; Aʳ–O4ᵛ 1–112 text.

Ars 4° BL 3626

5. Ouyn, *Thobie*

THOBIE / TRAGI-CO- / MEDIE NOV- / VELLE. Tiree de la S. Bible, par IACQVES / OVYN Louerien. / *Dediee à Madame du Roulet.* / [Du Petit Val's mark, without motto] / *A ROVEN,* / DE L'IMPRIMERIE, / De Raphaël du Petit Val, Libraire & Im- / primeur du Roy, deuant la grand porte / du Palais, à l'Ange Raphaël. / 1606. / *Auec Privilege de sa Maiesté.*

12°: Aᵛ blank; A2ʳ 3 Dedication; A2ᵛ 4 Sonnets to same; A3ʳ 5 Prosopopée de l'Autheur a son livre; A3ᵛ 6 encomiastic verse; A4ʳ–5ᵛ 7–10 Argument; A5ᵛ 10 list of Personnages; A6ʳ–c8ᵛ 11–64 text; C9ʳ–11ᵛ Hymne to Virgin; C12ʳ Privilège, 4 February 1597; C12ᵛ blank.

Ars 8° BL 14173

BN Rés Yf 2905 ⎫ in Du Petit Val's anthology, *Diverses Tragedies*
BN Rés Yf 4669 ⎬ *sainctes*, Rouen 1606, no. 97 (ii).

> The Privilège does not name this play, and gives no reliable indication that it was in Du Petit Val's hands by 1597: see no. 10 (i).

6. F.D.B.P., *Eglogues saintes*

Eglogue ou bergerie à quatre personnages, contenant l'Institution, Puissance, et Office d'un bon Pasteur and *Eglogue ou bergerie à cinq personnages, contenant les abus du mauvais Pasteur, et montrant, que bienheureux est qui a cru, sans avoir vu,* Lyons 1563 (La Vallière, vol. 1, p. 171).

7. Perrin, *Sichem ravisseur*

(i) SICHEM RAVISSEVR, / TRAGEDIE / EXTRAITE DV GE- / nese trente quatriesme / Chapitre. / *Par François Perrin Autunois.* / [mark: Renouard, *Marques* 162] / A PARIS, / Chez Guillaume

Chaudiere, ruë S. / Iacques, à l'enseigne du Temps & / de l'Homm‹
Sauuage. / M. D. LXXXIX, / *Auec Priuilege.*

12⁰, sigs by 8 and 4: ã˅ blank; ã2ʳ–6ʳ verse Discours to Pierre Jehanni›
ã6˅ sonnet to same; ã7ʳ sonnet to same; ã7˅–8˅ encomiastic verses; ‹
Au lecteur; ẽ˅ blank; ẽ2ʳ address to Jacques Arthault; ẽ2˅ blank; Aʳ–G4
1–40˅ *Sichem*; G5ʳ–N˅ 41–73˅ *Les Escholiers, comedie*; N2ʳ errata; N2
blank.

Ars 8⁰ BL 14055

(ii) SICHEM RAVISSEVR, / OV / LA CIRCON– / CISION DE
IN– / CIRCONCIS / TRAGEDIE. / *Par Françoys Perrin Autunois.*
[mark: Slvestre 445] / *A ROVEN,* / De L'IMPRIMERIE, / L
Raphaël du Petit Val, Libraire / & Imprimeur ordinaire du Roy. / 160‹

12⁰: A˅ blank; A2ʳ⁻˅ Argument; A3ʳ quatrain by I.D.H.; A3˅ list ‹
Aucteurs; A4ʳ–C12ʳ 7–71 text; C12˅ orn.

BN Rés Yf 4585

Some copies were issued in an anthology, with the title-page replace‹
by:
DIVERSES / TRAGEDIES / SAINCTES, DE / PLVSIEVR
AV– / theurs de ce temps. / *Recueillies par Raphael du / Pet*
Val. / [mark: Silvestre 445] / *A ROVEN,* / DE L'IMPRIMERIE,
De Raphaël du Petit Val, Libraire / & Imprimeur ordinaire de Roy. /
1606.

Text as above, save that verso of title-page bears a list of the plays i
the volume (in fact all printed separately): *Sichem*, Behourt's *Esa*
(no. 10 (ii)), La Taille's *Saül* and *Famine*, *Le Martyre des Macabe‹*
(no. 125 (iii)), *La Victoire des Maccabees* (no. 126 (i)) in fact this cop
contains Ouyn's *Thobie* (no. 95), and Montreux's *Joseph le chas‹*
(no. 89).

BN Rés Yf 4664

98. Philone, *Josias*

(i) *JOSIAS* / TRAGEDIE / de M. Philone. / *Traduite d'Italien e*
François. / Vray miroir des choses aduenues de / nostre temps.
A GENEVE, / De l'Imprimerie de François Perrin. / M. D. LXVI.

8⁰: A˅ blank; A2ʳ 3 Argument; A2˅ 4 list of characters; A3ʳ–F10˅ 5–1‹
text.

BL 11408.aaa.38

(ii) IOSIAS. / TRAGEDIE / de M. Philone. / *VRAY MIROI*
DES / choses aduenues de nostre temps. / [mark: Heitz 24] PA
GABRIEL CARTIER. / Pour Claude D'Augy. / 1583.

8⁰: A˅ blank; A2ʳ 3 Argument; A2˅ 4 list of Personnages; A3ʳ–G4˅ 5–1‹
text.

Ars 8⁰ BL 13970

99. Philone, *Adonias*

ADONIAS. / TRAGEDIE DE M. / PHILONE. / Vray Miroir, ou
Tableau, & Patron de l'Estat / des choses presentes, & que nous pourrons
voir / bien tost cy-apres: Qui seruira comme de Me- / moire pour
nostre Temps, ou plustost de leçon / & exhortation à bien esperer.
Car le bras du / Seigneur n'est point accourci. / 9. *Qu'est-ce qui a esté?*
ce qui sera. Qu'est-ce qui a esté fait? ce qui / se fera. Et n'y a rien de
nouueau sous le Soleil. / 10. Est-il quelque chose dequoi on puisse dire:
Regarde, cela est / nouueau, il auoit ia esté és Siecles qui nous ont
precedez. / ECCL 7. / Alors ADONIAS Fils d'Aggith s'esleua, disant:
Ie Re- / gneray. Et se feit des chariots, &c. / I. ROIS. 1.2.&3. /
20. *Le nom du Seigneur soit benit, depuis un siecle iusques à l'autre. /*
Car à luy est la sapience, & force. / 21. Et c'est luy qui change les temps
& les saisons: Il oste les Rois, & / establit les Rois: Il donne aux Sages
la sapience, & conoissance à ceux qui / sont entendus. Dan. 2. / A
LAVSANNE. / De l'Imprimerie de Iean Chiquelle, / *M. D. LXXXVI.*

8°: A^v list of Personnages; A2^r–3^r Argument; A3^v Argument plus brief, et
sommaire; A4^r–E6^r text; E6^v blank [38 ff].

BN Rés Yf 10 *bis*

100. Picou, *Le Deluge universel*

LE / DELVGE / VNIVERSEL. *TRAGEDIE, /* OV EST COMPRIS
VN ABREGE' / de la Theologie Naturelle, / *Dediée à Monseigneur*
l'Eminentissime / CARDINAL MAZARIN. / Par M. HVGVES DE
PICOV, Docteur és Droits, / Aduocat au Parlement de Paris. / [en-
graving of Ark] / *Noë seul resta, & ceux qui estoient auec luy dans*
l'Arche, Gen. 7. / A PARIS, / Chez MARTIN HAVTEVILLE, ruë
sainct / Iacques, au Rosier. / M. DC. XLIII. / *AVEC PRIVILEGE*
DV ROY.

4°: ã^v blank; ã2^r–3^r Dedication; ã3^v Advis; ã4^r verses Au lecteur; ã4^v list
of Acteurs; A^r–M4^v 1–96 text; N^r–2^r 97–99 Prière à la sacrée Trinité;
N2^r 99 Privilège, 3 August 1643, and achevé, 22 September 1643; N2^v, 3,
blank.

BN Rés Yf 4611

101. Poncet, *Colloque chrestien*

REGRETS SVR / LA FRANCE. / Composez par Simon Poncet Me- /
lunois, Thresorier & Secretaire / de monsieur le Cheualier / d'Aumalle. /
ENSEMBLE / *VN COLLOQVE CHRESTIEN, / composé par luy-*
mesme, / dedié à madame / de Chelles. / [orn] / *A PARIS, /* PAR
MAMERT PATISSON. / 1589.

8°: ã^v blank; cancel bearing portrait of Aumale; ã2^r–3^r Dedication;
ã3^v–4^r encomiastic verses; ã4^v blank; cancel bearing portrait of author;
a^r–c8^v 1^r–24^v sonnets; d^r half-title: COLLOQVE / CHRESTIEN. /
PAR / S. PONCET MELVNOIS / THRESORIER ET / Secretaire
de Monsei- / gneur le Chevalier d'Aumalle; d^v blank; d2^r–v 26 Dedica-

tion to Abbesse de Chelles; d3ʳ–e7ᵛ 27ʳ–39ᵛ *Colloque chrestien;* e8 blank.
BN Rés Ye 1943

102. Poytevin, *Saincte Catherine*

SAINCTE / CATHERINE / TRAGEDIE. / *Dediée à la ROYNE.* /
[orn] / A PARIS, / Chez MATHVRIN HENAVLT, / ruë Clopin,
derriere Bon-court, / deuant le petit Nauarre. / M. DC. XIX.

4°: Aᵛ blank; A2ʳ Dedication, signed E. Poytevin; A2ᵛ list of Acteurs;
A3ʳ–E3ʳ 1–73 text; E3ᵛ, 4, blank.
Ars 4° BL 3610

103. Prevost, *Clotilde*

LES / TRAGEDIES / ET AVTRES OEVVRES / poëtiques de Iean
Preuost, / Aduocat en la Basse- / Marche. / L'indice desquelles est en
la page suiuãte. PREMIERE PARTIE. / [mark] / *A POICTIERS,* /
Par IVLIAN THOREAV, Imprimeur / du Roy & de l'Vniversité.
1614. / *Auec priuilege de sa Majesté.*

12°: ãᵛ table of contents; ã2ʳ–4ʳ Dedication to Jacques de la Guesle;
ã4ᵛ, π r–v encomiastic verses; *†*ʳ Privilège, 23 December 1613; *†*ᵛ
Argument and list of Acteurs of *Edipe;* Aʳ–C4ᵛ 1ʳ–28ᵛ *Edipe;* C5ʳ–7ᵛ
29ʳ–31ᵛ verses to La Guesle; C8ʳ–D3ᵛ 32ʳ–39ᵛ, D4ʳ–F4ᵛ 38ʳ–62ᵛ *Turne;*
Gʳ title: LES / SECONDES / OEVVRES POETI- / QVES ET
TRAGIQVES / de Iehan Preuost Aduocat / en la basse Marche. /
Imprimees nouuellement. / [mark] / *A POICTIERS,* / Par IVLIAN
THOREAV, Li- / braire & Imprimeur de l'Vni- / versité, demeurant
pres le / gros Horloge. 1613.; Gᵛ blank; G2ʳ–ᵛ Argument of *Hercule;*
G2ᵛ list of Acteurs; G3ʳ–4ᵛ verses to Sainte-Marthe; G5ʳ–8ᵛ, Hʳ–K12ᵛ 1ʳ–40ᵛ
Hercule; Lʳ–2ʳ 41ʳ–42ʳ Dedication of *Clotilde* to L. de Chastenet; L2ᵛ
blank; L3ʳ 43ʳ Argument; L3ᵛ 43ᵛ list of Acteurs; L4ʳ–N8ʳ 44ʳ–72ʳ
Clotilde; N8ᵛ blank; oʳ title: APOTHEOSE / DV / TRES-
CHRESTIEN / ROY DE FRANCE / ET DE NAVARRE. / HENRY
IIII. / *A la Royne Regente.* / *Par I. PREVOST, Aduocat au Dorat.* /
[mark] / *A POICTIERS,* / Par IVLIAN THOREAV, Imprimeur /
ordinaire du Roy & de l'Vniversité. / M. DC. XIII.; oᵛ blank; o2ʳ–4ᵛ,
Pʳ–Y11ᵛ *Apotheose d'Henry IV* and other poems; Y12 blank.
BN Rés Yf 2973

> Although the three parts of Prevost's works had separate title-pages,
> they were clearly printed together, because the signatures run con-
> tinuously through all three; but no gathering runs from one part into
> the next, so they could easily be separated for sale independently.

104. *Richecourt*

RICHECOVRT / TRAGE-COMEDIE, / REPRESANTEE / PAR
LES PENSIONNAIRES / DES Rr. PERES BENEDICTINS / de
S. NICOLAS. 1628. / [woodcut of knight holding a shield bearing the
motto IE ESPERE EN DIEV QVI MAIDERA] / Imprimé à S.

NICOLAS, / Par Iacob François à l'Echequin à la grand rue / M. DC. XXVIII.

8º: A᎐ blank; A2ʳ⁻ᵛ 3–4 Dedication to Lenoncourt; A3ʳ 5 Sonnet in praise of Richecourt; A3ᵛ 6 Argument and list of Acteurs; A4ʳ–E6ᵛ 7–76 text.

I have not managed to see a copy of the original ed.; this description is taken from the facsimile ed. by Beaupré, Nancy 1860. He suggests that the author was Dom Simplicien Gody.

105. Rivaudeau, *Aman*

Crit. ed. by Keith Cameron, Geneva and Paris 1969 (TLF 154).

106. Rosier, *Isaac*

Poëmes François, / CONTENANS / PLVSIEVRS EPITHALAMES, / EPIGRAMMES, EPITAPHES, / ELEGIES, COMEDIES, ET / AVTRES DISCOVRS, PLEINS / de Moralité & Pieté. / *Diuise en quatre Liures.* / PAR M. IEAN ROSIER / Prestre, Pasteur d'Esplechin, au / Diocese de Tournay. / [mark] / *A DOVAY,* / De l'Imprimerie de PIERRE AVROY, / au Pelican d'or. M. DC. XVI.

8º: A᎐ Approbation, 17 October 1616; A2ʳ–5ʳ Dedication to Adrien de Bacquehem; A5ᵛ–7ʳ encomiastic verses; A7ᵛ–8ʳ Table; A8ᵛ Au lecteur; Bʳ–D2ᵛ 1–36 Premier livre des poëmes françois; D3ʳ–H5ᵛ 37–106 Deuxieme livre; H6ʳ–N4ᵛ 107–184 Troisieme livre; N5ʳ–Y4ʳ 185–327 Quatriesme livre (including *Isaac*, N5ʳ–Q7ᵛ 185–238); Y4ʳ 327 errata; Y4ᵛ blank.

Ars 8º BL 9963

107. Rotrou, *Saint Genest*

Crit. ed. by E. T. Dubois, Geneva and Paris 1972 (TLF 196)

108. Sainct André, *La Naissance de Nostre Seigneur*

Histoire / Pastoriale / sur la Naissance / de Nostre Seigneur / Jesus-Christ. / Dediée à Monseigneur l'Illustrissime / et Reverendissime / Guillaume d'Hugues, / Archevesque et Prince d'Ambrun, / Conseiller du Roy en ses Conseils, / et autres. Par le Sieur de Sainct André / d'Ambrum. / A Beziers / Par Pierre Claverie, 1644.

4º: A᎐ blank; A2ʳ⁻ᵛ Dedication; A3ʳ–Bʳ sonnets in praise of d'Hugues; Bᵛ Au lecteur; B2ʳ list of Acteurs; B2ᵛ Prologue; B3ʳ–F4ᵛ 1–36 text.

BN MS fonds français 9305, ff. 127–150

I have been unable to trace a printed copy of this work; this description is derived from the MS copy which Soleinne, despairing of possessing the printed text, had prepared from a copy belonging to an acquaintance. I have found in other cases that Soleinne's scribe reproduced the original with complete fidelity.

109. Saint-Balmon, *Les Jumeaux Martyrs*

LES / IVMEAVX / MARTYRS. / TRAGEDIE. / *Par MADAME DE S. BALMON.* / [Courbé's mark] / A PARIS, / Chez AVGVSTIN

COVRBE', Imprimeur & Libraire de / Monseigneur le Duc d'Orleans, dans la petite Sale / du Palais, à la Palme. / M. DC. L. / *AVEC PRIVILEGE DV ROY.*

4°: ã^v blank; ã2^r l'Imprimeur au lecteur; ã2^v list of Acteurs, and Privilège, 7 April 1650; A^r–s4^v 1–144 text.

BN Rés Yf 335

110. *Samson le fort*

TRAGEDIE / NOVVELLE DE / SAMSON LE FORT. / Contenant ses victoires, & sa prise par la trahison de / son Espouse Dalide, qui luy couppa ses cheueux, & / le liura aux Philistins, desquels il occit / trois mil à son trespas. / [large woodcut showing Samson standing over the bodies of some soldiers and drinking from a jaw-bone] / *A ROVEN,* / Chez ABRAHAM COVSTVRIER, ruë de l'Orlo- / ge, deuant les Cycoignes.

8°: A^v blank; A2^r 3 Argument; A2^v 4 list of Acteurs; A3^r–B8^v 5–32 text.

BN Rés Yf 3466

111. Soret, *La Ceciliade*

LA CECILIADE, / OV MARTYRE SANGLANT / DE SAINCTE CECILE, PATRONE / des Musiciens: / où sont entre-mélés plusieurs / beaux exemples Moraux, graues Sentences / naïues allegories, & com~ / paraisons familieres, / conuenables tant aux personnages qu'au / suiet: Auec les Choeurs mis en Musique. Par / ABRAHAM BLONDET Chanoine & Mai- / stre de la Musique de l'Eglise de Paris. / *Dedié à Messieurs les Venerables Doyen & / Chanoines de l'Eglise de Paris,* / Par N. SORET Rhemois. / [orn] / A PARIS, / Chez PIERRE REZE' demeurant au mont / S. Hilaire, pres de la Court d'Albret. / M. DC. VI. / *Auec priuilege du Roy & Approbation.*

4°: π^v Privilège, 17 November 1606, and Approbation, 18 November 1606; π2^r–3^r Dedication; π3^v–4^v, ẽ^r–ẽ3^r encomiastic verses; ẽ3^v–4^r Argument; ẽ4^v list of Acteurs; A^r–1 4^v 1–72, K^r–L3^v 77–90 text; L4^r errata; L4^v blank.

BN Rés Yf 3882

Bound with a book of music, *Choeurs de l'histoire tragique saincte Cecile*, by Abraham Blondet, Paris, Pierre Ballard, 1606, 4°, 16 ff.

112. Soret, *L'Election divine de S. Nicolas*

L'ELECTION DIVINE DE S. NICOLAS / *A L'ARCHEVESCHÉ DE MYRE / Auec un sommaire de sa vie en Poëme / dramatique sententieux et moral P. N. S. R.* / A Reims chez Nicolas Constant / Imprimeur ordinaire du Roy. a la Couronne. 1624.

8°: π^v blank; †^r–2^v Dedication to Coquillart, signed Soret; †3^r–4^v, ††^r–2^r verses; ††2^v Approbation, 24 March 1624; A^r–E6^r 1–75 text; E6^r 75 note of performance, 9 May 1624, in the church of S-Antoine, Rheims; E6^v 76 engraving of Nicolas; E7^r–F2^r 77–83 life of Nicolas in verse;

F2^v 84 engraving of Christ resurrected; F3^{r}–4^{r} 85–87 verses on Resurrection; F4^v blank.

Ars 8° BL 13886

The title-page consists mostly of an engraving; the title occupies only a small rectangle at the foot.

113. *Saincte Susanne*

L'HYSTOIRE / DE SAINCTE SVSANNE, / EXEMPLAIRE DE TOVTES / sages femmes, & de tous / bons Iuges. / [woodcut of enthroned King and courtiers] / A Troyes, chez Nicolas Oudot, demeurant / en la ruë nostre Dame: au Chappon d'Or.

8°: A^v list of Personnages; A2^{r}–E3^v text; E4^{r-v} song about Susanne, and some proverbs [36 ff].

BN Rés Ye 2980

Dated 1634 by Corrard de Breban, *Recherches sur l'imprimerie à Troyes*, p. 148.

114. *La Chaste et Vertueuse Susanne*

TRAGEDIE / DE LA CHASTE / ET VERTVEVSE SVSANNE, / OV L'ON VEOIT L'INNOCENCE / vaincre la malice des Iuges. / [large woodcut of Susanne at her bath] / *A ROVEN,* / Chez Abraham Cousturier, Libraire, tenan. sa / boutique au bas de la ruë Escuyere. / M. DC. XIIII.

4°: A^v 2 Argument and list of Entreparleurs; A2^{r}–F4^v 3–48 text.

BN Rothschild II 1107

115. D.L.T., *Josaphat*

IOSAPHAT / OV / LE TRIOMPHE / DE LA FOY / SVR LES / CHALDE'ENS. / TRAGI-COMEDIE. / [mark] / A TOLOSE, / Par FRANÇOIS BOVDE Imprimeur / à l'Enseigne S. Thomas d'Aquin, deuant / le College des PP. de la Com- / pagnie de IESVS. 1646. / *AVEC PRIVILEGE DV ROY.*

12°, sigs by 4 and 2: ã^v blank; ã2^{r}–4^v, B^r Epistle to d'Epernon, signed D.L.T.; B^{v}–2^v, C^r Au lecteur; C^v list of Acteurs; C2^{r}–4^v, D^{r}–2^v, E^{r}–4^v, F^{r}–2^v, G^{r}–4^v, H^{r}–2^v, I^{r}–4^v, K^{r}–2^v, L^{r}–4^v, M^{r}–2^v, N^{r}–4^v, O^{r}–2^v, P^{r}–4^v, Q^{r}–2^v, R^{r}–4^v, S^{r}–2^v, T^{r}–4^v, V^{r}–2^r 1–105 text; V2^v 106 Privilège, 4 August 1646.

Ars 8° BL 14133 (Rés)

Soleinne, no. 1223, suggests that the author was De la Thorillière; but see note 102, p. 326.

116. Thierry, *David persecuté*

DAVID / PERSECUTE / TRAGEDIE. / *AVEC LE TOMBEAV DE* / *haut & puissant Seigneur, Monseigneur* / *le Comte de SALM.* /

DEDIE A HAVTE ET / Puissante Dame Dame BARBE de Salm, / Abesse de Remiremont. / PAR / *PIERRE THIERRY SIEVR* / *de Mont-Iustin.* / [orn] / A PONTOISE, / M. DC.

8°: A^v blank; A2^r–v Dedication; A3^r–4^v Tombeau sur la mort du Comte de Salm; A5^r Tombeau anagramatique; A5^v–6^r Argument; A6^r–7^r encomiastic verses; A7^r list of Acteurs; A7^v text begins; A8^r–F2^r 1–69 text; F2^v blank.

BL 11475.aa.32

117. *Timothee chrestien*

TRAGEDIE / DE TIMOTHEE / CHRESTIEN, / [orn] / Lequel a esté bruslé iniquement / par le commandement du Pape: / pour ce qu'il soustenoit l'Euangile / de Iesus Christ. / Traduitte nouuellement de Latin / en François. / MATTH. V. / *Ainsi ont ils persecutez les prophetes, qui ont / esté par deuant nous.* / A LYON, / PAR IEAN SAVGRAIN, / 1563.

4°: A^v 2 Argument and list of Personnages; A2^r–E4^r 3–39 text; E4^v blank.

BN Rés Yf 4671

118. Tiron, *L'Histoire de Joseph*

L'HISTOIRE. / DE IOSEPH, EXTRAIC- / TE DE LA SAINCTE BIBLE, / *& reduitte en forme de Comedie, nouuellement / traduitte du Latin de Macropedius,* / *en langage Françoys, par Antoi-* / *ne Tiron.* / [mark: Silvestre 1021] / A ANVERS. / Chez Iean waesberghe au Cemitiere no- / stre Dame, à l'Escu de Flandres au / Marché à Toiles. / M. D. LXIIII.

8°: A^v Privilège, undated; A2^r–4^r Prologue (in fact a preface); A4^v–1 6^v text; 17^r Au lecteur; 17^v Approbation, 8 October 1563 [71 ff].

BN Rés Yf 2931

119. Troterel, *Sainte Agnes*

TRAGEDIE / DE SAINTE / AGNES. / PAR / Le Sieur d'AVES. / [Du Petit Val's mark, without motto] / *A ROVEN,* / DE L'IMPRI~ MERIE, / De DAVID DV PETIT VAL, / Libraire & Imprimeur ordi- / naire du Roy. / 1615.

12°: A^v blank; A2^r–3^r 3–5 Argument; A3^v 6 Dedication to Françoise d'Averton; A4^r–v 7–8 encomiastic verses; A4^v 8 list of Entre-parleurs; A5^r–D12^r 9–95 text; D12^v blank.

Ars 8° BL 12638

BN Yf 4728, in Du Petit Val's anthology, *Le Theatre des tragedies françaises,* Rouen 1620, along with other plays printed earlier and still unsold.

120. Troterel, *Guillaume d'Aquitaine*

LA VIE / ET SAINTE / CONVERSION / de GVILLAVME Duc / d'Aquitaine / *ESCRITE EN VERS ET DISPO-* / *sée en actes pour representer sur le Theatre,* / Par le Sieur D'AVES. / [mark: Silvestre 445] / *A ROVEN,* / De l'Imprimerie de DAVID DV PETIT VAL, / Imprimeur & Libraire ordinaire du ROY. / M. DC. XXXII.

12°: A^v blank; A2^r–3^r 3–5 Dedication to Dom Guillaume de Luysiere, prior of Sauvigny; A3^r 5 Au lecteur and epigram; A3^v 6 list of Acteurs; A4^r–D5^r 7–81 text.

Bibliothèque municipale, Versailles

This description was prepared from a photocopy.

121. Vallin, *Israel affligé*

ISRAEL / AFFLIGE', / *OV* / TRAGECOMEDIE / SVR LA PESTE AD- / VENVE DV TEMPS / DE DAVID. / *Israel, atten-toi à l'Eternel, car il y a gratuitè / par deuers l'Eternel, & y a redemption & abondan- / ce par deuers lui.* / *Et lui mesme rachetera Israel de toutes ses ini- / quitez.* Psalm. 130. / [orn] / *A GENEVE.* / Par IAQVES PLAN~ CHANT. / M. DC. XXXVII.

8°: A^v list of Acteurs; A2^{r-v} Dedication to municipality of Neuchâtel, signed Iean Vallin Genevois; A3^r–4^r sonnets to officials; A4^v Argument; A5^r–E3^r 1–61 text; E3^r–4^r application; E4^v errata.

Ars 8° BL 14130

122. *La Verité cachée*

La Verité cachée, / COMPOSEE EN RIME / Françoise à six person- / nages. / Auec les autoritez de la saincte Escriture: / Reueuë & augmentée tout de nouueau. / III *ESDRAS* III.*c.* / Sur toutes choses Verité sur~ monte. / [mark: see below] De l'Imprimerie d'Antoine Cercia. / M. D. LIX.

8°: A^v list of Personnages; A2^{r-v} 3–4 Preface; A3^r–G2^v 5–100 text; G3^r Rondeau; G3^v Dixain.

BN Rés Yf 4684

Paul Chaix, *Recherches sur l'imprimerie à Genève de 1550 à 1564,* Geneva 1954, lists Cercia as a printer in that city; the mark used here is as described by Chaix, p. 158, but lacks the motto.

123. Vesel, *Jephthé*

LA / TRAGEDIE DE / IEPHTHE', TRADVICTE DV LATIN DE / George Buchanan Escossois, PAR / CLAVDE DE VESEL GENTIL- / *homme François.* / [mark: Renouard *Marques* 304] / A PARIS, / Par Robert Estienne Imprimeur du Roy. / M. D. LXVI. / AVEC PRIVILEGE.

8°: A^v blank; A2^{r-v} Argument du Translateur; A2^v list of Personnes; A3^r–D7^v [3]^r–31^v text; D8^r sonnet; D8^v Privilège, 26 March 1560.

BN Rés p. Yc 1629

124. Ville-Toustain, *La Creation*

TRAGEDIE / DE LA NAISSANCE, OV / Creation du Monde. / Où
se void de belles descriptions des Animaux, Oi- / seaux, Poissons, Fleurs
& autres choses rares, qui / virent le iour à la naissance de l'Vnivers. /
Par le Sieur VILLE-TOVSTAIN. / [large woodcut showing temptation
of Adam and Eve, and behind, Cain striking Abel] / *A ROVEN,* / Chez
ABRAHAM COVSTVRIER, rue de la grosse / Orloge, deuant les deux
Cycoignes.

8°: A^v blank; A2^{r-v} 3–4 Argument; A2^v 4 list of Acteurs; A3^r–B8^v 5–32
text.

BN Rés Yf 3921

125. Virey, *La Machabee*

(i) LA / MACHABEE / TRAGEDIE, DV / MARTYRE DES / sept
freres, & de / Solomone leur / mere. / [mark: Silvestre 445] /
A ROVEN, / Chez Raphaël du petit Val, deuant / la grand' porte du
Palais. / M. D. XCVI.

12°: A^v blank; A2^r–3^v 3–6 Dedication to Maréchale de Matignon, signed
Virey; A4^{r-v} 7–8 encomiastic verses; A5^r–c6^r 9–59 text; c6^v blank.

BL 840.a.8.(1.)

(ii) LA / MACHABEE / TRAGOEDIE, DV / MARTYRE DES
SEPT / freres, & de Solomone / leur mere. / *Par Iean de Virey, sieur du
Grauier.* / [Du Petit Val's mark, without motto] / *A ROVEN,* / DE
L'IMPRIMERIE / De Raphaël du Petit Val, Libraire & / Imprimeur
du Roy, deuant la / grand' porte du Palais, / à l'Ange Raphaël. /
1598. / *Auec Priuilege de sa Majesté.*

12°: A^v blank; A2^r–3^v 3–6 Dedication; A4^r 7 list of Personnages; A4^v–5^r
8–9 encomiastic verses; A5^v 10 Priuilège, 4 February 1597; A6^r–c8^r 11–63
text; c8^v–12^r 64–71 Prayers; c12^v blank.

Ars 8° BL 13978(1)

Ars 8° BL 13979(1) ⎫
                    ⎬ dated 1599
BN Yf 4738   ⎭

(iii) LA / MACHABEE / TRAGEDIE, DV / MARTYRE DES SEPT /
freres, & de Solomone / leur mere. / *Par Iean de Virey, sieur du
Grauier.* / [mark: Silvestre 445] / *A ROVEN,* / Chez Raphaël du Petit
Val, Libraire & / Imprimeur du Roy, deuant la grand' / porte du
Palais. / 1603. / *Auec Priuilege de sa Maiesté.*

12°: A^v blank; A2^r–3^v 3–6 Dedication; A4^r 7 list of Personnages; A4^v–5^r
8–9 encomiastic verses: A5^v 10 Priuilège, 4 February 1597; A6^r–c8^r 11–63
text; c8^v–12^r 64–71 Prayers; c12^v blank.

BN Rés Yf 2904

In Du Petit Val's anthology, *Diverses Tragedies sainctes*, Rouen 1606
(see no. 97 (ii)).

Despite the similarity of the contents, (iii) is not simply a re-issue of unsold sheets of (ii) adorned with a new title-page: it is a genuine new ed.

(iv) LA MACHABEE / TRAGEDIE, DV / MARTYRE DES SEPT / freres, & de Solomone / leur mere. / *Par Iean de Virey, sieur du Grauier.* / [Du Petit Val's mark, without motto] / *A ROVEN.* / DE L'IMPRIMERIE / De Raphaël du Petit Val, Libraire & Im- / primeur du Roy, deuant la grand' porte / du Palais, à l'Ange Raphaël. / 1611.

12°: A^v blank; A2^r–3^v 3–6 Dedication; A4^r 7 list of Personnages; A4^v–5^r 8–9 encomiastic verses; A5^v blank; A6^r–C8^r 11–63 text; C8^v–12^r 64–71 Prayers; C12^v blank.

Ars Rf 7384

As with (iii), this is a genuine new ed., despite superficial similarities with both (ii) and (iii).

126. Virey, *Victoire des Machabees*

(i) TRAGEDIE / DE LA DIVINE ET / HEVREVSE VICTOIRE / des Machabees, sur le Roy / Antiochus: / *Auecques la Repurgation du Temple / de Hierusalem.* / [Du Petit Val's mark, without motto] / *A ROVEN,* / De L'IMPRIMERIE / De Raphaël du Petit Val, Libraire & / Imprimeur ordinaire du Roy. / 1600. / *Auec Priuilege de sa Majesté.*

12°: A^v blank; A2^r–3^v 3–6 Dedication to Bishop of Coutances, signed Jean de Virey sieur du Gravier; A3^v 6 list of Entreparleurs; A4^r–B11^v 7–46 text; B12 blank.

Ars 8° BL 13979(2)

(ii) TRAGEDIE / DE LA DIVINE ET / HEVREVSE VICTOIRE / des Macabees, sur le Roy / Anthiocus. / *Auecques la Repurgation du Temple / de Hierusalem.* / [Du Petit Val's mark, without motto] / *A ROVEN,* / DE L'IMPRIMERIE / De Raphael du Petit Val, Libraire & Im- / primeur du Roy, deuant la grand porte du Palais. / 1611.

12°: A^v blank; A2^r–3^v 3–6 Dedication; A3^v 6 list of Entreparleurs; A4^r–B11^v 7–46 text; B12 blank.

BN Rés p. Yf 15

127. Vivre, *Abraham et Agar*

(i) Trois / COMEDIES / FRANCOISES, / De GERARD DE VIVRE Gantois. / *La premiere,* / Des Amours pudiques & loyales de The- / seus & Dianira. / *La seconde,* / De la fidelité nuptiale d'vne honeste Matro- / ne enuers son Mary, & espoux. / *Et la troisiéme,* / Du Patriarche Abraham & sa seruante Agar. / *Le tout pour l'vtilité de la ieunesse & vsage des escoles / françoises, pour la seconde edition, reueu & / corrigé par Ant. Tyron.* / [mark: Marques des P–B, Antwerp, Hendricx] / A ANVERS, / Chez Henry Hendricx, à la fleur / de lis. 1580. / *Auec grace & Priuilege Royal.*

8°: A^v Privilège for all three plays, 5 December 1577; A2^{r-v} 3–4 Dedication to Heyns, dated 24 May 1577; A3^r–4^r 5–7 Aux lecteurs; A4^v 8 list of Personnages and key to the signs used to indicate how the actors should move and speak; A5^r 9 Argument of *Theseus et Dianira*; A5^v–D6^v 10–60 *Theseus et Dianira*; D7^r 61 list of Personnages of *La Fidelité nuptiale*; D7^v–G5^v 62–106 *La Fidelité nuptiale*; G6^r 107 list of Personnages of *Abraham et Agar*; G6^v–7^r 108–9 Argument; G7^v–K3^v 110–150 *Abraham et Agar*; K4^r Approbation, undated; K4^v blank.

BN Rothschild IV.2(*bis*).63

Although the Privilège dated 1577 names all three plays, I know of no earlier ed. of all three that Tiron could have revised; the declaration that this is a second, revised ed. may mean only that he had revised *La Fidelité nuptiale*, which Hendricx had already printed in 1577.

(ii) Trois / COMEDIES / FRANCOISES. / De GERARD DE VIVRE Gantois. / *La premiere,* / Des Amours pudiques & loyales de Theseus & Dianita. / *La seconde,* / De la fidelité nuptiale dvne honeste Matrone enuers son / Mari & espoux. / *La troisieme,* / Du Patriarche Abraham & sa seruante Agar. / Le tout pour lvtilité de la ieunesse & vsage des escoles francoises, / reueu & corrige par Ant. Tyron. / [orn] / A ROTTERDAM, / Chez Iean VVaesbergue, Rue haute / à l'enseigne de la Fame. 1589.

8°: A^v–2^v 2–4 Aux lecteurs; A3^r 5 list of Personnages of *Theseus et Dianira* and key to symbols; A3^v 6 Argument of *Theseus et Dianira*; A4^r–D^r 7–49 *Theseus et Dianira*; D^v 50 list of Personnages of *La Fidelité nuptiale*; D2^r–8^v 51–64, E^r–8^v 66–81, F^r–4^v 78–85 *La Fidelité nuptiale*; F5^r 86 list of Personnages of *Abraham et Agar*; F5^v–6^r 87–8 Argument; F6^v–H6^v 89–121 *Abraham et Agar*; H7^{r-v} Dedication to Heyns; H8^r blank; H8^v border and mark (Silvestre 305).

Ars 8° BL 12604

The mark belonged to Janssens of Antwerp, rather than Waesberghe; see note to (iii) below.

(iii) TROIS / COMEDIES / FRANCOISES. / DE GERARD DE VIVRE Gantois. / *La premiere,* / Des Amours pudiques & loyales de The- / seus, & Dianira. / *La seconde,* / De la fidelité nuptiale d'vne honeste Ma- / trone enuers son Mary, & espoux. / *La troisiéme,* / Du Patriarche Abraham & sa seruante Agar. / *Le tout pour l'vtilité de la ieunesse, & vsage des Escoles* / *Francoises, reueu & corrigé par Ant. Tyron.* / [mark: Silvestre 305] / A ANVERS, / Chez Guislain Ianssens, rue dicte Camer- / strate, au Coq Veillant. 1595. / *Auec grace & Priuilege Royal.*

8°: A^v 2 Privilège for all three plays in the name of Janssens, 15 November 1589; A2^{r-v} 3–4 Aux lecteurs; A3^r 5 list of Personnages of *Theseus et Dianira* and key to symbols; A3^v 6 Argument of *Theseus et Dianira*; A4^r–c8^r 7–47 *Theseus et Dianira*; c8^r 48 list of Personnages of *La Fidelité nuptiale*; D^r–F3^r 50–85 *La Fidelité nuptiale*; F3^v 86 list of Personnages of

Abraham et Agar; F4ʳ 87 Argument; F4ᵛ–H4ᵛ 88–120 *Abraham et Agar*;
H4ᵛ Approbation, undated.

Ars Rf 1576

If Janssens took a Privilège for the plays in 1589, it is strange that
Waesberghe could issue an ed. of them in the same year (ii); but the
presence in that ed. of a mark belonging to Janssens suggests that
Waesberghe may have prepared his ed. with the consent of the holder
of the Privilège.

(iv) TROIS / COMEDIES / FRANCOISES / DE GERARD DE
VIVRE Gantois / *La premiere,* / Des Amours pudiques & loyales de
The- / seus, & Dianira. / *La seconde.* / De la fidelité nuptiale d'vne
honeste Ma- / trone enuers son Mary, & espoux. / *La Troisiéme.* / Du
Patriarche Abraham & sa seruante Agar. / *Le tout pour l'vtilité de la
ieunesse, & vsage des Escoles* / *Françoises, reueue & corrigé par Ant.
Tyron.* / [mark: Silvestre 305] / A ANVERS. / Chez Guislain Ianssens,
rue dicte Camer- / strate, au Coq Veillant. 1602. / *Auec grace &
Priuilege Royal.*

8⁰: A ᵛ blank; A2ʳ⁻ᵛ Aux lecteurs; A3ʳ list of Personnages of *Theseus et
Dianira* and key to syymbols; A3ᵛ Argument; A4ʳ–c8ʳ *Theseus et
Dianira*; c8ᵛ list of Personnages of *La Fidelité nuptiale*; Dʳ Argument;
Dᵛ–F3ʳ *La Fidelité nuptiale*; F3ᵛ list of Personnages of *Abraham et Agar*;
F4ʳ⁻ᵛ Argument; F4ᵛ–H4ᵛ *Abraham et Agar*; H4ᵛ Approbation, undated
[60 ff].

BL 11737.a.12

Notes

Introduction

1. To avoid confusion, Classical with a capital C is used to designate the style used by Corneille, Molière, Racine and contemporaries; with a small c classical applies to the whole tradition stretching back to ancient Greece and Rome; and neo-classical refers to the version of that tradition current in the sixteenth and seventeenth centuries, of which the Classical style is one variant.

2. Notably the work of Richard Griffiths, *The Dramatic Technique of Antoine de Montchrestien: Rhetoric and Style in French Renaissance Tragedy*, Oxford 1970; and Stone (1974).

3. Lebègue's excellent *TR* is limited to the period 1514–73, and Pascoe to 1635–50. G. D. Jonker, *Le Protestantisme et le théâtre de langue française au XVIe siècle*, Groningen 1939, and P. Keegstra, *Abraham sacrifiant de Théodore de Bèze et le théâtre calviniste de 1550 à 1565*, The Hague 1928, are limited to a single genre, while the studies of Jacques Chocheyras, *Le Théâtre religieux en Savoie au XVIe siècle*, Geneva 1971, and *Le Théâtre religieux en Dauphiné du moyen âge au XVIIIe siècle (domaine français et provençal)*, Geneva 1975, are limited to a single region. Sacred plays are also considered in passing in more general studies, notably Dabney, Forsyth, and Lancaster's monumental *History*. With some exceptions (Lebègue, Forsyth and Chocheyras) these studies are vitiated by the supposition that modern expectations are automatically applicable to all plays.

4. Of Loukovitch it should also be noted that he apparently had not read a number of the plays that he did analyse, but reproduced without verification descriptions, quotations and even errors from previous studies, sometimes without attribution.

5. Studies of the evolution of dramatic forms are too numerous to catalogue: particularly useful for this period are H. B. Charlton, *The Senecan Tradition in Renaissance Tragedy*, Manchester 1946; Forsyth; Lancaster's *History*; R. Lebègue, *La Tragédie française de la renaissance*, Brussels and Paris 1954; and Stone.

6. Public and ecclesiastical attitudes are traced by Loukovitch, and for the

period 1628-1700 by Henry Phillips, *The Theatre and its Critics in Seventeenth-Century France*, Oxford 1980.

7. The neo-Latin tradition has been thoroughly studied by Paul van Tieghem, 'La Littérature latine de la Renaissance: étude d'histoire littéraire européenne', *BHR*, IV (1944), pp. 177-418; by Emile Faguet, *La Tragédie française au XVIe siècle*, 2nd ed., Paris and Leipzig 1897, pp. 57-79; and in *TR*, pp. 111-286. Having studied both the neo-Latin and French traditions, Lebègue concluded that they were separate: *TR*, pp. x-xi.

1. The inheritance of 1550: the *mystères*

1. *Mystères*, vol. I, p. 429.
2. The most grandiose performance of all was of the *Actes des apôtres*, with nearly 500 roles, staged in episodes by the Confrères de la Passion in Paris on holidays from 8 May to 25 September 1541 in a total of 35 *journées*: R. Lebègue, *Le Mystère des Actes des apôtres: contribution à l'étude de l'humanisme et du protestantisme au XVIe siècle*, Paris 1929, pp. 192-3.
3. See *TR*, pp. 47-8.
4. See *TR*, pp. 52-6.
5. The only long *mystère* performed frequently was the *Passion*, which in the versions by Greban or Michel occupies 4 *journées*. Petit de Julleville cites a record of a performance at Auxerre in 1551 'pendant 28 jours' (*Mystères*, vol. II, p. 158), which I take to mean not 28 *journées*, but on the holidays in a four-week period, i.e. 4 or perhaps 5 Sundays. The *Actes des apôtres* was performed in 1551 and 1571 in an unknown number of *journées*; if all the 35 used earlier in Paris were given, the fact would surely have been recorded.
6. Contemporary documents showing how a village set about preparing a text are quoted by Chocheyras, *Le Théâtre religieux en Savoie*, pp. 7-9, 33-4; none of the versions of which he describes the preparation was printed.
7. Grace Frank, *The Medieval French Drama*, Oxford 1954, p. 22.
8. About two-thirds of the performances of *mystères* noted in the Chronology concerned such subjects.
9. A second *mystère* concerning this saint was also still popular after 1550: this was a version in Breton, published in Paris in 1557 for Bernard de Leau of Morlaix, and reprinted at Morlaix by Jean Hardouyn in 1647: see Emile Ernault, ed, *Le Mystère de Sainte Barbe, tragédie bretonne*, *Archives de Bretagne* III (1885).
10. These plays were performed usually on a trestle stage in the open air. Lined up across the back of the wide stage were small sets, called *mansions*, representing all the locations needed for the whole action; these were visible throughout the performance, there being no curtain, and the actors indicated the location of the scenes by moving from one *mansion* to another. The *mansions* usually included Heaven and a grotesque entrance to Hell. The performers were amateurs; in a village the whole community might take part, while in towns performances

were given by religious and charitable fraternities or *confréries*, such as the Confrères de la Passion of Paris. See Gustave Cohen, *Histoire de la mise en scène dans le théâtre religieux français du moyen âge*, Paris 1906; and for the late development of the system of staging, Elie Konigson's copiously-illustrated *La Représentation d'un Mystère de la passion à Valenciennes en 1547*, Paris 1969. Details of preparations for performances are included in Lebègue, *Le Mystère des Actes des apôtres*, and Chocheyras, *Le Théâtre religieux en Savoie* and *Le Théâtre religieux en Dauphiné*.

11. References are to the edition by Pierre Rigaud, Lyons 1602.

12. It is to be supposed that Barbe's bosom has miraculously recovered.

13. Cf. Eleanor Prosser, *Drama and Religion in the English Mystery Plays*, Stanford 1961, pp. 81–5, who takes strong exception to the praise frequently lavished on comic realism in the English cycles, on the ground that it contributes nothing to the development of the religious theme.

14. The inability to omit any stage of an action was noticed in the medieval *mystères* by O. B. Hardison, Jr, *Christian Rite and Christian Drama in the Middle Ages*, Baltimore 1965, pp. 272–3, and by Sister Mary Faith McKean, *The Interplay of Realistic and Flamboyant Art Elements in the French Mystères*, Washington 1959, pp. 20–23; the latter complained that concentration on the 'process' was so strong as to cause neglect of the religious significance of the event. By the late sixteenth century this tendency had become more exaggerated.

15. Summary in *Mystères*, vol. ii, pp. 531–3.

16. Though the *mystère* is no longer staged, these events are still celebrated at Saintes-Maries-de-la-Mer, where legend placed the landing, in a carnival on the feast-day of the party's black servant, Saint Sara.

17. *Mystères*, vol. ii, pp. 533–5, where there is also a full summary of the plot.

18. I have not included in this chapter any discussion of the *Mystère de la vie et hystoire de sainct Martin*, because of uncertainty over whether it was printed within the period considered here (this problem is examined in the Catalogue). An analysis of the play would in any case add little to the present discussion. It took the usual course of recounting the whole of the saint's career, with many spectacular miracles (see the summary in *Mystères*, vol. ii, pp. 535–8). As in the *Patience de Job*, discussed below, a large place is given to military episodes not involving the hero: Martin resigns the throne of Hungary and so provokes a quarrel over the succession between his uncle and his brother-in-law which is fought on the stage for the space of several hundred lines.

19. See the edition by A. Meiller, Paris 1971, pp. 59–65 and 169–70. It is possible that if other *mystères* were studied with as much attention as Meiller has lavished on *Job*, similar numbers of performances would come to light. Meiller's text, based on a MS, differs slightly from the versions printed later; I have used his list of variants to reconstitute the text as it was published by Nicolas Oudot, Troyes 1621.

20. Variants, largely concerning orthography, in *VT*, vol. v.

2. Bèze and the classical tradition

1. In the *VT* Abraham's life forms episodes 13–18 (vols I–II).
2. It was only the insistence of friends who had read the plays in manuscript that induced Buchanan to have them printed: Lebègue, *TR*, pp. 244–7, quotes their letters.
3. The most recent biographical information is contained in the unpublished doctoral dissertation of Philip Ford, 'The Poetical Works of George Buchanan before his Final Return to Scotland' (1976; Cambridge University Library); for this period see pp. 32–45. I am grateful to Dr Ford for evidence that Bèze most probably had read Buchanan's plays before writing his own. At a later date Bèze certainly knew *Baptistes*: in a letter to Bèze probably written in the 1570s, Peter Young reported: 'D. Buchananus, quem tuo nomine salutavi, te resalutat officiossime mittitque ad te *Baptistam* suum una cum dialogo *de Jure Regni*' (Bodleian MS Smith 77, p. 161). That Young explained what the latter work was but did not feel it necessary to do the same for *Baptistes* suggests that he knew Bèze to be familiar with the play already. It is most probable that Bèze would have read the plays when he and Buchanan were both in Paris (1543–7).
4. La Croix du Maine, writing in 1584, mentions without date another translation, by Le Duchat; this seems never to have been printed (vol. II, p. 154).
5. The version followed here is that by Chrestian (tutor to Henri IV: see Haag), in the edition of 1587, recently made available by Donald Stone in *Four Renaissance Tragedies*, Cambridge, Mass. 1966. The differences between the translations are analysed in *TR*, pp. 248–51.
6. From the Greek: Storge is the voice of affection, while Iphis, besides recalling Iphigeneia, signifies strength.
7. Judges xi; Buchanan's action occupies only verses 34–9.
8. The classical sources are considered in *TR*, pp. 234–9.
9. It reappears in almost all the humanist plays studied in Chapter 5 below.
10. Cf *TR*, pp. 229–39.
11. The humanist style is the subject of Chapters 5 and 6 below.
12. The play did not share the popularity of *Jephthes* among Frenchmen: it was translated only twice, by Brisset (Tours 1589) and Brinon (Rouen 1613).
13. Summary in *TR*, pp. 206–10.
14. In the Bible, John's execution is attributed to Herod's anger at John's criticising him for taking his brother's wife as his own (Matthew xv, Mark vi); by Josephus to Herod's fear of an insurrection of the crowds John draws (*Antiquities*, book XVIII, paras 116–19): in neither account is John the victim of religious persecution.
15. The question of the form required for propaganda is pursued in Chapter 4 below.
16. The play was intended for performance by Bèze's pupils on speech-day at the Academy at Lausanne (see the edition by Cameron, Hall and Higman, Geneva and Paris 1967, pp. 11–12, and *TR*, p. 295). Buchanan

too wrote for performance by his pupils. The staging was no doub
improvised in college halls or courts, with the assistance of a few back
cloths and props; there was no curtain before the seventeenth centur
(see Georges Védier, *Origine et évolution de la dramaturgie néc
classique: l'influence des arts plastiques en Italie et en France, le rideat
la mise en scène et les trois unités*, Paris 1955).

17. Unlike the *fatiste* of the *Viel Testament*, where the sacrifice is repeatedl
described as a symbol of God's own sacrifice of His Son, Bèze ignore
the typological interpretation, as is correctly pointed out by John F
Elliott, Jr, 'The Sacrifice of Isaac as Comedy and Tragedy', *Studies i
Philology* LXVI (1969), pp. 36–59. However, Elliott is mistaken i
supposing that by omitting the traditional triumphant interpretation o
the sacrifice as a promise of the Redemption, Bèze deprived the stor
of Christian hope: Bèze replaced the traditional interpretation with th
no less triumphant vision of the victory of faith.

18. That Bèze invented the triple temptation shows that the typologic:
interpretation was not absent from his mind: Christ, of course, wa
tempted thrice in the wilderness. However, Bèze did not make this th
theme of his play: he wished to present, not Christian hermeneutic
but an inspiring example of faith at work in a man.

3. The explicit representation of Christian doctrine

1. Four earlier plays seem lost. Two, performed at the Jesuit College a
Billom in 1557, are known only through the principal's report to h
superiors (reproduced by F. de Dainville, S.J., *Les Jésuites o
l'éducation de la société française*, vol. II, *La Naissance de l'humanism
moderne*, Paris 1940, p. 187): one used allegorical figures to explain th
nature and function of the Eucharist, and the other celebrated th
Assumption of the Virgin. La Vallière describes (vol. I, p. 171) tw
pastoral allegories published at Lyons in 1563 by an author who gav
only the initials F.D.B.P.: the *Eglogue ou bergerie à 4 personnage
contenant l'Institution, Puissance et Office d'un bon Pasteur, dédiée
François de Lorraine* concerned Christ's appointment of Peter to foun
His church, and the *Eglogue à 5 personnages, contenant les abus a
mauvais Pasteur, et montrant, que bienheureux est qui a cru, sans avo
vu* vilified the Jews who saw Christ but did not believe, in contrast t
the Christians who believe without having seen Him.

2. Dedication, p. 10. The 'quatre temps' are periods of fasting markin
each of the four seasons (*Encyclopédie*).

3. The majority of dramatists during the religious wars preferred t
express their concern with divine retribution through historical plays c
Old-Testament subjects; dealing with the lives of men, their dramat
technique was naturally quite different from that used by the doctrin
playwrights, and is the subject of Chapter 5 below.

4. Summary in Dabney, pp. 93–6.

5. Summary in La Vallière, vol. I, pp. 443–6.

6. The play's date is discussed in *History* I, pp. 74–5.

7. In the Bible it is the tree of knowledge that is prohibited. The *V7*

ll. 852–61, makes the same error as Ville-Toustain, but there is no other sign that Ville-Toustain used the earlier work.

8. Summary in La Vallière, vol. I, pp. 461–2.
9. *History* I, p. 81.
10. Ibid.
11. In other plays he did use the classical form, at least to the extent of adopting acts and choruses: see pp. 148–52 below.
12. A theological treatise not apparently intended for the stage was nevertheless written in dialogue form. Charles Hersent's *La Pastorale sainte* (Paris 1635) consists of three pieces which give one literal and two allegorical accounts of the Song of Songs; heavy use is made of the fashionable pastoral conventions. See La Vallière, vol. II, pp. 505–7, and *History* I, p. 390.
13. See the title-page of the play.
14. The resulting plot is remarkably incoherent: summary in *History* II, p. 354.
15. See *History* II, p. 658.
16. Nevertheless, Lancaster complained from his usual standpoint that 'There is no thought of unity or characterisation' (*History* II, p. 658). It is difficult to imagine how subtle characterisation would have enhanced the mood of celebration or clarified the meaning of the nativity; and if the play lacks unity of plot, it possesses the more important unity of theme.
17. Thus he signed the Dedication, p. 5; but the title-page bore the name Louis Jaquemin Donnet. Claude Longeon, in the unpaginated introduction to Georges Couton's edition of the play (Saint-Etienne 1971), explains that Jaquemin was the family name, Donnet a 'prénom mystique'.
18. Summary in *History* II, pp. 658–9.
19. He is dissuaded by his court. Couton points out that the scene may not derive from *Cinna*: Jaquemin probably used the same source as Corneille.
20. P. 326. It is perhaps no coincidence that all the observations Loukovitch made were to be found in Lancaster's *History* II, pp. 658–9.
21. The name Théandre for Christ derives from the Greek; it epitomises his dual nature as God and man.
22. Summary in *History* II, pp. 662–3.

4. The theatre of sectarian propaganda

1. Badius, *Pape malade*, critical edition by Helen Shaw: p. 97. In view of Badius's declaration, it is strange that Shaw saw fit to interpolate divisions into acts and scenes into the text.
2. See Jonker, *Protestantisme et théâtre*, pp. 3–26; also Emile Picot, 'Les Moralités polémiques, ou la controverse religieuse dans l'ancien théâtre français', *BSHP* XXXVI (1887), pp. 169–90, 225–45, 337–64; XLI (1892), pp. 561–82, 617–33; LV (1906), pp. 254–62. The *Mystère du Concil de Basle* has appeared in an edition by Jonathan Beck, Leiden 1979, where the date of composition is given on p. 27.

3. Since these plays did not use sacred material, they are excluded from consideration here. The satires printed after 1550 were, in addition to Badius's play: *La Verité cachée* (Geneva 1559); the *Tragedie de Timothee chrestien* (Lyons 1563); Jacques Bienvenu, *Comedie du monde malade* (Geneva 1568) and *Comedie du voyage de frere Fecisti* (Nîmes 1589); and Antoine Lancel, *Commedie des quatre estats* (The Hague 1605). The success of the propaganda theatre was apparently such that two tracts were dressed up as plays to take advantage of the vogue, though not intended for the stage: the *Tragédie du Roy Franc Arbitre* (Villefranche 1559) and Pierre Viret, *Le Monde à l'empire et le monde démoniacle* (Geneva 1558).

4. A *Tragédie de l'homme affligé* by Gilbert Cousin or Cognatus, Erasmus's secretary, may have had a similar burden; the text was not printed, but according to La Vallière (vol. 1, p. 162) the author included a summary of it in a volume which he published at Lyons in 1561, and which I have been unable to trace. Jonker, *Protestantisme et théâtre*, supposes that the play was performed in the same year (p. 71).

5. Bèze wrote *Abraham sacrifiant* for a speech-day performance in the first instance, and other propagandists probably had similar functions in mind; certainly Heinz was writing for his pupils (see below pp. 54–6). La Croix, on the other hand, wrote with a view to a performance in the household of the King of Navarre, of which he was a member (see below p. 45). These few surviving details suggest that the propagandists expected to see their work mounted on improvised stages by amateurs. The inclusion in some of the printed texts of long prayers and canticles, complete in some cases with music to which they were to be sung, suggests in addition that the performance could on occasion have something of the value of a religious service for the spectators; it was partly the danger that such a tone could meet with a ribald reaction from the crowd in a public performance that eventually led the Protestants to proscribe the theatre (see pp. 52–3).

6. Coignac is also credited with two satires on the Pope and the papacy, published in the same year, which I have been unable to trace: see Brunet, and *Soleinne* II Supplément, no. 322.

7. Summary in Jonker, *Protestantisme et théâtre*, pp. 106–7.

8. The battle and the beheading of Goliath occur on the stage.

9. The author states his position in the Dedication to the Queen of Navarre.

10. Summary in H. C. Lancaster, *The French Tragi-Comedy: its Origin and Development from 1552 to 1628*, Baltimore 1907, pp. 48–52.

11. The Huguenots were in some difficulties to know whether to rebel against the King, God's anointed regent, when his actions ran counter to what their consciences told them was God's will; see Forsyth, pp. 168–74.

12. Summary in Jonker, *Protestantisme et théâtre*, pp. 86–90.

13. Lebègue, *TR*, p. 338, suggests the existence of an edition of Geneva 1563, of which I have found no other trace.

14. Desmasures was a considerable classicist, and translated the *Aeneid*: Lebègue describes his life and work in *TR*, pp. 327–44.

15. Desmasures, *Tragédies saintes*, ed. Charles Comte, Paris 1907, Epistre, ll. 169–86; all references are to this edition.
16. The constant references to the fickleness of Princes reflect Desmasures's own experience of disgrace (*TR*, p. 329): David was an example to the author personally.
17. The probable significance for the French after the massacre of Vassy of the refusal to act against the King despite his injustice is explored by Forsyth, pp. 169–71.
18. Historians are agreed that Philone is a pseudonym, but it is not certain whose identity it conceals. Brunet, Quérard and the Catalogues of the Bibliothèque nationale and the British Library identify the author as Desmasures, but I have seen no reason advanced for this attribution and find it improbable that Desmasures should have been content for his name to appear in his trilogy but concealed it for *Josias*. Stylistically the trilogy and *Josias* have little in common.
19. II Kings xxii–xxiii, II Chronicles xxxiv–xxxv. Josiah dies aged 39: the action thus extends over 32 years.
20. See James Westfall Thompson, *The Wars of Religion in France, 1559–1576*, Chicago and London 1909, p. 290; also Forsyth, p. 172, and *TR*, p. 323.
21. This opinion was a contribution to a contemporary controversy: see Forsyth, pp. 172–4.
22. This speech is some 500 lines long.
23. Jeremiah i–ii; Philone gives marginal references to his sources throughout.
24. *TR*, p. 325.
25. This was the fear expressed by La Croix in his Prologue: see above, pp. 45–6.
26. See Loukovitch, p. 17, and Keegstra, *Bèze et le théâtre calviniste*, pp. 5–12, 114–23.
27. The wording ran as follows: 'Il ne sera pas permis aux Fideles d'assister aux spectacles profanes, comme aux Danses de Theatre, aux Comedies, Tragedies, ou Farces, soit qu'on les represente en public, ou en particulier; parce qu'ils ont été defendus de tous temps par les Eglises de Dieu, comme des amusements illicites et qui corrompent les bonnes moeurs, particulierement lorsque la Sainte Escriture y est profanée. Mais si le College juge convenable pour exercer la jeunesse de representer des histoires qui ne soient pas contenuës dans la Sainte Escriture (laquelle ne nous a pas été donné pour nous servir de Passetemps, mais pour être prêchée, et pour nôtre Conversion et Consolation;) pourvû que cela se fasse rarement, et par l'avis du Colloque, qui en fournira le sujet, ces representations seront tolerées' (Jean Aymon, *Tous les Synodes nationaux des Eglises réformées de France*, 2 vols, The Hague 1710, vol. I, pp. 118–19).
28. Aymon, op. cit., vol. I, p. 142.
29. See below, p. 72. The plays of La Taille and Rivaudeau, being more humanist than propagandist, will be considered in the next chapter.
30. The attribution – in Brunet, Quérard and the Bibliothèque nationale Catalogue – to Desmasures of a play that appeared 12 years after his

death and referred to events of which he knew nothing is even less convincing than the attribution to him of *Josias*. Yves le Hir, in *Les Drames bibliques de 1541 à 1600: études de langue, de style et de versification*, Grenoble 1974, p. 67, has concluded on stylistic grounds that the authors of *Josias* and *Adonias* were in any case not the same.

31. See J.-H. Mariéjol, *La Réforme et la Ligue – l'Edit de Nantes (1559–1598)*, Paris 1904 (vol. VI, part 1 of E. Lavisse, ed., *Histoire de France*, 9 vols, Paris 1903–11), pp. 238–62.

32. See *Biographie nationale de Belgique*. Heyns's schools were for girls: in the two biblical plays there is only one male part.

33. *Susanne, miroir des mesnageres* (Amsterdam 1595). The heroine is an archetypical good wife, unrelated to the biblical Susannah.

34. Performed in 1580, according to the Dedication.

35. Summary in Lancaster, *Tragi-Comedy*, pp. 54–7.

36. Heyns had one male actor, whom he used to present, not Holofernes, as one might expect, but Achior, because of the latter's propaganda value. This is explained in a Conclusion, in which Allegorie tells Docilité the significance of all they have witnessed: Holoferne was a tyrant who, forgetful of God's might, sought to establish himself in His place. He persecuted the Jews (the church) and cut off their water (communion). Achior warned Holoferne of his error, but was persecuted for his good advice and joined the true servants of God. The people, increasingly oppressed, began to doubt God and the High Priest was unable to calm them, having only bookish devotion, and even fell into the error of prescribing limits to God's action (the five days). Judith, widow of Manassé (i.e. of forgetfulness of God), thought of nothing but God and was able to correct the Priest; inspired by her spiritual (as opposed to bookish) faith she left the city (as the pastor sacrifices all for his flock) and, dressed in the rich costume of virtue, went to Holoferne's camp. He got drunk on the wine of concupiscence and slept in the ignorance of God. Judith took his sword, the human strength on which he relied, and killed him with it, as God kills all tyrants by turning their own strength against them.

37. Only the few saint-plays performed in the Collèges are likely to have been new compositions: the *régents* wrote new plays for the annual prize-giving (see L.-V. Gofflot, *Le Théâtre au collège du moyen-âge à nos jours*, Paris 1907, pp. 46–87). These texts do not survive.

38. See below, p. 100.

39. He gives his credentials on the title-page.

40. Summary in Dabney, pp. 96–8.

41. *Pace* Loukovitch, p. 45.

42. Nevertheless, he retained the neo-classical formalities, excepting the unities: the action is divided into five acts, it starts *in medias res*, violence is kept off the stage, and the whole is disposed to provide opportunities for pompous tirades (mostly of rather poor quality, as Faguet pointed out in *La Tragédie française*, pp. 312–14).

43. The play's connections with contemporary politics are examined in more detail by Forsyth, pp. 189–91; he seems not to have been aware that it was written in the year of the formation of the Ligue.

44. Being primarily humanist tragedies, these plays are considered with others of that kind in Chapter 5 below.

45. The plays in question are Belyard's *Charlot* (Troyes 1592) and his *Le Guysien, ou perfidie tyrannique commise par Henry de Valois es personnes de Loys et Henry de Loraine* (Troyes 1592); and Fonteny's *Cleophon, tragedie conforme et semblable à celles que la France a veues durant les Guerres Civilles* (Paris 1600). The campaigns of Louis XIII against the Protestants of La Rochelle gave rise to two further Catholic propaganda plays, the *Tragedie des rebelles, ou sont les noms feints on void leurs conspirations, machines, monopoles, assemblees, prattiques et rebellions descouvertes* (Paris 1622) of an author who identified himself only as P.D.B. Parisien, and the work of another shy poet, P.M., *La Rocheloise, tragedie, où se voit les heureux succez et Glorieuses Victoires du Roy Tres Chrestien LOUYS XIII, depuis l'advenement de sa Majesté à la Couronne de France jusques à present* (Troyes 1629). All gave very partisan accounts of contemporary events.

5. Humanist drama: the themes and forms of the wars of religion

1. The sacred plays published between 1550 and the outbreak of fighting in 1562 have all been considered in the previous chapters.

2. Charlton, *Senecan Tradition*, p. xxii, draws attention to this aspect of Seneca's attraction for the Renaissance, and points out, p. xxxiii, that the Greeks were less favoured than Seneca partly because their plays were less bloodthirsty; among the Greeks the Renaissance most appreciated the violent Euripides, particularly his *Hecuba*, 'the most Senecan of Euripides's plays'. Charlton also describes the horror plays of Giraldi and his followers, pp. lxxii–xciv; the influence of Giraldi's *Orbecche* in France through Du Monin's translation is studied at greater length by A. T. Gable in his unpublished Cambridge Ph.D. thesis, 'The Rise of Irregular French Tragedy (1580–1630)' 1972, pp. 53–73.

3. The antecedents of this theme in classical literature are studied by Forsyth, pp. 109–15, and there is no need here to recapitulate his analysis of the preoccupation with horror in the Renaissance; he concludes that the peculiar form the theme assumed in France was inspired by the local condition of religious war.

4. See La Taille, *Oeuvres*, ed. René de Maulde, 4 vols, Paris 1878–82, vol. II, p. vi; and Garnier, *Les Juifves*, ed. Raymond Lebègue, Paris 1949, p. 10.

5. See Raymond Lebègue, 'Le Répertoire d'une troupe française à la fin du XVIe siècle', *Revue d'histoire du théâtre* I (1948), pp. 9–22, and S. W. Deierkauf-Holsboer, *Vie d'Alexandre Hardy poète du roi 1572–1632*, second edition, Paris 1972, p. 26.

6. See, for example, George R. Kernodle, *From Art to Theatre: Form and Convention in the Renaissance*, Chicago 1944, p. 170.

7. See his description of his position on the title-page of the play.

8. Rivaudeau was a Protestant (*TR*, pp. 375–6), as were the dedicatee of the play and François de la Noue, to whom the Avant-Parler is addressed. Uncertainty over the date of composition hinders identi-

fication of topical references, but it seems probable that Rivaudeau
intended the fall of Aman as a warning that the power of the Guises at
court would soon end, or that the play celebrated the death in 1563 of
François de Guise, perpetrator of the massacre of Vassy: see Françoise
Charpentier, 'Le Thème d'Aman dans la propagande huguenote: à
propos de l'édition critique de l'*Aman* de Rivaudeau par K. Cameron',
BHR XXXIII (1971), pp. 377–83. The play illustrates the common
Huguenot theme, that God protects the faithful from oppression.

9. Avant-Parler, ll. 39–49.

10. Also symptomatic of the more lettered approach and consciously
elevated tone of the humanists is Rivaudeau's use of Alexandrines.
The *mystères* were usually written in octosyllabic or sometimes decasyllabic couplets, with shorter lines and more complex rhyme-schemes
in lyrical passages. The same metres were used by many of the propagandists and doctrinal dramatists, at least until the end of the century.
The humanists almost all preferred the longer Alexandrine, attracted
perhaps by its greater capacity for pomp and dignity.

11. Rivaudeau's ideal was that the time of the action should be no longer
than the duration of the performance (Avant-Parler ll. 47–9). Before it
begins Aman has already persuaded Assuère to order the slaughter of
the Jews, and been forced to honour Mardochée, while Esther has
already fasted, entered the King's presence unbidden, and invited him
to the banquet. The *VT*, of course, omitted none of this: see vol. VI,
episodes 43–4. Rivaudeau's plot is limited to Esther vii.

12. The humanists' practice of using several characters and situations to
illuminate the same theme from different angles has been codified by
Marie-Madeleine Mouflard, in *Robert Garnier*, 3 vols, La Ferté–
Bernard and La Roche-sur-Yon 1961–4, vol. II, pp. 22–3.

13. The humanists placed *guillemets* or other typographical devices at the
beginning of a line to draw attention to a *sententia*: these are reproduced here as double inverted commas.

14. *Saül* was written before the autumn of 1562, when La Taille mentioned
it in the Dedication of his *Remonstrance pour le Roy* (*privilège*
19 October 1562): *Oeuvres*, ed. René de Maulde, vol. II, p. iv.

15. La Taille probably attended lectures at the Collège de Boncourt, around
which were grouped several dramatists identified with the Pléiade, but
there is no evidence that he had personal contact with members of the
band or even that he was enrolled at the Collège; usually so generous
with encomiastic verses, they wrote none for him, and he none for them.
The fullest biographical treatment is in C. N. Smith's unpublished
Ph.D. dissertation in the Cambridge University Library, 'The Tragedies
of Jean and Jacques de la Taille', 1969, chapter I, 'The early life',
pp. 8–34.

16. La Taille, *Dramatic Works*, ed. Kathleen M. Hall and C. N. Smith,
London 1972, p. 6.

17. Other humanist dramatists devoted scores of lines to the commonplace
that ill-fortune is not endless, but La Taille was not to be diverted from
deploying Saül's character and religious state.

18. Saül's treatment of Agag could have been the opportunity for debating

another of the humanists' favourite topics, the question whether a King rules more securely by a policy of rigour, earning his subjects' fear, or clemency, earning their love; but La Taille neglected the conventional development, to concentrate on the matter of Saül's reprobation.

19. Saül does not engage in the commonplace praise of *aurea mediocritas* (*pace* Loukovitch, p. 177): once again, La Taille did not deviate from the theme of Saül's refusal to submit to God's will.

20. See *TR*, p. 419, and the notes of the learned editors of the play.

21. These are not to be found in the edition by Hall and Smith, but may be consulted in Forsyth's, Paris 1968, pp. 15–16 and 90.

22. This is the interpretation advanced by Griffiths, *Dramatic Technique of Antoine de Montchrestien*, pp. 29–30.

23. *TR*, p. 416.

24. See Forsyth's introduction to the play in his edition, pp. xvii–xviii, xlvi–liv.

25. See Kathleen M. Hall and C. N. Smith, 'The Early Editions of the Tragedies of Jean de la Taille', *Kentucky Romance Quarterly* xx (1973), pp. 75–88.

26. Forsyth surmises in his edition of the plays that *La Famine* was written after the Saint Barthélemy and intended to warn the Valois of the punishment God would mete out to them for destroying the Protestants after making peace with them (p. lxv). It is not known when the play was written: La Taille informs us that it came after *Saül* (*Art de la tragédie*, l. 13), but it seems not to have been ready in 1562, when he mentioned only Saül in his *Remonstrance*; it must have been written between 1562 and 1573. No doubt *La Famine* took on an anti-Valois colour for Protestant readers when it appeared after the massacre, but there is no reason to suppose that La Taille intended his literary compositions to be *engagées*; when he wished to comment on contemporary affairs he did so explicitly, in a *Remonstrance*. Without firm evidence to the contrary, it seems more likely that *La Famine* was written shortly after *Saül* and, as a classical tragedy, did not refer to contemporary events. This is the conclusion of Hall and Smith in their edition, p. 2.

27. See *TR*, pp. 425–32, and the editors' notes.

28. II Samuel xxi 1–14; also *Antiquities* vii 294–7. These sources state only that David ended the drought afflicting Israel by sacrificing Saul's sons and grandsons to the Gibeonites' vengeance; La Taille contributed the mothers' attempt to save the children by hiding them in his tomb. According to *Antiquities* vii 296 and II Samuel xxi 7, David spared one of Saül's grandsons; wishing no doubt to avoid the moral problems this raises, La Taille omitted any reference to this child or his survival.

29. See Gabriel Spillebout's review of Forsyth's edition of the plays, *BHR* xxxii (1970), p. 190.

30. See *Biographie nationale de Belgique*.

31. Tiron also translated another play, Gnapheus's *Acolastus*, as *L'Enfant prodigue* (Antwerp 1564); he worked as a translator and editor for Plantin (*Biographie nationale de Belgique*).

32. *TR*, p. 153.

33. The plays must have been written around 1570; the Preface, which first

appeared with *La Fidelité nuptiale* in 1577, mentions performances five or six years earlier.

34. The plays written in schools outside the Netherlands were quite different: see below the analyses of the work of Fronton-du-Duc, Behourt and Soret, pp. 82–3, 104, 116–17.

35. The play appeared in a volume of verse in the style of the Pléiade. This must have been complete by 30 September 1576, the date of the prefatory letter in which Frère G. Vigerius describes how he became acquainted with Chantelouve when the latter visited Paris, and decided to see through the press work Chantelouve was too modest to publish himself. The views on persecution outlined here indicate a much more moderate attitude than the same author's *Gaspard de Colligny*; this leads me to suppose that *Pharaon* may have been written some years earlier, before events induced in the author the bitterness evident in the satire.

36. The contemporary significance of the portrayal of Pharaon as a vacillating tyrant is explored by Forsyth, pp. 187–9.

37. Nevertheless, Loukovitch criticised the plays as 'oratoire et sans action. Chaque acte n'est qu'un monologue avec choeur, d'un style ampoulé' (p. 59). This was precisely what Chantelouve intended, and he would have been surprised to find such observations used as a ground for complaint. A more admissible criticism is that his attempts at grandiloquence frequently resulted only in bathos or even nonsense, though the involvement of Vigerius in publication may partly account for the incoherence.

38. Charles Bellier-Dumaine, 'Thomas Le Coq et sa tragédie de *Caïn* 1580', *Normannia* XI (1938), pp. 181–230, gives the few available facts about Le Coq's life and from them draws an inspired psychological portrait. His life was considerably disturbed by the civil wars, which may have contributed to the play.

39. Rothschild drew attention to Le Coq's debt to the *VT*, vol. I, pp. lxvii–lxviii. Bellier-Dumaine, op. cit., defended the curé from the charge of plagiarism, pointing out correctly that the textual resemblances were few, but ignored the fact that many features of Le Coq's play are to be found in the *VT* but not in Genesis. However, Le Coq's order of events is different: he used the *VT*, but adapted it to suit his own requirements. Lebègue's assertion, *TR* p. 35 (repeated by Loukovitch, p. 59), that 'Les meilleurs scènes paraissent originales, mais tout le reste n'est qu'une imitation, souvent textuelle, de la partie correspondante du *Viel Testament*', cannot be sustained.

40. Lebègue points out, *TR*, p. 316, that this scene closely resembles one in Bèze's *Abraham sacrifiant* (ll. 735–8, 887–91), an unexpected source for the curé to have used.

41. These qualities earned the play sufficient popularity to be performed at least once some time after publication, at Rouen in 1630.

42. As *régent* at the Jesuit College at Pont-à-Mousson, Fronton-du-Duc wrote the play for performance during a visit of Henri III which was to have occurred in May 1580 but was prevented by plague; it was performed instead for the court of Lorraine in September: see Durand

de Lanson's introduction to his edition of the play, Pont-à-Mousson 1859. Another play by Fronton-du-Duc, *Julien l'apostat*, was performed in 1580, but it was never printed and has not survived. Subsequently Fronton-du-Duc made his career as a theologian (J. J. Soons, *Jeanne d'Arc au théâtre: étude sur la plus ancienne tragédie*, Purmerend 1929): he never again dabbled in the theatre, and took no further interest in his *Pucelle*, which was published later by one Jean Barnet, into whose hands the MS had fallen without his even knowing the identity of the author (Barnet's Dedication).

43. The same sentiment is apparent in the size of the role given to René of Lorraine (the author prefers this title to his more usual designation as duc d'Anjou) who insists on the loyalty of the province to France.

44. Full summary in La Vallière, vol. 1, pp. 236–40.

45. Apart from the appearance of Michel, the miracles in Joan's career are not staged, and the indecent gestures of the gaolers of which she complains are not enacted: the author of a *mystère* would not have denied himself such material.

46. On the basis of this speech, Clive R. Frankish has suggested that idolatry is Garnier's main theme ('The Theme of Idolatry in Garnier's *Les Juifves*', BHR xxx (1968), pp. 65–83); but idolatry is only one manifestation, albeit important, of the Jews' general forgetfulness of their debt of gratitude and obedience to God.

47. The play, and this speech in particular, was so popular that pastiches were still being written in the next century: there is one in Le Francq's *Antioche* (p. 154), and see also p. 150.

48. On average there was one edition of the plays each year until 1628; no other sacred play was printed so frequently between 1550 and 1650.

49. Full summary in La Vallière, vol. 1, pp. 256–9.

50. 'That eccentric and disorganised polymath who died too young to show anything more than longwinded promise': I. D. McFarlane, *A Literary History of France: Renaissance France 1470–1589*, London and New York 1974, p. 389.

51. Biographical details in Michaud.

52. Loukovitch's assertion, p. 45, that *Esther*, *Vasthi* and *Aman* form a trilogy, cannot be derived from an inspection of the texts.

53. In revising *Esther* in the same year as publishing the polemical *La Guisiade*, Matthieu took the opportunity to reinforce the *ligueur* criticisms voiced in the earlier version. The subtitles of the three plays give an indication of his opinion of the Valois, markedly less benign in 1589 than earlier. The Dedication of *Aman* to the Consuls of Lyons (at this stage a stronghold of the Ligue) is forthright: Matthieu's aim is to

vous faire veoir la malheureuse fin d'un Prince, qui d'un pernicieux conseil charmoit jadis l'entendement d'un Roy Payen, et disposoit de son authorité selon la passion de son traistre et ambitieux esprit, conjurant d'extirper l'union du peuple de Dieu, le massacrer, le proscrire et l'accabler de mille maux, pour seul manier à sa volonté et selon les ressors de son ambition la Monarchie des Medes et Perses, mais ce qu'il machinoit sur les innocens tomba sur sa teste et sur celle de ses Partizans, endurant le supplice qu'il avoit preparé pour ses ennemys.

Et par là se monstre à l'oeil comme les Roynes doivent appaiser les courroux des Roys sur l'oppression de leurs sujets, et qu'iceux ne doivent tant ceder à leur affection, que la grace qu'ilz portent à leurs Mignons soit au prejudice de ceux qui par leurs valeurs meritent d'estre favorisez et honnorez de la liberalité d'un Prince... (ff.†2ᵛ–3ʳ) Matthieu proceeds to give examples of the Mignons who have come to bad ends; the play was perhaps a warning in particular to Henri III's favourite d'Epernon.

54. The plays were substantially written during Matthieu's time as a teacher, though by 1589 he was practising as a lawyer in Lyons (see title-pages of *Vasthi* and *Aman*); in his new profession his old attitudes, and especially his fondness for rhetoric, remained with him, to judge from the evidence of the texts.

55. *Vasthi*, I, p. 10: Argument to the second scene. Each scene has a similar gloss.

56. In fact Assuere showed no patience; but for all that, it is a fine *sententia*.

57. He reveals his profession in the Dedication.

58. In fact Sara gives orders to her husband, forcing him to eject Ismael, and Isaac quarrels with his half-brother: like many humanists, George was rather blind to the sense of his story as a whole, and attended only to the instruction encapsulated in individual lines.

59. Anatole de Charmasse, *François Perrin, poète français du XVIe siècle; et sa vie par Guillaume Colletet publiée d'après le manuscrit aujourd'hui détruit de la Bibliothèque du Louvre*, Paris and Autun 1887.

60. Both acts II and III start with the same characters on the stage as at the end of the previous act: Perrin did not conceive of the acts as complete units but used the divisions like the *pauses* in the *mystères* to mark the passage of time in a continuous action. The Chorus speaks in the middle of the acts, never at the end.

61. F. A2ʳ. Perrin died in January 1606 (Charmasse, op. cit.), the year of the second edition, and it is possible that the printer issued it without the author's cooperation and contributed the Argument himself; but in that case it is still valuable as a contemporary appreciation of the play's sense.

62. P. 86.

63. Again, Stone has put this neatly: the humanists' technique consisted in 'expanding outward from misfortune to cover myriad didactic possibilities and feeling content when some elevation in tone and much moralizing could be included' (p. 90).

64. In performance, the actors doubtless similarly drew attention to fine lines by giving them special declamatory emphasis and pausing for applause.

65. Griffiths, *Dramatic Technique*, p. 81. Griffiths draws attention in this connection to the influence of the rhetorical exercise of *prosopopeia*,

for which see his 'The Influence of Formulary Rhetoric upon French Renaissance Tragedy', *MLR* LIX (1964), pp. 201–8.

6. Peace: new themes and forms

1. The only exception was Fronton-du-Duc's *Pucelle*.
2. Little is known of the performance conditions for which these plays were designed. La Pujade (pp. 114–15) wrote for performance at court, as presumably did the courtier Billard (pp. 126–9). Bardon (pp. 100–2) and Baudeville (p. 126) wrote *mystères* for the feast-days of saints, and Nancel had a commission from his town (pp. 120–4). *Jeanne d'Arques* was perhaps intended for the professional stage. Soret's play was performed by his pupils at choir school (pp. 116–17), and Loys's at a college (p. 126); this type of amateur presentation was perhaps the most common expectation. No single performance style predominated at this time.
3. See *DBF*.
4. According to the list of actors (f. ẽ4ᵛ), each Chorus was in fact represented by only one man.
5. Summary in Dabney, pp. 45–8.
6. The Argument summarises the life of Diocletian, making only passing reference to Sebastien: Laudun clearly intended this to be the emphasis of the play. Tracing the greater part of Diocletian's life was in keeping with Laudun's principle: 'La definition de la tragedie est, le recit des vies des Heros...' (*L'Art poétique françois*, Paris 1597, v ix, p. 295).
7. Summary in Dabney, pp. 42–5. Loukovitch's account of the play, p. 114, admittedly derived from La Vallière rather than the text, is highly misleading, omitting even Diocletian's suicide.
8. In the Dedication, p. 4, Virey records that early in the wars he had translated the Book of Maccabees into French verse, and the recent fighting had inspired him to publish a section of the larger work in play form.
9. In the Dedication he states that he was commander of the Garrison of Cherbourg, and fought elsewhere for Matignon.
10. Summary in Dabney, pp. 33–5.
11. Genesis xxv 19–34, and xxvii; Behourt omits chapter xxvi, the account of the drought. Summary in Dabney, pp. 19–20.
12. Stone makes a similar observation, p. 96.
13. Summary in Dabney, pp. 56–9.
14. So he states in the Dedication, p. 4.
15. I Maccabees ii–iv and II Maccabees viii–x, alternative versions of the same events; summary in Dabney, pp. 36–9.
16. By suppressing the lapse of two years between the rape and the murder of Amnon (II Samuel xiii 23), Thierry reinforced the connection between crime and retribution.
17. Elie's description of war and suffering imposed on the nation by the crimes and greed of the ruler seems to reflect Marcé's horror of civil war. The Dedication to Pierre Forget, Henri IV's trusted adviser, makes

it clear that Marcé intended the example of Achab to reflect on the excellence of Henri's rule:

> le ciel nous ayant faict naistre tres-fidelles vassaulx d'un prince aultant aimant et craignant Dieu, comme il est triomphant et invincible aux armes: J'ay pensé que le zelle fervent, la pieté et devotion de sa magesté (ainsi que son contraire) estant opposé à limpieté de ce Roy d'Israel, cela apporteroit un grand contentement au lecteur, et le convieroit souvent à jetter en hault la veuë, et la pensée, pour rendre graces à la bonté divine de la paix et repos duquel soubz son Empire et bon heur, jouist ápresent tout le peuple François (f. ã2ᵛ).

18. This occurs three years after the previous events (I Kings xxii 1); by not mentioning the delay, Marcé reinforced the connection between crime and punishment.

19. I Kings xxii 38: Ahab is killed in battle, as Micaiah warned, but the blood is licked from his chariot by dogs at the spot where Naboth was stoned, in fulfilment of Elijah's prophecy.

20. This aspect of Montchrestien's dramaturgy has been amply treated by Griffiths, *Dramatic Technique*, particularly p. 45 and chapter VI, 'Set Pieces'.

21. Montchrestien, *Tragédies*, ed. Louis Petit de Julleville, Paris 1899, f. d2ʳ⁻ᵛ. This Dedication to Condé was dropped when Montchrestien revised the texts in 1604, and replaced with one expressing the hope that the young Prince will imitate the virtues of the heroes of the tragedies. In both versions Montchrestien's moral concern is clear.

22. The dropping of 'vanité' in 1604 from the title did not indicate that Montchrestien had excised all reference to vainglory, but resulted from a new distaste for subtitles: he dropped all the original subtitles from the plays in the 1604 revision.

23. Ll. 130–5; references are to the 1604 version in the edition by Lancaster E. Dabney, Austin, Texas 1963.

24. Griffiths, *Dramatic Technique*, p. 67, considers that Montchrestien was interested only in the poetic content of David's speech, 'introduced for no other reason than to give (a) the picture of a man in love, (b) a description of a beautiful woman'. It seems to me that the tirade, besides offering poetic developments on those subjects, makes an important contribution to the theme of the pernicious effects of un-bridled passion.

25. *Pace* Griffiths, *Dramatic Technique*, p. 54, who describes the play as 'formless'.

26. See Rose-Marie Daele, *Nicolas de Montreux (Ollénix de Mont-Sacré), Arbiter of European Literary Vogues in the Late Renaissance*, New York 1946.

27. Summary in Dabney, pp. 14–16.

28. The play was apparently performed for Marguerite, for the Prologue addresses her in person. A performance would have been no small undertaking: the play totals some 6000 lines, and stage directions make such demands as 'quelques Bergers, menans des brebis et des aigneaux' (p. 193).

29. Summary in Lancaster, *Tragi-Comedy*, pp. 88–90.
30. Probably equally spectacular was *La Double Victoire, ou Eustache victorieux des Daces, et martyr, tragedie*, performed by the Jesuit college at Rouen in 1604; the text does not survive, but the printed programme was reproduced by P. le Verdier, ed., *Ancien Théâtre scolaire normand*, Rouen 1904. The matter seems not to have been the usual legend of Eustace: the author built an entirely new plot around the legendary names. The action involved several Kings and battles, and ranged over the length of the Roman Empire; it was supplemented by allegorical *intermèdes* and a ballet, and required a cast of 50.
31. As Ouyn scrupulously confides in the Argument, the play is not all his: as act IV it incorporates the one act of a projected play on Tobit published by Mlle des Roches in her *Oeuvres*, Paris 1579.
32. Summary in Dabney, pp. 28–33.
33. For example, when the Bible breaks into the narrative of the life of Tobit to record the death of Sarah's seventh husband (Tobit iii 7–17), Ouyn does not shift the scene to Sara's house (as the *VT* did) but remains with Tobit's family and shows only their reaction to the news.
34. In the play both father and son are named Thobie: for clarity, I shall use the English names, Tobit and Tobias respectively.
35. The lack of unity has already been pointed out by Faguet, *La Tragédie française*, p. 344.
36. In contrast to the practice in the *mystères*, violence is kept off the stage, Summary in Dabney, pp. 40–2.
37. Stone, p. 88, observes that the play seems to have been composed as a series of discrete lessons.
38. Cioranescu attributes the play to Jean de Virey, the author of the two *Maccabees*; I know no reason for doing so. La Vallière, vol. 1, p. 361, attributes it to 'le pasteur Calianthe'. The copy in the BL lacks the title-page, but has a MS copy, which names the author as Simon Fauconnier; this is crossed out and 'le pasteur Calianthe' substituted in another hand, possibly contemporary. Arbour, *Répertoire*, identifies Calianthe as a pseudonym of Gervais de Bazire, whose output consisted otherwise of pastorals.
39. The lack of a chorus at the end of act IV is unusual; it was perhaps omitted by an error of the printer's.
40. Jeanne apostrophises the Loire: 'Toy fleuve roul'argent aym-or porte bateaux' (III, p. 32).
41. For this reason I am tempted to speculate that the play was written for the professional stage, which set great store by such characteristics: see the discussion of the professional productions printed in Rouen, pp. 130–5 below.
42. Aux lecteurs, f. A4^r. The amphitheatre, which can still be visited, is now considered to be an ancient quarry, but was earlier thought to be of Roman construction.
43. Summary in Dabney, pp. 8–10.
44. Nancel nevertheless did not respect the Horatian proscription of violence, for in act v he showed the sack of the Shechemites' town: 'Pause; la ville se saccage' (stage direction, p. 76).

45. Forsyth comments drily: 'La morale qui anime la pièce...est assez peu logique', and bravely offers the hypothesis that *Dina* was intended to show that the sins of the Prince are visited on both him and his people (p. 247).
46. The sack of Jericho is staged: 'Pause; ils sonnent, tournent par sept fois, les murs tombent, ils mettent tout à sac' (stage direction, p. 145).
47. 'Pause; Icy Achan est lapidé par les soldats, avec ses petis enfans' (stage direction, p. 179).
48. Judges vi, vii; summary in Dabney, pp. 23–6.
49. Summary in Dabney, pp. 26–8.
50. II Samuel xiii; *Antiquities* vii 162–80. The motive of ambition may have been suggested by Thierry's *David*, but in that case Chrestien elaborated what was no more than a hint in Thierry's account.
51. Sigismond Ropartz, ed., *La Légende de Saint Armel*, Saint-Brieuc 1855; further details, particularly about the date of composition, are given by A. Guyot, 'La Tragèdie de S Armel par Messire Baudeville: étude historique et critique', Vannes 1910 (offprint from *Revue Morbihannaise*).
52. The next known Old-Testament play was the *Perfidie d'Aman*, p. 150 below.
53. The action is more broadly conceived than in La Taille's *Saül*, to which Billard seems to owe nothing.
54. According to Lancaster E. Dabney, *Claude Billard, Minor French Dramatist of the Early Seventeenth Century*, Baltimore, London and Paris 1931, Billard was born about 1549–50, and so was of the generation of Garnier and Matthieu. In the Preface of the 1610 edition Billard praises Ronsard and pours scorn on modern taste.
55. The battle is apparently fought on the stage.
56. This chorus was accidentally printed in act iv, where two choruses appear continuously, ff. 129^r–130^v.
57. Forsyth, p. 248, suggests that Billard was bound by his position as a courtier to insert comments approving of divine right.
58. Though few, Saül's speeches are long: he accounts for about one-third of the 1200 lines.
59. Performance conditions among the touring troupes were described above, p. 61. Relatively little is known about conditions in the indoor theatre that was struggling into existence at this time; its later development is better recorded (see below, pp. 161–7). In Paris, one purpose-built theatre existed, the Hôtel de Bourgogne, owned by the Confrères de la Passion, who had staged the *mystères* until the ban of 1548; otherwise stages were set up in *jeux de paume*. In either case the hall was long and narrow, with the stage across the narrow end. Boxes were ranged along the two long sides, and tiered seats up the back wall, while the floor was left free for standing spectators. Candles were used for lighting. Those in the auditorium were not extinguished during the performance. Those on the stage were fixed mostly round a proscenium arch; this, however, was not equipped with a curtain (except sometimes a curtain dropped to open the performance). There were no scene-changes: as in the *mystères*, the various sets required by the action were

represented by *mansions* all on view throughout the performance. See S. W. Deierkauf-Holsboer, *Le Théâtre du Marais*, 2 vols, Paris 1954–8, *Le Théâtre de l'Hôtel de Bourgogne*, 2 vols, Paris, 1968–70, and *L'Histoire de la mise en scène dans le théâtre français de 1600 à 1657*, 2nd ed., Paris 1960; Donald H. Roy, 'La Scène de l'Hôtel de Bourgogne', *RHT* XIV (1962), pp. 227–35; and Védier, *Dramaturgie néo-classique*.

60. See Deierkauf-Holsboer, *Le Théâtre de l'Hôtel de Bourgogne*, especially chapters II and III.

61. Roméo Arbour, 'Raphaël du Petit Val de Rouen et l'édition des textes littéraires en France (1587–1613)', *Revue française d'histoire du livre*, nouvelle série V (1975), pp. 87–141.

62. The authorship and dates of these plays have been settled as far as possible by Lancaster, *History* I, pp. 74–5.

63. Lacroix, *Soleinne* no. 958, also suggests that they were printed from old acting copies; Jules Marsan agrees, *La Pastorale dramatique en France à la fin du XVIe et au commencement du XVIIe siècle*, Paris 1905, p. 296.

64. When a text was printed it ceased to be the property of the troupe that had bought it from the author and could be performed by rival actors; a troupe would allow a text to be printed only when it could expect no more profit from performing. On this practice see Deierkauf-Holsboer, *Vie d'Alexandre Hardy*, pp. 87–8, 92–108.

65. 'Répertoire d'une troupe'.

66. One of these plays has already been discussed: Ville-Toustain's *Creation*, see pp. 34–5 above.

67. The play was declared lost by Lancaster, *History* I, pp. 83–4. A copy is available in the BN among the *imprimés* of the Rothschild collection.

68. Daniel's speech is taken from the Bible, where it has nothing to do with Susannah: Daniel ix.

69. Conviction is not absolute, however, for the stage world is not entirely coherent and independent of the spectator: at two points to understand what is happening he has to supply knowledge from outside the play (Daniel's intervention in act II and Susanne's apprehensions before her bath). The author similarly retained something of the conventions of the *mystères* in the intervention of the angel. However, neither this nor any other biblical play in the set seems to owe any debt to the corresponding section of the *VT*.

70. Perhaps the last revision of the text before it reached Cousturier was made for a performance before an audience drawn from the docks of Rouen, on a day when the troupe could call on the services of a magician to enliven proceedings!

71. It is an anagram of Pierre Mainfraie: *History* I, p. 75.

72. The plays exhibit sufficient similarities of style and tone to suggest that, if they had not all come from the same pen, they had all been revised by a single hand to suit the requirements of the troupe.

73. Similar qualities were exhibited in another play in this set, the *Comedie admirable intitulee la Merveille*. This resembled the old *miracles*, but is excluded from study here because it was not on a sacred subject.

A French captain escapes from the Soldam of Egypt with the help of a devil, then succeeds in recovering the pledge of his soul which he had given to the devil in exchange. He is helped to do so by God, who inspires him with the stratagem; but this is the only intervention of religion: like the others in the set, the play is an exotic and sensational secular drama with a satisfying ending.

74. *Mariamne* was written at some unknown date during the author's tours with professional troupes; historians generally ascribe it to the early part of his career, which started in the 1590s (see Deierkauf-Holsboer, *Vie d'Alexandre Hardy*, p. 155). Hardy sold his texts outright to his employers and they only permitted him to publish them years later, when they no longer had any use for them; how the version of *Mariamne* which has thus reached us compares with Hardy's earlier composition it is impossible to say.

75. *Antiquities* xv, 218–40; for a discussion of the sources and the many other plays on the subject, see M. J. Valency, *The Tragedies of Herod and Mariamne*, New York 1940.

7. The renewed vogue of the sacred chronicle

1. Of these plays one, *Richecourt*, is known to have been written for performance in a college (pp. 154–5 below). Soret's *S. Nicolas* was presented in Rheims cathedral (pp. 152–3 below). Prevost had a commission from his town (p. 138) and several other plays celebrated local patron saints, like the *mystères*. These were all no doubt performed on improvised stages, though possibly with some magnificence on occasion. Poytevin's *Saincte Catherine* (pp. 146–7 below), and the anonymous *Perfidie d'Aman* (p. 150 below), on the other hand, seem to have been designed for the professional stage in Paris. Other plays were perhaps intended for the touring troupes, performing often in the open air with rudimentary facilities.

2. As he indicates on the title-page.

3. *Hercule* and *Oedipe* (versions from Seneca), and *Turne*, qq.v. in *History* i, pp. 91–5.

4. Corneille has often been criticised for bothering with the conversions of Pauline and Félix after the death of Polyeucte; the example of *Sainte Agnes* suggests that it would have been more unsatisfactory had he not.

5. There are 15 in total; Martian and Censorin figure in 6 each, Simphronie in 7.

6. Vol. ii; Rosier transcribed ll. 9516–10598.

7. Although named Vincent in the title, he is known as Vincens throughout the action.

8. *Acta sanctorum*, 22 January; summary in *History* i, pp. 110–11.

9. The division into 5 acts is a meaningless formality; the play is conceived as a continuous narrative, for most acts begin where the previous one left off, with the same characters on the stage.

10. Summary in *History* i, p. 107.

11. Her speech is a transcription of the version given by Simon Meta-

phrastes, whom Boissin follows closely throughout (in Migne, *Patrologia graeco-latina*, vol. CXVI, cols 275–302).

12. Reputedly published at Liège in 1621: *History* I, p. 198.
13. Summary in *History*, I, pp. 186–8.
14. The play is followed by a farce about Gros-Guillaume, which may have been intended to be performed with it, or may simply have been added by the printer to fill up the last sheet.
15. These aspersions, for which there is no foundation in Jewish history, lend substance to the theory that the play was intended to refer to the assassination in 1617 of the favourite, Concini, who was satirised as a commoner (see *DBF*); Lancaster, however, considers this improbable, *History* I, p. 186.
16. *Acta sanctorum*, 17 September; summary in *History* I, pp. 199–200.
17. Lancaster's criticism of Coppée (*History* I, p. 199) for failing to exploit Pepin's dilemma between Alpayde and his wife and so make him the central figure is unfair: Coppée was not interested in a drama of dilemma, but in the *acta* of the saint. He followed the tradition of giving large roles to secondary figures so wholeheartedly, however, that Lancaster was misled into thinking of Pepin as the protagonist.
18. See *Gallia christiana*, vol. IX, cols 158–9.
19. Le Francq's version owes nothing to Virey's play on this subject.
20. I Maccabees i 16–19, 41–64, and II Maccabees vi, vii, ix; summary in La Vallière, vol. I, pp. 543–6.
21. The unnamed author was perhaps Dom Simplicien Gody, according to the editor of the edition of Saint-Nicolas-de-Port 1860.
22. Summary in *History* I, pp. 320–2.
23. Henri Busson, *La Pensée religieuse française de Charron à Pascal*, Paris 1933, p. 527.
24. 'Une Tragédie archaïsante à Plombières en 1628', *Annales de l'Est*, sixième série, IX (1958), pp. 187–94. M. Lebègue points out that only one copy survives, but has been unable to tell me where to locate it.
25. See *History* I, p. 679.
26. Reprinted by Jules Fréson, 'Un Mystère par Jean de Fies, curé de la paroisse de St-Remi, à Huy', in *Annales du Cercle hutois d'archéologie et d'histoire* XIII (1901), pp. 221–66; the date is given in de Fies's title on p. 224.
27. The location of a copy is given by Arbour, *Répertoire*: it was previously thought lost.
28. The rapid switching from one character to another was made possible by use of the system of simultaneous setting, as in the *mystères*.
29. See *Acta sanctorum*, 28 May. Troterel departs considerably from the Lives of the saint, and from the Chanson de Geste about him: these mostly concern war with the Saracens and are silent about the episode with Dorotée. Troterel was perhaps following a local variant of the legend. The literary sources concerning Guillaume (known also as Guillaume de Gellone) are studied by C. Revillout, 'Etude historique et littéraire sur l'ouvrage latin intitulé *Vie de S. Guillaume*', *Mémoires de la société archéologique de Montpellier* VI (1870–6), pp. 495–576.

30. The martyrdoms, the miracles and the battle are all presented on the stage.
31. Excluded from consideration here is the anonymous *Achab*, performed in a school in 1634, which survives only in a MS copy (Arsenal MS 3365): see *History* I, p. 681.

8. The early Classical period

1. *History* I, p. 703.
2. Stone, p. 156.
3. Cf. Chapter 2 above: between the publication of Ville-Toustain's *Creation* (*c.* 1613) and Picou's *Deluge* (1643) only one play was printed explicitly representing Christian doctrine, Coppée's *Passion*.
4. Corneille, 'Discours sur l'utilité des parties du poème dramatique', in *Oeuvres complètes*, ed. Charles Marty-Laveaux, vol. I, Paris, 1862, p. 20.
5. 'Naïf' is defined by Cotgrave (1611) as 'Livelie, quicke; naturall, kindlie, right, proper, true, no way counterfeit'.
6. Jean Chapelain, 'Lettre sur la règle des vingt-quatre heures', in *Opuscules critiques*, ed. A. C. Hunter, Paris 1936, p. 119. The letter is dated 1630, p. 113.
7. T. E. Lawrenson, *The French Stage in the Seventeenth Century: a Study in the Advent of the Italian Order*, Manchester 1957, and Védier, *Dramaturgie néo-classique*.
8. André Stegmann, *L'Héroïsme cornélien: genèse et signification*, 2 vols, Paris, 1968, vol. II, part I.
9. 'The Fate of the Humanist Aesthetic', chapter IV of his *French Humanist Tragedy*.
10. The advent of perspective on the stage has been studied by Kernodle, Lawrenson and Védier. The technique for creating perfectly convincing perspective scenes was described with mathematical precision by a number of theorists; their work is most conveniently consulted in B. Hewitt, ed., *The Renaissance Stage: Documents of Serlio, Sabbatini and Furttenbach*, Coral Gables 1958. The results may be seen in Mahelot's sketches of the sets he designed for the Hôtel de Bourgogne in the 1620s and 30s: *Le Mémoire de Mahelot, Laurent et d'autres décorateurs de l'Hôtel de Bourgogne et de la Comédie Française au XVIIe siècle*, ed. H. C. Lancaster, Paris 1920.
11. Védier, op. cit., p. 147.
12. The techniques are described in Hewitt, op. cit.
13. Védier, op. cit., pp. 91–146.
14. See the *Mémoire de Mahelot*; for Du Ryer's *Lisandre et Caliste*, for example, Mahelot required in one unified scene 'le petit Chastelet de la rue Sainct Jacques' and 'une hermitage sur une montaigne' (pp. 67–8; the result is illustrated between pp. 68 and 69).
15. Védier, op. cit., p. 50.
16. *La Pratique du théâtre*, ed. P. Martino, Algiers 1927, p. 101.
17. Ibid., p. 210.
18. A convenient summary account of physical conditions in Parisian theatres in the Classical period is provided by Chapter V of John

Lough's *Seventeenth-Century French Drama: the Background*, Oxford 1979.

19. Paris 1950.
20. 'Lettre sur la règle des vingt-quatre heures', *Opuscules critiques*, p. 116.
21. Ibid., p. 115.
22. The perspective stage framed by a proscenium arch was intended to promote realism, but by putting the actors into a separate box it established a barrier between characters and audience. The paradox inherent in this combination of a distancing effect with the demand for identification is explored by André Villiers, 'Illusion dramatique et dramaturgie classique', *XVIIe Siècle* LXXIII (1966), pp. 3–35.
23. Jules de la Mesnardière, *La Poëtique*, Paris 1640, pp. 70–1.
24. Ibid., p. 86.
25. Ibid., pp. 73–4.
26. Ibid., p. 73.
27. René Rapin, *Les Réflexions sur la poétique de ce temps et sur les ouvrages des poètes anciens et modernes*, ed. E. T. Dubois, Paris 1970, p. 70. Dubois places composition of the work between 1671 and 1673, pp. xxvi–xxxii.
28. Ibid., p. 99.
29. Octave Nadal, 'La Scène française d'Alexandre Hardy à Corneille', in Jean Tortel, ed., *Le Préclassicisme français*, Paris 1952, pp. 208–17: pp. 209–10.
30. Gordon Pocock, *Corneille and Racine: Problems of Tragic Form*, Cambridge 1973, p. 4.
31. La Bruyère, *Les Caractères*, 'Des Ouvrages de l'esprit' 51 (*Oeuvres*, ed. G. Servois, vol. I, part 2, Paris 1912, p. 138).
32. 'Défense de quelques piéces de théâtre de Mr. Corneille', in *Oeuvres en prose*, ed. René Ternois, 4 vols, Paris 1962–9, vol. IV, p. 429.
33. Ibid.
34. Antonin Artaud, 'Le Théâtre de la cruauté (deuxième manifeste)', in *Le Théâtre et son double*, Paris 1938, p. 131.
35. Jacques Truchet, *La Tragédie classique en France*, Paris 1975, p. 49.
36. The possible exceptions, described in Chapter 7 above, were the *Perfidie d'Aman* and Poytevin's *Saincte Catherine*, apparently professional productions in Paris; in the hope of pleasing the audience one subject was transformed into a comedy and the other into a romantic drama.
37. Social and ecclesiastical movements favouring the return of the sacred theatre to Paris are considered by Loukovitch, pp. 138–72; they are strictly peripheral to the present study.
38. The play's extraordinary success is detailed by N.-M. Bernardin, *Un Précurseur de Racine: Tristan l'Hermite, sieur du Solier (1601–1655), sa famille, sa vie, ses oeuvres*, Paris 1895, pp. 189–92.
39. Doubt surrounds the date of the first performance. Baro declared that he had been resisting attempts to persuade him to publish the play 'depuis dix ans' (Advertissement, f. ã4r); the Parfaict brothers consequently dated it 1639 (*Histoire du théâtre françois*, vol. VI, pp. 19–20). This has been generally accepted, though the ten years should perhaps be counted from the *privilège* (24 November 1648) as the date on which

Baro was writing, and 'dix ans' may in any case be a colloquial approximation. Loukovitch produced two documents suggesting that a 'renaissance du théâtre religieux à Paris' occurred between August and December 1637 (pp. 142-6). One names no play. The other records a discussion about a performance of a sacred play, *Le Favory solitaire*. This may be *Sainct Eustache*, for Eustache is a favourite at court before retreating into solitude. However, one speaker in the discussion mentions a chorus and quotes from memory some lines from the play: neither these lines nor a chorus appears in the printed text; but if the speaker's memory is not at fault, Baro may have introduced changes in the decade between composition and publication. While the documents do not prove that *Sainct Eustache* was performed in 1637, no other surviving play corresponds better to the title and description given. Even if it was not performed before 1639, *Sainct Eustache* was still the first in the Parisian renaissance of sacred drama.

40. Summary in La Vallière, vol. II, pp. 56-9.
41. Probably the Queen, Anne of Austria.
42. *Acta sanctorum*, 20 September.
43. See Bonjour, Offler and Potter, *A Short History of Switzerland*, Oxford 1952, pp. 181-3.
44. Summary in Pascoe, pp. 61-2.
45. Pascoe, loc. cit., draws attention to the lack of personal drama without allowing that its presence might not have suited Vallin's purpose.
46. The Dedication of the first edition mentions that the play had been known to the author's patron for four years, i.e. since 1638.
47. Sources are considered in *History* II, p. 227.
48. La Calprenède's *La Mort des enfans d'Herodes ou suite de Mariane*, *tragedie* (Paris 1639) was probably also first performed in 1638 (*History* II, p. 188). This was not a sacred play, being derived from *Antiquities* XVI rather than the Bible. La Calprenède attempted to follow the success of Tristan's *Mariane* by tracing Herod's subsequent execution of the two sons Mariamne bore him; the result is a tense and complex court intrigue, offering considerable pathos and psychological action.
49. H. C. Lancaster, *Pierre Du Ryer, Dramatist*, Washington 1912, p. 96. Du Ryer requested 'qu'on me sçache bon gré d'avoir au moins essayé de faire voir sur nostre Theatre la majesté des Histoires saintes', since 'j'ay eu cet avantage d'y faire paraistre le premier des subjets de cette nature avec quelque sorte d'applaudissement' (*Saül*, ed. H. C. Lancaster, Baltimore 1931, pp. 17-18; all references are to this edition). Assuming that Du Ryer had not simply forgotten Baro's *Sainct Eustache*, his claim suggests that we must revise our date for the first performance of that play; but by 'histoires saintes' Du Ryer probably meant biblical plays, excluding both Baro's *Sainct Eustache* and Tristan's *Mariane*. He naturally did not think of the *mystères* when he claimed that *Saül* was the first success on such a subject.
50. Thanks to Du Ryer's deliberate departure from the Bible to make Saül's punishment more just, it is difficult to see in the play the 'arraignment of Providence' discerned by Lancaster, *Du Ryer*, p. 97.

51. The first edition exists in three different states: for a discussion of which is to be treated as definitive, see the Catalogue of plays.

52. *History* II, p. 361.

53. This is not strictly a sacred subject, because More was beatified only in 1886; but it would have been as perverse to exclude him as Joan of Arc.

54. This play is the first of a small group written in prose, the others being the same author's *Sainte Caterine* (pp. 183–4 below) and La Calprenède's *Hermenigilde* (pp. 181–3 below); d'Aubignac's *Pucelle* (pp. 178–81 below), though published in prose, was performed in a versified text. The attempts to use prose were perhaps prompted by the preoccupation with realism, but the medium never gained acceptance outside comedy: *vraisemblance* as a *desideratum* was always tempered by the desire for heightened expression.

55. The play appeared simultaneously in verse and prose texts. The prose version is used here, since the versification was not d'Aubignac's work (see *History* II, p. 360) and only the prose edition included the Preface, and also a foreword by the printer recording the failure of the verse text in performance in 1641 (f. ā2ʳ).

56. Since the play is set in the courtroom, the unity of place required that she should be brought thither from the gaol for this scene, but there is no other reason why the angel could not appear to her in her cell: to preserve the unity of place d'Aubignac sacrificed *vraisemblance*, even though in his *Pratique du théâtre* he justified the unity principally on the ground that it was necessary if the all-important *vraisemblance* was to be preserved. In practice, it seems, the rule took priority over the principle which underlay it.

57. See W. S. Scott, *Jeanne d'Arc*, London 1974, pp. 113–17.

58. Loukovitch described the play as 'une sorte de moralité patriotique, plutôt qu'une tragédie religieuse' (p. 208).

59. The ultimate source, Gregory of Tours, is conveniently consulted in the *Acta sanctorum*, 13 April. See Pascoe, p. 124, for other sources, and Loukovitch, pp. 297–8, for a summary.

60. La Calprenède does not show the conversion of Recarède, who saved Spain from Arianism when he ascended the throne, though these events are prophesied by Hermenigilde (III i, p. 52); where the *fatistes* or the humanists would have traced the whole cycle by which God's will was accomplished, La Calprenède concentrated on the pathetic fate of the individual.

61. He is seconded by a sister, Matilde, invented by La Calprenède; she appears only in this scene, and merely echoes Recarède's arguments. Knowing that the arguments themselves would be repeated, La Calprenède attempted to introduce variety by putting them into various mouths.

62. *Acta sanctorum*, 25 November; summary in Loukovitch, pp. 303–4.

63. Confusingly, the saint is known throughout as Placide rather than Eustache; his wife and children likewise do not take new names at baptism.

64. Summary in Pascoe, pp. 95–8.

65. Stage directions, v ix, p. 88; references are to the 1644 4° edition.
66. With more vigour than justice, J. Lichtenstein wrote: 'Il y a du Corneille dans cette pièce: la plupart des défauts du grand poète. On y conspire, intrigue, combat, aime et hait. Aman est amoureux d'Esther. Son confident, Tharès, est épris de Thamar, suivante de la reine. Pourquoi cette complication bizarre? On l'ignore.' (*Racine, poète biblique*, Paris 1934, p. 100).
67. The other sources – the supplementary chapters of Esther printed in the Apocrypha, and *Antiquities* xi – agree with this order of events.
68. Pascoe's declaration that 'le personnage de Vasthi est superflu' (p. 58) is inaccurate; while Vasthi's presence may break the strict unity of action, for Du Ryer's purpose of extracting the maximum number of clashes from his source her role is very valuable.
69. The connection between Haman and the plot may have been suggested by ll. 1455–62 of Rivaudeau's *Aman*, but Lancaster denied that Du Ryer was influenced by the earlier play (*Du Ryer*, p. 107) and I have discovered no other sign of familiarity with Rivaudeau's text.
70. *Corneille et la dialectique du héros*, Paris 1963, pp. 247 and 251.
71. In the first three acts, Pauline and Polyeucte share only three scenes: i ii, in which Polyeucte leaves as fast as possible; ii iv, in which he ignores her fears; and ii v, a brief business scene. In these acts Pauline exchanges more lines with Sévère than with her husband.
72. Op. cit., p. 244.
73. Joseph Pineau, 'La Seconde Conversion de Polyeucte', *RHLF* lxxv (1975), pp. 531–54.
74. The question whether the hero has correctly understood the high ideals he claims to serve was a recurring preoccupation for Corneille. In *Le Cid* Rodrigue's devotion to honour seems right without question, since he is rewarded by winning Chimène's love by it; but in *Horace* the hero turns himself into a brute by blindly serving his ideal, and in many later plays (notably *Cinna, La Mort de Pompée, Sertorius*) Corneille was far from confident about the justification of apparently high-principled behaviour.
75. Pineau, op. cit., p. 549.
76. D. R. Clarke, in 'Politics and the Christian Ethic in the Theatre of Pierre Corneille, up to *La Mort de Pompée*', unpublished doctoral dissertation, Cambridge 1965, pp. 507–19, points out that it was the practice of the early Church to doubt the inspiration of any who seemed to seek martyrdom until miracles proved that his death had been welcome to God.
77. See Georges Mongrédien, *Dictionnaire biographique des comédiens français du XVIIe siècle suivi d'un inventaire des troupes (1590–1710) d'après des documents inédits*, Paris 1961.
78. Desfontaines suppressed Alexis's travels overseas and the passage of 34 years between conversion and death; see *Acta sanctorum*, 17 July, and Pascoe, pp. 102–4, for a summary.
79. Desfontaines perhaps derived from *Polyeucte* the idea of the pathetic sequence in which Olympie brushes off an importunate lover before meeting her husband from whom she is estranged by his faith; but,

whereas Desfontaines contrived this scene only for pathos, Corneille gave it a function in his argument as well.

80. Lancaster proposes 1644 as the date of first performance: *History* II, p. 536.

81. Summary in Pascoe, pp. 154–5.

82. Hardy's *Mariamne* seems to have started a minor fashion for endings in which the persecutor has a vision of his victim and begs forgiveness: this occurs also in Tristan's *Mariane*, La Serre's *Sainte Caterine*, and Cosnard's *Chastes Martirs*, qq.v. pp. 168–9, 183–4, 212. Such a conclusion was spectacular as well as gratifyingly just.

83. 1645 is the date usually accepted for the first performance. J. Trethewey and A. Howe, in 'Pierre Corneille's *Le Véritable* and Some Problems of Literary History', *French Studies* XXVI (1972), pp. 266–75, have shown that references to a play called *Le Véritable*, on which this dating is based, may not concern Rotrou's play; but if this weakens the reason for believing that it was first performed in 1645, no other date has yet been proposed.

84. Commenting on the vogue for plays containing inner plays, T. J. Reiss has written: 'The original stage illusion has been replaced by a game of multiple illusions, and it would seem that this game is more important than the story' (*Toward Dramatic Illusion: Theatrical Technique and Meaning from Hardy to 'Horace'*, New Haven and London 1971, p. 66). The comment is not without application to Rotrou's play.

85. Rotrou's careful contrasting of pagan and Christian values has been pointed out by numerous scholars. It is possible, however, to take this line of reasoning too far. J.-D. Hubert, in 'Le Réel et l'illusoire dans le théâtre de Corneille et dans celui de Rotrou', *Revue des sciences humaines* (1958), pp. 333–50, and in *Essai d'exégèse racinienne: les secrets témoins*, Paris 1956, pp. 12–15, and Jacques Morel, in *Jean Rotrou, dramaturge de l'ambiguïté*, Paris 1968, pp. 127–8, suggest that the first act provides a system of analogies with Genest's martyrdom, in which Maximin represents Christ and Diocletian God. This is to neglect the fact that the court's values are deliberately opposed to Genest's. To see Maximin as Christ and Diocletian as God is not helpful: the result is only confusion as to why in that case they should persecute him. The analogies described by Hubert and Morel would not help an audience as the play is performed, since at the end of this first act there is no hint that the ensuing action will concern a martyrdom, and so no reason for the spectator to seek Christian analogies in the court: this approach is illuminating, if at all, only to the critic who is not bound like the spectator to take the acts in order.

86. Cf. Alain Seznec, 'Le *Saint-Genest* de Rotrou: un plaidoyer pour le théâtre', *Romanic Review* LXIII (1972), pp. 171–89, who also explores the function of the theatre for Rotrou as a way to truth.

87. See pp. 9–10 of the Introduction to the edition of *Saint-Genest* by E. T. Dubois.

88. *Notice* to *Théodore* in *Oeuvres*, ed. Marty-Laveaux, vol. v, p. 3; see also *History* II, p. 516.

89. *Examen* to *Théodore*, p. 11.

90. Most conveniently consulted in the Marty-Laveaux edition, vol. v, pp. 103–11.

91. Henri Hauvette, 'Un Précurseur italien de Corneille, Girolamo Bartolommei', *Annales de l'Université de Grenoble* IX (1897), pp. 557–77, compares Bartolommei's two plays with *Polyeucte* and *Théodore*.

92. *Pratique du théâtre*, pp. 132–4; the conduct of the plot is also praised at p. 66. There was more than a little irony in d'Aubignac's description of the failure as Corneille's masterpiece, but this does not affect d'Aubignac's valuation of the qualities he singled out as desirable.

93. Professor Barnwell has suggested that Corneille habitually considered first the 'sujet' of his play – what we might call the theme – and only later found characters and actions to illustrate it: 'Some Reflections on Corneille's Theory of *Vraisemblance* as Formulated in the *Discours*', *Forum for Modern Language Studies* I (1965), pp. 295–310, particularly pp. 298–9.

94. Corneille was happy to use again the device which had been so successful in *Horace*.

95. The validity of the special revelations which the *illuminés* claimed to receive was the subject of much contemporary controversy: see Bremond's *Histoire littéraire du sentiment religieux en France*, especially vol. XI, *Le Procès des mystiques*.

96. Magnon's *Josaphat* (see pp. 207–8 below).

97. Loukovitch surveys the controversy over presenting sacred material on the stage, pp. 370–87; see also Phillips, *The Theatre and its Critics*, pp. 221–42.

98. For a summary history of the sacred theatre from 1650 to the Revolution, see Loukovitch, Chapters VIII and IX.

99. See *Biographie nationale de Belgique*. D'Ennetières wrote several lives of saints in his later years; this is the only one in dramatic form.

100. Aldegonde rightly does not share Théodore's dangerous confidence that any inspiration which seems to come from God dispenses her from obedience to the Law He imposes on all.

101. Father Binet's *La Vie admirable de la princesse Ste Aldegonde*, Paris 1626; the source was identified by Pascoe, pp. 78–9.

102. Lacroix, in *Soleinne* no. 1223, identifies him as de la Thorillière, later one of Molière's troupe; but this seems improbable since he was still a soldier at this date and took to the boards only ten years later (Lyonnet, *Dictionnaire des comédiens*). It is not certain in any case that T stood for the author's surname: it was common to add the locality of one's birth after one's surname, in which case he may have been D. L. Toulousain, if he was a native of the town where the play was published.

103. It is declared lost in *History* II, p. 663, Pascoe, p. 135, and Loukovitch, p. 323; a copy is available in the Arsenal.

104. Only Spire Pitou has studied the play, but he analyses its relationship to the Romance versions without giving any impression of the play itself in 'L'Autre Version dramatique de Josaphat au XVIIe siècle', *XVIIe Siècle* LXXXVIII (1970), pp. 19–29.

105. St John Damascene, *Vita Barlaam et Joasaph* (in Migne, *Patrologia*

cursus completus: patrologia graeca, vol. xcvi, Paris 1860); this had recently been reprinted in Latin, and also in two French translations.

106. According to St John, Joasaph was warned of the trick by a vision. I am unable to say why D.L.T. changed the agent to Zardan, since he was not shy of supernatural interventions in other scenes; perhaps he preferred not to devalue the supernatural by overuse.

107. According to St John, Abenner appointed Joasaph King of half his kingdom, hoping worldly cares would divert him from God, but Joasaph's exemplary Christian rule converted his father; later Joasaph succeeded on Abenner's death, but resigned his throne to join Barlaam in his desert hermitage. By altering this sequence D.L.T. avoided dissipating the pressures on Josaphat by the passage of time, made his triumph more sweeping, and made Abenner's conversion more sudden.

108. There was an earlier *mystère* on the subject, *Le Mystère du roy Avenir* by Jehan du Prieur (ed. A. Meiller, Geneva and Paris 1970); also a *Miracle de Notre Dame* (*Les Miracles de Nostre Dame*, ed. G. Paris and U. Robert, 8 vols, Paris 1876–93, vol. 3, pp. 241–304); and a number of romances (see Jean Sonet, S.J., *Le Roman de Barlaam et de Josaphat*, 3 vols, Paris and Namur 1949–52). D.L.T.'s treatment differs from the traditional works of piety by the thoroughgoing reorganisation of the material into a drama of human attitudes.

109. Both were dedicated to Bernard, duc d'Epernon; I have been unable to discover why he accepted dedications of similar plays in such quick succession. The connection between Magnon and d'Epernon is considered in *History* II, pp. 651–2.

110. Lancaster mentions a performance of *Josaphat* at the Hôtel de Bourgogne: *History* II, p. 652.

111. Summary in Pascoe, pp. 135–6.

112. See the title-page of the play.

113. Robert Denyau, *Vita sancti Clari*, Paris 1633. The *Acta sanctorum*, 4 November, mentions that Denyau also published French versions of this work in 1644, 1645, 1646; the Bollandists say these are very rare, and I have been unable to examine them, but the Bollandists assure that they add nothing to the Latin version. Mouffle acknowledged his debt to Denyau in a liminary poem, p. 8.

114. From the Book of Judith Bouvot omits only the accounts of Nebuchadnezzar's reign before the campaign against the Jews (Judith i) and of the campaign itself before the siege of Bethulia (Judith ii 21 – iii 10); he also omits the celebrations in Jerusalem after Holofernes's rout (Judith xvi 18 ff): otherwise he transcribes the whole. A version of the rest of Judith xvi (her canticle) is included after VI ii, which is headed 'Scene dernière': it is not clear from this if the canticle was to be included in the performance or was simply printed to fill the last gathering.

115. The play has been attributed to d'Aubignac, Saint-Germain and Desfontaines; Lancaster, in *History* II, pp. 668–9, dismisses these and claims that the author was an unknown provincial. The BN Catalogue enters one copy, Yf 4836, under the names of both d'Aubignac and Marthe Cosnard.

116. Summary in Loukovitch, pp. 396–9.
117. The author added the second favourite to the legend so as to imitate Auguste's consultation of the conspirators in Corneille's *Cinna*.
118. This version is independent of La Calprenède's, but owes much to Caussin's *Hermenigildus*, though Pascoe overstates the matter in concluding that it is almost a translation, pp. 127–30. The most important difference is that Olivier unlike the Jesuit allowed himself female characters; their roles are smaller than those La Calprenède supplied for the women in his version.
119. Summary in Pascoe, pp. 127–8.
120. Though his implication in the plot is a calumny, Hermenigilde does not deny that he is a Christian, and so the false accusation leads to his martyrdom.
121. For her exploits in her home of Lorraine, see Michaud.
122. Summary in Pascoe, pp. 141–3.
123. The action is extracted from the life of St Sebastian, in which Marcus and Marcellinus are minor figures (*Acta sanctorum*, 20 January). Sebastian is strictly irrelevant to their martyrdom, but Mme de Saint-Balmon felt unable to deny herself such an important figure, so he makes appearances at odd moments to deliver sermons (for an analysis of which see Busson, *La Pensée religieuse*, pp. 529–30).
124. The judges form another pair, but are differentiated. The parents are differentiated only by sex. Otherwise the members of each pair are indistinguishable: each takes alternate speeches with his other half, the two adding up to only one character.
125. As the author pointed out, the play derived from J.-P. Camus's fictional *Agathonphile* (Paris 1621), but I have included it briefly here because history at least provided the characters' names and Camus insisted that the story was true, p. 851. See P. Sage's introduction to his edition of excerpts, Geneva and Lille 1951, pp. xxix–xxxiv, for a discussion of the historical basis.
126. There is a ninth death: it is reported that Tryphine's old nurse died of sorrow on seeing her in chains, but not before she was herself converted.

Conclusion

1. Quoted above, pp. 164–5.
2. See for example La Mesnardière, quoted above, p. 165.
3. Euripides perhaps did not share the confidence of Aeschylus and Sophocles that our sufferings correspond to a divine justice, however inscrutable, that must be accepted. On this question see, among many other studies, Leo Aylen, *Greek Tragedy and the Modern World*, London 1964, and Hugh Lloyd-Jones, *The Justice of Zeus*, Berkeley and London 1971.

Bibliography

(i) Works of reference

Acta sanctorum, 2nd ed., Paris 1863 – (in progress)

Arbour, Roméo: *L'Ere baroque en France: répertoire des éditions de textes littéraires*, 4 vols, Geneva 1977–80 (Histoire des idées et critique littéraire, no. 165)

Barbier, A.-A.: *Dictionnaire des ouvrages anonymes*, 3rd ed., 4 vols, Paris 1872–9

Baudrier, Henri-Louis: *Bibliographie lyonnaise*, 12 vols, Lyons 1895–1921

Biographie nationale de Belgique, 28 vols, Brussels 1866–1944; supplements in progress

Bossuat, Robert: *Manuel bibliographique de la littérature française du moyen âge*, Melun 1951

Brunet, Jacques-Charles: *Manuel du libraire et de l'amateur de livres*, 6 vols, Paris 1860–5, and *Supplément*, 2 vols, Paris 1878–80

Chaix, Paul: *Recherches sur l'imprimerie à Genève de 1550 à 1564*, Geneva 1954 (THR xvi)

Cioranescu, Alexandre: *Bibliographie de la littérature française du XVIe siècle*, Paris 1959

Bibliographie de la littérature française du XVIIe siècle, 3 vols, Paris 1965–6

Corrard de Breban, M.: *Recherches sur l'établissement et l'exercice de l'imprimerie à Troyes*, 3rd ed., Paris 1873

Cotgrave, Randle: *A Dictionarie of the French and English Tongues*, London 1611

Dictionnaire de biographie française, Paris 1933 – (in progress)

Dictionnaire historique et biographique de la Suisse, 7 vols, Neuchâtel 1921–33

Du Verdier, Antoine: *Les Bibliothèques françoises de La Croix du Maine et de Du Verdier*, ed. Rigoley de Juvigny, 6 vols, Paris 1772–3

Gallia christiana, 16 vols, Paris 1715–1865

Gardy, Frédéric: *Bibliographie des oeuvres théologiques, littéraires, historiques et juridiques de Théodore de Bèze*, Geneva 1960 (THR xli)

Haag, E. and E.: *La France Protestante*, 10 vols, Paris 1846–58
2nd ed., 6 vols, Paris 1877–88 (incomplete: A-G only published)

Havre, G. van: *Marques typographiques des imprimeurs et libraires anversois*, 2 vols, Antwerp and Ghent 1883–4

Heitz, Paul: *Genfer Buchdrucker- und Verlagerzeichen in XV., XVI., und XVII. Jahrhundert*, Strasbourg 1908

Lacroix, Paul: *Bibliothèque dramatique de M. de Soleinne* and *Suppléments*, 5 vols, Paris 1843–4

La Vallière, Louis-César de la Baume le Blanc, duc de: *Bibliothèque du théâtre françois depuis son origine*, 3 vols, Dresden 1768

Lepreux, G.: *Gallia typographica, ou répertoire biographique et chronologique de tous les imprimeurs de France depuis les origines de l'imprimerie jusqu'à la Révolution*, 7 vols, Paris 1903–13

Lyonnet, Henry: *Dictionnaire des comédiens français*, 2 vols, Paris, no date

Marques typographiques des imprimeurs et libraires qui ont exercé dans les Pays-Bas, 2 vols, Ghent 1894

Michaud: *Biographie universelle ancienne et moderne*, 2nd ed., 45 vols, Paris 1843–65

Mongrédien, Georges: *Dictionnaire biographique des comédiens français du XVIIe siècle suivi d'un inventaire des troupes (1590–1710) d'après des documents inédits*, Paris 1961

Muller, Jean: *Dictionnaire abrégé des imprimeurs/éditeurs français du XVIe siècle*, Baden-Baden 1970

Parfaict, F. and C.; *Histoire du théâtre françois depuis son origine jusqu'à présent*, 15 vols, Paris, 1734–49

Picot, Emile: *Bibliographie cornélienne*, Paris 1876

Quérard, J.-A. *Les Supercheries littéraires dévoilées*, 2nd ed., 3 vols, Paris 1869–70

Renouard, Philippe: *Les Marques typographiques parisiens du XVe et XVIe siècles*, Paris 1926

 Répertoire des imprimeurs parisiens, libraires, fondeurs de caractères et correcteurs d'imprimerie depuis l'introduction de l'imprimerie à Paris jusqu'à la fin du XVIe siècle, 2nd ed., Paris 1965

Répertoire bibliographique des livres imprimés en France au XVIe siècle, Baden-Baden 1968 – (in progress)

Silvestre, Louis-Catherine: *Marques typographiques*, Paris 1853–67

Vigoureux, F.: *Dictionnaire de la Bible*, 5 vols, Paris 1895–1912

(ii) Non-dramatic sources of plays

Binet, Etienne, S.J.: *La Vie admirable de la princesse Ste Aldegonde, fondatrice des Dames chanoinesses de Mauberge*, Paris 1626

Camus, J.-P.: *Agathonphile*, Paris 1621; and ed. P. Sage, Geneva and Lille 1951 (TLF)

Caussin, Nicolas, S.J.: *La Cour sainte*, Paris 1645

Denyau, Robert: *Vita sancti Clari*, Paris 1633

John of Damascus, saint: *Vita Barlaam et Joasaph*, in Migne, ed., *Patrologiae cursus completus: patrologia graeca*, vol. xcvi, Paris 1860

Josephus, Flavius: *The Jewish Antiquities*, trans. H. St J. Thackeray, R. Marcus, A. Wikgren, L. H. Feldman, 6 vols, London and Cambridge Mass. 1967–9 (Loeb Classical Library)

Simon Metaphrastes: *Opera*, in Migne, ed., *Patrologiae cursus completus: patrologia graeca*, vol. CXVI, Paris 1864

(iii) Contemporary authorities

Aubignac, François Hédelin, abbé d': *La Pratique du théâtre*, ed. P. Martino, Algiers 1927

Aubigné, Agrippa d': *Les Tragiques*, ed. A. Garnier and J. Plattard, 4 vols, Paris 1932 (STFM)

Aymon, Jean: *Tous les Synodes nationaux des Eglises réformées de France*, 2 vols, The Hague 1710

Boileau-Despréaux, Nicolas: *L'Art poétique*, ed. C. H. Boudhors, Paris 1939

Chapelain, Jean: *Opuscules critiques*, ed. A. C. Hunter, Paris 1936

Hewitt, Barnard, ed.: *The Renaissance Stage: Documents of Serlio, Sabbatini and Furttenbach*, Coral Gables Fla. 1958.

La Bruyère, Jean de: *Les Caractères*, in *Oeuvres*, ed. G. Servois, vol. I, part 2, Paris 1912

La Mesnardière, Jules de: *La Poëtique*, Paris 1640

Lancaster, Henry Carrington, ed.: *Le Mémoire de Mahelot, Laurent et d'autres décorateurs de l'Hôtel de Bourgogne et de la Comédie Française au XVIIe siècle*, Paris 1920.

Laudun, Pierre de, sieur d'Aigaliers: *L'Art poétique françois*, Paris 1597

Rapin, René; *Les Réflexions sur la poétique de ce temps et sur les ouvrages des poètes anciens et modernes*, ed. E. T. Dubois, Paris 1970 (TLF 160)

Saint-Evremond, C. de: *Oeuvres en prose*, ed. René Ternois, 4 vols, Paris 1962–9 (STFM)

Tragédie du Roy Franc-Arbitre, Villefranche 1559

Viret, Pierre: *Le Monde à l'Empire et le monde démoniacle, fait par dialogues*, Geneva 1561

Young, Peter, letter to Bèze, Bodleian MS Smith 77 p. 161.

(iv) Other plays, including editions of sacred plays not mentioned in the Catalogue

Achab, Arsenal MS 3365

Le Mystère des Actes des apôtres, 2 vols, Paris 1540

Anouilh, Jean: *L'Alouette*, Paris 1953

Le Mystère de Sainte Barbe, tragédie bretonne, ed. Emile Ernault, *Archives de Bretagne* III (1885)

Bartolommei, Girolamo: *Tragedie*, 2nd ed., Florence 1665

Baudeville: *La Légende de Saint Armel*, ed. Sigismond Ropartz, Saint-Brieuc 1855

Behourt, Jean, S.J.: *Hypsicratée ou la magnanimité, tragédie*, Rouen 1604
La Polyxène, tragicomédie, Rouen 1598

Brecht, Bertolt: *Plays*, 2 vols, London 1960–2

Buchanan, George: *Baptistes, sive calumnia, tragoedia*, London 1577
Jephthes, sive votum, tragoedia, Paris 1554

Caussin, Nicolas, S.J.: *Tragoediae sacrae*, 2 vols, Paris 1620

Chrestien, Nicolas: *Les Amantes, ou la grande pastorelle, enrichie de plusieurs*

*belles et rares inventions et relevee d'intermedes Heroyques à l'honneur
des François*, Rouen 1613

*Le Concil de Basle (1434): les origines du théâtre réformiste et partisan en
France*, ed. Jonathan Beck, Leiden 1979 (Studies in the History of
Christian Thought, 18)

Coppée, Denis: *La Sanglante Bataille d'entre les Impérieux et Bohèmes,
donnée au Parc de l'Estoille, la reddition de Prague, et ensemble l'origine
du trouble de Bohème, tragédie*, Liège 1624

Corneille, Pierre: *Polyeucte, tragédie*, ed. Richard Sayce, Oxford 1949

Des Roches, Catherine: *Tobie*, in *Les Oeuvres de Mes-dames des Roches mère
et fille*, 2nd ed., Paris 1579

Du Prieur, Jehan: *Le Mystère du roy Avenir*, ed. A. Meiller, Geneva and Paris
1970 (TLF 157)

Du Ryer, Pierre: *Lisandre et Caliste*, Paris 1932

Euripides: *The Complete Greek Tragedies*, ed. D. Greene and R. Lattimore,
2 vols, Chicago and London 1969 (third impression)

Fies, Jean de, *Tragicomédie de S. Rémy*, ed. Jules Fréson, 'Un Mystère par
Jean de Fies, curé de la paroisse de St-Remi, à Huy', in *Annales du
Cercle hutois d'archéologie et d'histoire* XIII (1901), pp. 221–66.

Foxe, John: *Christus triumphans, comeodia apocalyptica*, Basle 1556

Gnapheus, G.: *Acolastus: de filio prodigi comeodia*, Antwerp 1529

Greban, Arnoul: *Le Mystère de la Passion*, ed. Omer Jodogne, Brussels 1965
(Mémoires of the Académie royale de Belgique, collection in-4, deuxième
série, tome XII, fasc. 3)

Hardy, Alexandre: *Théâtre*, ed. E. Stengel, 5 vols, Marburg and Paris 1883–4

Hersent, Charles: *La Pastorale sainte*, Paris 1635

Heyns, Pierre: *Susanne, Miroir des mesnageres*, Amsterdam 1595

La Calprenède, Gauthier de Costes, sieur de: *La Mort des enfans d'Herodes
ou suite de Mariane, tragedie*, Paris 1639

La Taille, Jean de: *Oeuvres*, ed. René de Maulde, 4 vols, Paris 1878–82
 Saül le furieux; La Famine, ou les Gabéonites, ed. Elliott Forsyth, Paris 1968
(STFM)

Macropedius, Georgius: *Omnes Georgii Macropedii Fabulae comicae*, 2 vols,
Utrecht 1552–3

Mairet, Jean de: *L'Athénaïs, tragi-comédie*, Paris 1642
 La Sophonisbe, tragédie, Paris 1635

Mauger, abbé Nicole: *Le Lavement des pieds*, ed. P. Le Verdier, Evreux 1893
(offprint from *Revue Catholique de Normandie*)

La Comedie admirable intitulee la Merveille, Rouen *c.* 1612–14

Michel, Jehan: *Le Mystère de la Passion*, ed. O. Jodogne, Gembloux 1959

Les Miracles de Nostre Dame, ed. Gaston Paris and Ulysse Robert, 8 vols,
Paris 1876–93 (SATF)

Montchrestien, Antoine de: *Tragédies*, ed. Louis Petit de Julleville, Paris 1899

Naogeorgus (i.e. Thomas Kirchmayer): *Mercator*, Augsburg 1540

Nichols, Peter: *A Day in the Death of Joe Egg*, London 1967

Lystoyre de monseigneur sainct Sebastien, ed. François Rabut, Chambéry 1872

Seneca, *Tragedies*, trans. Frank Justus Miller, 2 vols, Cambridge Mass. 1968
(Loeb Classical Library)

Stone, Donald, ed.: *Four Renaissance Tragedies*, Cambridge Mass. 1966

Tiron, Antoine: *L'Histoire de l'Enfant prodigue*, Antwerp 1564
Tristan l'Hermite, François: *La Mariane*, ed. Jacques Madeleine, Paris 1917
Troterel, Pierre de: *Tragédie de sainte Agnés*, ed. Deschamps, Paris 1875
   (Librairie des bibliophiles)
Le Mistére du Viel Testament, ed. James de Rothschild and Emile Picot,
   6 vols, Paris 1878–91 (SATF)
Vivre, Gérard de: *Comédie de la fidelité nuptiale*, Antwerp 1577

   (v) Modern authorities

Abraham, Claude K.: *The Strangers: the Tragic World of Tristan l'Hermite*,
   Gainsville Fla. 1966 (University of Florida Monographs, Humanities
   no. 3)
Adam, Antoine: *Histoire de la littérature française au XVIIe siècle*, 5 vols,
   Paris 1948–56
Adkins, Arthur W. H.: *Merit and Responsibility: a Study in Greek Values*,
   Oxford 1960
Angers, Julien-Aymard d': '*Polyeucte*, tragédie chrétienne', *XVIIe Siècle* LXXV
   (1967), pp. 49–69
Arbour, Roméo: 'Raphaël du Petit Val de Rouen et l'édition des textes
   littéraires en France (1587–1613)', *Revue française d'histoire du livre*,
   nouvelle série v (1975), pp. 87–141
Artaud, Antonin: *Le Théâtre et son double*, Paris 1938
Aylen, Leo: *Greek Tragedy and the Modern World*, London 1964
Baelen, Jacqueline van: *Rotrou: le héros tragique et la révolte*, Paris 1965
Balmas, Enea: *Un Poeta del Rinascimento francese: Etienne Jodelle: la sua
   vita, il suo tempo*, Florence 1962 (Biblioteca dell'Archivum Romanicum,
   series I, vol. 66)
Barbier, Pierre: 'Le Théâtre militant au XVIe siècle', in his *Etudes sur notre
   ancienne poésie*, Bourg 1875
Barnwell, H. T.: 'Some Reflections on Corneille's Theory of *Vraisemblance*
   as Formulated in the *Discours*', *Forum for Modern Language Studies* I
   (1965), pp. 295–310
Beaujour, Michel: '*Polyeucte* et la monarchie de droit divin', *French Review*
   XXXVI (1962–3), pp. 443–9
Bellier-Dumaine, Charles: 'Thomas Le Coq et sa tragédie de *Caïn* 1580',
   Normannia XI (1938), pp. 181–230
Bernardin, Napoléon-Maurice: *Un Précurseur de Racine: Tristan l'Hermite,
   sieur du Solier (1601–1655), sa famille, sa vie, ses oeuvres*, Paris 1895
Boas, Frederic Samuel: *University Drama in the Tudor Age*, Oxford 1914
Bolgar, R. R.: *The Classical Heritage and its Beneficiaries: from the Caro-
   lingian Age to the End of the Renaissance*, London 1954
Bonet-Maury, G. '*Le Monde malade et mal pensé*, ou la comédie protestante
   au XVIe siècle', *BSHP* XXXV (1886), pp. 210–22
Bonjour, E., Offler, H. S., and Potter, G. R.: *A Short History of Switzerland*,
   Oxford 1952
Bradbrook, M. C.: *Themes and Conventions of Elizabethan Tragedy*, Cam-
   bridge 1935

Bray, René: *La Formation de la doctrine classique en France*, Dijon 1927

Bremond, Henri: *Histoire littéraire du sentiment religieux en France depuis la fin des guerres de religion jusqu'à nos jours*, 12 vols, Paris 1916–36

Brereton, Geoffrey: *French Tragic Drama in the Sixteenth and Seventeenth Centuries*, London 1973

Brooks, William S.: 'Polyeucte's Martyrdom – "une autre explication"', *MLR* LXXII (1977), pp. 802–10

Buffum, Imbrie: *Studies in the Baroque from Montaigne to Rotrou*, New Haven 1957 (Yale Romanic Studies, series II, no. 4)

Bulard, Marcel: 'Un Manuscrit du Mystère de la Passion découvert en Savoie', *Mélanges de la Société toulousaine d'études classiques* I (1946), pp. 245–63

Busson, H.: *La Pensée religieuse française de Charron à Pascal*, Paris 1933

Calvet, Jean: *Polyeucte de Corneille: étude et analyse*, Paris 1932

Cave, Terence C.: *Devotional Poetry in France, c. 1570–1613*, Cambridge 1969

Chamard, Henri: 'Le Collège de Boncourt et les origines du théâtre classique', in *Mélanges Abel Lefranc*, Paris 1936, pp. 246–60

Charlton, H. B.: *The Senecan Tradition in Renaissance Tragedy*, Manchester 1946 (University of Manchester Publications, English series, no. 24)

Charmasse, Anatole de: *François Perrin, poète français du XVIe siècle; et sa vie par Guillaume Colletet publiée d'après le manuscrit aujourd'hui détruit de la Bibliothèque du Louvre*, Autun and Paris 1887 (Mémoires de la Société éduenne, nouvelle série, tome XV)

Charpentier, Françoise: 'Le Thème d'Aman dans la propagande huguenote: à propos de l'édition critique de l'*Aman* de Rivaudeau par K. Cameron', *BHR* XXXIII (1971), pp. 377–83

Chocheyras, Jacques: 'Les Editions de la *Passion* de Jehan Michel au XVIe siècle', *Romania* 1966, pp. 175–93

Le Théâtre religieux en Dauphiné du moyen âge au XVIIIe siècle (domaine français et provençal), Geneva 1975 (Publications romanes et françaises, no. CXXVIII)

Le Théâtre religieux en Savoie au XVIe siècle, Geneva 1971 (Publications romanes et françaises, no. CIX)

Clarke, David Robert: 'Politics and the Christian Ethic in the Theatre of Pierre Corneille, up to *La Mort de Pompée*', unpublished doctoral dissertation (1965), Cambridge University Library

Cohen, Gustave: *Histoire de la mise en scène dans le théâtre religieux français du moyen âge*, Paris 1906

'Le Personnage de Marie-Madeleine dans le drame religieux français au moyen âge', *Convivium* XXIV (1956), pp. 141–63

Le Théâtre en France au moyen âge, 2 vols, Paris 1928–31

Currie, Peter: *Corneille: 'Polyeucte'*, London 1960 (Studies in French Literature no. 3)

Dabney, Lancaster E.: *Claude Billard, Minor French Dramatist of the Early Seventeenth Century*, Baltimore, London and Paris 1931 (Johns Hopkins Studies in Romance Literatures and Languages, no. XIX)

French Dramatic Literature in the Reign of Henri IV: a Study of the Extant Plays Composed in French between 1589 and 1610, Austin Texas 1952

Daele, Rose-Marie: *Nicolas de Montreux (Ollénix de Mont-Sacré), Arbiter of European Literary Vogues in the Late Renaissance*, New York 1946

Dagens, Jean: *Bérulle et les origines de la restauration catholique, 1575–1611*, Paris 1952

Dainville, François de, S.J.: *Les Jésuites et l'éducation de société française*, 2 vols, Paris 1940

'Lieux de théâtre et salles des actions dans les Collèges de Jésuites de l'ancienne France', *RHT* II (1950), pp. 185–90

Daniel, George Bernard: *The Development of the 'Tragédie nationale' in France from 1552 to 1800*, Chapel Hill 1964 (University of North Carolina Studies in Romance Languages and Literatures, no. 45)

Dawson, F. K.: 'An Idea of Tragedy: Tristan l'Hermite's *Mariane* and *La Mort de Sénèque*', *Nottingham French Studies* II no. 2 (1963), pp. 2–10

Deierkauf-Holsboer, Sophie Wilma: *L'Histoire de la mise en scène dans le théâtre français de 1600 à 1657*, 2nd ed., Paris 1960

Le Théâtre de l'Hôtel de Bourgogne, 2 vols, Paris 1968–70

Le Théâtre du Marais, 2 vols, Paris 1954–8

Vie d'Alexandre Hardy poète du roi 1572–1632, 2nd ed., Paris 1972

Dodds, Eric Robertson: *The Greeks and the Irrational*, Berkeley 1951 (Sather Classical Lectures, no. 25)

'On Misunderstanding the *Oedipus Rex*', *Greece and Rome*, second series XIII (1966), pp. 37–49

Doubrovsky, Serge: *Corneille et la dialectique du héros*, Paris 1963

Dupont, Leopold C.: 'Denis Coppée: tradition religieuse, actualité politique et exotisme dans le théâtre à Liège au temps du Baroque', *Revue belge de philologie et d'histoire* LV (1977), pp. 791–840.

Elliott, John R., Jr: 'The Sacrifice of Isaac as Comedy and Tragedy', *Studies in Philology* LXVI (1969), pp. 36–59

Engel, C.-E.: 'Colligny dans la littérature', *Actes du Colloque de l'Amiral Colligny dans son temps*, Paris 1964, pp. 377–88

Faguet, Emile: *La Tragédie française au XVIe siècle*, 2nd ed., Paris and Leipzig 1897

Falk, Eugene H.: *Renunciation as a Tragic Form: a Study of Five Plays*, Minneapolis 1954

Ford, Philip J.: 'The Poetical Works of George Buchanan Before his Final Return to Scotland', unpublished doctoral dissertation (1976), Cambridge University Library

Forsyth, Elliott: *La Tragédie française de Jodelle à Corneille (1553–1640): le thème de la vengeance*, Paris 1962

Frank, Grace: *The Medieval French Drama*, Oxford 1954

Frankish, C. R.: 'The Theme of Idolatry in Garnier's *Les Juifves*', *BHR* xxx (1968), pp. 65–83

Fumaroli, Marc: 'Rhétorique et dramaturgie: le statut du personnage dans la tragédie classique', *RHT* XXIV (1972), pp. 223–50

Gable, Anthony Terence: 'The Rise of Irregular French Tragedy (1580–1630)', unpublished doctoral dissertation (1972), Cambridge University Library

Ginestier, Paul: '*Polyeucte*, essai de critique esthétique', *Revue d'esthétique* 1960, pp. 128–39

336   Bibliography

Gofflot, L.-V.: *Le Théâtre au collège du moyen âge à nos jours*, Paris 1907

Gombrich, Sir Ernst: *Art and Illusion: a Study in the Psychology of Pictorial Representation*, 5th ed., London 1977

Gras, Maurice: *Robert Garnier, son art et sa méthode*, Geneva 1965 (THR LXXII)

Griffiths, Richard: *The Dramatic Technique of Antoine de Montchrestien: Rhetoric and Style in French Renaissance Tragedy*, Oxford 1970
'The Influence of Formulary Rhetoric upon French Renaissance Tragedy', *MLR* LIX (1964), pp. 201–8

Guyot, A.: 'La Tragédie de Saint Armel par Messire Baudeville: étude historique et critique', Vannes 1910 (offprint from *Revue Morbihannaise*)

Hall, Kathleen M., and Smith, Christopher Norman: 'The Early Editions of the Tragedies of Jean de la Taille', *Kentucky Romance Quarterly* XX (1973), pp. 75–88

Hardison, O. B., Jr: *Christian Rite and Christian Drama in the Middle Ages*, Baltimore 1965

Hauvette, Henri: 'Un Précurseur italien de Corneille, Girolamo Bartolommei', *Annales de l'Université de Grenoble* IX (1897), pp. 557–77

Hérelle, Georges: *Les Théâtres ruraux en France (langue d'oc et langue d'oïl) depuis le XIVe siècle jusqu'à nos jours*, Paris 1930 (offprint from *Bulletin de la Société des sciences, lettres, arts et d'études régionales de Bayonne*)

Herland, L.: 'La Notion du tragique chez Corneille', *Mélanges de la Société toulousaine d'études classiques* I (1946), pp. 267–84

Hubert, J.-D.: *Essai d'exégèse racinienne: les secrets témoins*, Paris 1956
'Le Réel et l'illusoire dans le théâtre de Corneille et dans celui de Rotrou', *Revue des sciences humaines* (1958), pp. 333–50

Jeffery, Brian: *French Renaissance Comedy, 1552–1630*, Oxford 1969

Jondorf, Gillian: *Robert Garnier and the Themes of Political Tragedy in the Sixteenth Century*, Cambridge 1969

Jonker, G. D.: *Le Protestantisme et le théâtre de langue française au XVIe siècle*, Groningen 1939

Keegstra, Pieter: *Abraham sacrifiant de Théodore de Bèze et le théâtre calviniste de 1550 à 1565*, The Hague 1928

Kernodle, George R.: *From Art to Theatre: Form and Convention in the Renaissance*, Chicago 1944

Kitto, H. D. F.: *Form and Meaning in Drama: a Study of Six Greek Plays and of Hamlet*, 2nd ed., London 1964
Greek Tragedy: a Literary Study, 3rd ed., London 1966

Konigson, Elie: *La Représentation d'un Mystère de la Passion à Valenciennes en 1547*, Paris 1969

Lancaster, Henry Carrington: *Pierre Du Ryer, Dramatist*, Washington 1912 (Carnegie Institute Publication, no. 171)
The French Tragi-Comedy: its Origin and Development from 1552 to 1628, Baltimore 1907
'Alexandre Hardy et ses rivaux', *RHLF* XXIV (1917), pp. 414–21
A History of French Dramatic Literature in the Seventeenth Century, 9 vols, Baltimore, London and Paris 1929–42
'La Calprenède, Dramatist', *Modern Philology* XVIII (1920–1), pp. 121–41, 345–60

Lanson, Gustav, 'Etudes sur les origines de la tragédie classique en France',
RHLF x (1903), pp. 177–231, 413–36

'L'Idée de la tragédie en France avant Jodelle', RHLF xi (1904), pp. 541–85

Lawrenson, T. E.: *The French Stage in the Seventeenth Century: a Study in the Advent of the Italian Order*, Manchester 1957

Lawton, H. W.: *Handbook of French Renaissance Dramatic Theory*, Manchester 1949

Lebègue, Raymond: *Le Mystère des Actes des apôtres: contribution à l'étude de l'humanisme et du protestantisme au XVIe siècle*, Paris 1929

'Le Diable dans l'ancien théâtre religieux', *Cahiers de l'association internationale des études françaises* iii–iv (1953), pp. 97–105

Etudes sur le théâtre français, 2 vols, Paris 1977–8

'L'Evolution du théâtre dans les provinces du Nord', in François Lesure, ed., *La Renaissance dans les provinces du Nord*, Paris 1956, pp. 117–26

'Fêtes religieuses dramatiques en France sous la monarchie absolue', *Maske und Kothurn* x (1964), pp. 217–24

Robert Garnier: Les Juifves, Paris 1958 (Les Cours de Sorbonne)

'Noël Georges et le théâtre rural en Haute-Bretagne', in *Mélanges d'histoire littéraire offerts à Daniel Mornet*, Paris 1951, pp. 27–36

'Grâce et liberté dans les tragédies au temps de Louis XIII', in *Le Théâtre tragique*, ed. J. Jacquot, Paris 1962

'L'Influence du théâtre néo-latin sur le théâtre sérieux en langue française', *Humanisme et Renaissance* vi (1939), pp. 41–7

'Notes sur la tragédie française', BHR ix (1947), pp. 190–4

'Persistance, altération, disparition des traditions dramatico-religieuses en France', in *Dramaturgie et société: rapports entre l'oeuvre théâtrale, son interprétation et son public aux XVIe et XVIIe siècles*, ed. J. Jacquot, 2 vols, Paris 1968, vol. i, pp. 247–53

'Quelques survivances de la mise en scène médiévale', *Mélanges Gustave Cohen*, Paris 1950

'De la Renaissance au classicisme: le théâtre baroque en France', BHR ii (1942), pp. 161–84

'Le Répertoire d'une troupe française à la fin du xvie siècle', RHT i (1948), pp. 9–24

'La Représentation des tragédies au xvie siècle', *Mélanges Henri Chamard*, Paris 1951, pp. 199–204

'Rotrou, dramaturge baroque', RHLF l (1950), pp. 379–84

'Les Survivances des personnages des mystères français', *Studi in onore di Carlo Pellegrini*, Turin 1963, pp. 205–16 (Biblioteca di studi francesi, no. 2)

'Tableau de la comédie française de la Renaissance', BHR viii (1946), pp. 271–344

'Tableau de la tragédie française de 1573 à 1610', BHR v (1944), pp. 375–93

'Le Théâtre provincial en France', *Helicon* i (1938), pp. 141–9

'Une Tragédie archaïsante à Plombières en 1628', *Annales de l'Est*, sixième série ix (1958), pp. 187–94

La Tragédie française de la renaissance, Brussels and Paris 1954

La Tragédie religieuse en France: les débuts, 1514–1573, Paris 1929 (Bibliothèque littéraire de la Renaissance, nouvelle série, vol. xvii)

'La Vie dramatique en province au xviie siècle', *XVIIe Siècle* xxxix (1958), pp. 125–37

Leblanc, P.: *Les Ecrits théoriques et critiques français des années 1540–61 sur la tragédie*, Paris 1942

Le Hir, Yves: *Les Drames bibliques de 1541 à 1600: études de langue, de style et de versification*, Grenoble 1974

Léonard, E.-G.: *Histoire générale du protestantisme*, 3 vols, Paris 1961

Le Verdier, Pierre: *Ancien Théâtre scolaire normand*, Rouen 1904 (Société des Bibliophiles normands)

Lichtenstein, J.: *Racine, poète biblique*, Paris 1934

Lintilhac, Eugène: *Histoire générale du théâtre en France*, 5 vols, Paris 1904–10

Lloyd-Jones, P. H. J.: *The Justice of Zeus*, Berkeley and London 1971 (Sather Classical Lectures, no. 41)

Lough, John: *Paris Theatre Audiences in the Seventeenth and Eighteenth Centuries*, London 1957

Seventeenth-Century French Drama: the Background, Oxford 1979

Loukovitch, Kosta: *L'Evolution de la tragédie religieuse classique en France*, Paris 1933 (Bibliothèque de la Société des historiens du théâtre, vol. 2)

McFarlane, I. D.: *A Literary History of France: Renaissance France, 1470–1589*, London and New York 1974

McGowan, Margaret M.: *L'Art du ballet de cour en France, 1581–1643*, Paris 1963

McKean, Sister Mary Faith: *The Interplay of Realistic and Flamboyant Art Elements in the French Mystères*, Washington 1959 (Catholic University of America Studies in Romance Languages and Literature, vol. 60)

Mâle, Emile: *L'Art religieux après la Concile de Trente: étude sur l'iconographie de la fin du XVIe siècle, du XVIIe, du XVIIIe siècle; Italie, France, Espagne, Flandres*, Paris 1932

Mariéjol, Jean-H.: *La Réforme et la Ligue – L'Edit de Nantes (1559–1598)*, Paris 1904 (vol. vi part 1 of Ernest Lavisse, ed., *Histoire de France*, 9 vols, Paris 1903–11)

Marsan, Jules: *La Pastorale dramatique en France à la fin du XVIe et au commencement du XVIIe siècle*, Paris 1905

Martin, H.-J.: *Livre, pouvoirs et société à Paris au XVIIe siècle (1598–1701)*, 2 vols, Geneva 1969

Maurens, Jacques: *La Tragédie sans tragique: le néo-stoïcisme dans l'oeuvre de Pierre Corneille*, Paris 1966

May, Georges-Claude: *Tragédie cornélienne, tragédie racinienne: étude sur les sources de l'intérêt dramatique*, Urbana 1948 (Illinois Studies in Language and Literature, vol. xxxii no. 4)

Monnerot, Jules: *Les Lois du tragique*, Paris 1969

Morel, Jacques: 'Ordre humain et ordre divin dans *Saint-Genest* de Rotrou', *Revue des sciences humaines* (1972), pp. 91–4

Jean Rotrou, dramaturge de l'ambiguïté, Paris 1968

Mouflard, Marie-Madeleine: *Robert Garnier*, 3 vols, La Ferté-Bernard and La Roche-sur-Yon 1961–4

Nadal, Octave: 'La Scène française d'Alexandre Hardy à Corneille', in Jean
Tortel, ed., *Le Préclassicisme français*, Paris 1952, pp. 208–17

Nelson, Robert J.: *Immanence and Transcendence: the Theater of Jean
Rotrou, 1609–1650*, Ohio 1969
Play Within a Play, New Haven 1958 (Yale Romanic Studies, series II,
vol. 5)

Orlando, Francesco: *Rotrou: dalla tragicommedia alla tragedia*, Turin 1963
(Studi di Filologia Moderna of the University of Pisa, nuova serie no. 4)

Pascoe, Margaret E.: *Les Drames religieux au milieu du XVIIe siècle, 1636–
1650*, Paris 1932

Petit de Julleville, Louis: *Histoire du théâtre en France: les mystères*, 2 vols,
Paris 1880
*Histoire du théâtre en France: répertoire du théâtre comique en France au
moyen âge*, Paris 1886

Phillips, Henry: *The Theatre and its Critics in Seventeenth-Century France*,
Oxford 1980

Picot, Emile: 'Les Moralités polémiques, ou la controverse religieuse dans
l'ancien théâtre français', *BSHP* XXXVI (1887), pp. 169–90, 225–45,
337–64; XLI (1892), pp. 561–82, 617–33; LV (1906), pp. 254–62

Pineau, Joseph: 'La Seconde Conversion de Polyeucte', *RHLF* LXXV (1975),
pp. 531–54

Pintard, René, *Le Libertinage érudit dans la première moitié du XVIIe siècle*,
2 vols, Paris 1943
'Autour de *Cinna* et de *Polyeucte*: nouveaux problèmes de chronologie et
de critique cornéliennes', *RHLF* LXIV (1964), pp. 377–413

Pitou, Spire: 'L'Autre Version dramatique de *Josaphat* au XVIIe siècle',
XVIIe Siècle LXXXVIII (1970), pp. 19–29

Pocock, Gordon: *Corneille and Racine: Problems of Tragic Form*, Cambridge
1973

Poupé, Edmond: 'Les Représentations scéniques à Cuers à la fin du XVIe
siècle et au commencement du XVIIe', *Bulletin historique et philologique
du Comité des travaux historiques et scientifiques*, 1899, pp. 53–7
'Documents relatifs à des représentations scéniques à Correns, au XVIe et au
XVIIe siècle', *Bull. hist. et phil.*, 1900, pp. 95–7
'Documents relatifs à des représentations scéniques en Provence au XVIe
et au XVIIe siècle', *Bull. hist. et phil.*, 1903, pp. 26–39
'Documents relatifs à des représentations scéniques en Provence du XVe au
XVIIe siècle', *Bull. hist. et phil.*, 1904, pp. 13–28
'Documents relatifs à des représentations scéniques en Provence du XVIe au
XVIIIe siècle', *Bull. hist. et phil.*, 1906, pp. 33–42
'Documents relatifs à des représentations scéniques en Provence du XVe au
XVIIe siècle', *Bull. hist. et phil.*, 1920, pp. 145–58

Prosser, Eleanor: *Drama and Religion in the English Mystery Plays*, Stanford
1961 (Stanford Studies in Language and Literature, no. XXIII)

Reiss, T. J.: *Toward Dramatic Illusion: Theatrical Technique and Meaning
from Hardy to 'Horace'*, New Haven and London 1971 (Yale Romanic
Studies, series II, vol. 22)

Revillout, C.: 'Etude historique et littéraire sur l'ouvrage latin intitulé *Vie de*

S. Guillaume', *Mémoires de la société archéologique de Montpellier* VI (1870–6), pp. 495–576

Rey-Flaud, Henri: *Le Cercle magique: essai sur le théâtre en rond à la fin du moyen âge*, Paris 1973

Riddle, L. M.: *The Genesis and Sources of Corneille's Tragedies from Médée to Pertharite*, Paris and Baltimore 1926 (Johns Hopkins Studies in Romance Literatures and Languages, no. 3)

Rousset, Jean: *Forme et signification: essai sur les structures littéraires de Corneille à Claudel*, Paris 1962
L'Intérieur et l'extérieur: essais sur la poésie et sur le théâtre au XVIIe siècle, Paris 1968
La Littérature de l'âge baroque en France: Circé et le paon, Paris 1953

Roy, Donald H.: 'La Scène de l'Hôtel de Bourgogne', *RHT* XIV (1962), pp. 227–35

Ryngaert, J. P.: 'Un Exemple de codification du jeu de l'acteur au XVIe siècle: le théâtre de G. de Vivre', *RHLF* LXXII (1972), pp. 193–201

Salmon, J. H. M.: *Society in Crisis: France in the Sixteenth Century*, London and Tonbridge 1975

Sayce, Richard A.: *The French Biblical Epic in the Seventeenth Century*, Oxford 1955

Schérer, Jacques: *La Dramaturgie classique en France*, Paris 1950

Scott, Walter Sidney: *Jeanne d'Arc*, London 1974

Seidmann, Abraham David: *La Bible dans les tragédies de Garnier et Montchrestien*, Paris 1971

Seznec, Alain: 'Le *Saint-Genest* de Rotrou: un plaidoyer pour le théâtre', *Romanic Review* LXIII (1972), pp. 171–89

Smith, Christopher Norman: 'The Tragedies of Jean and Jacques de la Taille', unpublished doctoral dissertation (1969), Cambridge University Library

Smith, Pauline Mary: *The Anticourtier Trend in Sixteenth-Century French Literature*, Geneva 1966 (THR LXXXIV)

Sonet, Jean, S.J.: *Le Roman de Barlaam et Josaphat*, 3 vols, Paris and Namur 1949–52 (Bibliothèque de la Faculté de philosophie et lettres de Namur, vols 6, 7, 9)

Soons, J. J.: *Jeanne d'Arc au théâtre: étude sur la plus ancienne tragédie*, Purmerend 1929

Spillebout, Gabriel: review of Forsyth's ed. of La Taille's plays, *BHR* XXXII (1970), pp. 180–92

Stegmann, André: *L'Héroïsme cornélien: genèse et signification*, 2 vols, Paris 1968

Stone, Donald, Jr: *French Humanist Tragedy: a Reassessment*, Manchester 1974

Sutherland, N. M.: *The Massacre of St Bartholomew and the European Conflict, 1559–1572*, London 1973

Thiel, Maria Arendina: *La Figure de Saül et sa représentation dans la littérature dramatique française*, Amsterdam 1926

Thompson, James Westfall: *The Wars of Religion in France, 1559–1576*, Chicago and London 1909

Tieghem, Paul van: 'La Littérature latine de la Renaissance: étude d'histoire littéraire européenne', *BHR* IV (1944), pp. 177–418

Tobin, Ronald W.: 'Le Sacrifice et *Polyeucte*', *Revue des sciences humaines* XXXVIII (1973), pp. 587–98

Trethewey, J., and Howe, A.: 'Pierre Corneille's *Le Véritable* and Some Problems of Literary History', *FS* XXVI (1972), pp. 266–75

Truchet, Jacques: *La Tragédie classique en France*, Paris 1975

Valency, M. J.: *The Tragedies of Herod and Mariamne*, New York 1940 (Columbia University Studies in English and Comparative Literature, no. 145)

Védier, Georges: *Origine et évolution de la dramaturgie néo-classique: l'influence des arts plastiques en Italie et en France, le rideau, la mise en scène et les trois unités*, Paris 1955

Villiers, André: 'Illusion dramatique et dramaturgie classique', *XVIIe Siècle* LXXIII (1966), pp. 3–35

Zamparelli, Thomas L.: *The Theatre of Claude Billard: a Study in Post-Renaissance Dramatic Esthetics*, New Orleans 1978 (Tulane Studies in Romance Languages and Literature 9)

Index